OBJECT-ORIENTED C++ PROGRAMMING

OBJECT-ORIENTED C++ PROGRAMMING

By

HIRDAY NARAYAN YADAV

MCA, P.G.D.B.M., M.Tech. M.C.S.D.

Lecturer, Deptt. of Computer Application

V.B.S. Purvanchal University, Jaunpur

Uttar Pradesh

UNIVERSITY SCIENCE PRESS

(An Imprint of Laxmi Publications Pvt. Ltd.)

BANGALORE • CHENNAI • COCHIN • GUWAHATI • HYDERABAD
JALANDHAR • KOLKATA • LUCKNOW • MUMBAI • RANCHI
NEW DELHI • BOSTON, USA

Published by :

UNIVERSITY SCIENCE PRESS

(An Imprint of Laxmi Publications Pvt. Ltd.)
113, Golden House, Daryaganj,
New Delhi-110002

Phone : 011-43 53 25 00
Fax : 011-43 53 25 28

www.laxmipublications.com
info@laxmipublications.com

Price : **Rs. 250.00** *Only.* *First Edition* : 2008

OFFICES

India

© **Bangalore**	080-26 61 15 61
© **Chennai**	044-24 34 47 26
© **Cochin**	0484-239 70 04
© **Guwahati**	0361-254 36 69, 251 38 81
© **Hyderabad**	040-24 65 23 33
© **Jalandhar**	0181-222 12 72
© **Kolkata**	033-22 27 37 73, 22 27 52 47
© **Lucknow**	0522-220 95 78
© **Mumbai**	022-24 91 54 15, 24 92 78 69
© **Ranchi**	0651-230 77 64

USA

Boston
11, Leavitt Street, Hingham,
MA 02043, USA

UOO-9214-250-OBJECT ORIENTED C++ PROGRAM C—14927/07/11
Typeset at : Kalyani Computer Services, New Delhi. *Printed at* : Ajit Printers, Delhi.

Dedicated to
My Father Mr. Ram Nath Yadav
and
My Mother Smt. Pran Devi

CONTENTS

PREFACE

This book **Object-Oriented C++ Programming** has been written to serve as a textbook for M.C.A, B.Tech., M.Tech, B.C.A students of U.P. Technical University and several other universities of Uttar Pradesh, Rajiv Gandhi Prodyogki Viswavidyalaya, Bhopal, AAI Deemed University Allahabad and M.C.R.P University, Bhopal.

This book has been divided into four parts. Part I is for object oriented modeling and design which consists of four chapters. Chapter 1 is introduction of object oriented modeling techniques. Chapter 2 deals with object modeling, Chapter 3 deals with dynamic modeling and Chapter 4 deals with functional modeling. This book emphasise in Part I that object oriented technology is more than just a way of programming. Most importantly it is the way of thinking abstractly about a problem using real world concepts.

Part II deals with programming in C++ which covers introduction, data type, control flow, function, array, string, structure and union in chapters 5-8.

Part III is dedicated to concept of object oriented programming in C++. This part is divided into 8 chapters which cover class and objects, constructor and destructor, inheritance, operator overloading, and pointers in C++, polymorphism, virtual function and friend function, files and stream.

Part IV is dedicated to advance feature of object oriented programming in C++ which covers templates and exception handling, software development system. Chapter 19 in which five years' paper have been given is specially for U.P. Technical University students. In each chapter review questions, programming exercise and solved exercise have been given.

Appendix I deals with standard library function. Appendix II deals with standard library function and Appendix III deals with index and references.

Whenever necessary, concepts are explained in boxes with output to facilitate easy understanding and easy grasping and better understanding.

The author will feel highly obliged to all readers for their constructive suggestion and healthy criticism of the book which will go a long way in improving the text.

AUTHOR

ACKNOWLEDGEMENT

It is a pleasure to be able to thank all people who helped me to turn this first edition of **Object-Oriented C++ Programming** from the list of good ideas into a real book.

I am pleased to express my thanks to the following academician for allowing me to work under their valuable guidance.

- Prof K.P. Singh, Vice Chancellor, V.B.S Purvanchal University, Jaunpur
- Dr. Saurabh Pal, Head, Department of Computer Application, V.B.S Purvanchal University, Jaunpur
- Dr. S.K. Singh, Head, Department of Computer Science & Engg., V.B.S Purvanchal University, Jaunpur
- Prof G.C. Jaiswal, Professor, Department of Commerce, B.H.U, Varanasi
- Prof P.C. Patanjali, Ex. Vice Chancellor, V.B.S Purvanchal University, Jaunpur & Tlka Manji University, Bhagalpur
- Mr. Surjeet Kumar, Lecturer, Department of Computer Application, V.B.S Purvanchal University, Jaunpur
- Mr. Indresh Gangwar, Librarian, UNSIET, V.B.S Purvanchal University, Jaunpur.

I give special thanks to Dr. Anil K. Ankit, Dr. Saurabh Pal, Mr. Indresh Gangwar who played major role in the proofreading of this book.

I am thankful to my daughter Sneha Yadav and sons Dheeraj Yadav and Nitin Yadav for their love and encouragement.

Finally, I am very much grateful to my wife Smt. Kamlesh Yadav without whose personal attention and care, it would not have been possible for me to complete this book.

AUTHOR

1

INTRODUCTION

1.1 WHAT IS OBJECT-ORIENTED?

"Object-oriented" means the software components are organized as a collection of discrete object that incorporate both data and possible action over it. The four generally adopted aspects for object-oriented approach are: Identity, Classification, Polymorphism and Inheritance. "Object-Oriented Approach" is a different kind of expressive medium. As a result of using OOA, the tools start to look less like machine and more like part of our minds, and also like other forms of expression such as writing, painting, sculpture, animation, and filmmaking. Object-oriented programming (OOP) is part of this movement towards using the computer as an expensive medium. Following characteristics represent a pure approach to object-oriented programming.

- *Everything is an object.* Assume object as a fancy variable; that store data, but you can "make request" to the object, and can tell an object to perform operations on itself.
- A program is bunch of object telling each other what to do by sending message. To make a request of an object, you "send a message" to that object, by giving a request to call a method that belong to a particular object.
- Each object has its own memory made up of other object. i.e., you can create a new generation of object, by making a class containing existing objects. One can also say it like that you can build complexity in a program handling it behind the simplicity of objects.
- Every object has a type. Each object is an instance of a class, in which "class" is synonymous with "type".
- All object of a particular type can receive the same type of message. This is actually a loaded statement, as you will see later. Because an object of type "Square" is also an object of type "Rectangle", a square is guaranteed to accept rectangle message. This means you can write code that talks to rectangle and automatically handle anything that fits the description of a rectangle. This substitutability is one of the most powerful concepts in OOP.

1.1.1 Object

Identity signifies that data is quantized into discrete, distinguished entities called objects. A monitor on my desk, window on my workstation and an application on any desktop are examples of objects. Every object has a unique handler by which it can be referred. This could have being implemented in any way such as an address references, array index, or even with a unique value of attribute. Object references are uniform and are independent of the contents of the object, hence permitting mixed collection of object to be created.

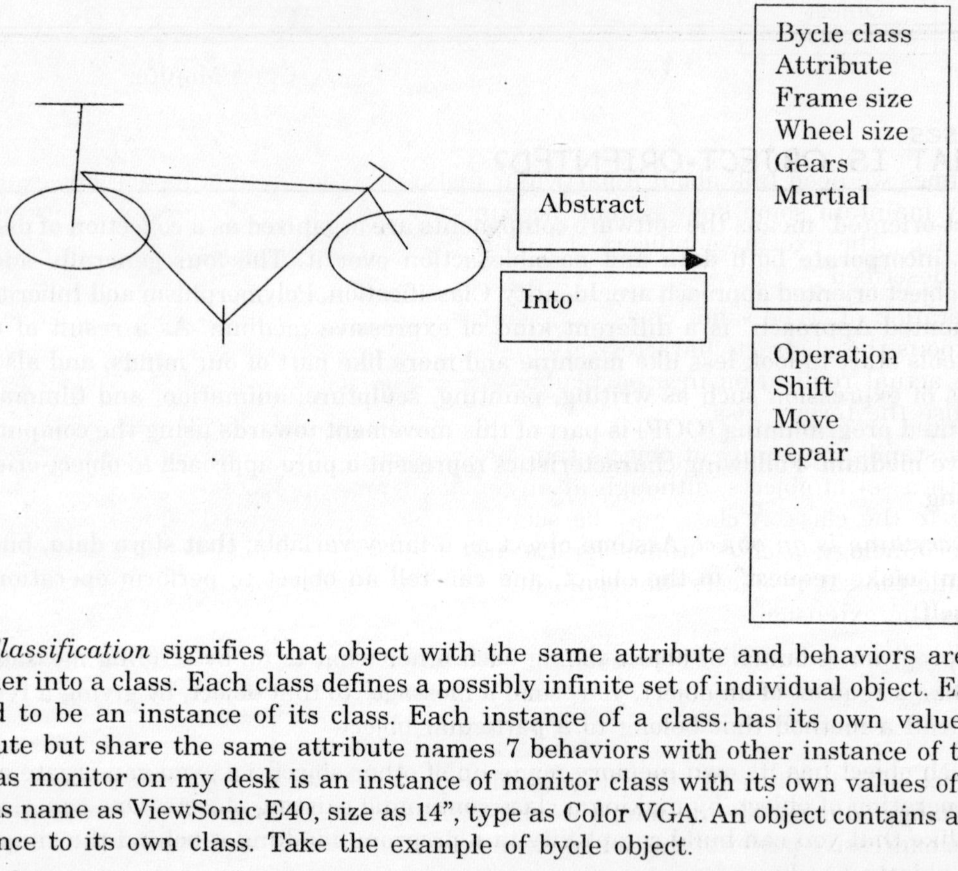

Classification signifies that object with the same attribute and behaviors are grouped together into a class. Each class defines a possibly infinite set of individual object. Each object is said to be an instance of its class. Each instance of a class has its own value for each attribute but share the same attribute names 7 behaviors with other instance of that class. Such as monitor on my desk is an instance of monitor class with its own values of attribute such as name as ViewSonic E40, size as 14", type as Color VGA. An object contains an implicit reference to its own class. Take the example of bycle object.

Polymorphism signifies that the same operation be behave different classes. A Move operation is defined with different rule for a window on desk top system and on Chess-Board. An operation is an action or transformation that an object performs or is subject to Right-Justify display and move as example of operation on a window a specific implementation of an operation by a certain is called a method. In OO approach a class may have more than one method implementing a single *Inheritance* is the sharing of attribute and operation among classes based on a hierarchical relationship. A class can be defined with generalized attribute and behaviors, and can be refined to more specialized attribute and behavior in its subclasses. Each subclass inherits all the properties of its parent class (Super Class) while adding to its own unique properties. For example window is a generalized class, while a fixed window is inherited and more specialized class.

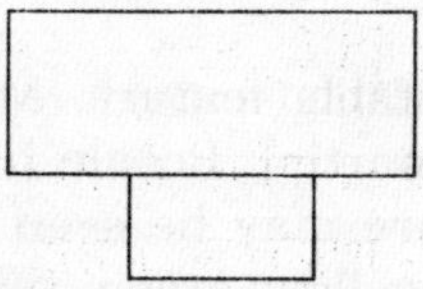

Object

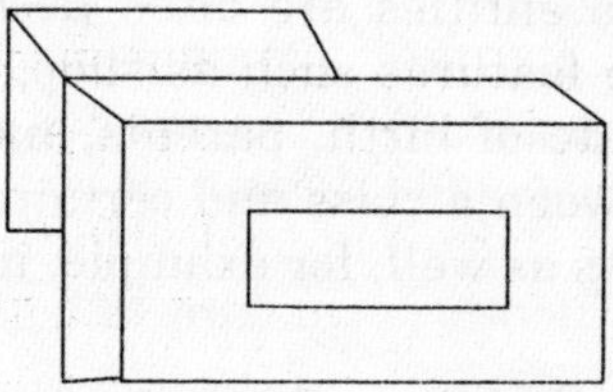

Class Monitor

1.1.2 Classes

Sometimes we need talk about a particular instance in our system model. For example, a bank may maintain some key "system" accounts. We may want to describe a few special employees, e.g., the executive officers. Usually, however, collections of objects, so called classes are described.

The notation of "type" and "class" are sometimes distinguished in the implementation realm. A type is the abstract characterization of a particular "family" of object, while a class is then the actual realization in a particular programming language of that type. We will uniformly use the term "class".

A class stands for family of objects that have something in common. A class is not be equated with a set of objects, although at any moment we can consider the set of instance that belong to the class. A class may be seen as what all these sets have in common. In technical terminology, a class stands for the intension of a particular characterization of entities, while the set of objects that conform to such a characterization in a certain period is known as the extension.

Notationally, a rectangle surrounds the name of class. For example, the Accounts is depicted as:

Accounts

An object is an instance of at least one and at most one class. Certain method allow an object to change, during its lifetime, the class of which it is an instance. This freedom increase the expressive power of the analysis method. But since most object-oriented software development method and language do not support this feature, and since the effect of Individual objects are primarily characterised by an indication of which class they belong. For example:

The arrow between the instance characterization is insufficient. At this stage, we do not have available the means, beyond naming, to distinguish multiple instance of the class Account. In general, we avoid using to describe individual objects; because usually objects do not have natural names. Just consider the examples given earlier — a bank transaction, a newspaper story, a phone call, a rental car contract, a utility bill, and an airline reservation. Instead, descriptions are used that somehow denote unique entities. Attribute of objects will do descriptive job.

1.1.3 Attributes

Real-life entities are often described with that indicate stable feature. Most physical objects have features such as shop, wheat, color, and type of martial. People have features including date of birth, parents, name, and eye color. A feature may be seen as a binary relation between a class and certain domain (brown, blue, and yellow, green, red). A domain can be a class as well, for example, in the case of the features parents, spouse, account owned by, etc.

The applicability of certain feature (i.e., the features themselves, not just their value) may change over time. For example, frog and butterflies go through some drastic changes in their lifetime. We avoid this kind of flexibility. Thus, a class is characterized by its set of defining features, or attributes. This collection of feature does not change.

The notation of (binary) relation crept into the previous discussion. The reader may wonder how we can discuss them here since we have relegated them to another model in our four component view. We make a distinction between attribute (binary) relationship that presents intrinsic, definitional properties of an object versus relationship that describe contingent, incidental connection between objects. Because we, as analysts, are in control, we can prescribe for an object what is definitional and what is incidental. For example in a particular system we may agree that for the class person a social-security-number is a defining attribute while a parent feature is seen as an incidental relationship. In another system, the reverse choice could be made.

We illustrate the notation for attribute with a class account that has:

- attribute account number of value domain account number and
- attribute currency of value domain currency.

A graphical notation for these attribute name and attribute values is

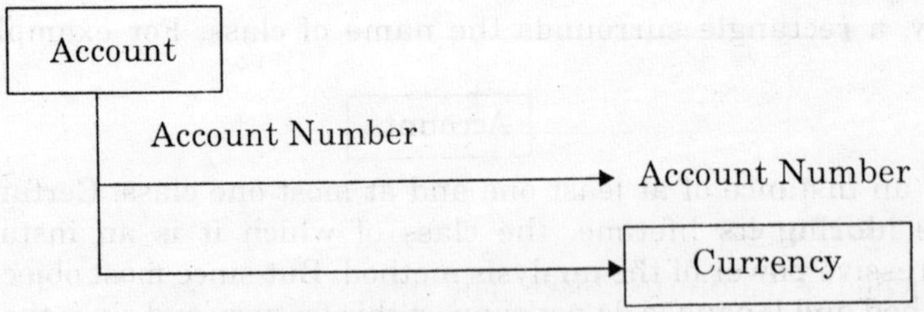

This representation indicates that account number is a "data value" domain and currency is a class. It is debatable whether we should make such a distinction between values and object. For instance, one can take the stance that integers, strings , and 32-bit reals are all objects as well. Although we will be very picky about the resulting distinction in part II, either way is fine with us. We use the convention that unboxed value domain do not represent classes. Consequently, if we change our mind and represent the currency attribute as a data value, we would unbox it.

1.1.4 Attribute of Instances

Attributes can be employed to describe an instance of a class by indicating how it "scores" with respect to the attributes. In the following example, we depict a particular instance of the class account:

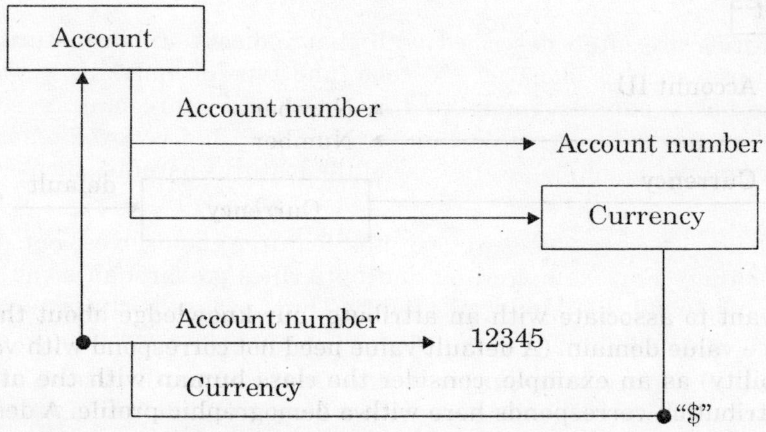

Note that attribute names have repeated in the instance. An alternative approach would use graphic notation to link up the attribute of the instance with the attribute in the class, as in:

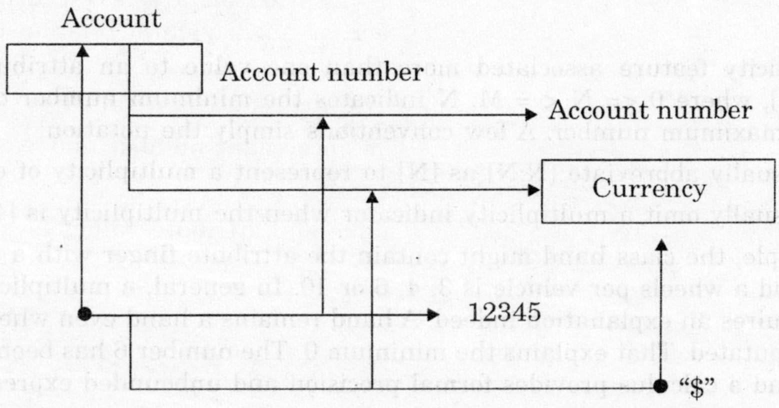

1.1.5 Attribute Features

We have attached attribute to object. The next step is to give, in a sense, attributes to attribute. We will call them feature to avoid too much confusion.

Two feature of attribute have been encountered already, the attribute relation name, which is some time called the role name, and the value domain. Here we expand the feature that can be associated with an attribute. We should stress that using these feature is optional and can be ignored in first rounds or even all together.

Defaults

Sometimes it is useful to indicate a default initial value for an attribute. A generous bank may, for example, give a surprised new customer an account with an initial balance of Rs. 100. Since sheep are usually white, their color attribute can be given default value.

A revised account class include a notation for indicating a default value of an attribute:

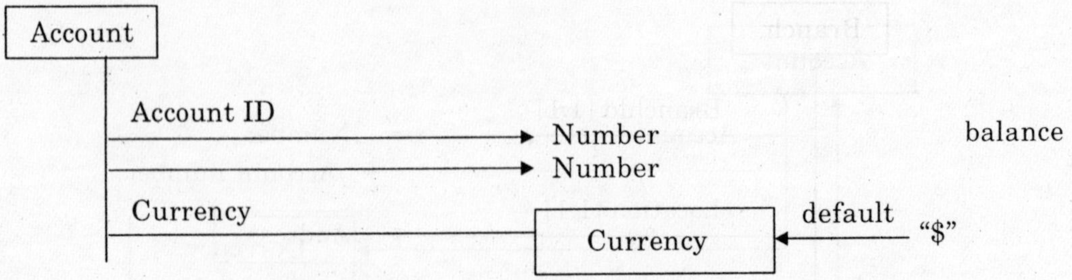

Probability

We may want to associate with an attribute our knowledge about the distribution of the values in the value domain. (A default value need not correspond with value that has the highest probability) as an example, consider the class human with the attribute age. The probability distribution corresponds here with a demographic profile. A designer may want to exploit this information.

We avoid introduction special notation. One option is to list (value, probability) pairs. For numerical domain, a probability distribution function may be specified. Any other mathematical notation may be invoked as needed.

Multiplicity

A multiplicity feature associated more than one value to an attribute. We use the notation [N:M], where 0 <= N < = M. N indicates the minimum number of values and M indicates the maximum number. A few conventions simply the notation:

- We usually abbreviate [N:N] as [N] to represent a multiplicity of exactly N.
- We usually omit a multiplicity indicator when the multiplicity is [1].

For example, the class hand might contain the attribute finger with a value domain of class finger and a wheels per vehicle is 3, 4, 6 or 10. In general, a multiplicity constraint of [0.6]. This requires an explanation indeed. A hand remains a hand even when all the fingers have been amputated. That explains the minimum 0. The number 6 has been chosen because Anne Bolen had a calculus provides formal precision and unbounded expressiveness.

Optional attributes

Using a zero lower bound in the multiplicity feature of an attribute indicate that possession of the attribute is "optional". This allows instance that effectively do not have that attribute. This is a way around the limitation of freezing a collection of attributes for class.

For example, a bank has branches, each having departments. We assume that departments consists of a department head and sub-departments. This creates a recursive structure that bottom out by making sub-departments optional. Thus, a non-managerial employee is a department head that does not supervise sub-departments. For illustration, we restrict the branching ratio of departments to six.

Multiplicity default and probability

Multiplicity indication may be dressed up with more knowledge if this information is beneficial for design and/or implementation. For example, a reasonable default multiplicity for the number of children per parent might be obtained through an empirical sampling.

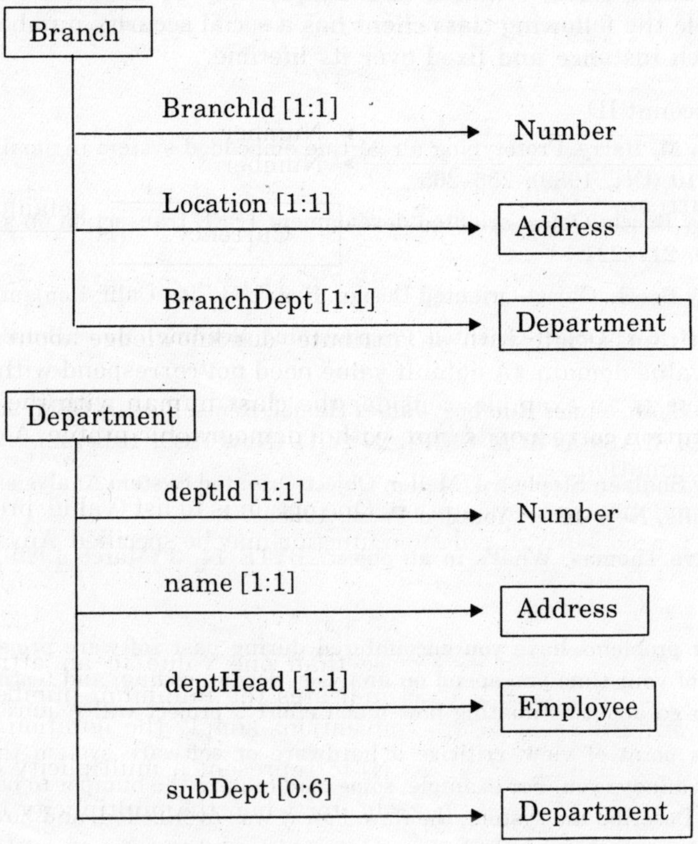

Qualifiers

The range of an attribute value can be restricted in any of several senses. We always fix an attribute to a particular domain. The values of an object must remain within the indicated domain throughout the lifetime of the object. The domain for an attribute listed in a class may be narrowed down to only one possible value. For example, the class Albino has for its color attribute the value white. Intermediate domain restriction that do not limit attributes to only one value may be expressed via constraints.

Several other senses of restriction are common enough to group under broad categories, allowing simpler qualification:

- We may require that an attribute value for each instance of the class to be fixed (immutable) when the object is created and initialized. This value may differ across different instances, but it may not vary across time for any instance. Fixed attribute differentiate from peer object that are members of the same class.
- We may require that the value of an attribute be common to all instance of a class, even without knowing what that value should be. The common value may also change across time. For example, all instance of class account might need to record transaction using a common logfile. The exact file may change over time.
- The category of unique attribute is the extreme opposite of common. A unique attribute is one whose value differs for each instance of a class. For example, the value of attribute acctId should be unique to each instance of class account.

Qualifiers including fixed, common and unique may be annotated in any convenient fashion. For example the following class client has a social security number attribute that is both unique for each instance and fixed over its lifetime.

References

[Barry-89] Brain M. Barry. Prototyping a real tine embedded system in small talk. OOpsla'89 as ACM SIGPLAN 24, 10 (Oct. 1989), 255–265.

[Booch-86] Grady Booch. Object-oriented development IEEE transaction on software engineering SE-12, 2 (Feb. 1989), 211–221.

[Booch-91] Grady Booch. Object-Oriented Design. Redwood City, Calif: Benjamin/Cummings, 1991.

[Cox-86] Brand J. cox. Object-Oriented Programming Reading, Massachusetts: Addison-wesley, 1986.

[Shah-89] Aswin Shah, James Rumbug, James Hamel, Renee Borsari DSM: an object-relationship modling language OOPSLA'89 as ACM SIGPLAN 24,11 (Nov. 1989, 191–192).

[Shlaer-88] Sally Shalaer, Stephen J. Mellor. Object-Oriented System Analysis: Modeling the world in data englewood cliffs, New Jersy: Yourdon Press, 1988.

[Thomas-89] Dave Thomas. What's in an object? BYTE 14, 3 (March 1989), 231–240.

Exercises

1. What major problems have you encountered during past software projects? Estimate what percentage of your time you spend on analysis, design, coding, and testing/debugging/fixing. How do you go about estimating how much effort a project will require?
2. From user's point of view, criticize a hardware or software system that has a flow that particularly annoys you. For example, some cars require the bumper to be removed to replace a tail light. Describe the system, the flaw, how it was overlooked, and how it could have been avoided with more through design.
3. All objects have identity and are distinguishable. However, for large collection of objects, it may not be trivial matter to devise a scheme to distinguish them. Furthermore, a scheme may depend on the purpose of the distinction, for each of the following collection of objects; describe how they could be distinguished:

   (*a*) All persons in the world for the purpose of sending mail.

   (*b*) All persons in the world for the purpose of criminal investigation.

   (c) All customers with safe deposit boxes in a given bank.

   (*d*) All telephone in the world for making telephone calls.

   (*e*) All customers of a telephone company for billing purposes.

   (*f*) All electronic mail throughout world.
4. Prepare a list of object that you would expect each of the following systems to handle:

   (*a*) A program for laying out a newspaper.

   (*b*) A program to compute and store bowling scores.

   (*c*) A telephone answering machine.

   (*d*) A controller for a video casette recorder.

   (*e*) A catalog store order entry system.

5. Define class for an object can be used to perform operations on paragraph written in english language. Operations that can be performed are left justify word count and search for a word in paragraph?

6. Discuss what the object in each of the following list have in common. You may add more class to each list.

   (*a*) Scanning electron microscope, eyeglasses, telescope, bomb sight, binoculars.

   (*b*) Pipe, check, valve, faucet, pressure, gauge.

   (*c*) Bicycle, sailboat, car, truck, airplane, glider, motorcycle horse.

   (*d*) Square root, exponential, sine cosine.

2

OBJECT MODELING

The object model shows the state data structure of the real world system and organizes it into workable pieces. The object model describes real-world object classes and their relationship to each other. Most crucial is the top level organization of the system into classes connected by associations: lower level partition within classes as less critical. The object model precedes the dynamic model and functional model because static structure is usually better defined, less dependent on application details, more stable as the solution evolves, and easier for humans to understand.

2.1 OBJECT AND CLASSES

2.1.1 Object

The purpose of the object modeling is to describe object. We define an object as a concept, abstraction, or things with crisp boundaries and meaning for the problem at hand. Object servers two purpose they promote understanding of the real world and provide a practical basis for computer implementation. Decomposition of a problem into object depends on judgment and the nature of the problem. There is no one correct representation.

All objects have identity and are distinguishable. Two apples with the same color, shape, and texture are still individual apples. The term identity means that objects are distinguished by their inherent existence and not by descriptive properties that they may have.

2.1.2 Class

An object class describes a group of objects with similar properties (attributes), common behavior (operations), common relationships to other objects, and common semantic, person, company, animal process and window are all objects classes. Each person has an age IQ and may work at a job. The abbreviation class is often used instead of object class. Object in a class have the same attributes and behavior patterns. Most objects drive their individuality from difference in their attribute values and relationship to other objects. However, classes with identical attribute values and relationship are possible.

Each object in a class "known" its class. Most object-oriented programming languages can determine an object's class at run time. An object's class is an implicit property of the object.

2.1.3 Object Diagram

Object diagram provide a formal graphic notation for modeling objects, classes and their relationship to another. Object diagrams are useful both for both abstract modeling and for designing actual program. Object diagrams are concise, easy to understand, and work well in practice.

A class diagram is a schema, pattern, or template for describing many possible instance of data. A class diagram describe object classes.

An instance diagram describes how a particular set of objects relate to each other. An instance diagram describes object instances. Instances diagram are useful for documenting test cases and discussing example.

The OMT symbol for class is a box with class name in boldface.

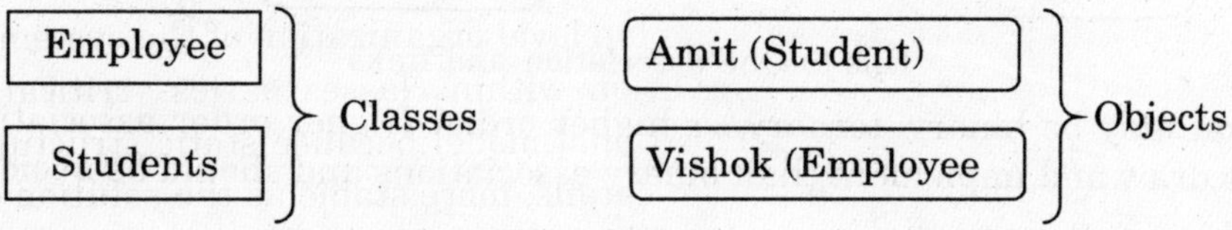

2.1.4 Attributes

An attribute is data value held by the objects in class. Name, date of join, salary, are attribute of employee objects. Color, weight, and model-year are attributes of a car object, each attribute has value for each object instance.

Different object instances may have the same of different values for a given attribute. Each attribute is unique within class. An attribute be a pure data value, not an object. Unlike objects, pure data value do not have identity.

Class with Attribute   Object with value

2.2 LINKS AND ASSOCIATIONS

A link is a physical or conceptual connection between object instances. Mathematically, a link is defined as tuple that is, an order list of object instances. A link is an instance of an association.

An association describes a group of link with common structure and common semantics. All the links in an association connect objects from the same classes. Association and link often appears as verbs in a problem statement. An association describes a set of potential links in the same way that a class describes a set of potential objects.

Association are inherently bidirectional, the name of a binary association usually reads in a particular direction, but the binary association can be traversed in either direction. The direction implied by the name is the forward direction.

The OMT notation for an association is a line between classes. Link is drawn as a line between object.

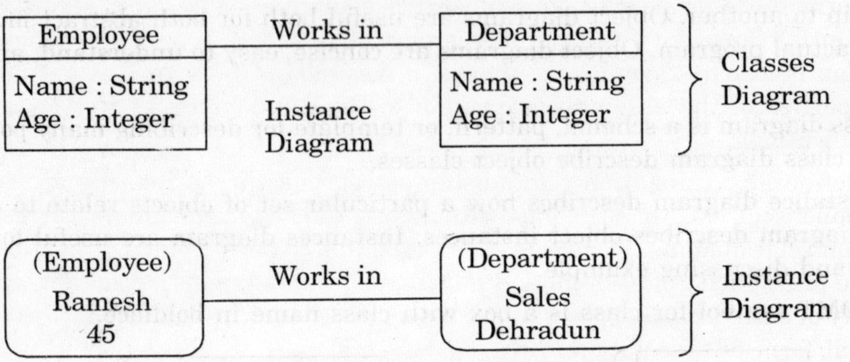

One-to-One association and links

Association may be binary, ternary, or higher order. Higher order association are more complicated to draw and implement than binary associations and should be avoided wherever possible.

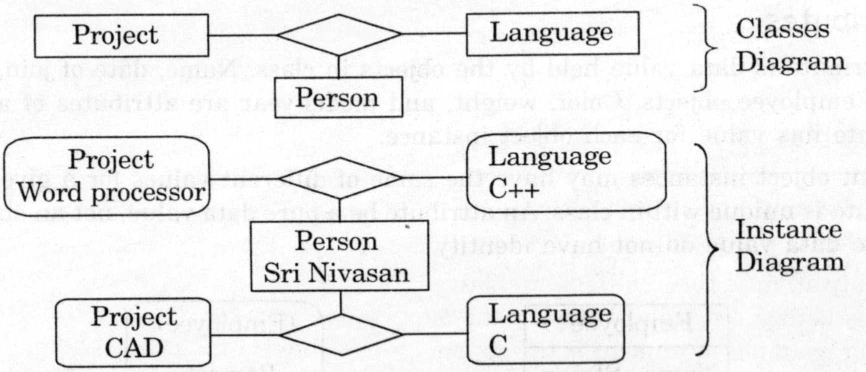

Ternary association and links

2.3 MULTIPLICITY

Multiplicity specifies how many instance of one class may relate to a single instance of associated class. Multiplicity constraints the numbers of related objects. Multiplicity is often described as being "one" or "many", but more generally it is a sub-set of non-negative integers.

Following figure illustrate Zero-or-one, or operational, multiplicity. A workstation may have one of its windows designated as the console to receive general error message. It is possible however, that no console exists. Multiplicity depends on assumption and how you define the boundaries of a problem.

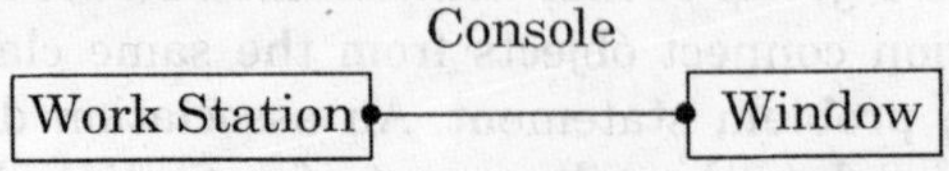

Zero-or-One multiplicity

2.4 AGGREGATION

Aggregation is the "part-whole" or "a-part-of" relationship in which objects representing the components of something are associated with an object representing the entire assembly. One common example is the bill-of-material or parts explosion tree. Aggregation is a tightly coupled form of association with some extra semantics. The most significant property of aggregation is transitivity, that is, if A is part of B and B is part of C, then A is part of C. Aggregation is also *antisymmetric*, that is, if A is part of B, then B is not part of A. Finally, some properties of the assembly propagate to the components as well, possible with some local modifications.

We define an aggregation relationship as relationship as relating an assembly class to one component class. An assembly with many kind of components corresponds to many aggregation relationships. We define each individual pairing as an aggregation so that we can specify the multiplicity of each individual pairing as an aggregation so that we can specify the multiplicity of each component within the assembly. This definition emphasizes that aggregation is a special form of association.

Aggregation is drawn like association, except a small diamonds indicate the assembly end of the relationship. A document consists of many paragraph, each of which consists of many sentences.

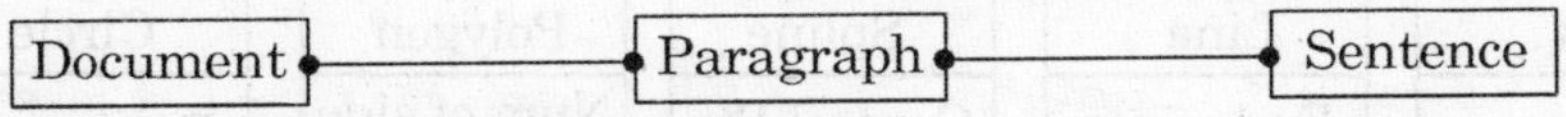

Aggregation

2.5 GENERALIZATION AND INHERITANCE

Generalization and inheritance are powerful abstraction for sharing similarities among while preserving their different.

Generalization is the relationship between a class and one or more redefine versions of it. The class being redefined is called the super class and each redefine version is called a subclass. For example equipment is the supper class of pump and tank. Attribute and operation common to a group of subclass are attached to the super class and shared by each subclass. Each subclass is said to inherit the feature of its superclass. Generalisation is sometimes called the "is-a" relationship because each instance of a subclass is an instance of the super class as well.

The notation for generalization is a triangle connecting a super class to its subclasses. The super class is connected by a line to the apex of the triangle. The subclasses are connected by lines to a horizontal bar attached to the base of the triangle. For the convenience, the triangle can be inverted, and subclass can be connected to both the top and bottom of the bar, but if possible the super class should be drawn on top and the subclasses on the bottom.

Following figure shows classes of graphical geometrical figures. This example has more of a programming flavor and emphasizes inheritance of operations. Move, select, rotate and display are operation inherited by all subclasses. Scale applies to one- and two-dimensional figures. Fill applies only to two-dimensional figure.

Do not nest subclass too deeply. Deeply nested subclass can be difficult to understand, much like deeply nested blocks of code in a procedural language. Often with some careful thorough and a little restructuring, you can reduce the depth of an overextended inherited hierarchy.

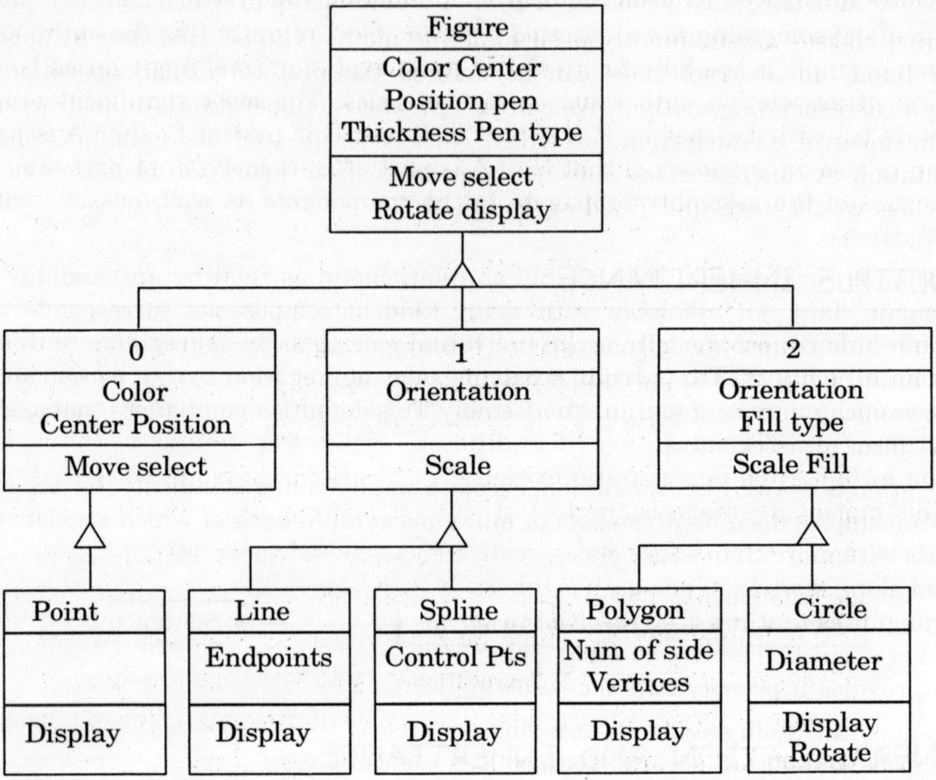

2.6 ABSTRACT CLASSES

An abstract class is a class that has no direct instance but whose descendent classes have direct instance. A concrete is a class that is instantiable; that have direct instances. A concrete class may have abstract subclass. A concrete class may be leaf class in the inheritance tree; only concrete classes may be leaf classes in the instantiable tree. Following employee class is an example of an abstract class. All employee must be hourly, salaried, or exempt.

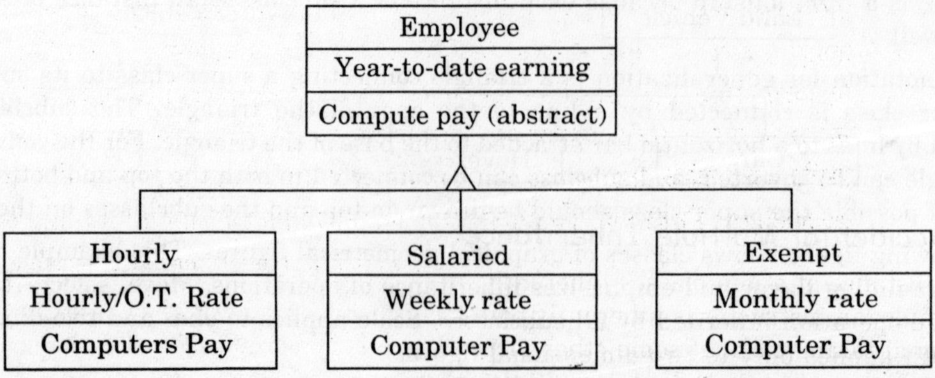

Abstract class organizes features common to several classes. It is often useful to create an abstract super class to encapsulate classes that participate in the same association or aggregation. Some abstract class appears naturally in the application domain. Other classes are artificially introduced as a mechanism for promoting code reuse.

Abstract classes are frequently used to define methods to be inherited by subclass. On the other hand, an abstract class can be defined the protocol for an operation without supplying a corresponding method. We call this an abstract operation. An abstract operation defines the form of an operation for which each concrete subclass must provide its own implementation. A concrete class may not contain abstract operation because object of the concrete class would have undefined operations.

2.7 MULTIPLE INHERITANCE

Multiple inheritance permits a class to have more than one super class and to inherit feature from all parents. This permit mixing of information from two or more sources. This is more complicated from generalization than single inheritance, which restrict the class hierarchy to a tree. The advantage of multiple inheritance is greater power in specifying classes and an inherited opportunity for reuse. It brings object modeling to the way people thinks. This major advantage is the loss of simplicity.

A class with more than super class is called a join class. A feature from the same ancestor class found along more than one path is inherited only once. Conflict among parallel definition create ambiguities that must be resolved in implementation. In practice, such conflict should be avoided or explicitly resolved to avoid ambiguities and misunderstanding, even if a particular language provides a priority rule for resolving conflicts.

Each generalization should cover a single property, for example where a vehicle travels. If class can be refined on several distinct and independent dimensions, then use multiple generalization. Recall that the content of an object model is driven by its relevance to an application solution, so do not list all possible generalization, just show the important ones. In the example given below Hovercraft is both Land Vehicle and Water Vehicle.

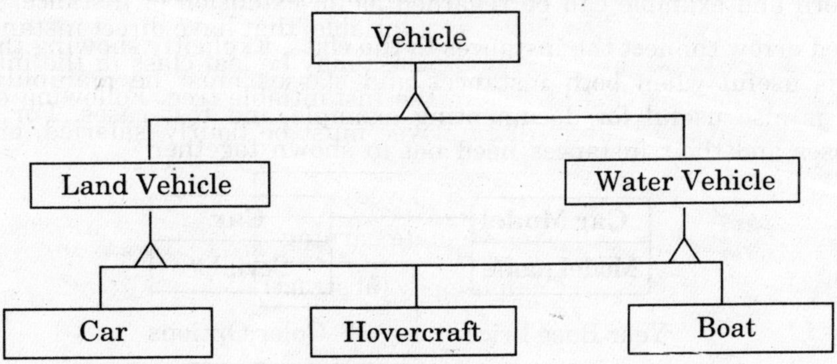

2.7.1 Accidental Multiple Inheritance

An instance of a join classes inherently an instance of all the ancestor of the join class. For example, an instructor is inherently both faculty and student. But what about a Harvard Professional taking class at some other place? There is no class to describe the combination. This is an example to accidental multiple inheritance, in which one instance happens to participate in two overlapped classes. The case is poorly handled by most object-oriented languages. Following figure shows the best possible approach using conventional languages is to treat person as an object composed of multiple university member object.

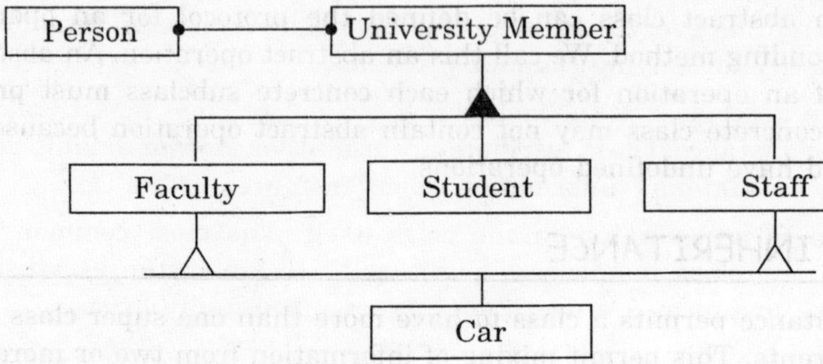

2.8 METADATA

Metadata is data that describes other data (i.e., is data about data). The definition of class is metadata. Models are inherently metadata, since they describe the things being modeled rather than being the things. Many real-world applications have metadata, such as part catalogs, blueprints, and dictionaries, computer language implementation also use metadata heavily. RDBMS also use metadata. Metadata is frequently confusing because it blurs the normal separation between the model and real world; the context of usage distinguished which is meant. With metadata, the context is not sufficient to distinguish the description from the thing being described, so more precise distinction must be made.

2.8.1 Patterns and Metadata

A class describe a set of object instances of a given form. Instantiation relates a class to its instances. In a broader sense, any pattern describe example of the pattern; the relationship between pattern and example can be regarded as an extension of instance.

The dotted arrow connect the instances to the class. Explicitly showing the instantiation relationship is useful when both instances and classes must be manipulated as object. Instantiation is also useful for documenting example and test cases. For most problem, however, classes and their instances need not to shown together.

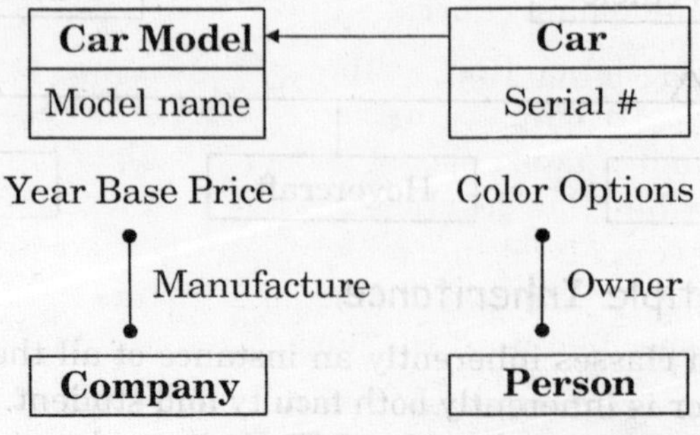

Real-world things may be metadata. There are real-world things that describe other real-world things. A part description in a catalog describes manufactured parts. A blueprint describes a house. An engineering drawing a system.

2.8.2 Class Descriptors

Classes can also be considered as object, but they are meta-objects and not real-world objects. Class description have feature, and they in turn have their own classes, which are called mata classes. Treating everything as an object provides a more uniform implementation and greater functionality for solving complex problem.

A class attribute describe a value common to an entire class object, rather that data peculiar to each other instance. Class attribute are useful for storing default information for creating new objects or summary information about instances of the class.

A class operator is an operator on the class itself. The most common kind of class operation to create new class instances. Operation to create instances must be class an operation because the instances are operated on does not initially exists.

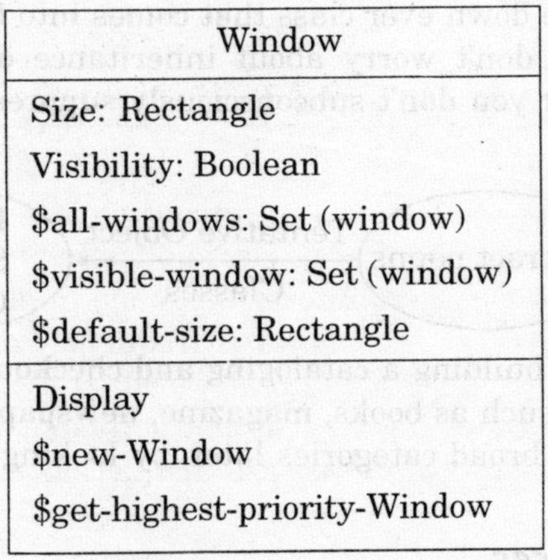

Class with class feature

2.9 CREATING OBJECT MODEL

Information for the object model comes from the problem statement, expert knowledge of the application domain, and general knowledge of the real world. If the designer is not a domain expert, the information must be obtained from the application expert and checked against the model repeatedly. Object model diagram promote communication between computer professional and application-domain experts.

Identify classes and association first, as they affected the overall structure and approach to the problem. Next add attribute to further describe the basic network of classes and association. Then combine and organize classes using inheritance. Attempt to specify inheritance directly without first describing low-level classes and their attributes often distort the class structure to much preconceived notions. Add operations to classes later as a by-product of constructing the dynamic and functional models. Operations modify objects and therefore cannot be fully specified until the dynamics and functionality are understood.

The following steps are performed in constructing an object model.

- Identify object and classes,
- Prepare a data dictionary,
- Identify association between objects,

- Identify attribute of object and links,
- Organize and simplify object classes using inheritance,
- Verify that access paths exist for likely queries,
- Iterate and redefine the model,
- Group class into modules.

2.9.1 Identifying Object Classes

All classes must make sense in the application domain; avoid computer implementation constructs, such as linked lists and subroutines. Not all classes are explicit in the problem statement; some are implicit in the application domain or general knowledge.

Start with listing candidate objects classes found in the written description of the problem. Don't be selective, just write down ever class that comes into the mind. Many a classes often corresponds to nouns. And don't worry about inheritance or high level classes; first get specific classes right so that you don't subconsciously suppress detail in an attempt to fit a preconceived structure.

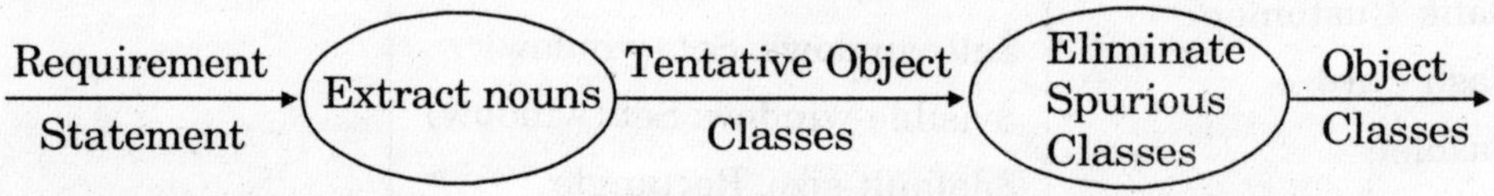

For example if you are building a cataloging and checkout system for a library, identify different kind of materials, such as books, magazine, newspapers, records, videos, and so on. You can organize them into broad categories later, by looking for similarities and difference among basic classes.

Keeping the right classes

As a next step we discard unnecessary and incorrect classes according to the following criteria.

- Redundant Classes: If two classes expressed the same information, the most descriptive one should be kept.
- Irrelevant Classes: If a class has very little or nothing to do with the problem, it should be eliminated.
- Vague Classes: Some of the tentative classes may have ill-defined boundaries or be too broad in scope. Hope a class should be specific.
- Attribute: Name that primarily describes individual object should be restated as attributes.
- Operation: If a name describes an operation that is applied to object and not manipulated in its own right, then it is not a class.
- Roles: The name of a class should reflect its intrinsic nature and not a role that it plays in an association. One physical entity sometimes may corresponds to several classes.
- Implementation Constructs: Constructs extraneous to the real world should be eliminated from the analysis model. They may be needed later during design, but not now.

2.9.2 Prepare a Data Dictionary

Isolated word have too many interpretation, so prepare a data dictionary for all modeling entities. Write a paragraph precisely describing each object class. Describe the scope of the class within the current problem, including any assumptions or restriction on its membership or use. The data dictionary also describes associations, attribute, and operations. For example let us see a data dictionary for the classes for an ATM system.

- Account: A single account in a bank against which transactions can be applied. Accounts can be of various types, like saving, current. A customer can hold more that one account.
- ATM: A station that allows customers to enter their own transaction using cash cards as identification. The ATM interacts with the customer to gather transaction information, sends the transaction information to the centralized computer for validation and processing, and dispenses cash to the user.
- Bank: A financial institution that holds accounts for customers and that issue cash cards authorizing access to accounts over the ATM network.
- Bank Customer
- Cash Card
- Cashier
- Cashier Station
- Central Computer
- Consortium
- Customer
- Transaction

2.9.3 Identifying Associations

Any dependency between two or more classes is known as association. A reference from one class to another is association. Associations often corresponds to stative verbs or verb phrases. These include physical location (next to, part of, contained in), directed actions (drives), communication (talks to), ownership (has, part of), or satisfaction of condition (works for, married to, manages). Extracts all the candidate from the problem statement and get them down on paper first.

Don't spend much time trying to distinguish between association and aggregation. Aggregation is just an association with extra connotations.

Following figure shows association for the above ATM example:

- **Verbal Phrases:**
  - ❑ Banking network include cashiers and ATM's,
  - ❑ Consortium shares ATM's,
  - ❑ Bank Provide bank computer,
  - ❑ Bank computer maintain accounts,
  - ❑ Bank computer process transaction against accounts,
  - ❑ Bank own cashier station,

- ❑ Cashier station communicates with bank computer,
- ❑ Cashier enter transaction for accounts,
- ❑ ATM's communicate with central computer about transaction,
- ❑ Central computer clears transaction with bank,
- ❑ ATM accepts cash card,
- ❑ ATM interacts with user,
- ❑ ATM dispenses cash,
- ❑ ATM prints receipts.

- **Implicit Verb Phrases:**
  - ❑ Bank holds accounts,
  - ❑ Consortium consists of banks,
  - ❑ Consortium owns central computer,
  - ❑ System provides security,
  - ❑ System provides record keeping,
  - ❑ Customer have cash cards.
- **Knowledge of Problem Domain:**
  - ❑ Cash card accesses accounts,
  - ❑ Bank employs cashiers.

Keeping the right associations

Now we have to discard all unneeded and incorrect associations, using the following criteria;

- Irrelevant or implementation associations: Elimination any associations that are outside the problem domain or deal with implementation constructs.
- Associations between eliminated classes: If one of the classes in the association is eliminated, then the association must be eliminated or restated in terms of remaining classes.
- Actions: An association should describe a structural property of the application domain, not a transient event.
- Derived Associations: Remove all association that can be defined in terms of other associations because they are redundant.

  But keep in notice that not all associations that form multiple paths between classes indicate redundancy.
- Ternary associations: Most associations between three or more classes can be decomposed into binary association or phrased as qualified associations.

Intel object diagram to the state is shown:

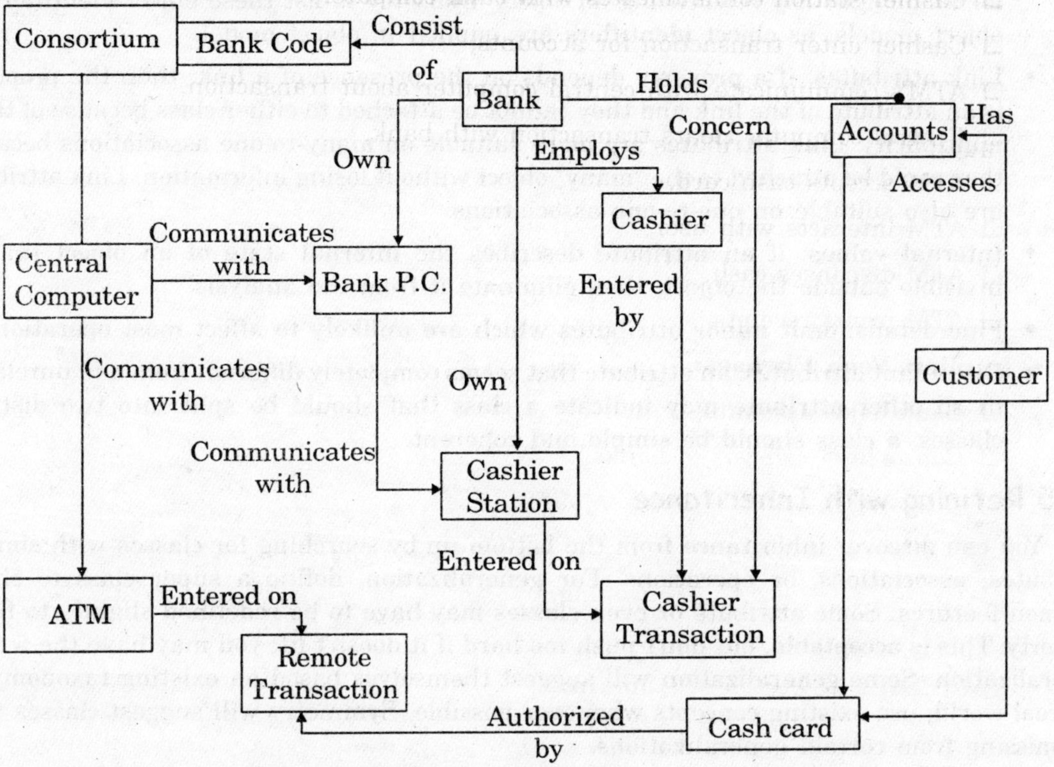

Object Diagram for an ATM System (initial Stage)

2.9.4 Identifying Attributes

Attribute usually corresponds to nouns followed by possessive phrase, such as 'the color of car' or 'the position of the cursor'. Adjective often represent specific enumerated attribute values, such as red, on or expired. Unlike classes and associations, attributes are less likely to be fully described in the problem statement. One must draw on his knowledge of the application domain and the real world to find them.

Only consider attribute that are directly related to a particular application and get the more important attribute first; fine details can be added later on. During analysis, avoid attribute which are solely for implementation purpose. And always remember to give each attribute a meaningful and identifiable name. Link attribute should also be identified. A link attribute is properly of the link between two objects, rather that being a property of an individual object.

Keeping right attribute

Now we have to eliminate all unneeded and incorrect attribute, using the following criteria;

- Object: if independent existence of an entity is important, rather than just its value, then it is an object not a attribute.
- Qualifiers: if the value of an attribute depends on a particular context, then consider restating the attribute as a qualifier.
- Names: Names are often better modeled as qualifiers rather that object attributes. Also for if check that names selected among object is a set? Or can an object in the set have more that one name? If so, the name qualifies an association.

- Identifiers: Object-oriented language incorporate the notion of an object identifiers for unambiguously referencing an object. Don't try to list these object identifiers in object models, as object identifiers are implicit in object model.
- Link attributes: if a property depends on the presence of a link, then the property is an attribute of the link and they cannot be attached to either class because of their multiplicity. Link attributes are more suitable on many-to-one associations because they could be attached to the "many" object without losing information. Link attribute are also suitable on one-to-one associations.
- Internal values: if an attribute describes the internal state of an object that is invisible outside the object, then eliminate it from the analysis.
- Fine details: omit minor attributes which are unlikely to affect most operations.
- Discordant attributes: an attribute that seems completely different from and unrelated to all other attribute may indicate a class that should be split into two distinct classes. a class should be simple and coherent.

2.9.5 Refining with Inheritance

You can discover inheritance from the bottom up by searching for classes with similar attributes, associations, or operations. For generalization, define a super class to share common features. Some attribute or even classes may have to be redefined slightly to fit in property. This is acceptable, but don't push too hard if it doesn't fit; you may have the wrong generalization. Some generalization will suggest themselves based on existing taxonomy in the real world; use existing concepts whenever possible. Symmetry will suggest classes that are missing from certain generalizations.

Multiple inheritance can be used to increase sharing, but only if it is necessary, because it increase both conceptual and implementation complexity. In using multiple inheritances, it is often possible to designate a primary super class which supplies most of the inherited structure and behavior. Secondary super class which supplies most of the inherited structure and behavior. Secondary super class adds orthogonal details. When the same association name appears more that once with substantially the same meaning, try to generalize the associated classes. Attribute and associations must be to the most general class for which it is appropriate.

2.9.6 Verifying Access Paths

Trace access paths through the object model diagram to see if they yield sensible results. Where unique values is expected, is three path yielding a unique result? For multiplicity "many" is there a way to pick out unique values when needed? Think about the questions you might like to ask about. If something seams simple in real world but look complex in the model it means you have missing something.

In ATM example if a cash card itself does not uniquely identifies an account, so the user must choose an account somehow. If the user supplies a account type, each card can access at most one savings and one checking account. This is probably reasonable, and many cash card actually work this way, but it limits the system. The alternative way is to require each customer to remember his account number. If a cash card accessed the single account, then transfer between accounts is impossible.

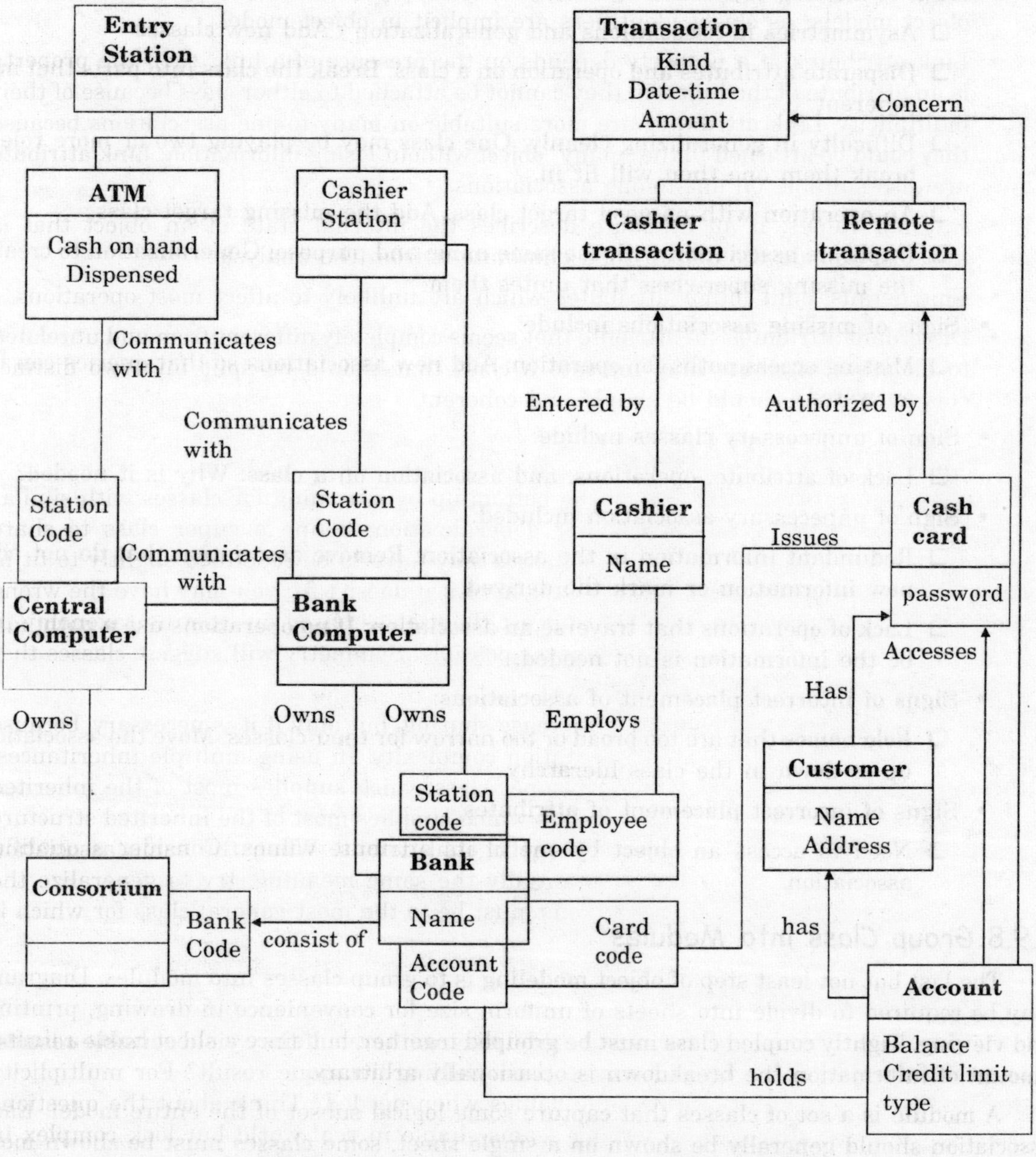

ATM Object Model (with attribute and Inheritance)

Real cash card machine today often serve overlapping networks of banks and accept credit cards as well as cash cards. The model would have to be extended to handle such a situation.

2.9.7 Iterate and Redefine the Model

The entire software development process is one of continual iteration, as an object model is rarely correct after a single pass. Different parts of a model are often at different stages of completion. If a deficiency is found, go back to the earlier stage if necessary to correct it.

- Sign of missing object are as:
  - ❑ Asymmetries in associations and generalization : Add new classes
  - ❑ Disparate attributes and operation on a class: Break the class into parts that are coherent.
  - ❑ Difficulty in generalizing cleanly: One class may be playing two or more roles, break them one then will fit in.
  - ❑ An operation with no good target class: Add the missing target class.
  - ❑ Duplicate association with the same name and purpose: Generalization to create the missing super-class that unites them.
- Signs of missing associations include:
  - ❑ Missing access paths for operation: Add new associations so that queries can be answered.
- Sign of unnecessary classes include:
  - ❑ Lack of attribute, operations, and association on a class: Why is it needed?
- Sign of unnecessary association included:
  - ❑ Redundant information in the association: Remove association that do not add new information or mark the derived.
  - ❑ Lack of operations that traverse an association: If no operations use a path, may be the information is not needed.
- Signs of incorrect placement of associations:
  - ❑ Role names that are too broad or too narrow for their classes: Move the association up or down in the class hierarchy.
- Signs of incorrect placement of attributes:
  - ❑ Need to access an object by one of its attribute values: Consider a qualified association.

2.9.8 Group Class into Modules

The last but not least step of object modeling is to group classes into modules. Diagrams may be required to divide into sheets of uniform size for convenience in drawing, printing, and viewing. Tightly coupled class must be grouped together, but since a sheet holds a limited amount of information the breakdown is occasionally arbitrary.

A module is a set of classes that capture some logical subset of the entire model. Each association should generally be shown on a single sheet, some classes must be shown more that once to connect different sheets. Looks for a cut-piece among classes: a class that is the sole connection between two otherwise disconnected parts of the object network, Such a class forms the bridge between two sheets or modules.

In earlier ATM example, the model we are using might have following modules:

- Teller: casher, entry station, cashier station, ATM.
- Accounts: account, cash card, card authorization, customer, transaction, cashier transaction, remote
- Bank: consortium bank.

References

[Atwood-85] Thomas M. Atwood. An object-oriented DBMS for design support application IEEE COMPAINT '85. 299–307.

[Balha-88] Michael Balha, William Premerlani, James Rumbug Relation database design using an Object-Oriented Methodology. Communication of ACM 31, 4 (April 1988) 414–427.

[Cardelli-85] Kuca Cardelli, Peter Wegner. On understanding types, data abstraction, and polymorphism. ACM Computing Surveys 17, 4, 471–522.

[Chen-76] P.P.S Chen. The Entity-Relationship model-towards a unified view of data ACM transaction on database system1, 1 (March 1976).

[Cox-86] Brad J. Cox. Object-Oriented Programming. Reading, Mass: Addison-Wesley, 1986.

[Goldberg-83] Adel Goldberg, David Robson. Smalltalk-80: The Language and its Implementation Reading Mass : Addison-Wesely, 1983.

[Khoshafian-86] S.N. Khoshafian, G.P. Copeland Object identity. OOPLA'86 as ACM SIGPLAN 21, 11 (Nov, 1986), 406–416.

[Loomis-87] Mary E.S. Loomis, Ashwin V. Shah, James E. Rumbaugh. An object modeling technique for conceptual design. European conference on Object-Oriented Programming, Paris, France, June 15–17, 1987, published as Lecture Notes in Computer Science, 276, Spring-Verleg.

[McAllester-86] David Mc Allester, Ramin Zabih. Boolean classes OOPSLA '87 as SIGPLAN 22, 12 (Dec. 1987), 417–424.

[Meyer-88] Bertrand Meyer. Object-Oriented Software Construction. Hertfordshire, England : Prentice Hall International, 1988.

[Rumbug-87] James E. Rumbugh. Relations as semantic constructs in an Object-Oriented Language OOPSLA'87 as ACM SIGPLAN 22, 12(Dec.1987), 466–481.

[Rumbug-88] James E. Rumbaugh. Controlling propagation of operation using attribute on relations OOPSLA' 88 as ACM SIGPLAN 23, 11 (Nov. 1988), 285–296.

Descriptive Questions

1. Differentiate between generalization and aggregation. **(UPTU-MCA)**
2. What is abstract class? Take suitable example from real life? **(UPTU-MCA)**
3. Design and draw class diagram fore house structure. Make realistic assumption about room kitchen etc. **(UPTU-MCA)**
4. Explain any four of the following **(VBSPU-MCA)**
   (*i*) abstraction (*ii*) encapsulation (*iii*) metadata (*iv*) synergy (*v*) derived attribute.
5. Explain aggregation with the help of example. How does it differ from generalization? What are recursive aggregate? **(VBSPU-MCA)**
6. How does abstract class differs from a concrete class? Is it possible for a concrete class to have an abstract subclass? Explain with help of example? **(VBSPU-MCA)**
7. What is Metadata? **(UPTU-MCA)**
8. Differentiate between aggregation and association with example. **(UPTU-MCA)**
9. Explain instantiation with a suitable example. **(UPTU-MCA)**
10. Distinguish between:
    (*i*) entry and exit action (*ii*) operation methods (*iii*) Link and association (*iv*) internal action and self transition (*v*) class diagram and object diagram. **(VBSPU-MCA)**
11. Discuss aggregation concurrency and concurrency within object with the help of suitable state diagram. **(UPTU-MCA)**

Exercises

1. Prepare an object model to describe undirected graph (fig). Your model should capture only the structure of graphs (i.e., connectivity) and need not be concerned with geometrical details such as location of vertices or length of edges. **(UPTU-MCA)**

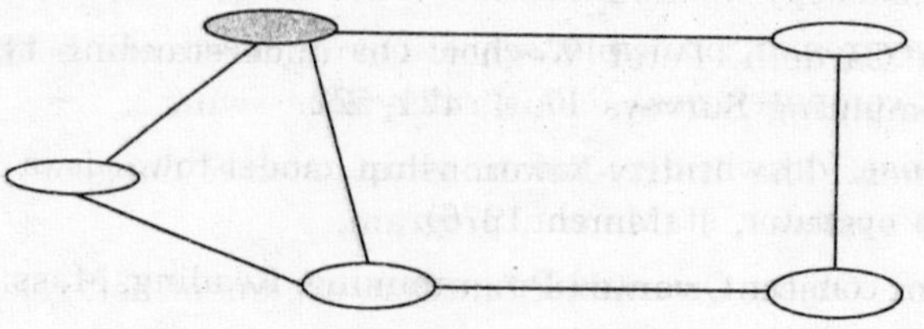

2. Draw an object model of workstation windows management system (e.g., X windows System). **(UPTU-MCA)**
3. Draw a class diagram that shows multiple inheritance from overloading classes. **(UPTU-MCA)**
4. Prepare object diagrams showing atleast 10 relationships among the following object classes include association, aggregation and generalizations. Use qualified association and show multiplicity balls in your diagrams. You do not need to show attributes or operations. Use association names where needed. You may add additional object classes, as you prepare diagram. **(UPTU-MCA)**
5. The following is a partial taxonomy of rotating electrical machine: Electrical machines may be categorized for analysis purpose into altering current (ac) or direct current (dc). Some machines run on ac, some on dc and some will run on either. An ac machine may be synchronous or induction. A few example of electrical machine include large synchronous motors, small induction motors, universal motors and permanent magnet motors. Most motors found in house are induction machines or universal motors. Universal motors are typically used in where high speed is needed such in blenders on vacuum cleaners. They will run on either ac or dc. Permanent magnet motors are frequently used in toys and will work only on dc. Prepare an object diagram showing how the categories and machines relate to one another. Use multiple inheritances where it is appropriate to do so. **(VBSPU-MCA)**
6. Tower of Hanoi is a problem frequently used to teach recursive programming techniques. The object is to move a stack of disks from one of three long pegs to another. Using the third peg for maneuvering. Each disk is a different size. Disk may be used from top of the stack on any other pages, one at a time, provided a disk is never placed on another disk that is smaller than itself. The details of the algorithms for listing the sequence of required moves will depend on structure of the object diagram used. Prepare object diagrams for each of the following descryptions. Show object classes and associations. Do not show attributes or operations:
   (*a*) A tower consists of several (3) pegs. Each peg has several disks on it, in certain order.
   (*b*) A tower consists of several (3) pegs. Disks on the pegs are organized into subsets called stack. A stack is an ordered set to disks. Every disks is in exactly in stack on it, in order.
   (*c*) A tower consists of several (3) pegs. Disks on the pegs are organized into subsets called stacks, as in (*b*) with several stack on a pag. However, the structure of a stack is recursive. A stack consists of one disk (the disk that physically on the bottom of the stack) and zero or one stack, depending on the height of the stack.
   (*d*) Similar to (*c*) except only one stack is associated with a peg. Other stacks on the peg are associated in a linked list. **(VBSPU-MCA)**

7. Prepare object diagrams showing at least 10 relationships among the following object classes. Include associations, aggregations, and generalisations. Use qualified association and show multiplicity balls in your diagrams. You do not need to show attributes or operations. Use association names where needed. As you prepare the diagrams, you may add additional object classes. **(UPTU-MCA)**

   (*a*) School, playground, principle, school board, classroom, book, student, teacher, cafeteria, rest room, computer, desk, chair, ruler, door, swing.

   (*b*) Castle, moat, drawbridge, tower, ghost, stairs, dungeon, floor, corridor, term, factor, arithmetic operator, statement, program.

   (*c*) Expression, constant, variable, function, argument list, relational operator, term, factor, arithmetic operator, statement, program.

   (*d*) File system, file, directory, file name, ASCII file, executable file, directory file, disk drive, track and sector.

   (*e*) Automobile, engine, wheel brake, brake light, door, battery, muffler, tail pipe.

   (*f*) Gas furnace, blower, blower motor, room thermostat, humidifier, humidity, sensor, gas control, blower control and hot air vents.

   (*g*) Chess piece, rank file, square, board, move, position, sequence of moves.

   (*h*) Sink, freezer, refrigerator, table, light, switch, window, smoke alarm, burglar alarm, cabinet, bread, cheese, ice, door, kitchen.

3

DYNAMIC MODELING

3.1 INTRODUCTION

Dynamic modeling tries to capture how objects behave and how they interact. In this way, we can find new operations, attribute and relationships for the objects model. Dynamic model are perhaps the most effective way of uncovering the behavior of systems. We shall meet functional modeling, later, which is another method of uncovering operation and attributes.

We shall look at dynamic modeling as a form of story telling. Do not think this trivializes it. The plot of a good novel is at least as complicated as the most intricate of computer programs, through usually less baroque (at least since Dickens). The approach we are going to adopt is to look at the stories in the world we are analyzing, call them scenarios (just so we have some jargon), and then see these stories affect each of the individual objects (which for the novelist would be characters and artifacts).

3.2 EVENTS AND STATES

An object model describes the possible patterns of object, attribute, and links that exist in a system. The attribute values and links held by an object are called its *state.* Over the time object simulate each other, resulting in a series of change to their states. An individual stimulate from one object to another is an *event.* The response to an event depends on the state of the object receiving it, and can include a change of *state* or the sending of another event to the original sender or the third object. The pattern of events, states and states and state transaction for a given class can be abstracted and represented as a state diagram. A state diagram is a network of states and events, just as an object diagram is a network of a classes and relationships. The *dynamic model* consists of multiple *state diagrams*, one state diagram for each class with important dynamic behavior, and shows the pattern of activity for an entire system. Each state machine executes concurrently and can change state independently.

3.3 EVENT

An *event* is something that happens at a point of time, such as *user depresses left mouse button*. An event has no duration; of course, nothing is really instantaneous; an event is simply an occurrence that is fast compared to the granularity of the time scale of a give abstract.

One event may logically precede or follow another, or the two events may be unrelated. Flight AI2432 must depart from Delhi before it can reach Mumbai, but Flight AI3421 Mumbai to Lucknow can depart before or after the arrival of AI2432. Two events that are causally unrelated are said to be *concurrent*, they have no effect on each other. If the communication delay between two locations exceeds the difference in event times, then the events must be concurrent because they cannot influence each other.

An event is a one-way transmission of information from one object to another. It is not like a subroutine call that returns a value. In real world, all object exists concurrently. An object sending an events to another object may except a reply, but the reply is a separate event under the control of the second object, which may not choose to send it.

The term event is often used ambiguously. Sometimes event refers to an event instance, at other to an event class. In practice this ambiguity is usually not a problem and the precise meaning is apparent from three context. Events include errors condition as well as normal occurrences. For example, *motor jammed transaction aborted, and time outs are* typical error events. There is nothing special about an error event; only our interpretation makes it an *"error"*.

airplane flight departs (airline, flight, number, city)

mouse button pressed (button, location)

phone receivers lifted

input string entered

3.3.1 Event Traces-Building Scenarios

A scenario is a sequence of events that occurs during one particular execution of a system. The scope of a scenario can vary from all events in the system to only those events impinging on or generated by certain objects in the system. A scenario can be the historical record of executing a system or a through experiment of executing a proposed system. Let us see the following scenario;

1. Caller lifts the receiver
2. Dial tone begins
3. Caller dials digits (2)
4. Dial tone stops
5. Caller dials digit (7)
6. Caller dials digit (5)
7. Caller dials digit (3)
8. Caller dials digit (2)

9. Caller dials digit (1)
10. Caller dials digit (7)
11. Called phone begins ringing
12. Ringing tone appears on the calling phone
13. Called party replies
14. Called phone stop ringing
15. Ringing tone disappears from caller's phone
16. Phones are connected
17. Called party hang up
18. Phones are disconnected
19. Caller hangs up

Each event transmits information from one object to another. For example, *dial tone begin* transmits a single from the phone line to the caller. The next step after writing a scenario is to identify the sender and receiver object for each event. The sequence of event and objects exchange can both be shown in an augmented scenario called an *event trace* diagram. This diagram shows each object as a vertical line and each event as a horizontal arrow from the sender object to receiver object. Time increases from top to bottom but the space is irrelevant.

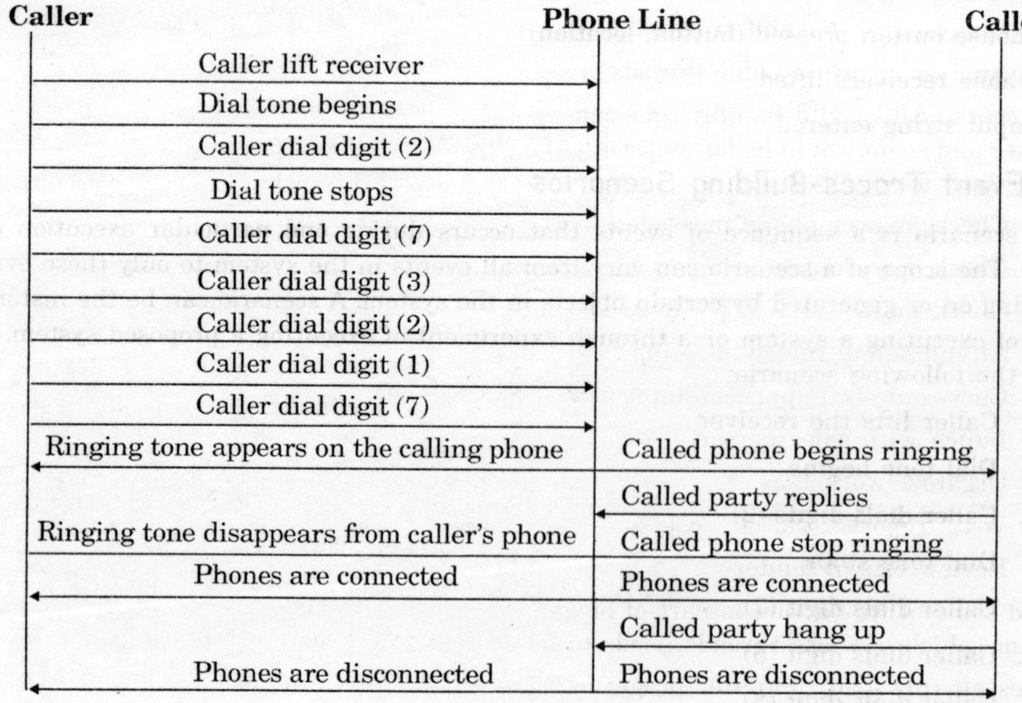

Event trace for a Phone call

We only pick up the bare bones of story. Stories tell us what things there are in the world, and how they interact. It is the basis of good analysis. The simple list considerably simplifies interviewing and recording. We do dot consider all cases, alternatives, and complex repetition. We work through individual cases. Complexity can be introduced later. Of course an individual may have many stories. The patients story varies with each disease and with any complications. The nurse story of caring for individual patients depends on the patient's problems. And indeed an patients and running the staff coffee club. We look for the simple sequences. It is the merging of those sequences, which makes the world, looks a messy and complicated place.

Analyzing the world is like unraveling a number of threads, which have wound together. The picking out of individual threads stops the feeling that the world is impossible to comprehend.

Taking each thread at a time, the overall pattern begins to make sense. And we not get buried in confusing knots and misleading patterns.

3.3.2 Story of an Initial Analysis Session

- Analyst contact manager
- Analyst arrange interview
- Analyst meet manager
- Analyst asks manager the first thing she does in a morning
- Analyst asks manager the next thing she does and so on
- Analyst ends enter view
- Analyst look for end of threads
- Analyst record possible threads

Of course, this could be quit time-consuming. Visits to the coffee machine, chats with colleagues and so on would be left out. Only the gross detail of the manager's activates would recorded such as

- Check answer phone message
- Check diary notes
- Check mail
- Attend safety review meeting
- Carry out staff appraisal interview
- Lunch with sales person
- Organize workshop
- Write report
- Review bits of tender

And some of this action is part of bigger, longer stories. The focus of the analysis will determine which of these threads needs to be examined in detail at later stage.

Does all this lead computer programs? The answer is, it can do, but not necessarily. However, to reassure those with aspirations to encode the whole on their PC, here is an example as part of the design for washing machine controller. A boil-wash may operate like this:

- Lock washing machine door
- Open hot water valve (Note: start of wash program)
- Switch on drum tumble
- Close hot water valve
- Set thermostat cut-out to 105 degrees
- Set thermostat cut-in to 100 degrees
- Switch on heater
- Switch off heater
- Switch off drum tumble
- Open drain valve
- Turn on pumps
- Start drum spin
- Stop drum spin
- Turn of pump
- Close drain valve
- Open cold water valve (Note: start of first rinse)
- Switch on drum tumble
- Close cold water valve
- Open drain valve
- Turn on pump
- Start drum spin
- Stop drum spin
- Turn off pump
- Close drain valve
- Open cold water valve (Note: start of second rinse)
- Turn on pump
- Switch off drum tumble
- Open drain value
- Turn on pump
- Start drum spain
- Turn off pump
- Close drain valve
- Unlock door

Pretty tedious, I know, but a comprehensive explanation of how a washing machine operates on a particular wash. It leaves out a lot of things, such as timing information, but that can be added in later if necessary. And of course, the hot wash, warm wash and cold wash cycle will be similar, but equally long-winded. Note also that are some stories hidden behind this. One even duller story is that of the drum. A single tumble story is:

(*i*) Set motor direction clockwise

(*ii*) Turn on motor

(*iii*) Turn of motor

(*iv*) Set motor direction anticlockwise

(*v*) Turn on motor

(*vi*) Turn of motor

And drum being the goldfish of the washing machine world will repeat this story endlessly until told to stop. "What do you do with the event traces"?

As you develop an event trace you will find the following:

(*i*) There are objects missing from your object model-so add them

(*ii*) There are operation missing from your object model-so add them

(*iii*) There may be attribute you have overlooked-so add them

(*iv*) Perhaps there are object and operation which you thought at first were appropriate, but now look unused-so remove them.

3.3.3 Stage

A stage is an abstraction of the attribute value and links of an object. Sets of values are grouped together into a state according to properties that affect the gross behavior of the object. For example, the state of bank is either solvent or insolvent, depending on whether its assets exceed its liabilities. A state specifies the response of the object to input event. The response to an event received by an object may vary quantitatively depending on the exact values of its attribute, but the response is quantitively same for all values within the same state, and may be qualitatively different for values in different state. The response of an object to an event may include an action or a change of state by the object. For example, if a digit is dialed in state *Dial Tone* the phone line drops the dial tone and enters state Dialing; if receiver is replaced in state *Dial Tone*, the phone goes dead and enters stage *Idle*.

A state has duration; it occupies an interval of time. A state is often associates with continuous activity, such as ringing of telephone, or an activity that to complete, such as flying from Delhi to Lucknow. Events and states are dual of one another; an event separate two states and separates two events. Both event and state depends upon the level of abstraction used.

A state can be characterized in different ways. Let us see an example showing various characteristics of the state Alarm Ringing on a watch.

State:

Alarm Ringing

Description:

Alarm on watch is ringing to indicate target time

Event sequence that produces the state:

Set Alarm to target time

Any sequence not including clear alarm

Current time=target time

Condition that characterize the state:

Alarm=on, and

target time<=current time+20 Sec and

No button has been pushed since target time

Event accepted in the state:

Event	Action	Next State
Current time=target time+20	Reset Alarm	Normal
Button pushed (any button)	Reset Alarm	Normal

3.3.4 State Diagrams

Computer system is built from objects, which responds to events. External events arrive at the boundary of the system; say when a mouse button is clicked. Some object picks up the event, responds to it, and perhaps generates some internal event by calling an operation on another object.

A *state* diagram relates events and states. When an even is received, the next stage depends on the current stage as well as the event; a change of the state caused by n event is called a transaction. A state diagram is a graph whose nodes are states and whose directed arcs are transitions labeled by event names. A state is drawn in a round box containing an optional name, a transition is drawn as an arrow from the receiving state, the label on the arrow is the name of the event causing the transaction. All the transition leaving a state must corresponds to different events.

The state diagram specifies the state sequence caused by an event sequence. If an object is in a state and an event labeling one of its transitions occurs, the object enters the state on the target end of the transition. The transition is said to *fire*. If more that one transition leaves a state, then the first event occur causes the corresponding transition to fire. If an event occurs that has no transition leaving current state, then the event is ignored. A sequence of events corresponds to a path through the graph.

Following figure shows a state diagram describing a simple digital watch having a display and two buttons to set it

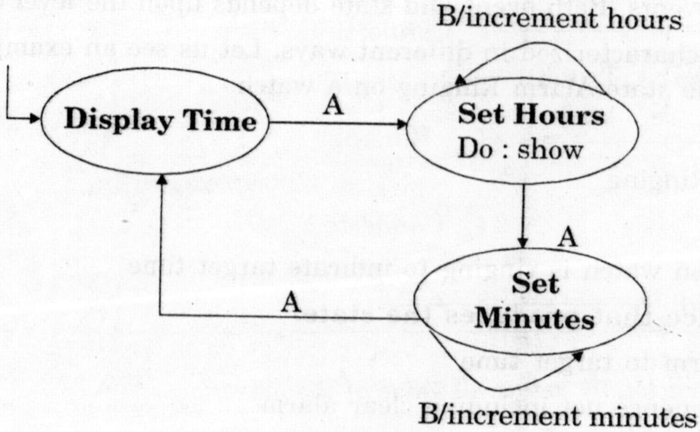

Digital Watch

as you can see, initial state are represented by a block blob. Intermediate states are represented by round-cornered boxes. Final states are represented by bulls-eyes. Events are represented by arrow with label giving a name. An event usually corresponds to an operation in the object model.

Basically any system which you can reasonably model on a computer jumps from state to state. Even those apparently continue games are made up of object which change their state very quickly.

State diagram allows you to further explore the operations and attributes that need to be defined for an object. They consist of set of states, which an object is in, and event, which take the object from one state to another.

The level of state decomposition must be decided on judgment. Too fine a grained model is inappropriate; say modeling all the possible ages of an employee as individual states. Too gross decomposition is useless; say modeling an employee as employed or not. Careful consideration of a state can often uncover more complicated behavior. Consequently we have a notation to describe sub-states.

A state diagram describe the behavior of a single class of object. Since all instance of the class have same behavior, they all share the same state diagram, they all share the same class features. But each object has its own attribute values, so to each object has its own state, the result of the unique sequence of events that it has received. Each object is independent of the other object and proceeds at its own pace. Let us see one more state diagram of phone line example we had taken earlier.

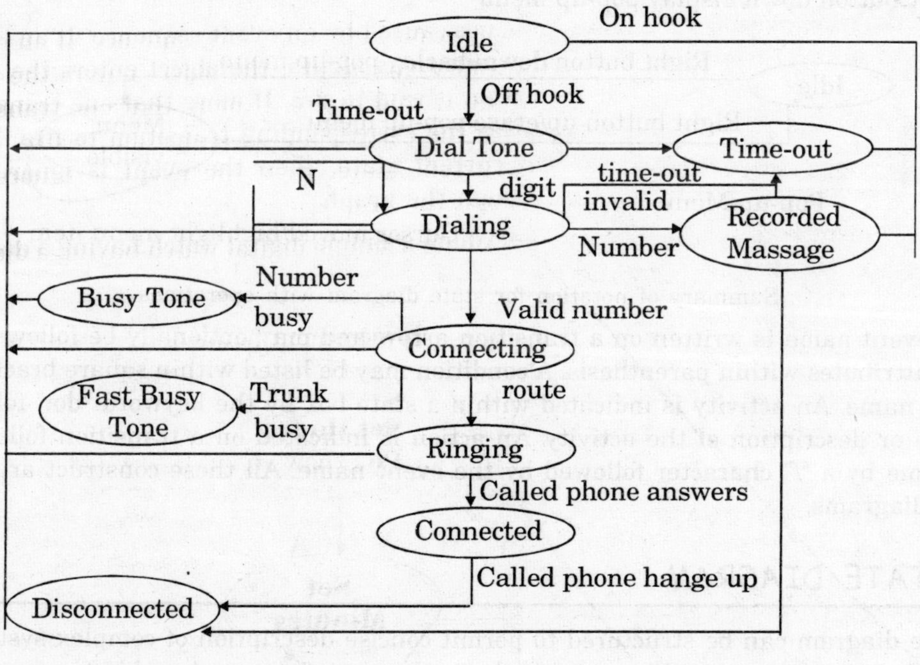

Note: The state do not totally define all value of the object.

3.4 OPERATIONS

3.4.1 Controlling Operation

State diagram is of little use if they just describe pattern of events. A behavioral description of an object must specify what the object does in response to an event. Operations attached to state or transitions are performed in response to the corresponding states of events.

An activity is an operation that takes time to complete. An activity is associated with a state. Activites include continuous operation, such as displaying a picture on a television screen, as well as sequential operations that terminate by themselves after an interval of time, such as closing a value or performing computation. A state may control a continuous activity, such as ringing telephone bell that persists until an event terminates it by causing a transition from state.

An action is instantaneous operation it is associated with event. An action represents an operation whose duration is insignificant compared to the resolution of state diagram. Action can also represent internal control operations, such as setting attribute or generating other events. Such events have no real world counterpart but instead are mechanisms for structuring control within implementation. The notation for an action on translation is a slash "/" and the name (or description) of an action, following the name of event that causes it. The figure shown below shows the state diagram of pop-up menu is displayed, when the right button is released, the menu is erased. While the menu is displayed, the highlighted menu item is updated whenever the cursor moves.

Right button down/display pop-up menu

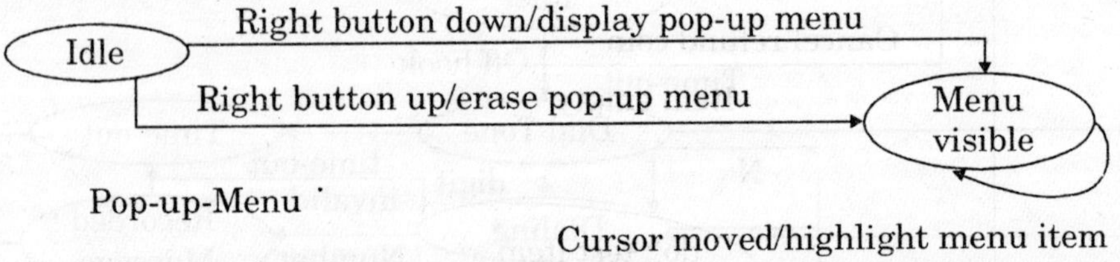

Summary of notation for state diagram with operations

An event name is written on a transition arrow and may optionally be followed by one or more attributes within parenthesis. A condition may be listed within square brackets after an event name. An activity is indicated within a state box by the keyword "do:" followed by the name or description of the activity. An action is indicated on a transition following the event name by a "/" character followed by the event name. All these construct are optional in state diagrams.

3.5 STATE DIAGRAM

State diagram can be structured to permit concise description of complex systems. The ways of structuring state machines are similar to the way of structuring objects: generalization and aggregation. Generalization is equivalent to expending nested activities. It allows an activity to be described at a high level, then expanding at a lower level by adding details, similar to nested procedure calls. In addition, generalization allows states and events to be arranged into generalization hierarchies with inheritance of common structure and behavior similar to inheritance of attribute and operation in classes. Aggregation is equivalent to concurrency of states. Concurrent states generally correspond to object aggregations, possibly entire systems that have interacting part.

3.5.1 Nested State Diagrams

An activity in a state diagram can be expanded as lower-level state each state representing one step of activity. Nested activities are on-shot state diagrams with input and output transitions. The set of the nested state diagrams from a lattice.

Following shows a top-level model for a vending machine. This diagram contain an activity dispense item and as event select item that are expanded in more detail in nested state diagrams. The diagram also shows a bit of alternate notation. The event coins in is written within the collecting money state. This indicates a transition that remains within a single state. Also, the transition from the unnamed state containing "do: dispense item" to state idle has no even label. The lack of event label indicates that the transition fires automatically when the activity in the state is complete.

Vending Machine Model: Following figure shows a sub-diagram for the select item from the above diagram, which actually involves several low-level events. The customer keys in an item number can start over by hitting clear; the selection is confirmed by hitting enter. The level on the bull's-eye indicates the event generated on the higher-level.

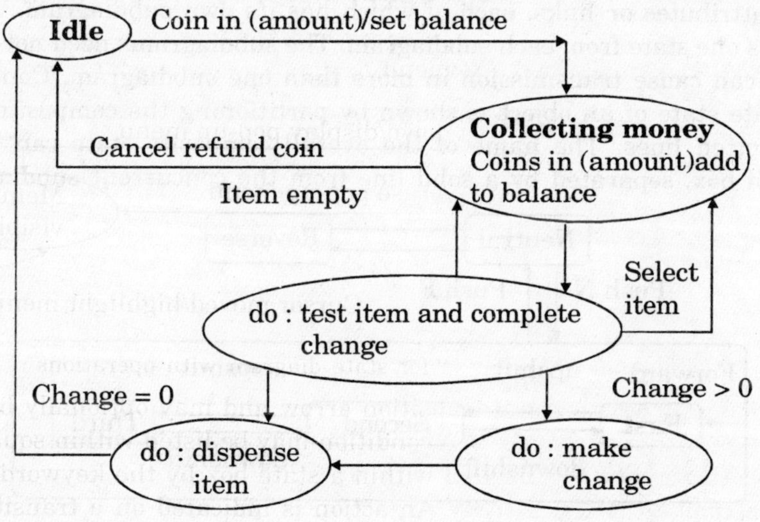

3.6 CONCURRENCY

A state diagram for assembly is a collection of state diagrams, one for each component. Aggregation implies concurrency. The aggregate state corresponds to the combined states of all the component diagram. Aggregation is the "and relationship". The aggregate state from the first diagram and, a state from each other diagram. In the more interesting cases, the component states interact. Guarded transition for one object can depend on another object being in a given state. This allows interaction between the state diagrams, while preserving modularity.

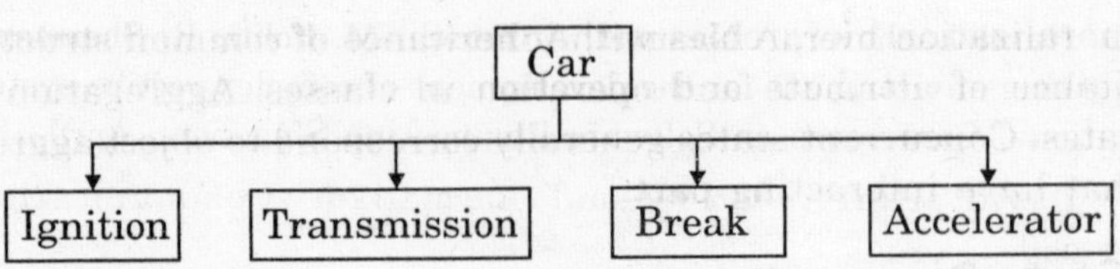

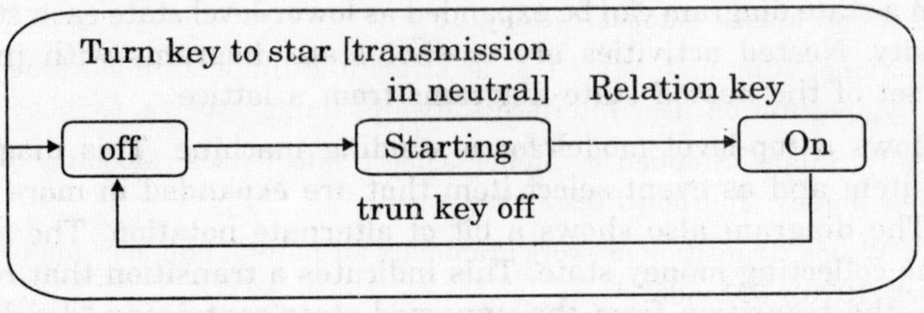

Next figure will show the state of car as an aggregation of component states the Ignition, Transmission, Accelerator, and Brake. Each component state also has substrates. The state of the car includes one subsets from each component each quit, independent: the car will not start unless transmission is in neutral.

3.6.1 Concurrency Within an Object

Concurrency within the state of a single object arise when the object can be portioned into subsets of attributes or links, each of which has its own subdiagram. The state of the object comparises one state from each subdiagram. The subdiagrams need not be independent; the same event can cause transmission in more than one subdiagram. Concurrency within a single composite state of an object is shown by partitioning the composite state into sub-diagram with dotted lines. The name of the overall composite state can be written in a seprate region of box, separated by a solid line from the concurrent subdiagram.

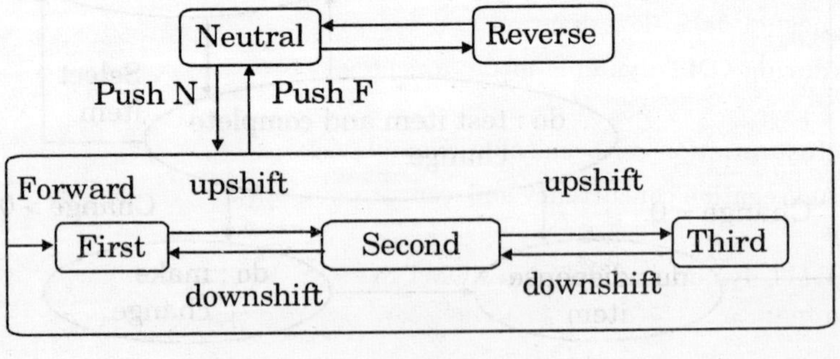

References

[Comer-84] David J. Comer. Digital Logic and State Machine Design. New York: Holt, Rinehart, 1984.

[Davis-88] Alan M. Davis. A comparison of techniques for the specification of extrnal system behavior. Communication of ACM 31, 9 (September 1988), 1098–1115.

[Green-86] Mark Green. Asurvey of three dialogue models. ACM transaction on Graphics 5, 3 (July 1986), 244–274.

[Herel-87] David Harel. Statecharts: a visual formalism for complex systems. science of computer programming 8 (1987), 231–274.

[Herel-88a] D. Harel Lachover, A Naamad, A. Pnueli, M. Politi, R. Sherman, A. Stul-Trauring. STATEMATE: A working environment for the development of complex rective systems. Proceedings of 10th IEEE International Conference on Software Engineering Singapore, April 1988.

[Herel-88b] David Harel. On visual formalism Communication of ACM 31, 5 (May 1988), 514–530.

[Hopcroft-79] J.E. Hopcroft, J.D. Ullman. Introduction to Automata Theory, Languages, and communication, Reading, Mass : Addison-wesley, 1979.

[Rembugh-88] James Rumbugh. state tree as structured finite state machine for user interfaces ACM SIGGRAPH symposium on user interface software, Banff, Alberta, October 17–19, 1988.

[Shlaer-90] Sally Shlaer, Stephen J. Mellor. Object Life Cycles: Modeling the world in states Englwood cliffs, New Jersey: Yourdon Press, 1990.

[Wood-70] W.A. Woods. Transition network grammars for natural language analysis, Communication of ACM 13, 10 (Oct. 1970), 591–606.

Descriptive Question

1. Explain how dynamic model is related to object and functional model. **(VBSPU-MCA)**
2. Explain and distinguish between : **(VBSPU-MCA)**
   (*i*) Entry and exist actions
   (*ii*) Operation and methods
   (*iii*) Links and association
   (*iv*) Internal action and self transition
   (*v*) Class diagram and object diagram. **(VBSPU-MCA)**
3. What are event and states. **(UPTU-MCA)**
4. How concurrency within state of single object represented.
5. Identify various state in which a cd-drive of computer can exist. **(UPTU-MCA, B.Tech.)**
6. Explain nested data flow diagram and functional constraints. **(UPTU-MCA, B.Tech.)**
7. Explain during OMT dynamic model are prepared. Describe content of these model. **(UPTU-MCA, B.Tech.)**
8. Explain Instantiation with suitable example. **(UPTU-MCA, B.Tech.)**
9. Discuss Aggregation concurrency and concurrency within object with the help of suitable state diagrams. **(UPTU-MCA, B.Tech.)**
10. What is OMT dynamic model? Draw OMT dynamic model for participants registration system for a seminar. **(UPTU-MCA, B.Tech.)**

Exercises

1. Decide which models object, functional and dynamic are related to computer chess player. The board and piece will be displayed graphically on video display. Human movies will be indicated via a cursor controlled by a mouse. Defend your answer:
   (*i*) User interface which displays computer moves and accept human movies.
   (*ii*) Representation of a configuration of pieces on the board.
   (*iii*) Consideration of a sequence of possible legal movies. **(VBSPU-MCA)**
2. Give the scenario of event trace for a phone call being made 4235278. Include conditions for individual number and time out. If the number does not response in 10 rings, the answering machine gets switched on 8. **(VBSPU-MCA)**

3. A single digital watch has a display and two buttons on it, the A button and the B button. The watch has two modes of operation, display time and set time. In the display time mode, hours and minutes are displayed, separated by flashing colon. The set time modes has two sub modes, set hours and set minutes. The A button is used to select modes. Each time it is pressed, Button must be released before they can generate another event. Prepare a state diagram of watch. **(VBSPU-MCA) (UPTU-MCA, B.Tech.)**
4. Discuss several ways of implementing DFD. Prepare a data flow diagram for computing the root $ax^2 + bx + c = 0$. Inputs are a, b, c. Outputs are roots R_1 and R_2 which may be real or complex depending on values of a, b and c.
5. Write scenario for the following activities moving bag of corn, a goose and a fox across a river in a boat. Only one thing may be carried in the boat at a time. If the goose is left alone with corn, the corn will be eaten. Prepare two scenarios, one in which something gets eaten and one which everything is safely transported across the river. **(UPTU-B.Tech., RML Avadh-MCA)**
6. An extension ladder has a rope, pully, and latch for raising, lowering and locking the extension. When the latch is locked, the extension is mechanically supported and you may safely climb the ladder. To release the latch, you raise the extension slightly with the rope. You may then freely raise or lower the extension. The latch may be reengaged while raising the extension by reversing direction just as the latch is passing a rung. Prepare state diagram of extension leader. **(VBSPU-B.Tech.)**
7. The telephone answering machine activated on first ring. Draw a state diagram that machine answer after 5 ring. If the telephone is answered before five ring, the machine should do nothing. Be careful to distinguish between five calls in which the telephone is answered on first ring and one call that rings five times. **(UPTU-B.Tech.)**

4

FUNCTIONAL MODELING

4.1 FUNCTIONAL MODELING

The functional model shows how value are computed, without referring to sequence, decisions or object structures. The functional model shows which values depends on, which other value and the function that relate them.

The processes on a data flow diagram correspond to activities or action in the state diagram of the classes. The flows on a data flow diagram correspond to object or attribute value in an object diagram. It is best to construct the functional model after the object and dynamic models.

The following steps are performed in constructing a functional model:

1. Identify input and output values
2. Building DFD showing functional dependencies,
3. Describe functions,
4. Identify constraints,
5. Specify optimization criteria

4.1.1 Identify Input/Output Values

Input and output are parameter of events between the system and the outside world. Start with preparing the list of input/output value. Examine the problem statement to find any input or output values that you may being missing. Following figure shows input and output values for the ATM example that we were earlier talking about.

Since all interaction between the system and the outside world pass through the ATM, all input and output values are parameters of ATM events. Input events that only affect the flow of control, such as *terminate, or cancel*, do not supply any input. Acknowledgement *event*, such as *take cash* or *take card* do not supply any data.

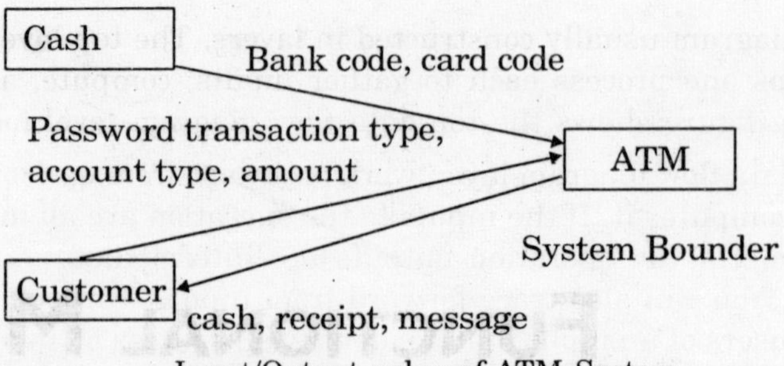

Input/Output value of ATM System

4.1.2 Data Flow Diagram

The functional model consists of multiple data flow diagrams which specify the meaning of operation and flow diagram (DFD) shows the functional relationship of values computer by a system, including input values, output values and internal data stored.

The data flow diagram solves two purposes

1. To provide an indication of how data transformed as they move the system.
2. To depict the functions and sub-functions that transforms the data flow.

The major components of data flow diagram are shown below:

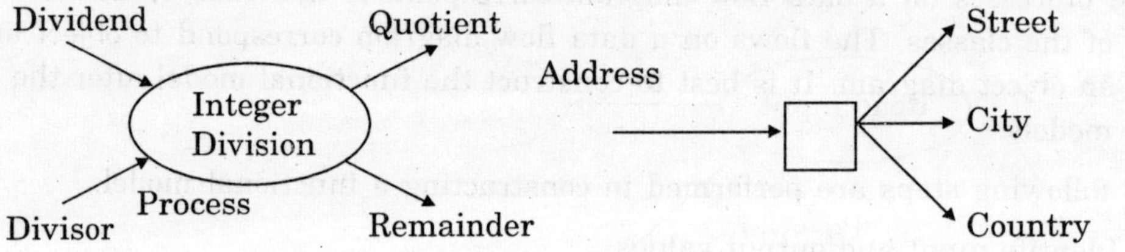

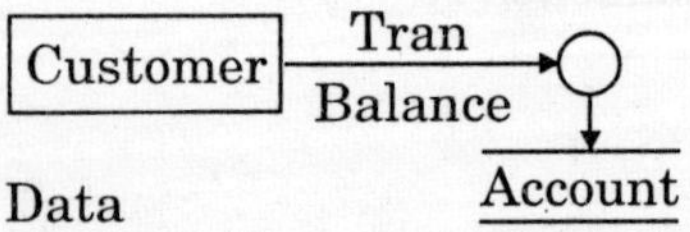

Data Stores

The Data Flow Diagram provides additional information that is used during the analysis of the information domain and serves as a basis for the modeling of function. A description of each function presented in the flow diagram is contained in a process specification.

Data flow diagrams are useful if:

- You have lots of calculations to carry out, and
- You are familiar with data flow techniques in a method you have used repeated before.

The approach to data flow diagramming should be as follows:

- Create a data flow diagram for each of the major outputs of the system,
- Work back from the outputs to the inputs to construct the diagram,
- Add new object, where necessary to the object model as you discover the need for them in the data flow modeling, and
- Add new operations and attributes to the object model as you discover the need them in the data flow modeling.

A data flow diagram usually constructed in layers. The top layer may consist of a single process, or perhaps one process each to gather inputs, compute, and values and generate outputs. Following figure shows the top data flow diagram level for the ATM example.

Within each data flow diagram layer, work backward from each output value to determine the function that computes it. If the inputs to the operation are all inputs the entire diagram, you are done. Some of the operation outputs are intermediate values that must be trace backward in turn. You can also trace forward from input to output, but it is usually header to identify all the users of an input than to identify all sources of an output. Expand each non-trivial process in the top-level diagram into lower level data flow diagram. If second level processes still contain non-trivial processes, they can be expanded recursively. Let us expand the perform transaction process from the earlier example. Data flow diagram specifies only dependencies among operations. They do not show decision or sequencing of operation; in fact, some operation can be optional of mutually exclusive. In the example below password must be verified before updating the account. Some data values affect the decisions in the dynamic model.

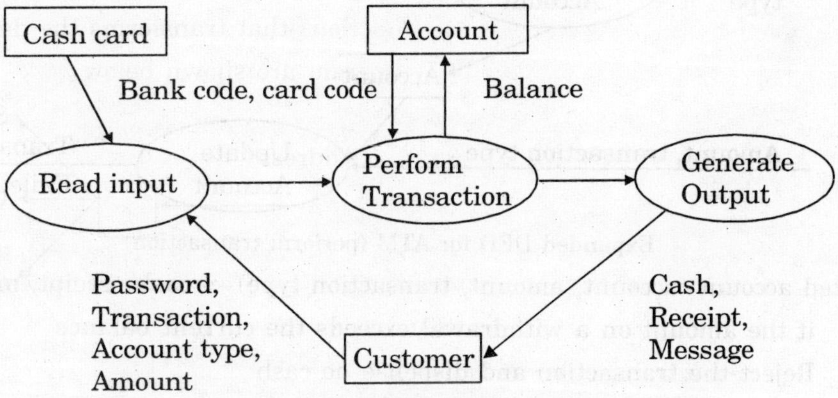

Top Level DFD for Application

Decision do not directly affect output values in the data flow model, as the data flow model shows all possible computation paths. However, it can be useful to capture decision functions in the data flow model, since they may be complicated function of input. Decision function can be shown on the data flow diagram, but their outputs are control signals, indicated by doted output arrows.

When the data flow diagram has been refined enough, write a description of each function. The description can be in natural language, mathematical equations, pseudo code, decision tables, or some other appropriate form on what the function does, not how to implement it. The description can be declarative or procedural. A declarative description specifies the relationship between input and output values and the relationship among the output values. A procedural description specifies a function by giving an algorithm to compute it. The purpose of the algorithm is only to specify what the function does; during implementation, any other algorithm that computes the same value can be substituted. Declarative description is preferable to procedural description, because they do not imply an implementation, but if the procedural description is much easier to write it should be used.

Following figure shows the functional description of the updated account function.

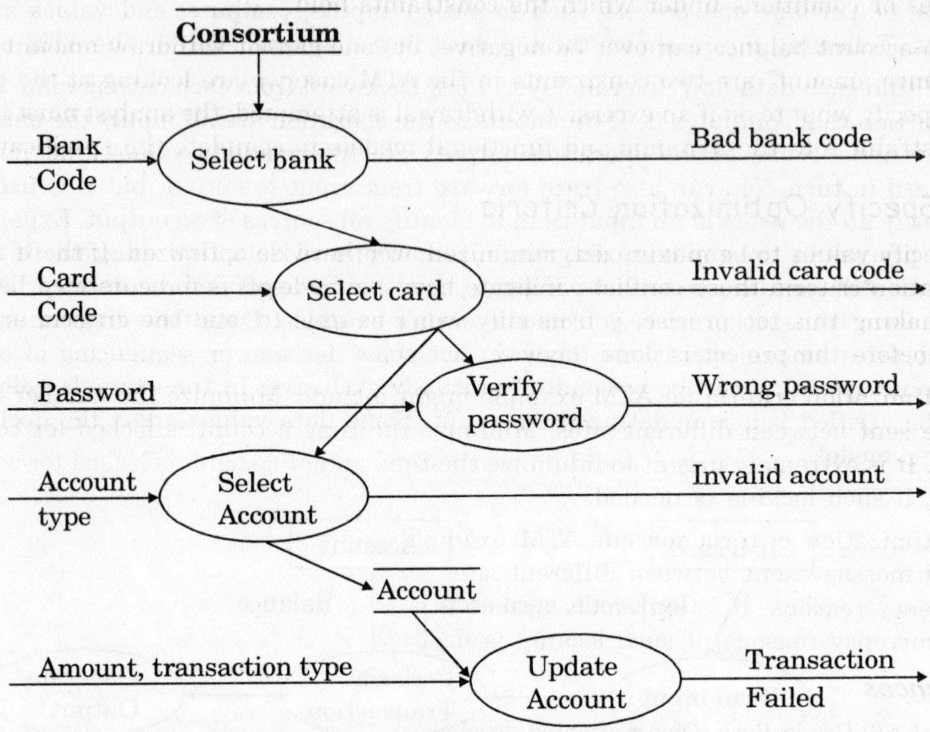

Expanded DFD for ATM (perform transaction)

Updated account (account, amount, transaction type) -> cash receipt, message

if the amount on a withdrawal exceeds the current balance

Reject the transaction and dispense no cash

If the amount on a withdrawal does not exceeds the current balance

Debit the and dispense cash requested

If the transaction is a deposit

Credit the account and dispense no cash

If the transaction is status request,

Dispense no cash

In any case,

The receipt shows ATM number, date, time, account number,

Transaction-type, amount transacted (if any) and new balance.

4.1.3 Identify Constraints

Identify constraints between objects. Constraints are functional dependencies between object that are not related by an input/output dependency. Constraints can be on two object at the same time, between instance of the same object at different time (an invariant), or between instance of different object at different times (although the latter are usually input/output functions). Preconditions on functions are constraints that the input values must satisfy and post-conditions are constraints that the output values are guaranted to hold. State the times or conditions under which the constraints hold.

"No account balance can ever be negative" or "one cannot withdraw amount more that the balance amount" are two constraints in the ATM case we are looking at the constraints do not specify what to do if an excessive withdrawal is attempted; the analyst must incorporate the constraint into the dynamic and functional models to complete the specifications.

4.1.4 Specify Optimization Criteria

Specify values to be maximized, minimized, or otherwise optimized. If there are several optimization criteria those conflicts, indicate how the trade-off is to be decided. Don't worry about making this too precise, you usually won't be able to, and the criteria are likely to change before the project is done anyway.

Optimization criteria for ATM example might include: Minimize the number of physical message sent between different sites. Minimize the time account is locked for concurrency reasons. It is extremely urgent to minimize the time an entire bank is locked for concurrency reasons, if such locking is needed.

Optimization criteria for our ATM example might include: Minimize the number of physical message sent between different sites. Minimize the time an account is locked for concurrency reasons. It is extremely urgent to minimize the time an entire bank is locked for concurrency reasons, if such locking is needed.

References

[Boch-86] Grady Boch. Object-oriented development IEEE Transaction on Software Engineering SE-12, 2 (February 1986), 211–221.

[Meyer-88] Bertrand Meyer. Object-Oriented Software Construction. Hertfordshire, England: Printice Hall International, 1988.

[Shah-89] Ashwin Shah, James Rumbugh, Jung Hamel, Renee Borsari. DSM: an object relationship moseling language. OOPSLA' 89 as ACM SIGPLAN 24, 11 (Nov. 1989), 191–210.

[Shlaer-88] Sally Shlaer, Stephen J. Mellor. Object-Oriented System Analysis Englewood Cliffs, New Jersay: Yourdon Press, 1988.

Exercises

1. Design and draw class diagram for house structure. Make realistic assumption about room, kitchen. **(UPTU-2001)**
2. Describe various symbol used in data flow diagram along with symbol. **(VBSPU-MCA)**
3. Write brief about following:
   (*a*) Nested Data Flow Diagram.
   (*b*) Functional Constraints. **(UPTU-2002)**
4. Discuss several ways of implementing DFD. Prepare a data flow diagram for computing the roots of a quadratic equation $ax^2 + bx + c = 0$. Inputs are a, b and c. Outputs are roots R1 and R2 which may real or complex depending on the values of a, b and c. **(UPTU-MCA- 2003)**
5. Describe the relation of function model to object and dynamic models. Also discuss how these modeling help in a system model. **(UPTU-MCA-2002)**
6. Prepare a data flow diagram for computing the volume and surface area of a cylinder. Inputs are the height radius of the cylinder. Output is volume and surface area. Discuss several ways of implementing the data flow diagram. **(UPTU-B.Tech.)**

7. Prepare a dataflow diagram for computing the mean of a sequence of input values. A separate control inputs is provided to reset the computation. Each time a new value is input, the mean of all values input since the last reset command should be output. Since you have no way of knowing how many values will be processed between resets, the amount of data storage that you should not depend on the number of input values. Detail your diagram down to the level of multiplication, division, and additions. **(UPTU-MCA)**
8. Using the quadratic formula as a starting points, prepare a data flow diagram for computing the roots of the quadratic equation $ax^2 + bx + c = 0$. Real number a, b and c is input. Output are values of $X = R_1$ and $x = R_2$, which satisfy the equation. Remember, R_1 and R_2 may be real or complex, depending on the values of a, b and c. The quadratic formula for R_1 and R_2 is $-b + \sqrt{b^{2-4ac}} / 2a$. **(UPTU-B.Tech.)**
9. Define data flow, data store, actors and control flow. **(VBSPU-MCA)**
10. Draw data flow diagram for a compiler. **(VBSUP-MCA)**
11. How functional model is related with object and dynamic model. **(VBSPU-MCA)**
12. Explain Object Modeling Vs Functional Modeling. **(UPTU-MCA)**
13. Identify various states in which a floppy drive in a computer system can exist. Draw state transition diagram. **(UPTU-MCA)**

5

INTRODUCTION OF C++

C++ was developed by Bjarne Stroustrup in the 1980 at Bell Labs. The name C++ comes from the C increment operator ++, which adds 1 to the value of a variable. The name C++ correctly suggests an augmented version of C.

The C++ is an extensive verson of language C. C++ supports for the structured programming and also it fully supports object-oriented programming, including the four pillars of object-oriented development: encapsulation, data hiding, inheritance, and polymorphism.

These are the main features of the C++ language.

(*i*) It provides functions for input and output statements.

(*ii*) The variable can be declared at point of use.

(*iii*) It provides techniques of object based programming.

(*iv*) It allow use of classes and objects to store large data.

(*v*) It provides new simplified method for file operation.

5.1 IDENTIFIERS

Given names to the program elements is known as identifiers these names is given by the programmer. An identifier is used for any variable, function, data definition, etc.

In the C++ programming language, an identifier is a combination of alphanumeric characters, the first being a letter of the alphabet or an underline, and the remaining being any letter of the alphabet, any numeric digit, or the underline.

The rules in C++ for identifiers are:

(*i*) Only alphabetic characters, digits and underscores are permitted.

(*ii*) The name cannot start with a digit.

(*iii*) Key words cannot be used as a name.

(*iv*) Upper case and lower case letters are distinct.

5.2 VARIABLE

A variable is a name that can be given to some variety of values. Or we can say that: "A values which varies continuously during the execution of programs is a variable of the programs."

Variables are declared like as follows:

Type variable;

For example → int n;

This shows that n is variable name, in which we can store int (integer) type values. There are different types of variables are used in different languages.

5.3 DATA TYPE

Given name to a set of values, which have common property, is known as data type. Classifications of C++ data types are:

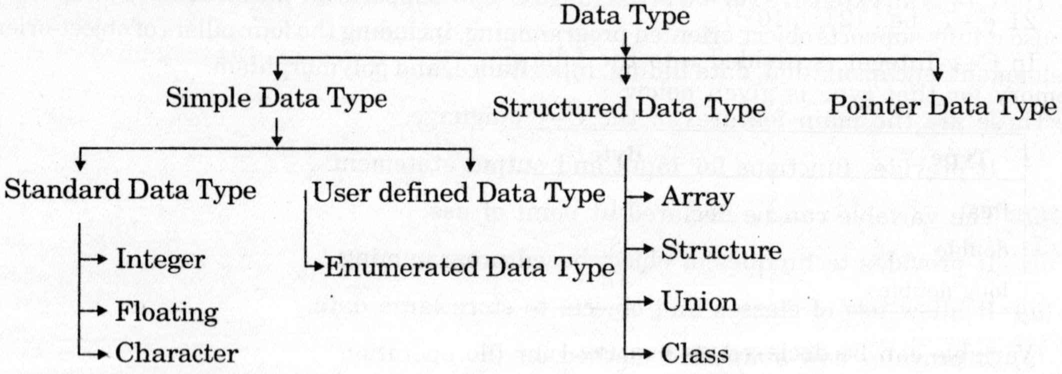

5.3.1 Integer Type

Integers are numbers with no fractional part, such as 2, 98, –5286, and 0. There are lots of integers, assuming you consider an infinite number to be a lot, so no finite amount of computer memory can represent all possible integers. Thus, a language only can represent a subset of all integers. Some languages, such as standard pascal, offer just one integer type (one type fits all!).

In C++ Integer is divided into the following types and their ranges and also required memory for that type is given below.

Type	Byte	Range
int	2	–32768 to 32767
unsigned int	2	0 to 65535
signed int	2	–32768 to 32767
short int	2	–32768 to 32767
unsigned short int	2	0 to 65535
signed short int	2	–32768 to 32767
long int	4	–2147483648 to 2147483647
signed long int	4	–2147483648 to 2147483647
unsigned long int	4	0 to 42949667295

Note: We can not store values which are out of range off that type, if we do so then that will give wrong results.

Variable can be declared as integer by the following way

```
int a, b;
long int x, y;
unsigned long int z;
```

a and b are int type; x and y are long int type; z is unsigned long int type.

5.3.2 Floating Type

Those numbers, which contains fractional part, also is called floating type data.

This type of data can be represented in mantissa and exponent form.

These are some examples of valid floating type data

51.45

251 E 11 i.e., $(251 * 10^{11})$

21 e –7 i.e., $(21 * 10^{-7})$

In C++ Integer is divided into the following types and their ranges and also required memory for that type is given below.

Type	Byte	Range
float	4	3.4 E – 38 to 3.4 E + 38
double	8	1.7 E – 308 to 1.7 E + 308
long double	10	3.4 E – 4932 to 1.1 E + 4932

Variable can be declared as floating type by the following way

```
float a, b;
double x;
long double y, z;
```

Means a and b are float type, x is double type and y and z are long double type.

5.3.3 Character Type

Character variables are declared by using type specifer char. Range is – 128 to + 127. Variable can be declared as floating type by the following way.

```
char ch;
```

means ch is a variable which is of character type.

There are some other character types in C++, they are following (other than char)

1. unsigned char
2. signed char

Types of character and their ranges and also required memory for that type is given below.

Type	Byte	Range
char	1	–128 to 127
unsigned char	1	0 to 255
signed char	1	–128 to 127

We can assign a single character to ch. This can be done via their ASCII value through a character constant, for example-

ch = 'a'

or

ch = 65 [65 is the ASCII value of A]

5.3.4 Enumerated Data Type

Enumerated data type enables you to create new types and then to define variables of those types whose values are restricted to a set of possible values. For example, you can declare COLOR to be an enumeration, and you can define that there are five

Values for COLOR: RED, BLUE, GREEN, WHITE, and BLACK.

The syntax for enumerated constants is to write the keyword enum, followed by the type name, an open brace, each of the legal values separated by a comma, and finally a closing brace and a semicolon. Here's an example:

enum COLOR {RED, BLUE, GREEN, WHITE, BLACK};

This statement performs two tasks:

1. It makes COLOR the name of an enumeration, that is, a new type.
2. It makes RED a symbolic constant with the value 0, BLUE a symbolic constant with the value 1, GREEN a symbolic constant with the value 2, and so forth.

Every enumerated constant has an integer value. If you don't specify otherwise, the first constant will have the value 0, and the rest will count up from there. Any one of the constants can be initialized with a particular value, however, and those that are not initialized will count upward from the ones before them. Thus, if you write enum Color {RED=100, BLUE, GREEN = 500, WHITE, BLACK = 700};

Then RED will have the value 100; BLUE, the value 101; GREEN, the value 500; WHITE, the value 501; and BLACK, the value 700.

You can define variables of type COLOR, but they can be assigned only one of the enumerated values (in this case, RED, BLUE, GREEN, WHITE, or BLACK, or else 100, 101, 500, 501, or 700). You can assign any color value to your COLOR variable. In fact, you can assign any integer value, even if it is not a legal color, although a good compiler will issue a warning if you do.

It is important to realize that enumerator variables actually are of type unsigned int, and that the enumerated constants equate to integer variables. It is, however, very convenient to be able to name these values when working with colors, days of the week, or similar sets of values.

5.4 OPERATOR IN C++

In C++ operator can be classified as follows

1. Arithmetic operator
2. Comparison and relational operator
3. Logical operator
4. Bitwise operator
5. Assignment operator
6. Special operator

5.4.1 Arithmetic Operator

Arithmetic operator are those *mathematical operator*, which are used for adding, subtracting, multiplying, dividing, and other operations. Arithmetic operators of C++ are given below.

Symbol	Meaning
*	Multiplication
/	Division and Integer Division
+	Addition
–	Subtraction
%	Modulus or Remainder

Most of these operators work in the familiar way you expect them to multiplication, addition, and subtraction produce the same results and the division operator *usually* does as those produced with a calculator although modulus operator gives the remainder. Given table will illustrates these simple operators.

Typical operator results.

Formula	Result
4 * 2	8
64/4	16
80 – 15	65
12 + 9	21
64 % 5	4

Note: Modulus operator can be used only with integer type data because 5.5%5 → not allowed because 5.5 is floating point type.

– operator is also some time used to negate a variable, for example suppose.

a = 5

then – a will be –5

This operator is unary because we need only one data with this but all the operators which we discussed before are binary operators because with every operator we need two data or operand.

If – operator is used with one data that is known as unary minus.

Order of precedence for arithmetic operator:

Order	Operator
First	unary minus
Second	Multiplication, division, modulus remainder (*, /, %)
Third	Addition, subtraction (+, –)

But if there is a parentheses () then compiler evaluates that first.

Given examples will show the order of precedence for arithmetic operations.

Example 1:

(4 + 2) * 5 – 4 / 2 + 2
↓
6 * 5 – 4 / 2 + 2
↓
30 – 4 / 2 + 2
↓
30 – 2 + 2
↓
28 + 2
↓
30

Looking back at the order of precedence table, you might notice that multiplication, division, and modulus are on the same level. This implies there is no hierarchy on that level. If more than one of these operators appear in a calculation, C++ performs the math from the left. The same is true of addition and subtraction C++ performs the operation on the extreme left first.

Example 2 : Illustrates an example showing this process.

10 / 5 * 2 – 2 + 1
↓
2 * 2 – 2 + 1
↓
4 – 2 + 1
↓
2 + 1
↓
3

In the above example C++'s order of operators from the left, with lines indicating precedence. Because the division appears to the left of the multiplication, so it is computed first.

5.4.2 Comparison and Relational Operator

Comparison and relational operator are used for comparing two operands (data). These operator given the result false or true (means 0 or 1). For example equal operator compares two values if both are equal, this result true i.e., 1 otherwise false i.e., 0. in C++

In C++ the following are comparison and relational operator.

Operator	Meaning
<	less than
>	greater than
< =	less than or equal to
> =	grater than and equal to
= =	equal to
! =	not equal to

Example:

1. 6 < 6 — This gives false result
2. (5 × 4) < (20 × 3) — This gives true result
3. 8 × 3 — This gives true result
4. 5 < = 5 — This gives true result
5. (8 × 5) > = 40 — This gives true result
6. 9 = = 6 — This gives false result
7. 5! = 6 — This gives true result

5.4.3 Logical Operator

Logical operator are symbol that used to combine or negate expression containing relational operator. Operator ! is equivalent to **Boolean** operation NOT, it has only operand, located at its right, and the only thing that it does is to invert the value of it, producing **false** if its operand is **true** and **true** if its operand is false.

Logical operator **&&** and **!!** are used when evaluating two expression to obtain a single result. They correspond with Boolean logic operation AND and OR respectively. The result of them depends on the relation between its operands:

The following logical operator are in C++

Operator	Meaning
& &	AND
! !	OR
!	NOT

First operand a	Second operand b	Result a && b	Resut a !! b
True	True	True	True
True	False	False	True
False	True	False	True
False	False	False	False

Example: If x = 3, y = 4 & z = 5 then calculate (x > y) && (z < x).

Ans: (x > y) && (z < x)

⇒ (3 > 4) && (5 < 3)

⇒ False && false

⇒ False (result)

Or operator (!!) The result OR operator is true if any condition is true (left to right) or both, otherwise false.

Example: If x = 4, Y = 6, Z = 3 calculate (x > y)!!(z< = y)

Ans: (x > y) !! (z< = y)

(4 > 6) !! (3< = 6)

false !! false

true (result)

NOT operator (!)

NOT operator change the value from false to true or from true to false.

The table for NOT operator

! false	Give result true
! true	Give result false

Example:

If x = 6, y = 3

Calculate

! (x, y)

Ans:

! (x, y)

! (6 < 3)

! false

true(result)

The precedence of logical operator:-

NOT (!)

AND (&&)

OR (!!)

Here also the parentheses is first evaluated

Example:

If x = 5, y = 6 and z = 8

Calculate

(x < y)!! (y > z) && (x. y) !! (x > z)

Ans:

(x < y)!!(y > z) && (x > y)!!(x > z)

(5 < 6)!!(6 > 8) && (5 > 6)!!(5 > 8)

True!!false&&false!!false

True!!false!!false

True!!false

True (result)

5.4.4 Bitwise Operator

Bitwise operator perform operation on the bit level. Generally the high level language do not suppot the bitwise operator. Bitwise operator is one of the salient feature of C++. In C++ the bitwise operator are as follows:

Operator	Meaning
&	Bitwise AND
!	Bitwise OR
^	Bitwise exclusive or (XOR)
>>	Bitwise Right Shift
<<	Bitwise Left Shift
~	Bitwise complement

Bitwise AND (&) : The bitwise AND (&) operator performs operation between two bit pattern.

Example: If x = 5 , y = 2 then calculate x and y

Ans: x = 5 binary pattern of 5 is 101 suppose we are using 8 bit for representing a value then binary pattern of 5 is → 000001, in eight bit form binary pattern of 2 is → 0000010 in eight bit form.

x and y ==> two

00000101

00000010

00000000

The answer is 00000000 means → 0 (zero)

Bitwise OR operator(!) : Bitwise OR operator performs OR operation between two bit pattern.

Example: Bitwise OR operator performs OR operation between two bit pattern.

Example: If x = 7 y = 2 calculate x!y

Ans: The bit pattern of 7 in eight bit form is –00000111

The bit pattern of 2 in eight bit form is –00000010

X!Y → (00000111)!(00000010)

→ 00000111

00000010

00000101

x!y → 00000101 ((Binary pattern)

→ 5 (value is decimal)

x!y → = 5 (result)

Bitwise X-OR operator: This operator perform exclusive OR operation between two bit pattern. The table for exclusive OR is as follows:-

Binary No.		**Result**
0	0	0
0	1	1
1	0	1
1	1	0

→ 0 ^ 0 = 0

→ 0 ^ 1 = 1

→ 1 ^ 0 = 1

→ 1 ^ 1 = 0

Example: If x = 7, y = 2 calculate x^y.

Ans: Bit pattern of → 00000111 → (5)

Bit pattern of y → 00000010 → (2)

x^y = (00000111) ^(0000010)

→ 00000111

x-OR between → 00000010

00000101

x^ y = 00000101(in bit pattern form)

= 5 (in decimal)

If x = 7, y = 2 then x^ y = 5

Bitwise right shift(>>): The right shift operator shifts the right to a binary pattern.

For example x >> 5 means shift the bit pattern of x into right side 5 times i.e., x >> n.

Means shift the bit pattern of x into right side n times, and in every shift drop the shifted bit and store in left side.

Example: If x = 41 the bit pattern of 41 is → 00101001

we have to right shift this three times (x >> 3)

x → 00101001

^after first shift → –0010100

This bit is dropped

zero stored here so the value is

00010100

After II shift → 00001010

After III shift → 00000101

So the resultant bit pattern is → 00000101

The decimal value of this is 5

Therefore

41 >> 3 equal to 5

Bitwise left shift(<<): Bitwise left shift is same as bitwise right shift only difference in this shift the pattern in left side and in every shift this drops the left bit and stress zero in right side.

For example, x << 5 means

Shift left bit pattern of x five times

Example: If x = 33 then calculate x << 3.

Ans: the bit pattern of x → 00100001 → (33)

x → 00100001

after I shift 0 → 01000010

after II shift 0 → 10000100

after III shift 1 → 00001000

dropped bit

The result is → 00001000 decimal equivalents is 8 so

So 33 << 3 equal to 8

Bitwise complement(~): The bitwise complement operator, complements the every bit of a bit pattern i.e., converts 0 to 1 or 1 to 0.

Example: If x = 32 calculate~x.

Ans: The bit pattern of 32 is 00100000

x → 00100000

~x→ 11011111

Decimal equivalent is

5.4.5 Assignment Operator

We can assign a value or variable to another variable. In C++ there are so many assignment operator but most important one is = assignment operator.

a = b means we are assigning the value of b to a

a = 30 means we are assigning 30 to a.

By using assignment operator we can assign a complete mathematical expression to a variable also, for example.

a = b * c + d/z

is also correct. We are assigning (b * c + d/z) value to a

In C++ following assignment operator are available:

Operator	Meaning
=	assign right side value to left side
+ =	a + = b means a = a + b
– =	a – = b means a = a – b
* =	a* = b means a = a – b
/ =	a/ = means a = a/b
% =	a% = b means a = a%b
>> =	a>> = n means a = a >> n
& =	a & = b means a = a & b
: =	a ? = b means a = a ? b
! =	a! = b means a = a!b

In all the assignment operator the right side value is assigned to left side variable. If in right side there is an expression is evaluated then the evaluated value is assigned to left side variable.

For example, x + = y

Equal to x = x + y

In this assignment operator first calculate them that value is assigned to x.

Suppose

x = 5 , y = 3

Then after x + = y → (x = x + y)

x = 5 + 3 = 8

now x is 8 not 5. y remain same.

5.4.6 Special Operator

In C++ there are some special types of operator which perform particular type of operation. Some special types of operator are:

1. Pointer Operator (*) : The pointer operator is used to get the content of the address operator pointing to a particular variable.
2. Address Operator (&) : The address operator is used to get the address of any variable.
3. Membership Operator: To represent the variable from a set of value membership operator are used they are → and [].
4. Scope Operator (: :) : Double colon :: is known as scope resolution operator in C++. With the help of this we can access a global variable within a particular function; if the global variable and local variable has the same name.

5. Size of Operator : Size of operator calculate the size of a variable. This is a unary operator.

6. Ternary Operator (?) S: In C++ this is a very special type of operator. The format of this operator is –

   Expression1? expression2: expression3

   If expression1 is true then expression2 is evaluated otherwise expression 3 is evaluated.

   Example: c = a > b ? a:b;

   In the above example if a is grater than b then a is assigned to c otherwise b is assigned to c.

7. Increment and Decrement Operator:- C++ also provide two special operator one for incrementing the value of a variable and other one is for decrementing the value of a variable.

   Increment operator (++):

   ++ x; equal to x = x + 1:

   Or

   x ++; equal to x = x + 1

There are two type of increment ++x (prefix increment) and x++ (postfix increment). If they use single variable then both act same.

if x = 5

then ++ x; is 6

if x = 5

then x ++; is also 6

But if they used in an expression then there is a difference. In this case they work follow. If prefix increment operator is used, first it increments the variable then expression is evaluated.

Example:

if x = 5;

then after y = ++x;

The value of x is 6 and the value of y is also 6.

If postfix increment operator is used first the expression is evaluated then it increment the value of variable.

Example: if x = 5

then after y = x ++

The value of y is 5 but the value of x is 6.

Decrement operator(--) : Like increment operator in C++ there are decrement operator also they are -- x and x --

x equal to x = x – 1

y = -- x

after these two statement y to 4 and x is also 4.

These operator come under unary operator.

5.5 EXPRESSION

An expression is a combination of operators, constants and variable arranged as per the rules of the language.

In other words an expression is a collection of operand (data) and operator that can be evaluated to a single value. Operator in one or more; operand zero and more.

Example:

1. C = 48 A + B * C
2. C = 4
3. M = (a > b) &&(c < d)
4. C = 4 * D + 5
5. 4 * 5 + 7
6. C + D * F above are the expression. If we write c = 4 * A + BC

Then compiler assumes BC as a single variable because there is no operator between B and C. If we write C = 4 A + B x C this gives an error because in between 4 and A there is no operator compiler assumes 4 A as a variable but this is not a valid variable name, because first character is digit.

5.6 TYPE CONVERSION

Type conversion means conversion of one type to other type. In C++ type conversion can be done by two way automatic and type casting.

Automatic conversion

If we have mix mode expression of one type to other type, some are float type i.e., different type of data in one expression then the lower type variable is converted to the type of the higher type variable.

Example:

```
int c =7;
float a = 155.5
double t = c * a;
```

In the above example int type c is converted to type float and stored in a temporary variable before being multiplied by float a the result is then converted to double so that it can assign to the double variable t.

Order of data type

long double double float long int char

Highest to lowest

By assigning one type variable to other type variable the type is also converted.

Example:

int x

float y

x = y is valid assignment statement, but keep in mind that the fractional part of *y* is truncted if y = 10.5 then after x = y , x is 10 but y remain same.

Type casting

The casting is a technique by which forcefully we can convert one type to other type. The operator used for this purpose is known as cast operator.

The cast operator takes on the format:

(cast type) expression:

Or

cast type (expression)

The cast operator may be a single variable.

Example: int a,b

```
float c,
a = 200; b = 400;
c = (float) a * b;
```

In the above example first a is converted to float then multiplied by b now result is also float then result is assign to c.

now c = 80000;

Example:

```
int a = 5, b = 2;
float c;
c = a/b;
```

In the above case c is 2 not 2.5 why 2 because a and b both are integer type therefore a/b is also integer type.

After calculating a/b that is int type is assigned to c which is float type. But a/b is int type i.e., 5/2 is 2 not 2.5. Therefore c is also 2.

If we want the correct answer then the statements are modified as follows:

```
Int a = 5, b = 2;
float c;
c = a/b;
```

Now c is 2.5 because in above expression first a is converted into float therefore a/b is also float type 5.0/2 is 2.5. Then that is assign to c.

5.6.1 Simple Program

Example 5.1:

```
# include <iostream.h>
void main ( )
{
cout << "Hello, How are you";
}
```

In the first line of the program # include <iostream.h> is necessary. This line means we are adding iostream.h header file in our program. By iostream.h the information about cout object is provided. iostream.h also provides the information about other input and output object and function. If we want to use these functions in our program then we have to add iostream.h in our program like above (example 5.1).

We can add more than one header file in one program, if necessary. For example, suppose we need string function in our program, then we have to add string.h header file also. If suppose we are using getche() function and clrscr() function in our program, then we need conio.h header file. In this case the starting lines of program look like:

```
#include <iostream.h>
#include <conio.h>
#include <string.h>
```

Here there is a question how you know; for a function, what type of header file is needed. The answer of this question, you will automatically get as soon as you cover this book.

In second line program void main () is necessary for every program. From this line onward the program body starts. Before main there is a word void. This means main return nothing. The parentheses ( ) following main are also required, main is treated as a function, in C++.

Third and fifth line of program contain only braces {and}. These enclose the body of main i.e., body of our program. The header are also part of program but *i* am saying only this part as program body because the main aim of the program is written here.

The forth line of program contains a statement cout << "Hello, How are you."

This tells the system to send the message "Hello, How are you," to the cout ("see-out") object. The cout object sends this message to standard output device i.e., screen. The output of above program like: HELLO, HOW ARE YOU

Example 5.2:

```
# include <iostream.h>
# include <conio.h>
void main ( )
{
clrscr ( );
cout << "HELLO, How are You";
getch ( );
}
```

In the above program we have added one more header file conio.h, because we have used clrscr () and getch () function in above program. The above program first clears the screen, because we have written clrscr (). Which is first means this wait for a character.

The message HELLO HOW ARE YOU

Remains on the screen upto when we do not press a key.

The output of above program is :

HELLO, HOW ARE YOU

When we press enter, the program comes onto the screen. Therefore, in every example of this book getch ( ) is written.

Example 5.3: Following program read two no and then print the sum of these two.

```
# include <iostream.h>
# include < conio.h>
void main ( )
{
int a,b,d;
clrscr ( );
cout << "Enter second no.;"
cin >> "Enter first no.;"
cout << "Enter second no;"
cin >> b;
s = a + b;
cout << "The sum of a and b:" <<s;
getch ( );
}
```

The output of above program is:

Ener first no. : 8
Enter second no. : 5
The sum of a and b : 13

In the above program there are two header file iostream.h and conio.h iostream.h is for cout and cin and conio.h is for clrscr ( ) and getch ( ).

After main braces { the statement int a, b, s means we are declaring three variable a, b and s all are integer.

clrscr ( ); which clear screen

cout << "Enter first no.:"; this statement print a message onto screen the message is: Enter first no.

cin>>a; this statement takes the value from standard input i.e., keyboard and assign the value to variable a.

cout >> "Enter second no.:" print the message. Enter second no onto screen.

cin >> b reads a value from keyboard and assign that value to b.

s = a + b; first calculate a + b and then assign the sum of a and b to s.

cout << "The sum of a and b:" <<s this statement print message.

"The sum of a and b :" and in front of that the value of s. If we give from keyboard first no value 8 and second no value 5. Then this statement print like follow:-

The sum of a and b: 13

5.6.2 Input Output Operator

Output Operator

```
cout << " Hello";
```

The above statement print the string Hello on to screen.

In above statement cout is a predefined object that represent the standard output stream in C++. In above example the standard output stream represent the screen. It is also possible to redirect the output to other output devices, we will cover IO stream in file chapter.

In the above statement the operator << is called insertion or put to operator. It inserts the content of the variable on its right to the cout object.

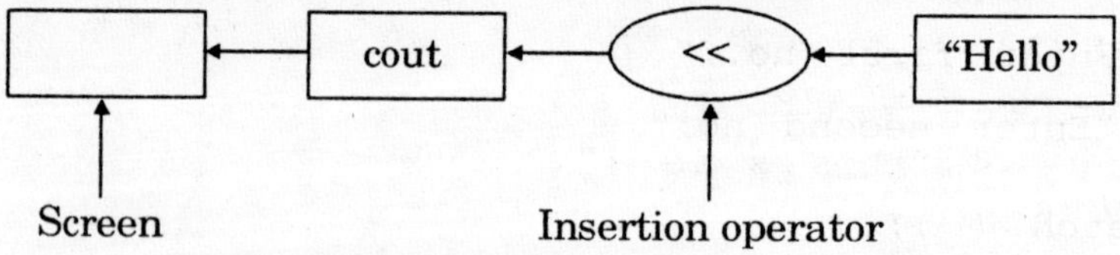

The above statement takes a value that value to n.

Same like cout –cin is also predefined object in C++. Cin represent standard input stream.

The operator >> is known as extraction or get from operator. It extract the value from the keyboard and assign it to variable like:

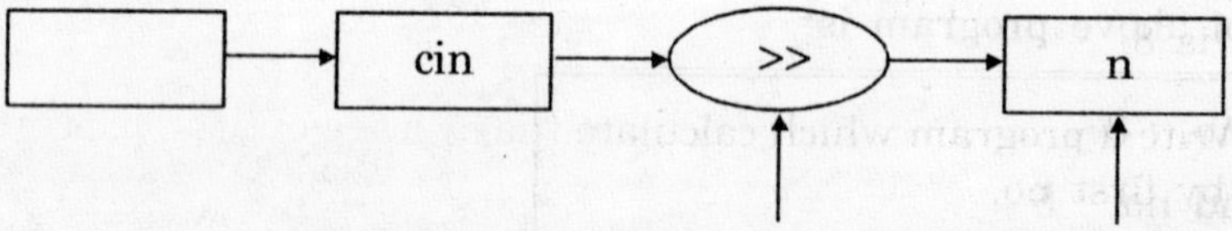

Cascading of input and output operator is also possible. If suppose we want to read the value for variable n1, n2 and n3 then we can write statement:

```
cin >> n1 >> n2 >> n3;
```

This is equivalent to

```
cin >> n1;
cin >> n2;
cin >> n3;
```

Same we do with output operator also for example suppose we want to print the value of a and b then we can write the statement like:-

```
cout <<" a =" << a <<" b = " <<b;
```

Above statement is equivalent to

```
cout << "a = ";
cout << a;
cout << "b = ";
cout << b;
```

Example 5.4: Write a program which read three no. u, a and t and then calculate function s where s=u*t+ ½ * a * t².

```
# include <iostream.h>
# include <conio.h>
void main ( )
    {
        float s, u, a, t ;
        clrscr ( );
        cout << "Enter value of u, a and t:";
        cin >> u >> a >> t;
        s = u * t +(½ ) * a * t* t;
        cout << "this s is :"<< s;
        getch ( );
        }
```

The output of above program is:

Enter first no. 7
Enter second no. 8
Generator no. is 8

Example 5.5: Write a program which calculate the average of two no, print the reminder if second is divided by first no.

```
#include < iostram.h>
# include < conio.h>
void main ( )
    {
    float avg;
    int first, second, reminder;
    clrscr ( );
    cout << "Enter first no. :"
```

```
cin >> first;
cout << "Enter second no.";
remainder = second % first;
avg. = (first + second)/2.0;
cout << "The average is :" <<avg. << endl;
cout << " The reminder is :" <<remainder;
getch ( );
}
```

Output of the above program is:

Enter first no. : 8
Enter second no : 5
The avg. is : 6.5
The reminder is 1

In the above example we have written a statement

Avg. = (first + second)/2.0;

In the above statement we have written 2.0 and not 2 because if we write 2 in place of 2.0 and suppose first = 8 second = 5 then

Compiler calculates

(first + second)/2.0

→ (8 + 5)/2.0

→ 13/2.0 = 6.5

2.0 is float so the final answer is also float type so answer is 6.5 not 6.

Example 5.6: Write a program which reads two nos. and then print greater no.

```
# include <iostream.h>
# include <conio.h>
void main ( )
{
int a, b, c;
clrscr ( );
cout << "Enter first no. :"
cin >> a;
cout << " Enter second no. :";
cin >> b;
c = (a > b) ? a : b;
cout << " Greater no. is :" << c:
getch ( );
}
```

Output of the above program is:

```
Enter first no : 6
Enter second no : 7
Generator no. : 7
```

In above example we are using ternary operator (?)

c = (a > b) ? a:b if a > b is true a is assigned to c otherwise b is assigned to c.

5.6.3 Comment in C++

In C++ the comment can be written by two methods

1. If the comment is one line long, then double slash "//".

   Example: //* Hi! How are you

2. If the comment is multiple line is given by "/*" and "*/".

   Example: /*This is multiple line comment */

Example 5.7: Demonstrate Comment

```
//   This Program Demonstrate Comments
     # include < iostream.h>
     # include <conio.h>
     /* above two line are for header file*/
     void main ( ) //Program main
     {
     int a =10;
     cout << " A="<< a << endl;
     getch ( );
     }
```

The statement which is written in comment is not executed.

Solved exercises

Exercise 1. Write a program to enter two integers and display their sum.

```
# include <iostream.h>
# include <conio.h>
void main ( )
{
clrscr ( );
int A, B, C;
cout <<("\n Enter the first number:");
cin >> A;
```

```
cout <<("\n Enter the second number:");
cin >> B;
C = A + B;
cout <<("\n Sum of two number is:");
getch ( );
}
```

Output of the above program is:

```
Enter the first number :3
Enter the second number : 4
Sum of two number : 7
```

Exercise 2. Write a program to read length and breadth of a rectangle and display it's area.

```
#include <iostream.h>
# include <conio.h>
void main ( )
{
int Length, Breadth, Area;
cout <<("\n Enter the length:");
cin >> Length;
cout <<("\n Enter the Breadth:");
cin >>Breadth;
Area = Length*Breadth;
cout <<("\n Area of rectangle is");
getch ( );
}
```

Output of the above program is:

```
Enter the length: 3
Enter the breadth : 4
Area of rectangle: 12
```

Exercise 3. Program to read principal amount, rate of interest and time from user and display calculated simple interest.

```
# include <iostream.h>
# include <conio.h>
void main ( )
{
```

```
clrscr ( );
float p,r,t, simple_interest;
cout <<("\Enter the principal amount:");
cin>>p;
cout <<("\n Enter the rate:");
cin>>r;
cout<<("Enter the time:");
cin>>t; simple_interest = (p*r*t)/100;
cout<<("/n simple_interest:"<<simple_interest;
getch ( );
}
```

Output of the above program is:

```
Enter the principal amount :1000
Enter the rate: 10
Enter the time : 5
Simple Interest : 500
```

Descriptive Questions

1. Why do we need header file in our program?
2. Explain difference between insertion and extraction operator, how they are used with cout and cin object?
3. What do you understand the term data type?
4. How many data type are available in C++?
5. What is expression?
6. What is identifier state rule for identifier?
7. What is processor directive?
8. What is use of reference variable?

Exercises

1. Write a program which calculate a function F where $F = A^2 + 4BC + 8$, where A, B, C are input ?
2. Write a program which calculate F where $\frac{F-32}{9} = \frac{C}{5} =$ where C is input?
3. Write a program to display the following output using a single cout statement

   Data structure = 85

   Programming in C++ = 95

DBMS = 87

Computer Network = 80

4. Find out the errors in the following C++ statement:
   1. cout << x
   2. cin >> x;
   3. cout<< ("The value of x is") >> x;
5. Write a program in C++ which would ask the user the student 's roll number and english marks and display it as "Roll number X score Y marks in english", X represent the roll number whereas Y represent english Marks?
6. Write a program in C++ using structure to initialize the birthday of person born on 15th August 1947 and also display the same?
7. Program to read principal amount, rate of interest and time from user and display calculated compund interest?

6

CONTROL FLOW

Depending upon requirement of a problem, it is often required to alter the normal sequence of execution in the program. This means desire to selectively or repetitively execute a program segment.

A number of C++ structure, known as control structure, are available for the flow of processing. We study structure under following topics:-

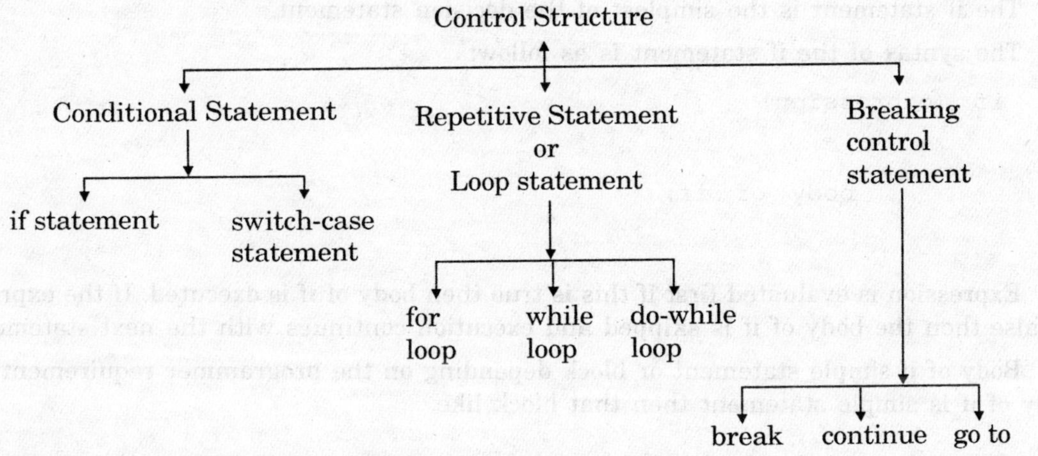

Before studying above structure we will study statement and block.

Statement: An expression such as

c = o or x – – or cout << x;

Because a statement when it is followed by a semicolon as in

c = o;

x ––;

cout << x;

In C++ semicolon is a statement terminator. The above statement is also known as simple statement.

Block: Block are also known as compound statement. Braces {and} are used to group declaration and statements together into a compound statement, or block, so that they are

syntactically equivalent to a single statement. There is no semicolon after the right brace that ends a block.

For example,

```
{ x1 = y + z;
  x2 = y * z;
  x3 = y – z;
  x4 = y/z;
}
```

6.1 CONDITIONAL STATEMENT

Conditional statements are mainly used for making decision. Depending on value of an expression decision can be made. Following are the conditional statements in C++.

6.1.1 If Statement

The if statement is the simplest of the decision statement.

The syntax of the if statement is as follow:

```
if (expression)
    {
        body of if;
    }
```

Expression is evaluated first if this is true then body of if is executed. If the expression is false then the body of if is skipped and execution continues with the next statement.

Body of if simple statement or block depending on the programmer requirement i.e. If body of if is simple statement then that block like.

```
if (expression)
    statement;
```

or

```
if (expression)
    statement;
```

If the body of if is compound or block then that look like:

```
if (expression)
{statement1;
statement 2;
        :
statement n;
}
```

If expression is true then all the statements within the block are executed. In case expression is false all the statements within the block are skipped.

Following diagram shows the execution of if statement.

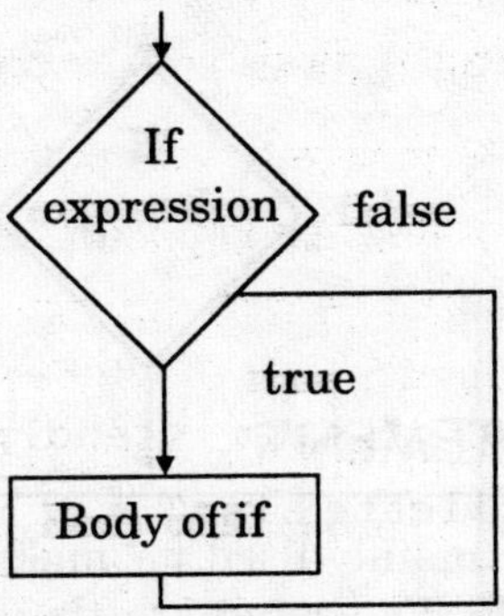

Example 6.1: Write a program which reads two numbers and then print greater one.

```
# include <iostream.h>
# include <conio.h>
void main ( )
    { int a, b;
    clrscr ( );
    cout << "Enter two no. :";
    cin >> a >> b;
    if (a>b)cout << "Greater is :" <<a;
    if (b > a) cout << "Greater is : "<<b;
    getch ( )·
}
```

Output of the above program is:

Enter two no.	: 7 8
Greater is	: 8

In above program we have used two if statement

Example 6.2: Write a program which calculate sum of two numbers and multiplication of two numbers if first number is greater than second one otherwise print sorry.

```
# include <iostream.h>
# include <conio.h>
void main ( )
    {
    int   a,b, sum, multi;
    clrscr ( );
```

```
        cout << "Enter first no. :";
        cin >>a;
        cout << "Enter second no. :"
        cin >>b;
        if (a>b)
        {
        sum = a + b;
        multi = a * b;
        cout << "sum is :"<<sum <<endl;
        cout << "multiplicate is:" << multi << endl;
        }
if (b >=a) cout << "Sorry";
        getch ( );
        }
```

6.1.2 If Else Statement

The syntax of if else statement is

```
if (expression)
    body of if;
else
    body of else
```

Body of if and body of else may be simple or may be block. If body of if and body of else is simple then the structure look like this.

```
if (expression)
    statement 1;
else
    statement 2;
```

If body of if and else is compound then the structure looks like.

```
if (expression)
    {
    Statement 1;
    Statement 2;
    :
    Statement n;
    }

else
```

```
{
Statement 1;
Statement 2;
:
Statement n;
}
```

If else structure execute like this-

Expression is evaluated first if that is true then the if body is executed otherwise else body is executed. Following diagram shows its execution.

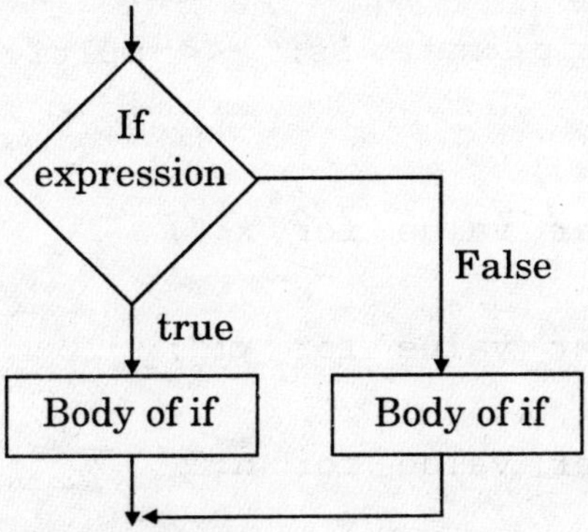

Example 6.3: Write a program which reads a number then prints the message for that number (that is even or odd).

If we divide a number by two and remainder is 0 that means that number is even otherwise odd. With the help of this concept we can write program.

```
#include <iostream.h>
#include <conio.h>
void main ( )
    { int n;
    cout << "Enter a number":;
    cin >> n;
    if (n%2 = = 0)
    cout << "The number is even";
 else
    cout << "The number is odd";
    getch ( );
    }
```

If we give n = 11 then output is:

```
Enter a number : 11
The number is odd
```

If we give n = 12 from keyboard then output is:

```
Enter a number : 12
The number is even.
```

Example 6.4: Write a program which calculate a function F where F is equal to-

F = { x + y if n > 0

x – y if n < = 0 where x, y and n is input.

```
# include <iostream.h>
#include <conio.h>
    void main ( )
    {
    clrscr ( );
    int x,y,n,f;
    cout << "Enter value for x:";
    cin >> x;
    cout << "Enter value for y:";
    cin >>y;
    cout << "Enter value for n:"
    cin >> n;
    if (n>0)
        {
        f = x + y ;
    cout << "f :" << f;
    }
    else
    {
    f = x - y;
    cout << "f is :" << f;
    }
    getch ( );
    }
```

If we give value x = 6 y = 7 and n = 2 then output is:

```
Enter value for x : 6
Enter value for y : 7
Enter value for n : 2
    f is : 13
```

6.1.3 Nested if-else Statement

In if statement of if-else statement in place of body we can also use again if or if-else this concept is known as nested structure. Following example give idea about this.

Example 6.5: Write program which reads three numbers and then find the largest one.

```
#include <iostream.h>
#include <conio.h>
void main ( )
{
float  a, b, c;
clrscr ( );
cout << "Enter three no. :";
cin >> a >> b >> c;
    if (a > b)
    {
        if (a>c)
cout << "largest value :" <<a<<endl;
    else
cout << "largest value :"<<c<< endl;
    }
else
    {
    (if (b>c)
    cout << "largest value :" <<b << endl;
        else
    cout << "largest value :" << c << endl;
    }
getch ( );
}
```

Output of program:

```
Enter three no.: 10 20 30
largest value: 30
```

Example 6.6: Write a program which reads a date and check whether that is valid or not.

```
# include <iostream.h>
# include <conio.h>
void main ( )
{
int month, day, year;
clrscr ( );
cout << "Enter month of date:";
cin >> month;
```

```
cout << "Enter day of date:";
cin >> date;
cout << "Enter year of date:"
cin >> year;
if (month = = 1)
{ if (day < = 31)
    cout << "Date is valid";
else cout << "Date is invalid"; }
if (month = = 2) { if (year  % 4 = = 0)
        { if (day < = 29)
    cout << "Date is valid";
else cout << "Date is invalid"; }
else { if (day < = 28)
cout << "Date is valid";
else cout << "Date is invalid";
else if (month = = 3)
    { if (day < = 31)
cout << "Date is valid";
    else
cout << "Date is invalid";
    }
else if (month = = 4)
    { if (day <= 30)
cout << "Date is valid";
    else
cout << "Date is invalid";
    }
else if (month = = 5)
    { if (day <=31)
cout << "Date is valid";
    else
cout << "Date is invalid";
    }
else if (month = = 6)
{ if (day < = 30)
cout << "Date is valid";
    else
cout << "Date is invalid";
```

```
    }
else if (month = = 7)
    { if (day < = 31)
cout << "Date is valid";
    else
cout << "Date is invalid";
    }
else if (month = = 8)
    { if (day < = 31)
cout << "Date is valid";
    else
cout<< "Date is invalid";
    }
else if (month = = 9)
    { if (day < = 30)
cout << "Date is valid";
    else
cout << "Date is invalid";
    }
else if (month = = 10)
    { if (day < = 31)
cout << "Date is valid";
    else
cout << "Date is invalid";
    }
else if (month = = 11)
    { if (day < = 30)
cout << "Date is valid";
    else
cout << "Date is invalid";
    }
else if (month = = 12)
    { if (day < = 31)
cout << "Date is valid";
    else
cout << "Date is invalid";
    }
getch ( );
    }
```

Output of Program is as follows:

```
Enter month of date: 7
Enter day of date 32
Enter year of date 2000
```

Or the output is as follows:

```
Enter month of date: 8
Enter day of date 25
Enter year of date 2000
Date is invalid
```

If you give valid date print date is valid otherwise if date is not valid this print date is not valid. Nested if-else statement sometimes leads to continue especially when an else is omitted from a nested if-else sequence.

For example

```
if  (expression)
        if  (expression)
                statement1;
else
                statement2;
```

Above statement are wrong. In above example there is a syntactic ambiguity.

```
if  (expression)
        {  if  (expression)
                statement1;
        }
else
                statement2;
```

Now this is correct, because in this there are braces. In this it is clear that the statement is for the second if.

6.1.4 Switch Statement

The switch or switch-case statement is an alternate of nested if-else structure. This is a multi way decision maker that test whether an expression matches one number of values.

```
switch  (expression)
        {
case  value 1:
        statement  1;
        statement  2;
        :
```

```
        statement n;
        break;
    case value 2:
        statement 1;
        statement 2;
        :
        statement n;
        break;
        ______
        ______
        ______
    case value n:
        statement 1;
        statement 2;
        :
        statement n;
        break;
        default :
        statement 1;
        statement 2;
        :
        statement n;
        }
```

The expression must be **integer or character** type. That means the value 1, value 2,.... value n all are also **integer or character** type.

In switch statement, switch, case break are reserve word. Switch first calculate the expression then match that expression with case value 1 if both are equal then first case body is executed and switch is terminated because of break statement, which is written. If we skip, the break statement then after executing first body switch is not terminated this match with next value and so on.

If expression is not equal to value 1, then expression checked with value 2 if equal executed second case body and switch is terminated.

If expression is not equal to value 2 then expression checked with value 3 if there is no match process continue to last value.

If expression is not match with any other value from 1 to value n then default body is executed.

The diagram for execution of switch statement is :→

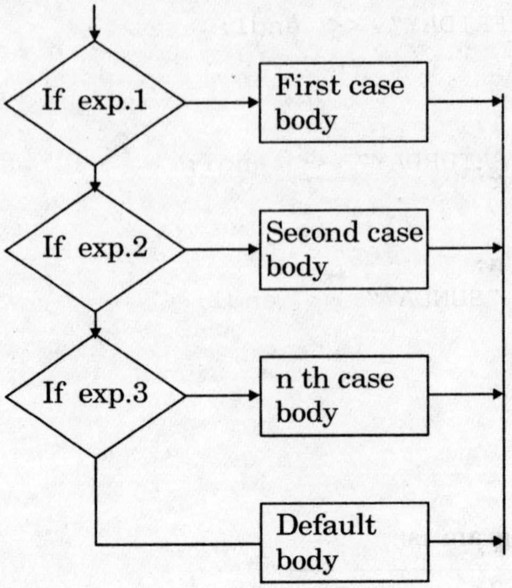

Example 6.7: Write a program which reads a number between 1 to 7 and then print the day corresponding to that number.

```
# include <iostream.h>
# include <conio.h>
void main ( )
{
int n;
clrscr ( );
cout << "Enter a number between 1 to 7";
cin >>n;
switch (n)
    {
Case 1 :
    cout << "MONDAY" << endl;
    break ;
Case 2 :
    cout << "TUESDAY" << endl;
    break;
Case 3 :
    cout << "WEDNESDAY" << endl;
    break;
Case 4 :
    cout << "THURSDAY" << endl;
    break;
```

```
Case 5 :
     cout << "FRIDAY" << endl;
     break;
Case 6 :
     cout << "SATURDAY" << endl;
     break;
Case 7 :
     cout << "SUNDAY" << endl;
     break;
     }
getch ( );
}
```

Output of above program is:

Enter number between 1 to 7 : 5 **FRIDAY**

In above from keyboard we are giving value 5. Output of above program depends on the value given from keyboard.

6.2 LOOP STATEMENT OR REPETITIVE STATEMENT

Loop cause a section of our program to be repeated a certain number of times. The repetition continues upto when a condition is true.

There are three kind of loop in C++. They are for loop, while loop and do while loop.

6.2.1 For Loop

For loop is easiest loop. This consists three expressions. The syntax of for loop is as follow:-

```
for (initialization expression; test expression; assignment)
     {
     (body of loop)
     }
```

If in body of loop there is single statement then for loop look like:

```
for (initialization expression; test expression; assignment)
     statement;
```

If body of loop consists multiple statements that look like:

```
for (initialization expression; test expression; assignment)
    {
    statement 1;
    statement 2;
    statement 3;
    :
    statement n;
    }
```

Example 1: `for ( i = 0; i < = 9 ; i ++)`

```
        statement;
```

Example 2: `for ( i = 0; i <= 9 ; i ++)`

```
        {
        statement 1;
        statement 2;
        }
```

The for statement execute like following

First the initialization expression execute. Then test expression is checked if it is false loop terminate, if this is true body of loop is executed. After this assignment assign a new value (that increment or decrement the variable) to variable. Then again test expression is checked if false loop terminate otherwise body of loop again execute.

This process repeat until the test expression becomes false.

The diagram for this is as follow:

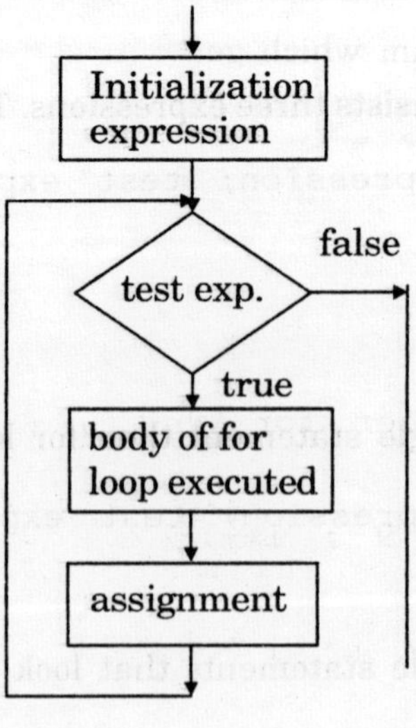

Example 6.8: Write a program which calculates the factorial of a given number.

```
# include <iostream.h>
# include <conio.h>
void main ( )
{
long int n, fact;
clrscr ( );
cout << "Enter a number :";
cin >> n;
fact =1;
for (int i=2; i < = n ; i++)
fact = fact * i;
cout << "The factorial of "<<n<<" is : "<<fact;
getch ( );
}
```

In the above example we have declared n and fact long int because if user give larger number. Then the factorial is also too large. In chapter 2 we have seen that every data type has a fixed range. Long int range is large than int range.

In for loop we have written int i=2 that means we are declaring also here. In C++ we can declare variable anywhere within the program when we read.

The output of above program looks like following if we give 5 from keyboard:

Enter a number : 5
The factorial of 5 is : 120

Example 6.9: Write a program which generate the table of number.

```
# include <iostream.h>
# include <conio.h>
void main ( )
{
int n;
cout << "Enter a number for which you need table:";
cin >> n;
for (int i=1; i < = 9 ; i++)
fact = fact * i;
cout << n<< i<< "="<< n* i <<endl;
getch ( );
}
```

The output of above program look like if we give 4 from keyboard:

```
Enter a number which
you need table : 5
5 * 1 = 5
5 * 2 = 10
5 * 3 = 15
5 * 4 = 20
5 * 5 = 25
5 * 6 = 30
5 * 7 = 35
5 * 8 = 40
5 * 9 = 45
5 * 10 = 50
```

Note: **In for loop we can initialize more than one variable also**

Example 1:
```
for (i=0, f=2; i<=5; i++, f--)
    statement;
```

Example 2:
```
for (i=0, j=3; j<=5; j++)
    statement;
```

If we write more than one initialization expression they are separated by comma, same for assignment expression is also.

Example 6.10

```
# include <iostream.h>
# include <conio.h>
void main ( )
{
int i, j;
for (int i=1; j = 9; i < = 9; i++, j--)
cout << "I=" << i << "J =" << j << endl;
getch ( );
}
```

The above program gives the following output:

```
I = 1    J = 9
I = 2    J = 8
I = 3    J = 7
I = 4    J = 6
I = 5    J = 5
I = 6    J = 4
I = 7    J = 3
I = 8    J = 2
I = 9    J = 1
```

Note: We can write following type of loop also

Initial loop

```
for (; ;)
      statement;
```

The statement executes infinite time, because there is no condition checked within the for loop.

That means we can say that in for loop all the expression are optional we can skip any one or more if we need but semicolon is necessary.

For example, in following loop the initialization expression is skipped.

```
for (; i < = 5; i++
statement;
```

Nested for loop:

In C++ any loop can be placed inside other loop. One for loop can be placed inside other for loop that is known as nested for loop.

For example,

```
for (i =0; i <= 7; i++)
for (j = 0; j <= 6; j++)
      Statement;
```

In the above example inside the first loop there is a second loop. Second for loop body has one statement.

```
for (i =0; i <= 7; i++)
      {
      for (j = 0; j <= 6; j++)
            {
            statement1;
            statement2;
            }
            statement3;
            statement4;
                  }
```

In above example statement1 and statement2 are body part of for (j = 0; j <= 6; j++) loop. But statement3 and statement4 are not the body part of for (j = 0 ; j <= 6; j++) loop. That means the first loop body has two part one is a loop for (j = 0; j <= 6; j++) and second are two statements statement3 and statement4.

Example 6.11: Write a program which generate the following pattern.

```
1
1    2
1    2    3
1    2    3    4
```

1	2	3	4			
1	2	3	4	5		
1	2	3	4	5	6	
1	2	3	4	5	6	7

We can write the program for above pattern with the help of nested for loop.

```
# include < iostream.h>
# include < conio.h>
void main ( )
    {
    int i, j;
    for (i =1; i<= 7; i++)
    {
    for (j=1; j<=i; j++)
        cout << j;
        cout << endl;
        }
    getch ( );
}
```

Note: In the above program we write cout << i in place of cout << j the output of program is different that is

1						
2	2					
3	3	3				
4	4	4	4			
5	5	5	5	5		
6	6	6	6	6	6	
7	7	7	7	7	7	7

Example 6.12: Write a program which generate the following pattern:

6	6	6	6	6	6
5	5	5	5	5	
4	4	4	4		
3	3	3			
2	2				
1					

We can write the program for above pattern with the help of nested for loop. In all loop we have used a variable which is known as index or control variable.

```
# include <   iostream.h>
# include < conio.h>
void main ( )
    {
    int  i, j;
    for  (i =6;  i<= 1;  i--)
    {
    for  (j=1;  j<=i;  j++)
        cout    << j;
        cout << endl;
        }
    getch ( );
}
```

6.2.2 While Loop

For loop is best if we fixed number of repetition. But if we don't know how many times you want to do something you start the loop then while loop is used.

The syntax of while loop is:

```
while  (condition)
body of loop;
```

If body of loop consists one statement that look like:

```
while  (condition)
     statement;
```

If body of loop consists multiple statements that looks like:

```
while  (condition)
{
statement1;
statement2;
statcment3;
:
statementn;
}
```

Condition is any expression which gives true or false value. Note in C++, zero value means false any non-zero means true.

Execution of while loop:

First the condition in evaluated if that is non-zero means true the body of loop executed otherwise loop terminates. After execution of body again condition is checked if it is zero or false the loop is terminated otherwise again the body of loop executes.

The body of loop is executed again and again upto when the condition is not false. The diagram for this is as follows:

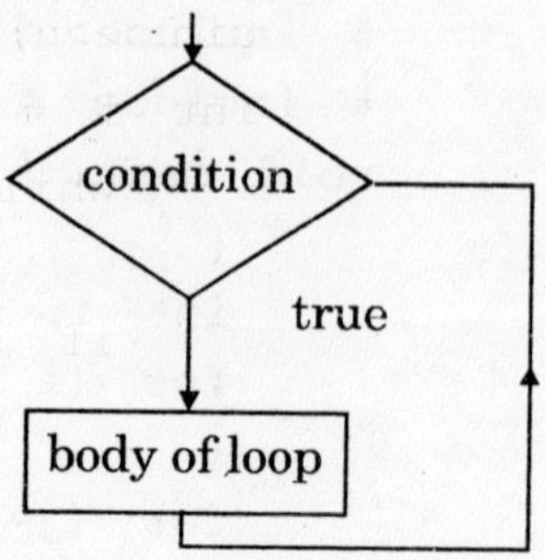

Example

```
while  (i <=9)
{  cout  <<  "i  ="  <<i;  i++;
}
```

Example 6.13: Write a program which reads integer number from keyboard until you do not give zero number.

```
# include <   iostream.h>
# include < conio.h>
void main  ( )
    {
    int n =5; // make sure n is not 0
    cout << "Enter 0 for termination otherwise any number";
    while  (n  ! = 0)
    cin >> n;
}
```

The above program terminate when we give 0 from keyboard otherwise this number reads. Here's some sample output:

```
Enter 0 for termination otherwise any number
    9
    10
    15
    20
    25
```

Example 6.14: Write a program which reads a number and then check whether that number is prime or not.

Prime number is number which is divisible by itself and 1 for example 7 is prime but 9 is not because 9 is divisible by 3.

```
# include <   iostream.h>
# include < conio.h>
void main  ( )
    {
    int n;
    cout << "Enter a number:";
```

```
cin >>n;
int i = 2, c= 0;
    while (i<= (n-1))
        {
    if (n % i = = 0)
        c++;
        i++;
        }
    if (c = = 0)
    cout << "Number is PRIME";
    else
    cout<< "Number is NOT PRIME";
    getch ( );
    }
```

Output of the program is:

Enter a number : 7
Number is PRIME
Enter a number : 9
Number is NOT PRIME

Example 6.15: Write a program which generate the Fibonacci series. Series is for more than one number.

If a1, a2, a3, a4....is Fibonacci series then a1= 1; a2 =1; a3=a1 + a2; a4= a2+a3 and so on

```
# include < iostream.h>
# include <conio.h>
void main ( )
    {
    int n;
    int a1,a2,a3;
    clrscr ( );
      cout << "Enter how many number series you need.'';
      cin >>n;
      a1 = 1;
      a2 = 1
      cout << a1<<endl;
      cout << a2<<endl;
      int c = 2;
    while (c < n)
        {
```

```
        a3 = a1 + a2;
        a1 = a2;
        a2 = a3;
        cout << a3 << endl;
        c++;
        }
    getch ( );
}
```

We can write above program with the help of for loop also. Try for that. The sample output for this program is if we give 6 from keyboard.

Output of the program is:

```
Enter how many number series you need 6
1
1
2
3
5
8
```

6.2.3 Do-While Loop

In a while loop, the condition is evaluated at the beginning of loop. If condition is false when the loop is entered, the loop body won't be executed at all. But in do-while loop first the body of loop is executed then the condition is evaluated. In do-while loop the body of loop always executes at least one time if the condition is false also.

The syntax of do-while loop is

```
do
body of loop;
while (condition);
```

If body of do-while loop consists one statement then that look like:

```
do
statement;
while (condition);
```

If body of do-while loop consists multiple statements then that look like:

```
do
{
statement1;
```

```
statement2;
    :
statementn;
    }
while  (condition);
```

The diagram of do-while loop execution is as follow:

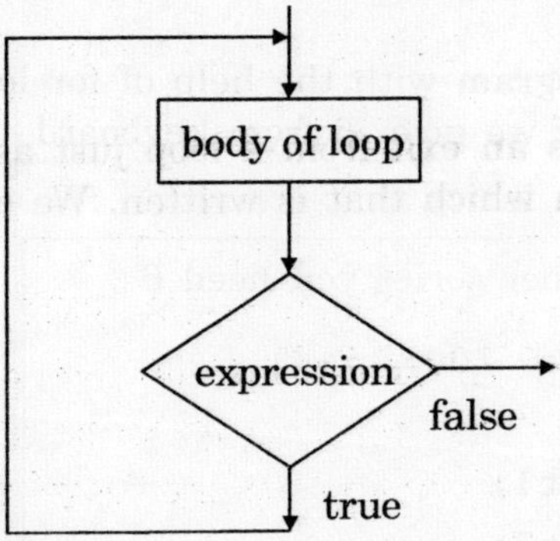

Example 6.16: Write a program which calculate the sum of odd number.

Sum = 1 + 3 + 5 + 7 +....n

```
# include < iostream.h>
# include <conio.h>
void main ( )
    {
    int n;
    cout << "Enter any no.:";
    cin >>n;
    int sum=0, i=1;
    do
        {
        sum=sum + i;
        i = i+2;
        }
        while (i <=n);
        cout <<"1+2+3+......"<<n<< "=" <<sum;
    getch ( );
}
```

Above program takes n first, then n different value from keyboard and calculate sum and average for these values.

6.3 BREAKING CONTROL STATEMENT

C++ provides three different type of breaking control statements. With the help of breaking control statement the control structure power is improved.

The breaking control structure is improved.

1. break statement
2. continue statement
3. goto statement

6.3.1 Break Statement

Break statement causes an exit from a loop just as it does from a switch statement. Break terminate the loop in which that is written. We can use break in any loop.

Example 1

```
for  (i  =  0;  i  <=  100;  i++)
     {
          statement1;
          statement2;
          break;
          statement3;
               }
          statement4;
```

Loop terminate here statement 3 not executed because before that there is a break statement.

Example 2

```
while  (condition)
       {
       statement1;
       statement2;
if  (a  <b)
       break;
       statement3;
       }
       statement4;
```

The above loop terminates if a>b is true

Example 3

```
do
       {
       statement1;
```

```
statement2;
break;
statement3;
} while (condition);
statement4;
```

In the above example loop terminate therefore statement 3 never executed.

6.3.2 Continue Statement

The continue statement is used for inverse operation of break statement. The continue statement transfers control to start of loop. The syntax of continue statement is similar to break.

Syntax of break is

```
break;
```

Syntax of continue is

```
continue;
```

both are reserve words.

Example

```
while (condition)
    {
    statement1;
    statement2;
if (a >b)
    continue;
    statement3;
    }
```

In the above example is a>b is true the control is transferred to start means again condition is checked and statement executed. The arrow shows the flow of control.

Example 6.17: Write a program which reads an integer and then calculates

(*a*) The sum of individual digit in the number

(*b*) The number of digit is the number.

```
# include <iostream.h>
# include < conio.h>
void main ( )
{
int n;
cout << "Enter a number:";
cin >>n;
int sum =0,c=0;
do
{
sum = sum + n %10;
```

```
n = n/10;
c++ ; }while (n>0);
cout << " Number of digit is the" <<n;
cout << " are :"<<c<<endl;
cout << "sum of digit:" <<sum << endl;
getch ( );
}
```

Example 6.18: Write a program which converts binary number to decimal number.

```
# include <iostream.h>
# include < conio.h>
# include <math.h>
void main ( )
{
int bin, int dec = 0.0; base = 0, bit;
clrscr ( );
cout << "Enter a binary number:";
cin >>bin;
while (bin)
{
     bit = bin %10;
     dec = dec +bit * pow (2, base);
     base ++;
     bin = bin/10;
}
cout << "Decimal equivalent is: "<<dec<<endl ;
getch ( );
}
```

In the above program we have used math.h header file because in program we are using pow (2, base) function. pow ( ) is a mathematical function which calculate power of a variable → pow (x, n) = x^n. This is an inbuilt function in C++, but for this we have to add math.h header file. In while loop in place of condition we have written only bin that also right. When bin becomes zero loop terminate. Because in C++ zero means false and number means true.

6.3.3 Goto Statement

By goto statement we can transfer the control to some other part. Means by goto we can change the execution sequence of the program.

The general syntax of goto is

```
goto label;
```

goto is reserved word. Label name given by user or programmer but be valid identifier.

Example:

```
goto start;
goto 23
```

But goto 23A; is invalid identifier because 23A is not valid identifier.

Example 1

```
statement1;
statement2;
start : statement3;
statement4;
goto start;
```

Example 2

```
statement1;
statement2;
start : statement3;
statement4;
if (a>b) goto start;
```

Solved Exercises

Exercise 1. Write program to find series sum for the following series

$$x + \frac{x^3}{3!} + \frac{x^5}{5!} + \ldots \frac{x^{2n-1}}{(2n-1)!}$$

```
#include <iostream.h>
#include <conio.h>
#include<math.h>
void main ( )
{
    clrscr( );
    float i, sum =0, o, n, x, j, fact =1, term;
    cout << "\n enter the number of terms in the series:";
    cin>>n;
    cout << "\n Enter the value of x:";
    cin>>x;
    cout << "\n the required series is:\n";
    for (i=1; i<=2*n-1; i=i+2)
```

```
{
        fact  =  1;
        for(j=1;  i<=2*n-1;  i=i+2)
        {
        fact  =1;
        for  (j=1;  j<=1;  j++)
        fact  =  fact*j;
        term  =  pow(x,i)/fact;
        if  (j<i)
            cout<<term<<  "+";
            else
            cout  <<term;
            sum  =  sum  +  term;
            }
            cout  <<  "\n  sum  of  series:"<<sum;
            getch(  );
            }
```

Output of the program is:

Enter the number of terms in series :5
Enter the value of x :3
The required series is :
3 + 4.5 + 2.025 + 0.433929 + 0.054241

Exercise 2. Write a program to find series sum for the following series:

$$1 + \frac{x}{2!} + \frac{x^2}{4!} + \frac{x^3}{6!} + ... \frac{x^n}{2n!}$$

```
#include  <iostream.h>
#include<conio.h>
#include<math.h>
void main  (  )
{
     clrscr  (  );
     float  i,  sum  =  1,  n,x,j,  fact  =1,  term;
     cin>>n;
     cout  <<  "\n  Enter  the  value  of  x:";
     cin  >>x;
```

```
cout << "\n series is :\n ";
for(i=1, i<=n; i++)
{
    fact =1;
    for (j =1; j <=n; j++)
    fact = fact *j;
    term = pow(x,i)/fact;
    if (j <n)
        cout <<term << "+";
    else
        cout <<term;
    sum = sum + term;
    }
    cout << "\n sum of series :" <<sum;
    getch ( );
    }
```

Output of the program is

Enter the number of terms in the series : 5 Enter the value of x: 3 Series is : 1 + 1.5 + 0.375 + 0.0375 + 0.002009 + 6.696429e-05

Exercise 3. Write a program to display Fibonacci series upto terms (obtain n from user) and display sum of these terms

Fibonacci Series. The Fibonacci series wherein every third element is the sum of previous two element e.g., if first two element are 0 and 1 respectively, third element will be 1(0+1), fourth will be 2(1+1), fifth will be 3(1+2), and so on.

Element

First 0

Second 1

Third 1 (First+Second)

Fourth 2 (Second+Third)

Fifth 3 (Third+Fourth)

```
#include<iostream.h>
#include<conio.h>
void main ( )
```

```
{
    clrscr ( );
    long t1=0,t2=1,t3, n,i, sum =1;
    cout << "\n Enter the number of terms(>2):";
    cin>>n;
    if (n>2)
        {
        cout << "\n t1\t<<t1;
        cout << "\n t2\t<<t2;
        for (i=3; i<=n;i++)
        {
        t3 = t1 + t2;
        cout << "\n t" <<i<< "\t=\t"<<t3;
        t1=t2;
        t2=t3;
        sum = sum + t3;
        }
        cout << "\n sum of" << n << "terms of Fibonacci series :"sum;
        }
        else
        cout << "No of terms should be more than 2\n";
        getch ( );
        }
```

Output

```
Enter the number of terms (>2): 5
t1 = 0
t2 = 1
t3 = 1
t4 = 2
t5 = 3
```

Descriptive Questions

1. Explain nested if structure?
2. What is while loop explain how while loop varies from do-while loop?
3. How many times loop body is executed in do loop?
4. What is break statement. Explain the use of break and goto statement?
5. The loop-body of the do-while loop is executed one or more times justify?
6. Write syntax for switch-case-default?
7. Explain relational operators and what are their associativetey?
8. Explain type casting?

Exercises

1. Write a program reads three number and display them in ascending order.
2. Write a program to three integer and display the largest order.
3. Write a program reads marks in three subjects, calculate average marks and assigns grade as per following specification:

   for marks (> = 90) grade A; for marks (75 – 90) grade B; for marks (60 – 75) grade C; for marks (50 – 60) grade D; and for marks (< 50) 'fail'.
4. Write a program that reads two numbers and perform arithmetic operations as per the optional opted from given menu.
5. Write to calculate area of square/rectangle/circle/triangle depending upon user's choice.
6. Write a program to check whether a given year is leap year or not.
7. Write a program to find roots of quadratic equation.
8. Write a program to read a day-number and print corresponding day of week.
9. Write a program to read a digit and display it in words.
10. Write a program to read two integer and check whether first number is divisible by second number.
11. Write a program to find the sum for series 1 + 2 + 3 + 4 + 5....n
12. Write a program to find sum of series 2 + 4 + 6 + ... + n.
13. Write a program to find a 3 digit number below 1000 such that the sum of cubes of digits of the number is equal to the number.
14. Prepare a program to read 10 digit number and rewrite in reverse order.
15. The displacement is given by:

    $s = ut + 1/2\ at^2$. Write a program to prepare a table of displacement versus time for given values of initial velocity u and acceleration at uniform increments of 1 second and 0 to 50 second.
16. Write a program to evaluate $x = \sum cy^k$.
17. Write a program to evaluate for different values of x

    $$P = x.\ \frac{x^2}{3}.\frac{x^3}{5}......\frac{x^{10}}{19}.$$

    where x value varies as

    $x = 0.9, 0.95, 1.0, ..., 1.4.$
18. Write a program to check whether the number is ARMSTRONG or not.
19. Write a program to display all factors of a given positive integer.
20. Write a program to check whether number is PALINDROM or not.
21. Write a program whether the number is perfect number or not.
22. Write program to generate PERFECT NUMBERS.
23. Write a program to generate MERSENNE NUMBERS.

    [**Hint:** Mersenne numbers are the one which are one less than power of two. 1, 3, 7, 15, 31, 63, 127,.....]
24. Write a program to display pyramid of digits 1-5.
25. Write program to find least common divisor of two given numbers.

7

FUNCTION

A function groups a number of program statement into a unit and give its name. This unit can then invoked from other part of program.

In C++, the main ( ) itself is a function. The main ( ) function invoke the other functions to perform its various tasks. In C++ there is no difference between function and subroutine or procedure. The function may or may not transfer back, value to a called function block.

7.1 STRUCTURE OF FUNCTION

The general syntax of the function definition is

```
function_return_type  function_name  (data_types  arg 1,data_type 2
arg 2...)
{
_

_

body of function

_

return  (value);
}
```

7.2 EXPLANATION ABOUT SYNTAX

***(i)* Function _Return _Type:** In place of this we write the type of value which return by the function to the calling portion of the program for example int, float, char etc. If functions return nothing to the calling portion of the program then we write **void** in place of function return type.

Note that if a function return type is **void** then there is no need of return statement within the function body.

Example 1

```
int  function_name(type 1  arg 1,  type  2  arg2,...)
    {
```

```
        —
        —
        —
        return  (int  type  value);
        }
```

Example 2

```
float  function_name  (type 1 arg 1,  type 2 arg 2...)
    {
        —
        —
        —
        return  (float  type  value);
        }
```

Example 3

```
void  function_name  (type 1 arg 1,  type 2 arg 2...)
    {
        —
        —
        —
        }
```

Note: The return type value must be same as function return type. But if function return type is void then no need of return statement.

***(ii)* Function_name:** Function name can be any name conforming to the syntax rules of identifier.

Example

```
    display  ( );
        square_of_a  ( );
        etc.
```

***(iii)* Data_Type and Arg**: Arg means argument. The data type of argument depends on the application of function. An argument is a data passed from a program to a function. The data_type of arg. tells about the type of arg. Note that the each argument variable must be declared independently inside parentheses.

Example. Write a function which calculates sum of two integer type numbers.

```
int  sum  (int  a,  int  b)
{
    int  sum;
    sum  =  a  +  b;
    return  (sum);
```

***(iv)* Body of Function**: The body of function is same like the body of main ( ) program. Statement or a block of statements enclosed between two braces; { and }.

In above example the body of function is also written.

***(v)* Return Statement:** The return is a reserve word. It is used to terminate function and return a value to its caller.

The syntax of return statement is-

return (value);	or	return value;

The value can be expression also. We can skip the value part i.e., return;

Example.

```
return  (a  -  b);
return  (j  -  -);
return;
```

Note: A function can also have more than one return statements.

Example.

```
int  smaller  (int  a,  int  b)
     {
     if  (a  <b)  return  (a);
          else  return  (b);
     }
```

Example 7.1 Write a function which calculate the multiplication of two numbers, call this function in main program.

```
# include <iostream.h>
# include <conio.h>
void main ( )
     {
     int  x,  y;
     int  mul  (int  a,  int  b);  //  function  prototype
     clrscr  (  );
     cout  <<  "Enter  the  value  of  first  no.:";
     cin  >>  x;
     cout  <<  "Enter  the  value  of  second  no.  :";
     cin  >>  y;
     cout  <<  "  The  multiplication  is  :"  <<endl;
     int  m  =  mul(x,y);  //  calling  function.
     cout  <<m  <<  endl;
     getch  (  );
          }  //  end  of  main  program
          int  mul  (int  a,  int  b)
          {  int  temp  =  a  *  b;
               return  (temp);
               }
```

Output of above program is:

```
Enter the value of first no. 6
Enter the value of second no. 7
The multiplication is : 42
```

In the above program within the function body we can write the following statement in place of

```
int temp = a * b;
return (temp);
   ⇓
return (a * b);
```

7.3 PROTOTYPE OF FUNCTION

The prototype describes the function interface to the compiler by giving details such as the number and type of argument and type o return values.

Note that in C++ prototype is must.

In example 7.1 the prototype declaration is:

```
int mul (int a, int b);
```

In place of above we can write

```
int mul (int , int );
```

That means the name of argument is optional in prototype declaration but the type is must. Each argument variable must be declared independently inside parentheses. If we write.

```
int mul (int a, b)
```

This is illegal. The general syntax of prototype declaration is

```
type function_name (argument list);
```

If function return type is void and suppose we are not passing any variable to function then that look like

```
void function_name ( );
```

or

```
void function_name (void);
```

Note: Prototype declaration must match with the function header.

7.4 CALLING THE FUNCTION

The syntax of the call is also following if function return type is void.

```
function_name  (parameter  name);
```

If the function return int, float or any other type value then we have to assign the call to same type value like.

```
m  =  function_name  (parameter  name);
```

In the above example 7.1 we have written following statement for call

```
int  m  =  mul(x,y);
```

The type of m is int type and the return type of mul function is also int type. We can write mul(x,y) directly in cout also. i.e., above program example 7.1 we write in place of following two statements.

```
int  m  =  mul  (x,y);
cout  <<m<<endl;
```

Call statement causes the function to execute; that is control is transferred to the function; the body of function executes and then function returns to the statement following the function call.

Example 7.2: Write a function which calculate the root of $x^2 + bx + c = 0$, call that into main program root are $x = \frac{-b \pm \sqrt{b^2} - 4ac}{2a}$.

```
# include <iostream.h>
# include <conio.h>
#include <math.h>
void main  ( )
    {
        float  a,b,c;
        void root  (float,  float,  float);
        clrscr  ( );
        cout  <<  "Enter  the  value  of  a,b  &  c:";
        cin  >>a>>b>>c;
        root  (a,b,c);
        getch  ( );
    }//  end  of  main
void root  (float  x,  float  y,  float  z)
```

```
        {
        float temp = y * y - 4 * x * z;
if  (temp <0)
    {
    cout << "The root's are imaginary";
    }
else if (temp = = 0)
    {
    cout << "Both roots are equal"<<endl;
        float r = -y/(2*x);
    cout << " roots are :" <<r<<endl;
    }
else
    {
    float r1 = (-y + sqrt (temp)/2 *x;
    float r2 = (-y - sqrt (temp)/2 * x;
cout << "First root is :"<<r1<<endl;
cout << "Second root is :" <<r2<,endl;
    }
}// end of function root
```

Simple output of above program if we give a,b,c 1, 4 3

Enter the value of a,b & c: 1 4 3
First root is : –1
Second root is : –3

7.5 ACTUAL AND FORMAL PARAMETER

The argument are classified into

(*i*) Actual (*ii*) Formal

Actual: When a function is called some parameters are written within parenthesis. These are known as actual parameter. In above program example 7.2 the calling statement is:

```
root (a,b,c);
```

a, b and c are known as actual parameters.

Formal: Formal parameter are those who are written in function header. In above program example 7.2 the header of function is:

```
void root(float x, float y, float z );
```

x, y and z are formal parameters in example 7.2 when we give the statement root (a,b,c);

execute, the control transfers to function, and the value of a is copied into x, the value of b is copied into y and the value of c is copied to z.

The formal parameter and the variable which declare inside the body of function are created when function is called and they exist only upto control remain on function.

We can give same name to actual and formal parameter, but their implementation is different. If in any function there is no formal parameter then we can write

Void in place of formal parameter.

```
# include <iostream.h>
void main ( )
    {
        void power (void); //prototype
        ___
        power ( ); // function calling
        ___ ;
        void power (void) // function header
        {
        _____;
        _____; // function body
        _____;
        }
```

Example 7.3: Write a program which calculate $\overset{n}{\underset{r}{C}}$ where $\overset{n}{\underset{r}{C}} = {!n}/{!n-r*!r}$

Ans. To solve above problem we are writing a function which calculate factorial and then we are passing different value to that.

```
# include <iostream.h>
# include <conio.h>
void main ( )
    {
    long int n; fact (long int);
        float ncr; clrscr ( );
        cout << "Enter the value of n:";
        cin >> n;
        cout << "Enter the value of r :";
        cin >> r;
        ncr = (float) fact (n)/fact (n-r) * fact (r) ;
        cout << "ncr is: "<< ncr << endl;
        getch ( );
    }
long int fact (long int temp)
```

```
{
long int t = 1, i;
for (i =2; i <= temp; i++)
t = t * i;
return (t);
}
```

Output of above program is:

```
Enter the value of n : 3
Enter the value of r : 2
ncr is : 3
```

Example 7.4: Write a Program which calculate the sum of following series

$$sum= x + \frac{x^2}{!2}+\frac{x^4}{!4}+\frac{x^6}{!6}+...+\frac{x^n}{!n}$$

```
#include <iostream.h>
#include <conio.h>
#include <math.h>
void main ( )
    {
    float x;
    long int n, i, fact (long int);
    clrscr ( );
    cout << "Enter N (even no.) :";
    cin >> n;
    cout << "Enter x:";
    cin >>x;
    float sum = x;
    for (i = 2; i <=n; i = i + 2)
    sum = sum + pow (x, i)/ fact (i);
    cout << "sum of series is : "<<sum<<endl;
    getch ( );
    }
    long int fact (long int m)
        {
        long int temp = 1, i;
        for (i = 2; i <= m; i ++)
        temp = temp * i;
        return (temp);
        }
```

Example 7.5: Write a program which calculate the sum of following series

$$\text{Sum} = 1 - x + \frac{x^2}{!2} + \frac{x^3}{!3} + \frac{x^4}{!4} + \frac{x^5}{!5} + \frac{x^6}{!6} + ... + \frac{x^n}{!n}$$

```
#include <iostream.h>
#include <conio.h>
#include <math.h>
void main ( )
    {
    float  x;sum;
    long int n, i  , fact (long int);
    clrscr ( );
    cout << "Enter n:";
    cin >> n;
    cout << "Enter x:";
    cin >> x;
    sum = 1;
    int j  = -1;
    for ( i = 1; i < = n; i++)
        {
    sum =sum + (j) * pow (x, i)/fact (i);
    j = -j;
    cout << "sum of series is : "<< sum << endl;
    getch ( );
        }
long int fact (long int n)
        {
        long int temp = 1, k;
        for (k =2; k<=n ; k++)
            temp = temp * k;
        return (temp);
        }
```

7.6 PASSING ARGUMENT TO FUNCTION

An argument is a data passed from a program to the function. In function we can pass variable by following three ways:

1. Passing value, 2. Passing by reference, 3. Passing by address or pointer

7.6.1 Passing by Value

In this value of actual parameter is passed to formal parameter when we call the function. But actual parameter is not changed.

Example

```
#include <iostream.h>
#include <conio.h>
void main ( )
    {
    int x, y;
    void swap (int, int);
    clrscr ( );
    x = 10;
    y = 20;
    swap (x, y);
    cout << "x =" << x << endl;
    cout << "y =" << x << endl;
    getch ( );
        }
void swap (int a, int b)
        {
        int  t ;
        t = a;
        a =b;
        b = t;
        }
```

Output of above program is:

```
x = 20
y = 10
```

In the above program the value of actual parameter x and y are copied into a and b but the change in a and b does not affect into x and y. This is the property of call by value or passing by value.

7.6.2 Passing by Reference

Passing argument by reference uses a different approach. In this the reference of original variable is passed to function. But in call by value the value of variable is passed.

The main advantage of passing by reference is that the function can access the actual variable in the calling program. The second advantage is this provide a mechanism for

returning more than one value from the function back to the calling program. It can change the actual parameter.

```
#include <iostream.h>
#include <conio.h>
void main ( )
    {
    int x, y;
    void swap (int &, int&);
    clrscr ( );
    x = 10;
    y = 20;
    swap (x, y);
    cout << "x =" << x << endl;
    cout << "y =" << x << endl;
    getch ( );
        }
void swap (int &a, int &b)
    {
    int  t ;
    t = a;
    a =b;
    b = t;
    }
```

Output of above program is:

x = 20
y = 10

The variable followed by & is a reference of that. In above program a and b are reference name for x and y respectively they refer to the same region. i.e., the change in a and b reflected the change in x and y.

7.6.3 Passing by Address or Pointer

This is similar to passing by reference but only difference in this case we pass the address of a variable.

Example

```
#include <iostream.h>
#include <conio.h>
```

```
void main ( )
    {
    int x, y;
    void swap (int *, int *);
    clrscr ( );
    x = 10;
    y = 20;
    swap (&x, &y);
    cout << "x =" << x << endl;
    cout << "y =" << x << endl;
    getch ( );
    }
void swap (int * a, int * b)
    {
    int  t ;
    t = * a;
    * a = * b;
    * b = t;
    }
```

Output of above program is:

x = 20
y = 10

In the above program we are passing the address of x and y by the statement

```
swap(&x,&y)
```

& x means address of x.

& y means address of y.

In function header we have written

```
void swap(int * a, int * b)
```

Int * a means a is pointer type which point to integer type data i.e., a can store the address of integer type data. Similarly int * b. In the function body we have written.

```
t = * a;
* a = * b;
* b = t;
```

`t = * a;` The * a means value which store at the address a i.e., the value of variable which is pointed by a.

This statement takes the value from address a means value x assign that value to t.

```
* a = *b;
```

This statement takes the value from address b means the value of y and assigns that value to a means at the address point by a means to x.

```
* b = t;
```

This statement assign the value of t to *b means y by using above three statement automatically the value of x and y is changed.

7.7 RETURN BY REFERENCE

A function can return a reference also.

```
int & min ( int &a; int &b)
    {
    if (a<b) return (a);
        else return (b);
        }
```

In above example return type of min is int & reference type. That means the function call such as min (x, y) will yield a reference to either x or y depending on their values. This means.

```
min (x, y) =10;
```

Is illegal and assign 10 to all to a if a<b is true otherwise 10 assign to b.

7.8 CONST ARGUMENT

In C++ we can declare constant like following:

```
const x = 10;
```

Const is reserved word. Above declaration means x is constant type i.e., the value of x remains constant through the program. In C++, argument to function can be declared as constant.

Example

1. int add (const c);
2. float mul(const char * m);

The qualifier const tells the compiler that the function should not modify the argument. If we violate the condition compiler will generate error.

7.9 INLINE FUNCTION

When we call a function control jump to function and come back to caller program when execution of function is completed. This takes lot of time. One solution of this problem is to use macro. Usual error checking does not occur during compilation in macro because they are not function. In C++ a different solution of above is also possible, that is inline function. When we call inline function compiler replace function call with the corresponding function code but control not jump to function.

Declaration of inline function

Inline function declare like follows

```
inline function_name (argument list)
    {
    _
}
```

Example

```
inline plus (int a, int b)
    {
    return (a+b);
    }
```

Example 7.6: Write a inline function which calculates cube of number and call that into main program.

The program of above problem is:

```
# include<iostream.h>
# include <conio.h>
inline double cube (double x)
    {
        return (x * x * x);
        }
void main ( )
    {
        double a;
        clrscr ( );
        cout << "Enter a no. :";
        cin >> a;
        cout << "The cube of"<<a<< "is :";
        cout << cube (a);
        getch ( );
        }
```

The simple output of above program is

```
Enter a no. :3
The cube of 2 is : 8
```

Explanation

In the above program the complete function is written before main. If we write the complete function body before main then there is no need of prototype declaration. We can write every function like above program function. But if we need the declaration of prototype of inline function name.

```
inline name_of_function(argument)
```

The syntax is similar to normal function but here there is a inline word is used before function name.

```
inline double cube (double)
```

Inline is reserved word in C++ for example the prototype for above function if we write the body of function after main is calling of inline function is same as calling normal function.

7.10 DEFAULT ARGUMENT

A function in C++ can be called without specifying all its argument. In case the function declaration must provide default values for those arguments that are not specified. The compiler looks at the prototype to see how many arguments a function uses and alerts the program for possible default values. One important point to note that only the trailing argument can have default values. That is the default argument must add from right to left. We cannot provide a default to a particular argument in the middle or first of an argument list.

```
float add (int a, int b = 2, int c = 5);
```

This illegal because trailing argument is default

```
int add (int a = 5, int b);
```

This illegal because trailing argument is not default

```
int add (int a, int b = 6, int c);
```

This illegal because trailing argument is not default

```
int add (int a = 4, int b = 5, int c = 6);
```

This is legal because arguments are default from right to left.

Example 7.7: Write a function which calculate A where $A = P(1 + r/100)^n$ for data p,r.n. But for some cases the value of r is fixed that is 50. Call this function in main program.

For solving this problem we can use the default argument concept because r is fixed for some case.

```
#include <iostream.h>
#include <conio.h>
#include <math.h>
void main ( )
      {
      float p,r,A;
      int n;
      float fun (float, int, );
      clrscr ( );
      cout << A < endl;
      cout << "Enter value of p, n; and r :";
      cin >> p >> n;
      A = fun (p,n)
      cout << "The value of A for default r :";
      cin>>p>>n>>r;
      A = fun (p,n,r);
      cout << "The value of A:"<<A<<endl;
      getch ( );
      }
      float fun (float p, int n, float r)
      {
      float temp = 1+r/100;
      float final = p * pow (temp, n);
      return (final) ;
      }
```

The output of the program is:

```
Enter the value of p and n : 100
                             2
The value of A for default r : 225
Enter the value of p,n and r : 300
                               1
                               25
The value of A : 350
```

Explanation: In the above program there is on default argument r. That means if suppose we do not pass the r in function then function automatically assume the default value of r, in our program we have assigned 50 to r see the prototype declaration.

```
float fun (float, int, float =50);
```

In this declaration we have skipped the name of argument. We can write this like follow also.

```
float fun (float p, int n, float r = 50);
```

In the above program we have called the function fun two times. In first call

```
A = fun (p,n);
```

The compiler automatically takes the value of default argument r and calculates according to that

```
A = fun (p,n,r);
```

We are passing all three arguments. Therefore compiler calculates according to the value of p, n and r does not take the default value in this case. i.e., I we do not pass the default argument function compiler take default value for that otherwise if we pass the default argument to function then compiler takes this value and not default value.

7.11 RECURSION

If a function calls itself is called recursion

```
# include <iostream.h>
void main ( )
    {
        _
        _
        fun ( );
        _
        _}
    void fun ( )
        { void fun ( )
        fun ( );
        _
        _
        }
```

Example 7.8: Write a program which calculate the factorial of number using recursion

Factorial of n is !n = n * ! n-1

!n-1 = (n-1) * !n-2

```
# include <iostream.h>
# include <conio.h>
void main ( )
    {
    long int fact (long int);
    long int f, n;
    cout << "Enter a number :";
    cin >> n;
    f = fact (n);
    cout << "Factorial is : << f << endl;
        getch ( );
        }
        long int fact (long int); // local fun prototype
        long int value = 1;
        if (n = = 1) return (value);
        else
            {
            value = n * fact (n-1);
        }
    }
```

The simple output of above program is:

Enter a number : 6
Factorial is : 720

Explanation: The value calculates like follow:

Value for n = 6 → 6 * fact (5)

For fact (5) → 5 * fact (4)

For fact (4) → 4 * fact (3)

For fact (3) → 3 * fact (2)

For fact (2) → 2 * fact (1)

For fact (1) → 1

Now fact (1) is passed to fact (2) → 2 * 1 = 2, now fact (2) value is passed to fact (3) → 3 * 2 = 6, now fact (3) value is passed to fact (4) → 4 * 6 = 24, now fact (4) value is passed to fact (5) → 5 * 24 = 120, now fact (5) value is passed to fact (6) → 6 * 120 = 720.

Note: If a function is used in a module (main or any other function) then we have to declare the prototype of that function in that module, In the above example local function prototype is used because function fact using fact function i.e., call to itself. But if function use itself i.e., call itself then we can skip local function prototype. In above example we can skip the local function prototype.

7.12 STORAGE CLASSES

The storage class of a variable tells about which part of a program can access it and also tells about its existence. In C++ the storage classes are following type:

1. Automatic
2. Static
3. Global or External
4. Register

7.12.1 Automatic

If a variable defined within a function that is known as automatic variable or local variable. Variable defined inside main ( ) are also automatic because in C++ main ( ) is also a function. A keyword auto is used to specify automatic variable. The general syntax of automatic variable is:

```
Auto data type variable 1, variable 2, ...;
```

For example

```
auto int a, b;
auto char c,d;
```

But we can skip the word auto. That means above variable can also be written as

```
int a,b;
int c,d;
```

Variable defined inside a function is automatically automatic variable. Therefore auto is default.

Example

```
void fun ( )
{
auto int a,b;    // a &b are automatic variable
  –
  –}
```

Example

```
void fun ( )
    {
    auto int c,d;
    –    // c and d are automatic
    –
    }
```

In the above example we can skip auto word

Example

```
void fun ( )
{
int a,b;   // a &b are automatic variable
—
—}
```

Example

```
void fun ( )
{
int c,d;
—   // c and d are automatic
—
}
```

Lifetime of automatic variable: An automatic variable created only when the function is called in which they are defined and are automatic variable are destroyed when we return from the function. The time period between the creation and destruction of a variable is called its lifetime. The lifetime of automatic variable is the execution time of a function. But if a automatic variable is inside main ( ) then that remain until main is executing.

Scope or visibility of automatic variable: The scope of a variable where within a program it can access. Automatic variable are accessed only within the function in which they are defined.

Example

```
# include <iostream.h>
void main ( )
    {
    int a,b;   // automatic variable
    void fun ( );
    —
    a = 10;
    — }
void fun ( )
    {
    int c, d;    // automatic variable
    a = 10; // wrong statement because a is
            // not accessed here
    c = 20;
    d = 30;
        }
```

In the above example a and b accessed only within main and not within fun ( ) function, and similarly c and d can accessed only within the fun ( ) function.

Initialization of automatic variable

When we create automatic variable then compiler does not initialize this. Thus it will take arbitrary value which may be 0 or something else. But if we want to initialize we can do like in place of simple a, b;

```
int a =10, b = 20;
```

7.12.2 Static

Here we will study static automatic variable. There are static external variables, but they are used only when program is multiple program. A static automatic variable is defined like-

```
static int a;
```

Lifetime and scope of static variable: A static automatic variable has the scope of local variable but the lifetime of external variable.

Initialization: Static variable initialized only once at the beginning, they are not reinitialized each time the function is called.

7.12.3 Global or External

Global variable or external variable are also called global variable. External variable defined outside of any function i.e., the variable which defined in between the header of program and main.

```
# include <iostream.h>
int a,b; // global variable
float c,d ; // global variable
void main ( )
    {
    void fun ( );
    _
    _
    _
    }
void fun ( )
    {
    _
    _
    }
```

For declaring global or external variable the keyword extern is used but we can skip this as like above example. The general syntax of external variable is

```
external data type variable 1, variable 2, .....
```

Lifetime of global variable: Global variable exist for the life of program. This takes memory space when program begins and remain until the program ends.

Scope of global variable: External or global variable are accessed in file in which they are defined. That means in above a, b, c and d can access within main ( ) and within function fun ( ). In the example a and b are global variable therefore they can access within main and within fun ( ).

```
# include <iostream.h>
void main  ( )
    {
    void  fun  ( );
    a  =  10;
    b  =  20;
    _
    _
    }
void  fun  ( )
    {
        a  =  30;
        b  =  40;
    _
    _
}
```

Initialization of external or global variables: If external or global variables are not initialize by the programmer then it is initialized 0 (zero) automatically when they are created.

7.12.4 Register

All variable are stored in memory. As accessing a memory location takes time more than accessing one of the machine register. We can store a variable in register with the help of register storage class. But if the machine register is not free then compiler stores that variable like others in memory.

The general syntax of register variable is:

```
register data type v1, v2, .....;
```

Register is keyword.

Example

```
void fun ( )
{
    register int n;
    -
    -
    }
```

Example 7.9: By using following example we understand the difference between static and automatic variable.

```
# include <iostream.h>
# include < conio.h>
void main ( )
    {
    void f1 ( );
    void f2 ( );
    f1 ( );
    f1 ( );
    f1 ( );
    f2 ( );
    f2 ( );
    f2 ( );
    getch ( );
    }
void f1 ( )
    {
    int n = 1; // automatic variable
    n ++;
    cout << "N: "<<n<<endl;
        }
    void f2 ( )
    {
    static int m = 1; // static variable
    m ++;
    cout << "m :"<<m<<endl;
    }
```

Output of the above program is:

```
N : 2
N : 2
N : 2
N : 2
N : 3
N : 4
```

Explanation: The value of n is 2 in every call. Because n is automatic variable, this creates when we call the function and destroy when we come back from function, so in every call to f1 n is created with value 1 and then n++ means n is 2 after that, the value is printed. When function terminates n also destroy. In next call again n is created with value 1, then n++ means n is 2 and then this value is printed.

In next call again same process is repeated but in case of m; because it is static variable is equal to life time of external variable and static is variable initialized once. That means m is not destroyed like n and the statement

static int m = 1 is execute only in first call to function f2 ( ).

In a program the local and global variable has same name then within the function in which local variable has high priority, but we can access global variable also with the help of scope resolution operator (: :).

Example 7.10

```
# include <iostream.h>
# include <conio.h>
int x = 20; // global variable
void main ( )
    {
    int x= 15;   // Local variable
    clrscr ( );
    cout << "local x is :"<<x<< "global x is :"<<: : x;
    x = x + 25;
    : : x = : : x + 25;
    cout << "\n local x is:" <<x<<" global x is:"<<: : x;
    }
```

Output of above program is:

```
Local x is : 15 and Global x is: 20
Local x is : 40 and Global x is : 45
```

Solved Exercises

Exercise 1. Program to check whether passed value is positive or not. The check function return 1 if the passed value is positive, otherwise return 0(zero).

```
# include <iostream.h>
# include <conio.h>
int check(int n);
void main ( )
    {
    int x, result;
    cout << "Enter any number :";
    cin >> x;
    result = check (x);
    if (result = = 1)
        cout << "The number you entered is positive";
        else
        cout << "The number you entered is negative";
        getch ( );
        }
    int check (int n)
        {
        if (n >0)
            return 1;
        else
        return 0;
        }
```

Output of the above program is:

Enter any number : 3
The number you entered is positive.

Exercise 2. Program to print power of number without using a library function. The power ( ) function should accept two parameter m and n to complete m^n. If only m is passed, then it should return m^2.

```
# include <iostream.h>
# include <conio.h>
int power(int m, int n=2)
void main ( )
{
    clrscr ( );
```

```
        int  P,Q,  m,n;
        cout << "Enter values m and n to complete m^n(m raised to
power n):";
        cin >>m>>n;
        P=power(m,n);
    cout<<"\n"<<m<<" to the power<<n<<n is (both argument were
passed):"<<p;
        Q=power(m);
    cout<<"\n"<<m<<" to the power 2 is (one argument is passed):"<<Q;
    getch ( );
    }
    int power (int m, int n)
    {
    int i, p=1;
    if(n = =0)
        return 1;
  else
    {
    for (i = 1; i <= n; i++)
        p=p * m;
        return p;
        }
    }
```

Output of the above program is:

Enter value m and n to compute m^n (m raised to power n) : 5 4
5 to the power 4 is (both argument were passed) :625
5 to the power 2 is (one argument is passed) : 25

Exercise 3. **Program to read time hh:mm:ss hrs format and display how many seconds have passed since midnight.**

```
    #include<iostream.h>
    # include <conio.h>
    long secPassed(long hh, long mm, long ss);
    void main ( )
        {
        long h,m,s;
        clrscr ( );
        cout << "Enter the time (hh mm ss) hrs :";
```

```
        cin >> h >> m >> s;
        if ( h > = 0 && h <24)
            if (m > = 0 && m<60)
            if (s > = 0 && s < 60)
            cout << "\n Second Passed since midnight:" <<
secPassed(h,m,s);
        else
            cout << "Invalid time entered /n";
        else
            cout << "Invalid time entered/n";
            else
            cout << "Invalid time entered/n";
            getch ( );
            }
            long secPassed (long hh, long mm, long ss)
            {
                long res;
                res ss;
                res + = mm * 60;
                res + = hh * 3600;
                return res;
                }
```

Descriptive Type Questions

1. What is function? What is use of function?
2. What is inline function explain with example?
3. What is different between static variable and automatic variable explain with example?
4. Explain what is scope of variable. Explain what is storage class?
5. What is difference between register variable and automatic variable explain with example?
6. Explain call by value parameter, call by reference parameter and call by address.

Exercises

1. Write a program print sum, average, maximum, and minimum, of some real number that are entered through keyboard?
2. Write a program to calculate volume of box whose dimensions are provided. If no value is provided, it (by default) should calculate volume of 1 × 1 × 1 inch box.
3. Write a program to calculate distance between two points. It should accept rectangular coordinate of two points(x1, y1) and (x2, y2), calculate the distance of each point from the origin and the distance between given two points.

4. Write a program to read amount in rupees and find the minimum number of notes required. Use function Deter ( ) that has an integer parameter for amount (no paise) and nine reference parameters thousands, five hundreds, hundreds, fifties, twenties, tens, fives twos and ones respectively.
5. Write a program to compute surface area and volume of a cylinder using two separate functions. Each of these two functions should accept the radius and length of the cylinder as parameters.
6. Write to swap the values of two variable.
7. Write to perform specific arithmetic operation on given two integers.
8. Write a program to check whether $a^3 + b^3 + c = d^3$ is satisfied or not.
9. Write a program to perform palindrome test on a given number.
10. Write program that uses a function to sum **n** natural numbers starting from number **a**.
11. Write a program to print largest element of an array using a function.
12. Write program to sum positive or negative (as per the passed choice) elements of an integer array.
13. Write a program to search for a given character in a string.
14. Write a program to calculate frequency of a given character in a string.
15. Write program to calculate length of a string without using library function strlen( ).
16. Write a program to count the number of words in given string.
17. Write a program in C++ which calculates the root of $ax^2 + bx + c = 0$, call this function in main program. Where root of equation are $x^1 = \frac{-b+\sqrt{b^2-4ac}}{2a}$ and $x^2 = \frac{-b-\sqrt{b^2-4ac}}{2a}$.
18. Write a program to print series $s = x = x + \frac{x}{!2} + \frac{x}{!3} + \ldots + \frac{x}{!n}$.
19. Write to compute sum of sine series $x = x - \frac{x^3}{!3} + \frac{x^5}{!5} + \ldots + \frac{xn}{!n}$.
20. Write program to compute sum of **cosine series** $1 - -\frac{x^2}{!2} + \frac{x^4}{!4} + \ldots + \frac{x^n}{!n}$.
21. Write program to set smaller of two numbers to value –1 using call by reference.
22. Write a program to set larger of two numbers to its square and smaller one to its cube using call by reference.
23. Write a program to determine frequency of each character of a given string.
24. Write program to compute mean, variance and standard deviation from a given list of numbers.
25. Write a program which calculate F where F = $\frac{a * b^n}{!c}$.
26. Write a program which calculate F where F = $1 + 2^2 + 3^3 + \ldots + n^n$.

8

ARRAYS AND STRING

An array is collection of similar data type which are stored in consecutive memory location under common name. In everyday life we commonly group similar object into unit. Array group together same data type so it is very useful data structure.

8.1 DECLARATION OF ARRAY

The array must be declared before using it in C++ program like other variable. The syntax for declaration of array is:

```
data_type array_name
[size]
```

Or if we want to add storage classes then that look like:

```
storage_class data_type array_name
[size]
```

Example

```
int marks [30];
static int page [40];
storage_class is optional
```

Data Type: In declaration data_type tell the compiler about data items type. For example all data item are integer type i.e., in marks array we can store only integer type data.

```
int marks.
[30]
```

Array name: In declaration array_name is the name of array. Any name you can give but follow the identifier rule.

Size: Size tell the size of array. We can use expression in place of size also. The size must positive integer type. If we use expression the value of expression must be positive integer. For example

```
int marks
[30]
```

In the size of array is 30 i.e., we can store 30 data item in marks array.

Example

```
int subject [5];
```

For this array 5 memory location is reserved. But from 0 to 4 like follow

Subject:

0 ← subject [0]
1 ← subject [1]
2 ← subject [2]
3 ← subject [3]
4 ← subject [4]

That means the array index in C++ starts from 0 to n-1 if the size of array is n.

The size of one memory location reserve for array depends on what is the type of array. In above example the array type is int. Therefore the compiler reserves 2 byte, length for every data item. In above example total memory reserve by compiler for array is → 5 × 2 = 10 Byte.

8.2 INITIALIZATION OF ARRAY

The array is initialized like follow if we need at the time of declaration.

```
data_type  array_name [size] = value1,  value2, . . ., value n
```

For example: Ex.1 int subject[5] = {45,40,55,65,35};

Ex.2 char sex [2] = {'M', 'F'};

Ex.3 float marks [3] = {30.5, –2.5, 3.5};

Example

```
{int element  [5] = 4,5,6}
```

In this example elements are five but we are assigning only three values. In this case the value to each element is assigned like following.

element [0] = 4

element [1] = 5

element [2] = 6

element [3] = 0

element [4] = 0 i.e., the missing element is set to zero.

8.3 ACCESSING ELEMENT OF ARRAY

If we have created an array the next thing is how we can access (read or write) the individual element of an array. The accessing function for array is:

```
array-name [index or subscript]
```

Example int marks [30];

```
marks [0] = 30;
```

Then 30 is assigned to first element of array mark.

0	1	2	3			29
30				—	—	

If we write

```
cin >> marks [2];
```

Then compiler takes value from keyboard and assigns that value to marks[2]; i.e., third element array mark. If we write.

```
cout << marks [4];
```

That means the marks [4] i.e., the fifth element of array value is printed into standard output device (monitor).

If we write

```
marks [0] = mark [0] * 10;
```

Then this means 10 is multiplied with mark [0] then assigned to mark [0]. If originally mark [0] is 30 after above statement the mark [0] is 300.

So if we want to read all the elements of array marks from keyboard then we can write the following loop for that-

```
for (i = 0; i<= 29; i++)
cin >> marks [i];
```

Similarly if we want to print all the element of array marks we can write he following loop:

```
for (i = 0; i<=29; i++)
cout >> marks [i];
```

Note that C++ does not check the range of array index. Therefore this is the responsibility of programmer. The programmer must make sure that the range of array index does not go out of its highest index.

In above example we have written the test condition in loop is i<=29 because the highest index of array marks is 29 (from 0, 1, 2, 3...29).

Example 8.1: Write a program which stores the marks of 5 students in an array and then print marks. The marks of student are 65, 75, 70, 85, and 80.

```
# include <iostream.h>
# include <conio.h>
void main ( )
{
int marks [5] = {65, 75, 70, 85, 80};
clrscr ( );
cout << "The marks of students are:" <<endl;
for (int i = 0; i<= 4; i++)
cout << "Marks of" << i++<<"student is :"<<marks[i] <<endl;
getch ( );
}
```

Output of above program is:

The marks of students are:
Marks of 1 student is : 65
Marks of 2 student is :75
Marks of 3 student is :70
Marks of 4 student is :85
Marks of 5 student is :80

Example 8.2: Write a program which reads a set of number from keyboard and find out smallest element. Use array for store number.

```
# include <iostream.h>
# include <conio.h>
void main ( )
{
int a [100], i n;
clrscr ( );
cout << " How many number you want to read";
cin >> n;
for (i = 0; i<=(n-1); i++)
{
```

```
cout <<"Enter "<<i+1<<"element:";
cin >> a[i] ;
}
int small = a [0];
for (i =1; i < = (n-1); i++)
{
if (small > a [i])
small = a [i];
}
cout << "smallest element is :"<<small;
getch ( );
}
```

Output of above program is:

How many number you want to read: 5
Enter first element : 5
Enter second element : 10
Enter third element : 15
Enter forth element : 20
Enter fifth element : 3
Smallest element is : 3

Example 8.3: **Write a program which read an array. Sort that array and then print.**

```
# include <iostream.h>
# include <conio.h>
void main ( )
{
int a [50];
int i, j, temp, n;
clrscr ( );
cout << " how many element you want to read";
cout << "Enter element less than or equal to 50";
cout <<endl;
cin >> n;
cout << "Enter elements one by one" <<endl;
    for (i = 0; i <= (n-1); i++)
```

```
{
    cout << a [i] << endl;
    }
    for (i = 0; i < = n-2; i++)
    for (j = i+1; j <=n-1; j++)
    if (a [i] < a [j])
    {
    temp = a [i]
    a[i] = a[j]
    a[j] = temp;
    }
    cout << "The array is after sorted form :";
    cout <<endl;
    for (i =0; i<=n-1; i++)
    {
    cout << "The" << i +1 <<, "element is :";
        getch ( );
        }
```

Output of above program is:

```
How many element you want to read
Enter element less than equal to 50: 4
Enter element one by one
50
35
30
65
The array in unsorted form
The 1 element is : 50
The 2 element is : 35
The 3 element is : 30
The 4 element is : 65
The array after sorted form:
The 1 element is : 30
The 2 element is : 35
The 3 element is : 50
The 4 element is : 65
```

8.4 PASSING ARRAY AS ARGUMENT TO FUNCTION

We can pass entire array to a function in C++. An array name can be used as an argument for the prototype declaration and in function header. When we call the function no need to use subscript or square brackets.

Example

```
#include <iostream.h>
void main ( )
{
void sort array (int a [ ] , int n);
int a [5];
—
—
sort array (a,n) //calling array;
—
}
void sort array (int a [ ], int n)
{
—
—
—
}
```

Note: we pass array that pass call by reference because the array name is address for that array. In the example above a is starting address for array a[5]..

Example 8.4: Write a program which read 11 number from keyboard store these numbers into array and then calculate sum of these number using function.

```
#include <iostream.h>
#include <conio.h>
void' main ( )
{
int sum (int a [ ] );
void output (int a [ ] );
int a [10], s;
clrscr ( );
cout << "Enter 11 element :";
cout <<endl;
for (int i = 0; i<= 9; i++)
```

```
cin >> a[i];
output (a);
s = sum (a);
cout << "sum of array element is :";
cout <<s<<endl;
getch ( );
    }
int sum (a [ ])
{
int n = 0;
for (int i = 0; i < = 9; i++)
n = n + a [i];
return (n);
}
void output (a[ ])
{
cout << "the elements of array are:"<<endl;
for (int i =0; i <= 9; i++)
cout < a [i] < endl;
}
```

Example 8.5: **Write a program which read the marks of student and then print the marks of only those students who got first division i.e., 60 or more marks and print location of those students within array.**

```
# include <iostream.h>
# include <conio.h>
void main ( )
{
void input (int m [ ], int n);
void output (int m [ ], int n);
int m [100];
int n;
cout << "How many marks to read";
cin > n;
input (m,n);
output (m,n);
getch ( );
```

```
} // end main
void input (int m[], int n)
{
cout <<"Enter the marks of student:"<<endl;
for (int i =0; i<= n-1; i++)
{
cout << "Enter" <<i<<"student marks:";
cin >> m [i];
}
void output (int m [], int n)
{
cout << "The first division student are:";
cout <<endl;
for (int i = 0; i < = n-1; i++)
{
if (m [i] > = 60)
{ cout << "Student"<<i<< "marks are:" <<m [i]<<endl;
}
}
}
```

8.5 MULTIDIMENSIONAL ARRAY

An array of arrays is called multidimensional array. For example a one dimensional array of one dimensional array is called two dimensional arrays.

A one dimensional array of two dimensional arrays is called three dimensional arrays etc. The two dimensional array are very useful for matrix operation.

8.5.1 Declaration of Two Dimensional Array

Multidimensional array are declared in the same manner as one dimensional array except that a separate pair of square bracket; three dimensional array require three pair of square bracket; four dimensional array require four pair of square brackets etc.

The general format for declaring multidimensional array is:

```
data-type array-name [size 1] [size 2]....[size n];
```

We can add storage class in above declaration if necessary like follows.

```
storage-class data-type array-name [size 1] [size]… [size n];
```

Storage part is optional.

For example,

```
int n [5] [6] ;
float a[6] [7] [8];
static char line [5] [6];
double add [6] [7] [8] [9];
```

8.5.2 Initialization of Multidimensional Array

Similar to one dimensional array multidimensional array can also be initialized.

Example 1

```
int a [3] [2] = {1, 2, 3, 4, 5, 6};
```

The value is assigned like follows:

a[0] [0] = 1;

a[0] [1] = 2;

a[1] [0] = 3;

a[1] [1] = 4;

a[2] [0] = 5;

a[2] [1] = 6;

Example 2 **Initialization can be done also**

```
int a [3] [2] = { (1,2), (3,4), (5,6) };
```

In the above example the value in first inner pair of braces are assigned to the array element in the first row; the value in the second pair of braces are assigned to the array element second row and so on i.e.

a[0] [0] = 1; a [0] [1] = 2;

a[1] [0] = 3; a [1] [1] = 4;

a[2] [0] = 5; a[2] [1] = 6;

Example 3

```
int n [3] [3] = { {1, 2,} ,{ 4, 5,},{7,8,9}};
```

In the above example the values are less than element of array. The value assign like follows by above example:

a [0] [0] = 1; a [0] [1] = 2 ; a [0] [2] = 0;

a [1] [0] = 4; a [1] [1] = 5 ; a [1] [2] = 0;

a [2] [0] = 7; a [2] [1] = 8; a [2] [2] = 9;

In the above example the value zero is assigned to [0] [2] and a[1] [2] because no value assigned to these.

Example 4

```
int n[3] [3] = {1, 2, 4, 5, 7, 8, 9};
```

The value assign like follow by above example:

a[0] [0] = 1; a[0,1] =2; a [0,2] = 4;

a[1] [0] = 5; a[1,1] =7; a [1,2] = 8;

a[2] [0] = 9; a[2] [1] =0; a[2] [2] =0;

Note that the order of assignment in different in this case.

8.5.3 Accessory Elements of Multidimensional Array

We can access the multidimensional array with the help of following accessing function.

```
array-name [index 1] [index2] ....[index n]
```

Example

```
int a[5] [6];
```

We can write the following statement:

```
a [0] [2] = 5;
x = a [3] [2];
cout << a [0] [0];
cin >a[2] [2];
```

If we want to read all the elements of above array we can make a loop like:

```
for (i = 0; i < = 4; i++)
for (j = 0; j < = 5; j++)
cin >> a [i] [j];
```

If we want to print all the element of above array a then the loop is:

```
for (i =0; i <=4; i++)
for (j = 0; j <=5; j ++)
    cout << a[i] [j];
```

But if we want to print the output of above array like a matrix than the loop is:

```
for (i =0; i < = 4; i++)
{
for (j = 0; j <= 5; j++)
cout << a [i] [j];
cout << endl;
}
```

Example 8.6: Write a program which initialize a two dimensional array and print all the element in matrix form.

```
# include <iostream.h>
# include <conio.h>
void main ( )
{
int a [2] [3] = {1,2,3,4,5,6};
int i, j;
clrscr ( );
cout << "The array is :" <<endl;
for (i = 0; i < = 1; i++)
{
for ( j =0; j <= 2; j++)
cout << a [i] [j];
cout << endl;
}
getch ( );
}
```

Output of above program is:

```
The array is:
1 2 3
4 5 6
```

Example 8.7: Write a program which read two matrix and then print a matrix which is addition of these two matrix.

```
# include <iostream.h>
# include <conio.h>
void main ( )
{
int a[2] [2], b[2,2], s[2,2];
clrscr ( );
cout << "Enter first matrix :"<< endl;
for (int i = 0; i <=1; i++)
for (int j = 0; j < 1; j++)
{
cout << "Enter" << i+1 << j +1 << "element:";
cin >> a [i] [j] ;
}
cout << "Enter second matrix :" <<endl;
```

```
for (i = 0; i < = 1; i++)
for (j = 0; j < = 1; j++)
{
cout << "Enter" << i+1 << j+1 << "element:"
cin >> b [i] [j];
}
for ( i = 0; i < = 1; i++)
for (j = 0; j <= 1; j++)
s [i] [j] = a [i] [j] + b [i] [j] ;
cout << "The addition matrix is :" <<endl;
for (i = 0, i <= 1; i++)
{
for ( j = 0; j < = 1; j++)
cout << s [i] [j] << '\t';
cout << endl;
}
getch ( );
}
```

The output of above program is:

Enter first matrix:
Enter 11 element : 1
Enter 12 element : 2
Enter 21 element : 3
Enter 22 element : 4
Enter second matrix:
Enter 11 element : 1
Enter 12 element : 2
Enter 21 element : 3
Enter 22 element : 4
The addition of matrix is:
4
8

Example 8.8: Write a program which reads two matrices and multiply them if possible.

```
# include <iostream.h>
# include <conio.h>
void main ( )
```

```
{
int a [9] [9], b[9] [9] , s[9] [9];
int m,n,l,p;
cout << "Enter row of first matrix ( <=9) :")
cin >>m;
cout << "Enter column of first matrix (<=9):";
cin >>n;
cout << "Enter row of second matrix (<=9) :";
cin >> l;
cout << "Enter column of second matrix (<=9) :";
cin >> p;
cout << "Enter first matrix :" <<endl;
for (int i =0; i < = m-1; i++)
for (int j =0; j < = n-1; j++)
{
cout << "Enter" << i+1 << j+1 << "element :";
cin >> a[i] [j];
}
cout << "Enter second matrix :"<<endl;
for (i = 0; i < = l-1; i++)
for (j = 0; j < = p-1; j++)
{
cout << "Enter" << i+1 << j+1 << "element:";
cin >> b [i] [j]; }
    if ( n ! = l)
{
cout << "Multiplication is not possible:";
cout <<endl;
}
else
{
for ( i = 0; i < = m-1; i++)
for (j = 0; j < = p-1; j++)
s [i] [j] = 0;
for ( i = 0; i < = m-1; i++)
for (j = 0;  j < = p-1; j++)
for (int k = 0; k< = n-1; k++)
```

```
s [i] [j] = s [i] [j] + a [i] [k] * b[k] [j];
cout << "Matrix Multiplication is:" <<endl;
for (i =0; i < = m-1; i++)
{
for (j = 0; j < = p-1; j++)
cout << s[i] [j] << '\t';
cout << endl; }
}
}
getch ( );
}
```

Sample output of above program:

```
Enter row of first matrix (<=9) : 2
Enter column of first matrix (<=9) : 1
Enter row of second matrix (<=9) : 1
Enter column of second matrix (<=9): 2
Enter first matrix:
Enter 11 element : 2
Enter 21 element : 2
Enter second matrix :
Enter 11 element : 3
Enter 12 element : 3
Matrix Multiplication is:
6
6
```

8.5.4 Passing Two Dimensional Array as an Argument to Function

We can pass entire two dimensional arrays to function like one dimensional array.

Example 8.9: Write a program which read two matrixces A and B of order 2 × 2 and subtract B from A, using function.

```
# include <iostream.h>
# include <conio.h>
void main ( )
{
int a[2] [2] , b[2] [2];
void input (int t [ ] [2]);
void output (int t1 [ ] [2], int t2 [ ] [2];
```

```
clrscr ( );
cout << "Enter first array:"<<endl;
input (a);
cout << "Enter second array :"<<endl;
input (b);
cout << "subtraction is :" <<endl;
output (a,b);
getch ( );
}
void input (int t  [ ] [2])
{
int i, j;
for ( i = 0; i <=1, i++)
for (j = 0; j < =1; j++)
cin >> t [i] [j];
void output (int t1 [ ] [2], int t2 [ ] [2])
{
int i, j;
int s [2] [2];
for (i =0; i <=1; i++)
for (j =0; j <= 1; j++)
s[i] [j] = t1 [i] [j] -t2 [i] [j];
for (i=0; i < = 1; i++)
{
for (j = 0; j < =1; j++)
cout << s [i] [j] << '\t';
cout <<endl;
}
}
```

The sample output of above program:

```
Enter first array:
4
3
2
4
Enter second array:
1
```

```
2
3
2
Subtraction is
1
     -1        2
```

Example 8.10: Write a program which reads a 3 × 2 matrix and then calculate the sum of each row and store that in one dimension array.

```
# include <iostream.h>
#include <conio.h>
void main ( )
{
int a [3] [2], s[3];
int i, j;
void input (int a [3] [2];
clrscr ( );
cout << "Enter Matrix :"<<endl;
input (a);
for (i =0; i <= 2; i++)
s[i] =0;
for (i =0; i <=2; i++)
for (j =0; j < =1; j++)
s [i] = s[i] + a [i] [j];
cout << " Sum of row elements is:" <<endl;
for (i = 0 ; i < = 2, i++)
    {
    cout << "Sum of" <<i+1<< "row is:";
    cout <<s [i] <<endl;
    }
    getch ( );
    }
    void input (int a [3] [2]
    {
        for (int i = 0; i <= 2; i++)
for (int j = 0; j <= 1; j++)
    {
```

```
cout << "Enter" <<i+1<<j+1<< "element:";
cin >>a [i] [j];
}
}
```

The simple output of above program is:

```
Enter Matrix:
    Enter 11 element : 2
    Enter 12 element : 3
    Enter 21 element : 4
    Enter 22 element : 5
    Enter 31 element : 6
    Enter 32 element : 7
Sum of row element is:
    Sum of 1 row is :  5
    Sum of 2 row is : 9
    Sum of 3 row is : 13
```

8.6 STRING

Array of character type which is terminated by null character is known as string. In other words we can say that a string is a sequence of contiguous character in memory terminated by null character '\0'.

In C++ header file string.h provides special function for multiplicating strings. The general format for declaring a string is:

```
storage-class char array-name
[size];
```

Storage class is optional.

Example

char a [10];

static char page [20];

The basic structure of character array (or string) is:

H I R D A Y \0

The string ends with a null character '\0'. That means if we declare a character array of size n then we can store only n-1 character in that array.

For Example

char a [6] = "ALPANA"

give an error because in this there is no space for null character.

a [0] = 'A'

a [1] = 'L'

a[2] = 'P'

a[3] = 'A'

a[3] = 'N'

a[4] = 'A'

But we write

char a [7] = "ALPANA"

This is right now array a has space for null character '/0'. Which automatically stored by C++ compiler.

Note: In C++ anything written within the "and" is string constant.

The C++ compiler automatically calculates the size.

We can initialize string like other array. See the following example:

```
char name [ ] = 'KAMLESH';
```

The C++ compiler automatically calculates the size. We can initialize string like other array. See the following example:

```
char name [ ] = { 'K', 'A','M', 'L', 'E', 'S', 'H'};
```

That means we can treat string as a one dimensional array

Note: null character '\0' is a back-slash followed by a letter zero

Example 8.11: Write a program which assigns KAMLESH YADAV to a string and then print the string.

```
# include <iostream.h>
#include < conio.h>
void main ( )
{
char name [ ] = "KAMLESH YADAV";
clrscr ( );
cout << "The Name Is :"<<endl;
cout << name;
getch ( );
}
```

Output of above program is:

The Name is: KAMLESH YADAV

Example 8.12: Write a program which read a string and then print that.

```
# include <iostream.h>
#include < conio.h>
void main ( )
{
char str [90];
clrscr ( );
cout << "Enter string :"<<endl;
cin >> str;
cout << "The string is:" <<str;
getch;
}
```

Note: We use the insertion operator >> to read a string from the keyboard and place it in string variable str. This operator known how to deal with strings because compiler understands that they are array of character. If the user enters the string "vinod" in above program, the array str will look like:

String Str

0	V
1	I
2	N
3	O
4	D
5	\0
6	
7	

When the << operator displays the string, it display characters until it encounters the null character. But we know that in C++ there is no built in mechanism to check the array range; therefore this is the responsibility of programmer to check the range. For example in the above program example 8.12 you can not enter more than 79 characters. Last space is needed for null character. If you entered more than 79 character there will be problem. We can solve this problem with the help of stew manipulator. See the following example:

```
# include <iomanip.h>
# include <iostream.h>
# include <conio.h>
void main ( )
{
char str [75];
```

```
clrscr ( );
cout << "Enter string:" <<endl;
cin<< setw (75) >>str;
cout << "The string is:" <<str;
getch ( );
}
```

Above program uses the stew manipulator to specify the maximum number of character the input buffer accepts. The user may type more characters but the >> operator won't insert them into the array.

Actually one character less than the number specified is inserted, therefore there is a space for terminating null character. iomanip.h header file is needed for stew.

8.6.1 Array of String

Array of string means two dimensional array of character.

Example

```
char str [5]
[8];
```

The first dimension tells how many strings are in the array. The second dimension tells the maximum length of each string. In above declaration we can store 5 strings each can store maximum 7 characters; last 8th space is for null terminator in each string.

Initialization of Array of string: The array of string initialized like follow:

Example 1

```
char str [2] [7] = {"Sunday", "Monday"};
```

Accessing of array of string: The array of string access like follow i.e., see the following example.

Example 2

```
char a[4]
[7];
```

If we want to read all the string from keyboard. We can use the following loop:

```
for (i =0; i <=3; i++)
cout << a[i]
```

Example 8.13: Write a program which store name of week days and then print all?

```
# include <iostream.h>
# include <conio.h>
void main ( )
{ int i;
char day [7] [10] = {"sunday", "monday",
"tuesday", "wednesday", "thursday", "friday",
"saturday";
clrscr ( );
cout << "Weekday are :"<<endl;
for (i = 0; i <= 6; i++)
{
cout <<day [i] <<endl;
getch ( );
}
```

Simple Output of above program:

```
Sunday
Monday
Tuesday
Wednesday
Thursday
Friday
Saturday
```

8.6.2 Reading String with Blank Space

If we read the string using cin and >> anything typed after a space is thrown away.

For example

```
# include <iostream.h>
# include <conio.h>
void main ( )
{
char s [80];
clrscr ( );
cout << "Enter string:";
cin >> d;
cout << "string is:" <<d;
getch ( );
}
```

In above program if we enter deeraj yadav from keyboard the output is only dheeraj i.e., the output like:

```
Enter string : dheeraj yadav
String is : dheeraj
```

The program print only dheeraj because insertion >>considers a space to be a terminating character anything typed after a space is thrown away. This problem can be solved with the help of member function get of the cin stream class. The get written like follow:

```
cin.get (string-name), length) ;
```

Example 8.14

```
# include <iostream.h>
# include <conio.h>
void main ( )
{
char str [75];
clrscr ( );
cout << "Enter a string :";
cin.get (str, 75);
cout << "string is:" << str;
getch ( );
    }
```

The sample output of above program is:

```
Enter a string : Sneha Yadav
String is : Sneha Yadav
```

Note: Get is also used for reading multiple line for this in get a third argument is used, this argument takes a character that tells the function to stop reading. The default value of this argument is new line character ('\n') like is above example 8.14 when we pass enter reading stop.

Example 8.15: Write a program which reads lines of text from keyboard until we give asterisk sign(*)

```
# include <iostream.h>
#include <conio.h>
void main ( )
{
char str [75);
clrscr ( );
cout << "Enter multiple line";
```

```
cout << "Press enter after each line";<<endl;
cout << "For terminating program enter *";
cout << " and then press enter :" <<endl;
cin.get (str, 75, '*');
cout << Entered multiple line :" <<endl;
cout << str << endl;
getch ( ) ;
}
```

The Sample output of above program is:

Enter multiple line press enter each line
For terminating program enter * and then press enter
Hello, where are you
Inheritance support C++
    *
Enter multiple line:
        Hello, where are you
Inheritance support C++
Polymorphism supported in C++
    *

Example 8.16: Write a program which read a string and then copy that string into another string.

```
# include <iostream.h>
# include <conio.h>
void main ( )
{
char a [75] , b [75];
void string_copy ([char b [ ], char a [ ]);
cout << "Enter a string :" <<endl;
cin.get (a, 75);
string_copy (b,a);
cout << "First string is:" <<endl;
cout << a << endl;
cout << "second string is :" << endl;
cout <<b<<endl;
getch ( );
}
```

```
void string_copy (char b [ ], char a [ ] )
{
int i, j;
i = 0; While (a [i] ! = '\0');
    {
    b[i] = a[i]; i++
    }
    b[i] = '\0';
    }
```

The sample output of above program is:

Enter a string : Hello sneha
First string is : Hello sneha
Second string is : Hello sneha

Example 8.17: Write a program which reads two strings, concatenates these two and prints the result.

```
# include <iostream.h>
# include <conio.h>
void main ( )
{
char a  a [35] , b [35], t[75];
void string cat (char t [ ] , char [ ], char b[ ];
clrscr ( );
cout << "Enter first string :" <<endl;
cin.get (a, 35);
cout << "Enter second string:"<<endl;
cin get (b,35); cout << "First string is :" <<endl;
cout << a << endl;
cout << "second string is:" <<endl;
cout << b << endl;
string cat (t,a,b);
cout << "Final string is :" <<endl;
cout << t <<endl;
    getch ( );
    }
void string cat (char t [ ], char a [ ], char [ ])
    {
```

```
int i, j;
i= 0;
while (a [i] ! = '\0')
{
t [i] = a [i]; i++ }
{
j = 0;
while (b [j] ! = '\0')
{
t [i] = b[j];
j++;
i++;
}
t [i] = '\0';
}
```

The sample output of above program is:

Enter first string : NITIN
Enter second string : YADAV
First string is : NITIN
Second string is : YADAV
Final string is : NITIN YADAV

Solved Exercises

Exercise 1. Write a program to convert decimal (non-fractional) number to binary number.

```
# include <iostream.h>
# include <stdio.h>
# include <string.h>
# include <conio.h>
void main ( )
  {
  clrscr ( );
  int dnum, qu, reme, i, R[16];
  long binum=0;
  cout << "Enter the decimal number:"
  cin >> dnum;
  i = 0;
  while (dnum !=0)
  {
```

```
qu = dnum/2;
reme = dnum%2;
R[i++] = reme;
dnum = qu;
}
while (--i>=0)
binum = binum*10+R[i];
cout << "Binary equivalent of given number is" << bnum << endl;
return 0;
}
```

The sample output of above program is:

Enter the decimal number : 200
Binary equivalent of given number is 11001000

Exercise 2. Write Program to print non-diagonal elements of a matrix.

```
# include <iostream.h>
# include <conio.h>
void main ( )
{
    clrscr ( )
    int A[10][10],i,j,size;
    cout << "\n Enter the size of the matrix:"
    cin >> size;
    cout << "\n Enter the elements of the matrix (row wise):\n":
    for (i = 0; i < size; i++)
        for (j = 0; j < size; j++)
    {
    cin >> A [i] [j];
    cout << "\n given matrix is :"
    for (i = 0; i < size; i++)
    {
        cout << "\n"
        for (j = 0; j < size; j++)
        cout << A[i] [j]<<"";
        }
        cout << "\n Non-diagonal element of given matrix are :";
        for (i=0; i<size; i++)
        {
            cout << "\n"
            for (i = 0; i < size; i++)
```

```
        if  (i  !=  j  &&  ((i+j)  !=  2))
        cout  <<  A  [i]  [j]  <<  "";
        else
        cout  <  "";
    }
    getch  ( );
    }
```

Exercise 3. Write a program to print transpose of matrix.
Transpose of matrix is obtained by switching the row and columns of matrix.

```
# include < iostream.h>
# include < conio.h>
void main  ( )
{
    clrscr  ( );
    int A[3]  [3],  B[3]  [3],  I,  j;
    cout  <<  "\n  Enter  the  elements  of  the  matrix  :\n";
    for  (i  =  0;  i  <  3;  i++)
        for  (j  =0;  j  <3;  j++)
        cin  >>  A  [i]  [j];
    cout  <<  "\n  given  matrix  is  :"
    for  (i=0;  i  <3;  i++)
        for  (j =0;  j<3;  j++)
        cin  >>  A  [i]  [j];
    cout  <<  "\n  given  matrix  is:";
    for  (i=0;  i  <  3;  i++)
        {
        cout  <<  "\n"
        for  (j  =0;  j  <3;  j++)
        cout  <<  A[i]  [j]  <<  "";
    }
    cout  <<  "\n  Transpose  of  given  matrix  is":;
    for  (i  =  0;  i  <  3;  i++)
    {
        cout  <<  "\n"
        for  (j  =  0;  j  <3;  j++)
        {
        B[i][j]  =  A[j]  [i];
        cout  <<  B  [i]  [j]  <<  "";
        }
      }
```

The output of above program is:

```
Enter the element of the matrix:
1 2 3 4 5 6 7 8 9
Given matrix is:
    1 2 3
    4 5 6
    7 8 9
Transpose of given matrix is:
    1 4 7
    2 5 8
    3 6 9
```

Exercise 4. Write a program to concatenate two string.

```
# include <iostream.h>
# include <stdio.h>
# include <conio.h>
void main ( )
    {
    clrscr ( );
    char str1[80], str2[80], str3[160];
    int i,j;
    cout << "\n Enter the first string (max 80 chars):"
    gets(str1);
    cout << "\n Enter the second string (max 80 chars):"
    gets(str2);
    for (i = 0; str1[i] != '0';i++)
        str3[i] = str1[i];
        for (j = 0; str2[j] !='\0'; j++)
        str3[i+j] = str2[j];
        str3[i+j] = '\0';
        cout << "\n concatenated string is :" <<str3;
        getch( );
        }
```

The sample output of above program is:

```
Enter the first string (max 80 chars) : anu
Enter the second string (max 80 chars) : alok
Concatenated string is :anualok
```

Descriptive Questions

1. Explain with example what is array?
2. How two dimensional array passed to a function.
3. What is string? Explain array of string.
4. Explain multidimensional array.
5. Explain how array is initialization (explain in case of one dimensional array).
6. How one dimensional array passed to function?
7. What is difference between a character array and string?
8. Explain how individual element of one dimensional array are accessed.
9. How the individual elements of two dimensional array are accessed.

Exercises

1. Write program to read one dimensional (1-D) array, display its elements in reverse order and print the sum of its elements.
2. Write a program to check each element of 1-D integer array for evenness/oddness.
3. Write a program to count number of positive and negative in a 1-D integer array.
4. Write a program to check primness of 1-D array
5. Write a program to check 1-D array is **Armstrong** number or not.
6. Write a program to find sums of even-positive, even-negative, odd-positive, odd-negative numbers in a given 1-D array.
7. Write a program to calculate length of string without using library function.
8. Write a program to count number of occurrence of given character in a string.
9. Write a program to count number of words present in a line.
10. Write a program to print each word of a string in a separate line.
11. Write a program of uppercase and lowercase character, digits and special character in a string.
12. Write a program to reverse string.
13. Write a program to search given character in string.
14. Write a program check whether string is **Palindrome** or not.
15. Write a program to compare length of two string.
16. Write a program to read element of a matrix and print it in matrix form.
17. Write a program to print diagonal element of matrix.
18. Write a program to determine inverse of a matrix.
19. Write a program to convert 2-d array into 1-D array.
20. Write a program to short 10 string/names.
21. Write a program to print all possible combination from letter of a given string.
22. Write a program to count maximum and minimum element from 3-D array.
23. Write a program to indicate whether the given matrix is symmetrical or not.

9

STRUCTURE AND UNIONS

Structure is a collection of data item. The data item can be different type, some can be int, some can be float, and some can be char and so on. The data item of structure is called member of the structure.

In other words we can say that heterogeneous data types can be grouped to form a structure. In some language structure is known as record.

The difference between array and structure is the element of an array has the same type while the element of structure can be of different type. Another difference is that each element of an array is referred to by its position while each element of structure has unique name.

9.1 DECLARATION OF STRUCTURE

The general syntax for declaration of a structure is:

```
storage-class  struct  name  {
     data-type  1 member1;
     data-type  2 member2;
     ----
     ----
     data-type  n  member  n;
     };
```

The storage-class is optional. The struct is a keyboard. The name is written by the programmer. The rule for writing name is rule for identifier.

Example 1

```
struct   student
     {
     char  name  [75];
     int  roll_no;
     char branch  [10];
     int  semester  ;
     };
```

Example 2

```
static struct date {
    int day;
    char month_name [15];
    int year;
    };
```

9.2 CREATING STRUCTURE VARIABLE

In section 9.1 we have studied about how we declare structure but we have not created the structure variable. Note that the space in memory for a structure is created only when we create the structure variable. The structure variable is created by the following way:

9.2.1 We can also create Structure Variable at the time of Declaration

Example

```
struct student
    {
    char name [75];
    int roll_no;
    char branch [10];
    int semester;
    } var1, var2, var3;
```

In this example three structure variable name var1, var2, and var3 are created. We can create one or more than one variable. The space is created like:

name	var1
roll_no	
branch	
semester	

name	var2
roll_no	
branch	
semester	

name	var3
roll_no	
Branch	
Semester	

name	var 4
roll_no	
branch	
semester	

9.2.2 We can Create Structure Variable like following also

Example: Structure declaration:

```
struct student
    {
    char name [80];
    int roll_no;
    char branch [10];
    int semester;
    };
```

Structure variable creation

```
struct student var1, var2, var3;
```

By using this element three structure var1, var2, var3 are created like:

name	Var1
roll_no	
branch	
semester	

name	var2
roll_no	
branch	
semester	

name	var3
roll_no	
branch	
semester	

9.2.3 We can Create Structure Variable like following also

Example: Structure declaration:

```
struct student
    {
    char name [80];
    int roll_no;
```

```
char branch [10];
int semester;
};
```

Structure variable creation

```
student var1, var2, var3;
```

By using this statement three structure variable var1, var2, and var3 like in above sections 9.2.1 and 9.2.2 are created.

9.3 ACCESSING MEMBER OF STRUCTURE

The accessing concept of member is:

```
structure-variable-name.member
```

The dot(.) is known as period.

Example

```
struct mca
    {
    char name [80];
    char semester [80];
    long int roll_no;
    };
    mca m1,m2;
```

(1) If we write

```
m1.roll_no = 61450;
```

The above statement store 61450 into member roll_no of m1 structure.

If we write

```
m2.roll_no = 61451;
```

This statement means 61451 is assigned to member roll_no of m2 structure.

(2) If we write

```
cin.get (m1.name, 80);
```

This statement reads a string (i.e., name) from keyboard assign that string to member name of m1 structure.

If we write

```
cin.get (m2.name, 80);
```

This statement reads a string from keyboard assign that to member name of structure m2.

(3) If we write

```
cout << m1.name;
```

This statement prints the value of member name of m1 structure onto screen.

If we write

```
cout << m2.address;
```

This statement prints the value of member address of m2 structure onto screen.

9.4 INITIALIZATION OF STRUCTURE

A structure is initialized like other data type in C++.

Example 1

```
Struct semester
    {
    int rn;
    int age;
    char sex;
    };
```

We can initialize the structure at the time of variable creation like:

```
semester sem (10, 22, 'm'};
```

By this 10 is assigned to rn of sem; 22 is assigned to age of sem and m is assigned to sex of per structure.

Example 2

```
struct mca
    {
    char name;
    int age;
    int rn;
    char sex;
    int mark;
    }
```

If we write following statement:

```
mca m = {'anju', 22, 10, 'f', 65} ;
```

In the above initialization we have not assigned value to each member of m. In this type of case C++ compiler will automatically initialize zero to those members who are not initialized.

Note that there is one correspondence between the members and initialized value. In the above example C++ compiler assign following value to each member:

age = 22
rn = 10
sex = m
phno = 0

Zero is assigned to phno because no value is initialized to phno.

Note: C++ compiler will not read or write an entire structure as a single command like.

```
cin >> m; //wrong
```

We can read complete structure by reading member of structure one by one. But we can copy one complete structure to another if both are same type.

Example 9.1: Write a program which initializes a structure and then copy that to another.

```
# include <iostream.h>
# include <conio.h>
struct mobile
    {
    int model_no1;
    float cost;
    };
    void main ( )
    {
        mobile model 1 = {  2600,  3700.00 }
        mobile model 2 = { 6500,  9000.00}
        model 2 = model 1 ;
        clrscr ( );
        cout << " The copied mobile model is :"
        cout << "model_no is :"<<model_no<<endl;
        cout << "cost is:" << model2.cost <<endl;
        getch ( );
            }
```

The output of above program is:

```
The copied mobile model is :
Chip number is : 2600
Cost is : 3600.00
```

9.5 ARRAY WITHIN STRUCTURE

We can also use array as a member of structure.

Example

```
structure A{int n;
      float  x  [4];
      };
      A  a1;
```

If we want to store 10.5 at x[2] location of a1 then we write the following statement.

```
a1.x  [2]  =  10.5
```

x is member of a1 so we can go to x by a1.x. Because x is an array so a1.x is an array within the array we can go by a1.x [index].

We can initialize this like:

```
A a2 = { 4, {10, 20, 30, 40, 50} };
```

9.6 ARRAY OF STRUCTURE

We can create array which each element is a structure type. i.e., structure within an array is also possible.

Example

```
struct  A  {
      int  n;
      float  x;
      char  c;
      };
      A  a1  [20];
```

The above declaration means a1 is an array of 20 elements is A type i.e., structure type.

a1:

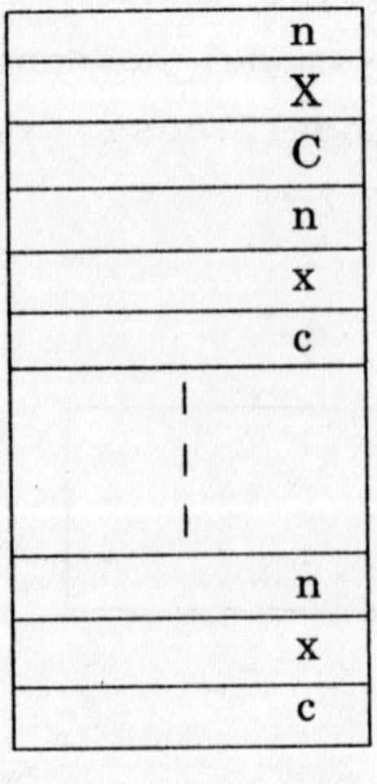

A a2 [3] = {{1,2.5, 'm'}, {2,3.5, 'f'}, {3,4.5, 'm'}};

Example 9.2: Write a program which reads the bio-data of 5 students and then prints the bio-data of those students which has more then 400 total marks. The bio-data consists the following field:

Name, roll-no, branch, semester subject marks, (array of five element); total marks.

```
# include <iostream.h>
# include <conio.h>
void main ( )
    {
    struct bio-data
      {
        char name [80];
        int roll_no;
        char branch [20];
        int semester;
        float subject_marks [5];
        float total_marks;
        };
        bio-data student [5];
        clrscr ( );
        cout << "Enter the bio-data of five students:";
        cout << "endl;
        for (int i =0; I <= 4; i++)
        {//start of reading loop
        cout << "Enter bio data of" <<i + 1<< "student:";
        cout <<endl;
        cout << "Enter name:";
        cin.get (student [i].name, 80);
        cout << "Enter roll no:";
        cin >> student [i].rollno;
        cout << "Enter branch:";
        cin.get (student [i].branch, 20);
        cout << "Enter semester:";
        cin >> student [i].semester;
        cout << "Enter marks of five subjects:" <<endl;
        for (int j = 0; j < = 4; j++)
            {
            cout << "Enter marks of" << j+1 << "subject:";
```

```
          cin >>student [i].subject_marks [j] ;
          }
      Student [i].total_marks = student [i].subject_marks [0]
          + student [i].subject_marks [1]
          + student [i].subject_marks [2]
          + student [i].subject_marks [3]
          + student [i].subject_marks [4]
          } //end of reading loop
      clrscr ( );
      cout << "Bio-data of students who get more";
      cout << "then 400 marks:" <<endl;
      for (i =0; i< =4; i++) // start of for loop
          {
      if (( student [i].total_marks) >400)
          {
      Cout << "BIO-DATA . . ."<<endl;
  cout << "name :"<<students [i] .roll_no <<endl;
  cout << "roll no. :"<<student [i] .roll_no <<endl;
  cout << "branch :" <<student [i].branch <<endl;
  cout << "semester :" <<student [i].semester<<endl;
  cout << "The marks of five subject are :" <<endl;
  for (j = 0; j < = 4; j++)
  cout << student [i].subject_marks [j] <<endl;
  cout << "Total marks :" <<student [i].total_marks;
  cout << endl << endl;) // end of if
      }
      getch ( );
      }
```

9.7 STRUCTURE WITHIN STRUCTURE

We can use structure within another structure.

```
# include <iostream.h>
# include <conio.h>
struct date
    {
    int day;
```

```
      char month-name [20];
      int year;
      };
struct bio-data
      {
      char name [80];
      date dob;
      };
void main ( )
      {
      bio-data student;
      clrscr ( );
      cout << "Enter name:" <<endl;
      cin >> student.name;
      cout << "Enter date of birth:" <<endl;
      cout << "Enter day:"
      cin >> student.dob.day;
      cout << "Enter month name :"
      cin >> student.dob.month-name;
      cout << "Enter year:";
      cin >> student.dob.year;
          // output is following
      cout << "The bio-data is:" <<endl;
      cout << "Name:" <<student.name <<endl;
      cout << "date of birth:"
      cout << student.dob.day << student.dob. month-name;
      cout << student.dob.year << endl;
          getch ( );
          }
```

The simple output of above program is as:

Enter name : dheeraj
Enter date of birth:
Enter day : 10
Enter month name : march
Enter year : 1992
The bio-data is :
Name : dheeraj
Date of birth : 10 march 1992

In above example the bio-data structure has two members' name (string type) and dob which is data type. Date is also a structure which has three members day, month name and year. Student is the structure variable bio-data. If we want to access dob then we first go to dob which is member of student like student dob; student dob is also a structure variable of data type, day is member of student.dob so we can access day like.

```
student.dob.day
```

9.8 FUNCTION AND STRUCTURE

A structure can be passed to a function like array. The structure can be passed like following:

Example

```
# include <iostream.h>
struct A
    {
    int n1;
    int n2;
        };
        void main ( )
        {
        A a1;
        void output (A a1);
        --
        --
        --
        Output (a1);
        --
        --
        }
        void output (A a2)
        {
            --
                --
            cout << a2.n1<<endl;
            cout << a2.n2 <<endl;
            --
            --
            }
```

Note The member data should be same throughout the program either in the main or in a function, when we pass entire structure. A function can return a structure also. See the following example.

Example 9.3: Write a program which reads two complex number and then perform multiplication of these two.

If the complex number are a1+ib1 and a2 +ib2 then multiplication is:

$$(a1 + ib2) * (a2 + ib2)$$
$$\rightarrow \quad a1a2 + i^2 b1b2 + a1b2i + a2b1i$$
$$\rightarrow \quad (a1a2 - b1b2) + (a1b2 + a2b1)\, i$$
$$(\text{because } i^2 = -1)$$

```
# include <iostream.h>
# include <conio.h>
struct complex
       {
            float realpart;
            float imagepart;
       };
void main ( )
       {
       complex a,b,c;
       complex mul (complex a, complex b);
       clrscr ( );
       cout << "Enter first complex no. :"<<endl;
       cout << "Enter real part:";
       cin >> a.realpart;
       cout << "Enter imagepart:";
       cin >> b.imagepart;
       c = mul (a,b);
       cout << "First no. is : <<b.real part << "+i" << a.imagepart <<endl;
       cout << "Second no. is :" <<b.realpart << "+i" <<c.imagepart <<endl;
       getch ( );
       }
       complex mul (complex a, complex b)
       {
         complex c;
         c.realpart = (a. realpart * b.realpart) - (a.imagepart *
b.imagepart);
         c.imagepart = (a.imagepart * b.realepart) + (b.imagepart * a.
realepart);
         return ( c) ;
       }
```

Sample output of above program is:

```
Enter first complex no. :
Enter real part : 2
Enter image part :4
Enter second complex no. :
Enter real part : 3
Enter image part : 5
First no. is 2 + i4
Second no. is 3 + i5
Multiplication is : –14 + i22
```

9.9 UNION

Union is similar to structure data type but union store value of different types in a single location. Union will contain many different type of value but only one is stored at a time. If a new assignment is made, the previous value is automatically erased.

The declaration of union is same as the structure. Only difference is in place of struct keyword the union keyword is used. The accessing of union member is also same like structure member.

Example

```
union  data
    {
        int  a;
        float  b;
            };
```

The union variable are declared like structure variable for example

```
data  d1,  d2
```

If we write the statement

```
d1.a  =  10;
```

Then that means the field is valid but if we want to print the value of b after above assignment the value is wrong because a is valid only. After above assignment if we write d1.b = 10.5; now b is valid not a i.e., only that field value is valid in which we have assigned value currently.

Example 9.4: A Program assigns and display union member.

```
# include  <iostream.h>
# include  <conio.h>
```

```
void main ( )
    {
        union data
        {
        int i;
    float f;
    };
    data d;
    clrscr ( );
    d.f = 10.5; d.i = 10;
    cout << "First member :" <<d.i <<endl;
    cout << "second member :" << d.f <<endl;
    d.f = 10.5;
    cout << "First member" <<d.i <<endl;
    cout << "Second member" <<d.f <<endl;
    getch ( );
        }
```

9.9.1 Anonymous Union

If we define a union without a name or tag that is called anonymous union. The syntax is:

```
union {
    data-type 1 member 1;
    data-type 2 member2;
    --
    --
    data-type n member n;
```

In anonymous union the member access directly by their name.

Example 9.5

```
# include <iostream.h>
# include <conio.h>
void main ( )
    {
    union
        {
        int n1;
        float n2;
        };
```

```
clrscr ( );
cout << "Enter integer no. :";
cin >> n1;
cout << "Enter float no. :"
cin >> n2;
cout << "n1 = "<<n1 <<endl;
cout << "n2 = "<<n2 <<endl;
getch ( );
    }
```

Above program print the value of n2 is correct but the value of n1 is wrong, because cin >>n2 statement is after statement cin >>n1 that means currently the value of n2 is read therefore n2 valid.

The output of above program is:

```
Enter integer no. : 24
Enter float no. : 10.5
n1 = 64412 // wrong value
n2 = 10.5 // correct value
```

9.9.2 Space Created for Union

We know that union store one value at a time so the question is how much space is created for union. C++ compiler first calculate the size of all members and then reserves the space which is highest among them. For example:

```
union A {
    int i;
    float f;
    char c;
    };
A a;
```

The space is created for a 4 byte. Because i needs 2 byte, f needs 4 byte and c needs 1 byte; 4 byte is highest in these.

Descriptive Questions

1. What is structure?
2. What is difference between array and structure?
3. What are rules of declaring structure?
4. How the structure is initialized?
5. How data member of structure are accessed?
6. How structure is passed to function?

7. List out few real life of structure?
8. Can function return structure?
9. What is union?

Programming Exercises

1. Write a program to implement a student structure having data member's admission number, name, address and marks.
2. Write a program to arrange ascending order. The student records are available in the form of array?
3. Write a program to add given number of days to a given date.
4. Write a program to implement a 2-D point and its two units.
5. Write a program to read and print details of member's phone details.
6. Write a program to read and display employee details.
7. Write a program to store countries details (name, capital, president) and then search for a specific country-detail based on given information such as capital or name of country.
8. Write a program to receive two dates and print the later date.
9. Write a program to store distance distances (km, mts) and add two unit of distance.
10. Write a program with help of structure which reads Emp. name, Emp. code, Emp. Design., Emp. Experience. Emp. Age.

10

CLASSES AND OBJECT

Like structure we have another derived data-type called class. As discussed, structure is a group of element of different data-type; class is group of elements of different data-types and functions. C++ structure can also have function defined in it.

There is very little syntactical difference between structure and classes in C++ and, therefore, they can be used interchangeably with minor modifications.

Since class is a specially introduced data-type in C++, most of C++ programmer tend to use the structure for holding only data and functions.

Specifying Class

A class is a way to bind data and its associated function together. It allows the data (and function) to be hidden, if necessary, from external user. When defining a class, we are creating a new abstract data-type that can be treated like any other built-in-data-type. Generally, a class specification has two parts:

1. Class declaration
2. Class function definitions

The class declaration describes the type and scope of its members. The class function definition describe how the class functions are implemented.

10.1 CLASS

A class is user defined data type which holds both the data and function. The data inside the class are called member data and the functions are called member function. The binding of data and functions together into single class type variable is called encapsulation, which is one of the benefits of object-oriented programming.

10.2 DECLARATION OF CLASS IN C++

Now we know that inside the class data and function (associated with data) bind together. The body of function can be written inside class or outside the class.

The class declaration describes the type and scope of its member (i.e., data and function).

The general form for declaring a class is:

```
class  class-name
     {
     access-specifier1:  member-data1;
     access-specifier2:  member-data2;
     ___
     ___
     ___
     member-function1;
     ___
     ___
     ___;
     access-specifier2:  member-data;
     ___
     ___
     ___
     member-function;
     access-specifier:
     ___
     member-function;
     };
```

In above declaration class is keyword. Class-name is any identifier name. The number of member data and member function depends on the requirements. In C++ there are three type of access-specifier:

1. Private
2. Public
3. Protected

The access specifier tells about the visibility of member.

The keyword private, public and protected are also known as visibility label. Study the following example.

```
class  student
     {
          private:  char  name [80];
                int  age;
                int  rn;
          protected:  int  semester;
          public:
                void  getdata  ( )
                {
```

```
            cout << "Enter name:";
            cin >> name;
            cout << "Enter age:"
            cin << "age;"
            cout >> "Enter roll no. :"
            cin >> rn;
            cout << "Enter semester:"
            cin >> semester;
                 }
            void showdata ( )
                 {
            cout << "Name:" <<name <<endl;
            cout << "Age :"<<age<<endl;
            cout << "Roll no.:" <<rn<<endl;
            cout << "semester:" <<semester<<endl;
                 }
                      };
```

In above example the body of function written inside the class we can also write body of function outside the class, we will study this in next section.

The member that has been declared as **private** can be accessed only from within class. In above example name, age and rn are private member.

The member that has been declared **public** can be accessed from outside the class. Generally the functions are written under public access specifier because generally function is called from outside the class in real life program.

We will study the **protected** access specifier with inheritance.

The member that has been declaring private can be accessed only within the class i.e., they are hide for outside the class. This is data hiding the key feature of object-oriented programming.

In above example public member are getdata ( ) and showdata ( ); private member are name, age and rn; protected data is semester; student is the name of class.

10.3 WRITING BODY OF MEMBER FUNCTION OUTSIDE CLASS

We can write the body of member function outside the class also with the help of scope resolution operator (::). We can write the above example as written in section 10.2 follow also: (Note that in scope resolution operator (: :) there is no space between : and : if you give space compiler generate error).

Example

```
  class student
       {
            private: char name [80];
```

```
            int  age;
            int  rn;
        protected  :  int  semester;
        public  :
            void  getdata  ( );
            void  showdata  ( );
        };
        void  student  :  :  getdata  ()
                {
                cout  <<  "Enter  name:";
                cin  >>name;
                cout  <<  "Enter  age:";
                cin  >>age;
                cout  <<  "Enter  roll  no.:"
                cin  >>  rn;
                cout  <<  "Enter  semester:";
    void  student  :  :  showdata  ( )
                {
                cout  <<  "name:"  <<name<<endl;
                cout  <<  "Age:"  <<age<<endl;
                cout  <<  "roll  no."  <<rn<<endl;
                cout  <<  "semester:"  <<semester  <<endl;
```

To write the body of function outside the class is better approach.

The general format to write a member function outside class is:

```
return-type  class-name  :  :  function-name  (argument)
    {
    body  of  function
        }
```

The class-name: : tells the compiler that the function, function-name belongs to the class, class-name. If in our program there are more than class and in each class there is a function getdata ( ) then class-name: : resolve their scope. (i.e., which function belong to which class).

Note that when body of function written inside the class it is treated as inline function. Normally the body of small function is written inside the class. We can make the function as inline which is written outside by writing inline in front of function header; like follow:

```
inline  return-type  class-name  :  :  function-name  (argument)
    {
    body  of  function
    }
```

10.4 CREATING OBJECT

Object is instance of class i.e., variable of a class. The declaration of an object is as follow:

```
class-name  object-name;
```

We can declare more than one object of class as follows-

```
class-name  object-name1,  object-name2,  ....,  object-name n;
```

When we declare object space is allocated to that.

For above class student which is written in section 10.2 and 10.3 we can create object as:

```
student  s1;
```

or

```
student  s1,s2,s3;
```

Object can also be created at the time of class declaration, as follows:

```
class  student
     {
     _____
     _____
     _____
     }  s1,  s2,  s3;
```

10.5 ACCESSING MEMBER OF CLASS

We know that private member can not access outside the class. Therefore the private data of a class can be accessed only by the member functions of that class. We have seen this in example section 10.3, the private member of student class like name, roll number, and age directly accessed by member function of student class getdata ( ) and showdata ().

The public member can be access outside the class like from main ( ). The format for calling a member function is:

```
object-name  member-name
```

If member is function then calling format is:

```
object-name.  function-name  (argument);
```

That means the public member of a class can access through the object of that class. The calling procedure of a public member function is same as calling procedure of function. Only difference is the object-name is also necessary in case of member function.

For class student written is 10.3 we call the getdata ( ) and showdata ( ) as follow (if s1, s2 and s3 are object of class student.)

```
s1.  getdata  (  );
s2.  getdata  (  );
```

```
s3. show data ( );
s4. getdata ( );
```

s1.getdata ( ) means we are calling getdata ( ) function for object s1.

s2. show data ( ) means we are calling get data ( ) function for object s2.

s1. show data ( ) means we are calling show data ( ) function for object s1.

If we write the following statement:

```
getdata ( );
```

is illegal because getdata ( ) is a member function of class student therefore we call this through the object of class student like:

```
s1.getdata ( );
```

The statement:

```
s1.age = 25;
```

Is also illegal because age is private member of class student therefore age can be accessed only through a member function and not by the object directly. But if a member is public that can be accessed directly inside class also and outside the class through the object.

Example

```
class abc
    {
    private :
            int i, f;
            void idata ( );
    public : int k;
        void getdata ( );
            };
        void abc : : getdata ( )
            {
            cin >> f >> k;
            }
        void abc : : idata ( )
            {
            i = 20;
            }
        void main ( )
            {
            abc s1;
```

```
        s1.k =20;   //ok,  k is public
        s1.getdata ( ); //ok getdata ( ) is public
        s1.i   = 30; //error, idata is private
        s1.idata ( ); //error, idata is private
        _____
        _____
        }
```

Example

```
class abc
    {
    private : int i, f;
        void idata ( );
    public : int k;
        void getdata ( );
    void abc : :getdata ( ) {cin >> f >> k;
    }
    void abc :  : idata ( ) {idata ( ) {i=20;}
    void main ( )
        {
            s1.k = 20; // ok, k is public
            s1. getdata ( ); //ok getdata ( ) is public
            s1. i = 30; //error, i is private
            s1.idata ( ); //error, idata is private
            _____
            _____
                }
```

Example 10.1: Write a program which reads two numbers calculate the smallest one and then print the smallest one by using object-oriented programming.

Ans. For above problem we will create a class small. Note that the class are written before main ( ).

```
#include <iostream.h>
#include <conio.h>
    class small
        {
        private: int x,y;
        public:
```

```
void readdata ( );
void output ( );
};
void small : : readdata ( )
{
cout << "Enter first number: ";
cin >>x;
cout << "Enter second number:";
cin >> y;
}
void small : : output ( )
{
if (x<y)
cout << "Smallest is :" <<x<<endl;
else
cout << "Smallest is:" <<y <<endl;
void main ( )
{
small s;
clrscr ( );
s.readdata ( );
s.output ( );
getch ( );
}
```

The sample output of above programme is:

```
Enter first number: 10
Enter second number: 20
Smallest is: 10
```

Note: A member function can be called by using its name inside another member function see the following example.

Example 10.2: Write a program which reads the sum of two numbers and then print sum.

```
# include <iostream.h>
# include <conio.h>
class add
{
private: int a,b;
public: void getdata ( );
```

```
        void output ( );
        int calculate ( );
        };
    void add : : getdata ( )
        {
        cout << "Enter a :";
        cin >> a;
        cout << "Enter b :"
        cin >> b;
        }
    int add :  : calculate ( )
        {
        int s;
        s = a + b;
        return (s);
        }
    void add : : output ( )
        {
        int temp;
        temp = calculate ( );
    cout << "SUM IS :" <<temp <<endl;
        }
    void main ( )
        {
        add obj;
        clrscr ( );
        obj.getdata ( );
        obj.output ( );
        getch ( );
        }
```

The sample output of above program is:

```
Enter a : 50
Enter b : 60
SUM IS : 110
```

Note: By default the member of class are private i.e., if we don't write the access specifier then member are automatically assumed private.

Example

```
class XYZ
    {
    int a;
    float b;
    public: getdata ( );
    int c;
```

10.6 ARRAYS WITHIN A CLASS

The array can be used within a class as a member. For example:

Example 1

```
class XYZ
    {
    int a[10];
    public:    ______;
               ______ ;
               ______
               };
```

Example 2

```
class abc
    {
    int a[5] [6];
    public:    ______;
               ______ ;
               ______
               };
```

Example 10.3: Write a program which performs the following operation—(a) addition of matrix (b) subtraction of matrix (c) multiplication of matrix

The above program is:

```
# include <iostream.h>
#include <conio.h>
class matrix
    {
    int a[2], [2], b[2] [2];
```

```
public : void readmatrix ( );
void addmatrix ( );
void submatrix ( );
void mulmatrix ( );
    };
void matrix : : readmatrix ( )
    {
    cout << " Enter first matrix:" <<endl;
    for (int i =0; i <= 1; i++)
    for (int  j=0; j<=1; j++)
        {
    cout << "Enter"<<i+1<<j+1<< "element:";
    cin >> a[i] [j];
        }
    cout << "Enter second matrix:"<<endl;
    for (i =0; i<=1; i++)
    for (j=0; j<=1; j++)
        {
    cout << "Enter" <<i +1<<j+1 << "element:";
    cin >> b [i] [j];
        } //end of read
    void matrix : : addmatrix ( )
        {
        int temp [2] [2];
        int i, j;
    for (i =0; i<=1; i++)
    for (j =0; j<=1; j++)
    temp [i] [j] = a [i] [j] + b [i] [j];
        cout << "Addition of matrix is:" <<endl;
        for (i =0; I <= 1; i++)
{ for (j =0; j < =1; j++)
    cout << temp [i] [j] <<'\t';
    cout << endl;
    } //end of add matrix
void matrix : : submatrix ( )
    {
    int t [2] [2];
    int i, j;
```

```
for ( i=0; i <= 1; i++)
for (j =0; j <=1; j++)
    t [i] [j] = a[i] [j] - b [i] [j];
cout << "subtraction of matrix is:" <<endl;
    for (i =0; i <=1; i++)
        {
        for (j =0; j <=1; j++)
        cout << t [i] [j] << '\t';
        cout <<endl;
        } //end of sub matrix
    void matrix : : mulmatrix ( )
        {
        int m [2] [2]
        int i,j,k;
    for (i =0; i <=1; i++)
    for (j =0; j <= 1; J++)
        for (k=0; k <=1; k++)
        m [i] [j] = m[i] [j] + a [i] [k] * b[k] [j];
cout << "multiplication of matrix is :"<<endl;
for (i =0; i <=1; i++)
    {
for (j =0; j<=1; j++)
cout << m [i] [j] << '\t';
cout << endl;
    }
} //end of mul matrix
void main ( )
    {
matrix mobj;
mobj.readmatrix ( );
mobj. addmatrix ( );
mobj.submatrix ( );
mobj.mulmatrix ( );
getch ( );
    }
```

10.7 MEMORY ALLOCATION FOR OBJECT

We know that memory is allocated to a object when we decide the object. Actually when we create the object space for member data variable is allocated separately for each object but no separate space for member function, the space for member function are created only once when they are declared as a part of class. Because all the objects belong to that class, therefore all use the same member function. For example:

```
class  abc
      {
      member-variable1;
      member-variable2;
      member-variable3;
public  :
      member-function1;
      member-function2;
      member-function3;
            };
      ______
      ______
      ______
abc  obj1,  obj2,  obj3;
```

The scope for obj1, obj2, obj3 is as follows

member_var1	**member_var1**	**member_var1**
member_var2	**member_var2**	**member_var2**
member_var3	**member_var3**	**member_var3**
Obj1	**Obj2**	**Obj3**
member_Fun1	**member_Fun1**	**member_Fun2**

Member function and member variable are in memory.

Example 10.4 Write a program which reads two complex number stores in different object and then print.

```
# include <iostream.h>
# include <conio.h>
class  complex
      {
            float  realpart;
            float  imagpart;
```

```
public : void getdata ( );
    void showdata ();
    };
void  complex :  : getdata ( )
    {
    cout << "Enter real part :";
    cin >> realpart;
    cout << "Enter imag part:"
    cin >> imagpart;
    }
void complex :  : showdata ( )
    {
    cout << "complex number is :" <<endl;
    cout << "realpart <<" +i <<imagpart <<endl;
    }
void main ( )
    {
    complex c1,c2;
    clrscr ( );
    cout << "Enter first complex no." ; << endl;
    c1.getdata ( );
    cout << "Enter second complex no.;" <<endl;
    c2.getdata ( );
    cout << "First no. :"<<endl;
        c1.showdata ( );
    cout << "second no. :"<<endl;
        c2.showdata ( );
    getch ( );
        }
```

The simple output of above program is:

```
Enter first complex no.:
Enter real part : 5
Enter image part : 6
Enter second complex no.
Enter real part : 4
Enter imag part : 2
```

```
First no. :
complex number is :
    5 + i6
second no. :
complex no is :
    4 + i2
```

The memories allocated for above objects are:

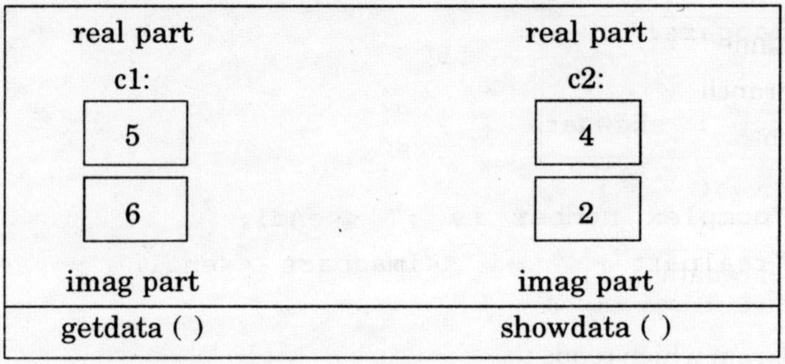

10.8 ARRAY OF OBJECT

Array is collection of homogenous data item. Therefore we can create an array in which each data item in class type such array is called array of object. For example,

```
class student
    {
    char name [80];
    char branch [20];
    int rn;
    public : void getdata ( );
         void showdata ( );
             };
         student biodata [30];
```

Biodata is an array of 30 elements each is student type i.e., biodata [0]; biodata[1], biodata[29] are all object of student class.

The accessing of public member as follows:

```
biodata [i].getdata ( );
```

(i is 0 to 29) for example if we want to access getdata( ) for object biodata [2] then we will write

```
biodata [2].getdata ( );
```

The space in memory is created like follow for above example:

biodata[0]	name
	branch
	rn
biodata [1]	name
	branch
	rn
biodata[29]	name branch rn
getdata ( )	
	showdata( )

Example 10.5: Write a program which reads the bio-data of four students and then prints.

```
# include <iostream.h>
# include <conio.h>
class bio
    {
    char name [80];
    char address [20];
    int phno;
public : void getdata ( );
    void showdata ( );
        };
void bio : : getdata ( )
    {
    cout << "Enter name :"; cin >>name;
    cout << "Enter address :"; cin >>address;
    cout << "Enter phno. :"; cin >> phno;
          }
void bio :   : showdata ( )
    {
    cout << "Name :" <<name <<endl;
    cout << "Address :" <<address <<endl";
    cout << "ph no. :" << phno <<endl;
```

```
        }
  void main ( )
        {
        bio obj [4];
        clrscr ( );
        for (int i =0; i <=3; i++)
        {
  cout << "Enter bio data of " i+1 << "Person:" <<endl;
  obj [i].getdata ( );
        }
        for (i =0; i <=3; i++)
        {
  cout << "Biodata of" << i +1 <<"person is:" <<endl;
  obj [i].showdata ( );
        }
  getch ( );
        }
```

Example 10.6: Write a program which assigns a mobile manufacturer name, model number and cost of two mobile and print all information by oop.

```
# include <iostream.h>
# include <conio.h>
# include <string .h>
class mobile
     {
     char mobilename [30];
     int modelnumber;
     float cost;
public : void assign (char p [ ], int n, float c);
     void output ( );
        };
void mobile : : assign (char p [ ], int n, float c);
     {
     strcpy (mobilename, p);
     modelnumber = n;
     cost = c;
        }
void mobile : : output ( )
```

```
        {
    cout << "mobile name:" <<mobilename <<endl;
    cout << "model number:" <<modelnumber <<endl;
    cout << "cost :" <<cost <<endl;
        }
void main ( )
    {
    mobile c1,c2;
    clrscr ( );
    c1.assign (6600, 5400);
    c1.assign (2600, 3500);
    c1.output ( );
    c2.output ( );
    getch ( );
        }
```

The sample output of above program is:

```
Mobile name : nokia
Model no. : 6600
Cost : 5400
Mobile name : nokia
Model no. : 2600
Cost : 3500
```

10.9 OBJECT AS FUNCTION ARGUMENTS

An entire object can be passed to a function. There are two concepts for passing an object to function

1. Call by value
2. Call by reference or call by address

If we pass object value to function that is called call by value, in this case any change made to the object inside the function do not affect actual object.

If we pass object as a call by reference or call by address, we pass the reference or address of the object. Therefore any change made to the object inside the function will reflect in the actual object.

The object which used as an argument when we call the function is known as actual object, and the object which is used as an argument within the function header is called formal object.

Example 10.7: Write a program which reads two complex number and then calculate sum of these two.

```
# include <iostream.h>
#include <conio.h>
class complex
    {
    float realp;
    float imagp;
public : void getdata ( );
    void sum (complex c1, complex c2);
    void output ( );
        };
void complex : : getdata ( )
        {
    cout << "Enter real part:";
    cin >> realp;
    cout << "Enter imag part:";
    cin >>imagp;
void complex :  : sum (complex c1, complex c2)
    {
    realp = c1.realp + c2.realp;
    imagp = c1.imagp + c2.imagp;
        }
void complex : : output ( )
    {
    cout << realp << "i" <<imagp <<endl;
void main ( )
    {
    complex x,y,z;
    clrscr ( );
    cout << "Enter first complex no.:" <<endl;
    x.getdata ( );
    cout << "Enter second complex no.:" <<endl;
    y.getdata( );
    z.sum (x,y);
cout << "First number :"<<endl;
    x.output ( );
cout << "Second number:"<<endl;
    y.output ( );
cout << "Sum of two number:" <<endl;
```

```
z.output ( );
getch ( );
     }
```

The sample output of above program is:

```
Enter first complex no.:
Enter real part : 4
Enter image part : 2
Enter second complex no.:
Enter real part : 3
Enter image part : 4
First number :
4 + i2
Second number:
3 + i4
Sum of two numbers:
7 + i6
```

In above program the member function sum ( ) is called by object Z and we have passed two arguments x and y both are object. When the statement → z sum (x,y);

Is execute the value of actual object X is copied to formal object C1 and actual object y is copied to formal object c2 and after that body of function sum ( ) is executed. Inside the body of sum ( ) there are following statements:

```
realp = c1.realp + c2.realp;
imagp = c1.imagp + c2.imagp;
```

By the first statement the realp of c1 is (i.e., the realp of object x) added with realp of c2 (i.e., the realp of object y) and assigned to realp variable. This realp is member of object z because the function sum ( ) is called by object z.

Similarly imagp is calculated by the statement.

```
imagp = c1. imagp + c2. imagp;
```

10.10 RETURNING OBJECT FROM FUNCTION

A function can return object. As shown in the example:

```
# include <iostream.h>
# include <conio.h>
class complex
     {
     float realp;
```

```
        float  imagp;
    public  :  void  getdata  (  );
        complex  sum  (complex  c1);
        void  output  (  );
            };
    void  complex  :  :  getdata  (  )
        {
            cout  <<  "Enter  real  part:";
            cin  >>  realp;
            cout  <<  "Enter  imag  part:";
            cin  >>imagp;
    complex  complex  :   :  sum  (complex  c1)
        {
        complex  temp;
        temp.realp  =  c1.realp  +  realp;
        temp  imagp  =  c1.imagp  +  imagp;
            return  (temp);
            }
    void  complex  :  :  output  (  )
        {
        cout  <<  realp  <<  "i"  <<imagp  <<endl;
    void  main  (  )
        {
        complex  x,y,z;
        clrscr  (  );
        cout  <<  "Enter  first  complex  no.:"  <<endl;
        x.getdata  (  );
        cout  <<  "Enter  second  complex  no.:"  <<endl;
        y.getdata  (  );
            z.sum  y.sum  (x);
        cout  <<  "First  number  :"<<endl;
            x.output  (  );
        cout  <<  "Second  number:"<<endl;
            y.output  (  );
        cout  <<  "Sum  of  two  numbers:"  <<endl;
            z.output  (  );
            getch  (  );
            }
```

In the above program the function sum is called by object y therefore inside the function sum ( ) in statement:

```
temp.realp  =  c1.realp  +  realp;
```

Realp is member of y.

c1.realp is actually X.realp because X is copied to C1 at the time of calling by the statement:

```
z  =  y.sum  (x);
```

So,

```
temp.realp  =  c1.realp  +  realp;
```

means realp of x is added with realp of y and assigned to realp of temp.

Similarly,

```
temp.imag  =  c1.imagp  +  imagp;
```

means the imagp x is added with imagp of y and assigned to imag p of temp.

```
return  (temp);
```

Statement object temp is returned to main and copied to z because we are assigning y. Sum(x) to z in main program by the calling statement.

```
z  =  y.sum  (x);
```

10.11 STATIC MEMBER OF CLASS

The member of class be made static; (data member and function member both).

10.11.1 Static Data Member

If we create the data member of a class is static then the properties of that is:

1. **It is initialized zero and only once when the first object of its class is created.**
2. **Only one copy of that member is created for the entire class and is shared by all the objects of class.**
3. **It is accessible only within the class, but its lifetime is the entire program.**

The static variables are declared as follows:

```
class  abc
        {
        static  int  c;
        -------
public  :  -------
        ---------
        };
```

The type and scope of each static member must be defined outside the class for example for above class abc c is defined as follows:

```
int abc  :   : c;
```

Or

```
int abc  :   : c = 10;
```

If we write

```
int abc  :   : c;
```

then c is automatically assigned to zero.
But by statement

```
int abc  :   : c = 10;
```

c is initialized 10.

Static variable are normally used to maintain values common to entire class.

```
#include <iostream.h>
#include <conio.h>
class counter
      {
      int n;
      static int count;
public :
      void getdata (int number)
            {
            n = number;
            count ++;
            }
            void showcount ( )
            {
            cout << "cout:" << cout <<endl;
            };
                  };
            int counter :   : count;
                  void main ( )
                        {
                        counter c1,c2,c3,c4;
                        clrscr ( );
                        c1.showcount ( );
                        c2.showcount ( );
                        c3.showcount ( );
```

```
            c4.showcount  ( );
            c1.getdata  (20  );
            c2.getdata  (40  );
            c3.getdata  (60  );
            c4.getdata  (80  );
      cout  <<"value  of  count  after  calling";
      cout  <<"getdata  function:" <<endl;
            c1.showcount  (  );
            c2.showcount  (  );
            c3.showcount  (  );
            c4.showcount  (  );
            getch  (  );
            }
```

The output of above program is as follows:

```
Count : 0
Count : 0
Count : 0
Count : 0
value of count after calling get data function
Count : 80
Count : 80
Count : 80
Count : 80
```

In the above example count in static variable this is initialized zero when the object are created. The variable count is incremented whenever the getdata ( ) function is called. Since the getdata ( ) function called four times by object c1, c2, c3 and c4, the variable count is incremented four times. Because there is only one copy of count shared by all four objects. All the four output statements print the value 80.

The memory taken by c1, c2, c3 and c4 as follows:

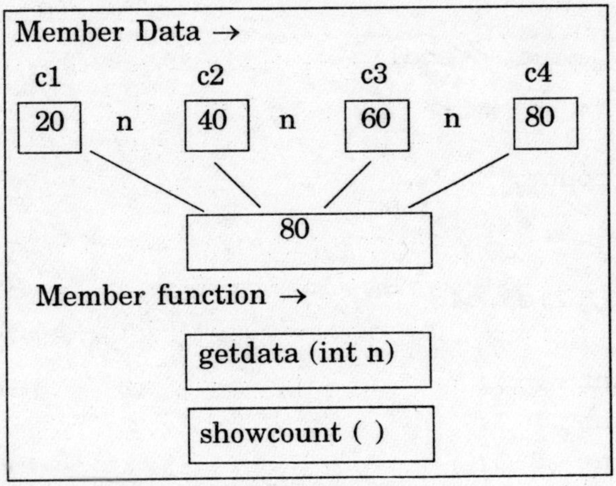

10.11.2 A Static Member Function is also Possible Like Static Member Variable

The static member functions declare as follows:

```
class  abc
    {
    int n;
    static  int  count;
    public  : —
              —
          static  void  output  (  )
               {  —// body  of  output
               ——
               ——}
                 };
int  abc  :    :  count  =  100;
```

If a member function is declared static that has following properties:

1. **A static function can access to only other static member (static member data and static member function) declare in the same class.**
2. **The calling procedure of static member function is as follows:**

```
class-name  :    :  function  -  name;
```

For above example output is called as follows:

```
abc  :  :  output  (  );
```

Example 10.8

```
#  include  <conio.h>
#  include  <iostream.h>
class  counter
    {
    int  a;
    static  int  count;
public  :
    void  assign  (  )
    {  +  +  count;
        a  =  count;
    }
void  output  (  )
```

```
        {
        cout  <<  "A ="  <<a <<endl;
        }
    static  void  outputc  ( )
        {
        cout  <<  "count  :  <<count  <<endl;
        };
        int  counter  :   :  count;
            void  main  ( )
            {  counter  c1,c2,c3;
    //By  above  statement  0  is  assigned
    //to  count
    counter  :    :   outputc
    c1.assign  ( );
    c2.assign  ( );
    c3.assign  ( );
    counter  c4;
    c4.assign  ( );
    counter  :   :  outputc;
    c1.outputn  ( );
    c2.outputn  ( );
    c3.outputn  ( );
    c4.outputn  ( );
       getch  ( );
            }
```

The output of above program is:

```
count : 0
count : 4
A : 1
A : 2
A : 3
A : 4
```

The memory space for object c1, c2, c3 and c4 is:

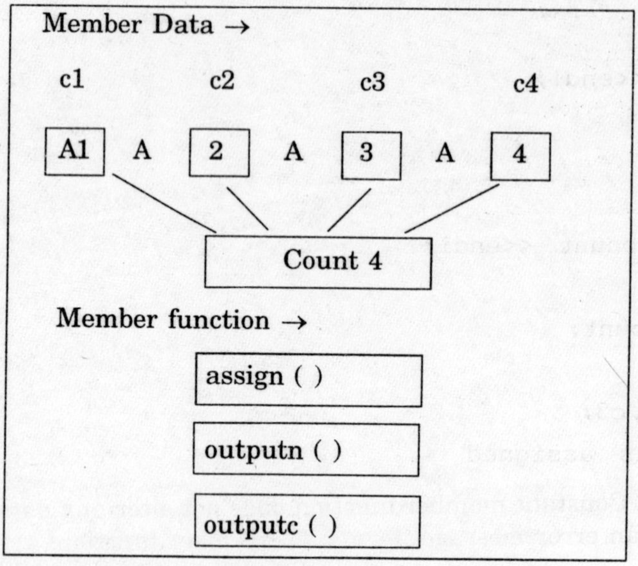

10.12 CONST MEMBER FUNCTION

We can declare a member function constant as follows:

```
class  abc
     {
          int  a,b;
          public  :  void getdata  (  )
               {
               —
               —
               —}
          void  printdata  (  )  const
               {
               —
               —
               — }
                    };
```

In above example printdata function is declared as constant. If we write the body of function outside then qualifier const is appended in both declaration and defined as follows:

```
class  abc
     {
          int  a,b,c;
     public  :  void  getdata  (  );
          void  printdata  (  )  const;
               };
```

```
void abc : : getdata ( )
    {
    —
    —
    }
void abc : : printdata ( )
    const
    {
    —
    —
    —
    }
```

The property of constant member is: Constant member function does not alter any data in the class. The compiler will generate an error message if constant member functions try to alter the data value.

Example

```
# include <iostream.h>
class abc
    {
    private : int data;
    public :
    void assign ( )
        {
        data = 20;
        }
    void change data ( ) const
        {
        data = 40; //error
    void showdata ( ) const
        {
        cout <<data << endl;
        };
    void main ( )
        {
        abc s1;
        s1. assign ( );
        s1. change data ( );
        s1. showdata ( );
        }
```

In the above statement

```
data = 40;
```

Give error because that is inside a constant member function. Similarly if we pass object as an constant argument to a function then function cannot modify these argument; if modify compiler give error message.

If we pass object as a call by value then no need of constant but if we pass as call by reference or call by address then we can use const, for safety. See the following example:

```
# include <iostream.h>
class abc
    {
        int a;
            public : void assign ( )
    {
    a = 10;
    }
void add (abc const & c1, abc const & c2)
    {
    a =c1.a + c2.a;
    }
void show ( )
    {
    cout << "a=" <<a<<aendl;
    }
    };
void main ( )
    {
    abc x,y,z;
    x.assign;
    y.assign;
    z.add (x,y);
    z.output ( );
    }
```

In above program the argument to the function add ( ) are passed by reference and we want to make sure that add ( ) won't modify these argument. To ensure this we have declare the argument as constant.

10.12.1 Structure and Class

Structure is a group of data while class is a group of data and function both. In fact, we can use structure in almost exactly same way that we use class.

The only formal difference between class and structure is that in a class the members are private by default, while in a structure they are public by default.

The format we have been using for classes:

```
class  xyz
        {
        private : int  data;
        public  :  void  func  (  );
        };
```

Since in classes private is the default, we can write above class xyz like:

```
class  xyz
        {
        int  data;
        public  :  void  func  (  );
        };
```

The member data will still be private.

If we want to use structure to do the same things as this class, we can dispense with the keyword public, provided you put public members before the private ones:

```
struct  xyz
        {
        void  func  (  );
                private  :
                        int  data  ;
                                };
```

Since public is the default therefore func( ) is public.

However in most situations we use structure to group data and classes to group data and functions.

Solved Exercises

Exercise 1. Write a program to represent a book in library book class.

```
# include  <iostream.h>
# include  <conio.h>
# include  <stdio.h>
class  book
        {
        int  book_no;
        char  author[25];
        char  publisher[40];
        float  price;
```

```
        int No_of _copies;
        int No_of_Issues;
        public:
            void readdata( );
            void display ( );
            void issue ( );
            void return ( );
        };
    void book :: readdata ( )
        {
            cout << "\n Enter the book number:";
            cin >> book_no;
            cout << "\n Enter the name of author:";
            get(Author);
            cout << "\n Enter the name of Publisher:";
            gets(Publisher);
            cout << "\n Enter the Price:";
            cin >> price;
            cout << "\n Enter the number of copies in library:";
            cin >> No_of _copies;
            cout << "\n Enter the number of copies issued:";
            cin >> No_of_Issues;
            }
            void book :: display ( )
            {
            cout << "\n book number:" << book_no;
            cout<< "\n Author:"<< Author;
            cout << "\n Publishor:" << Publishor;
            cout << "\n Price:" << Price;
            cout << "\n number of copies:" << No of copies;
            cout << "\n number of copies issued:" << No_of _Issue;
            }
            void book :: issue ( )
            {
                if(No_of_copies>No_of_Issues)
                {
```

```
                No_of_Issues++;
                cout << "\n book is issued";
            }
                else
                    cout << "\n book canot be issued";
            }
            void book::return ( )
            {
            if (No_of_Issue >0)
                {
                No_of_Issue—;
                cout << "\n book is returned";
                }
                else
                cout << "\n book cannot be returned";
                }
                void main ( )
                {
                Book bk;
                clrscr ( );
                cout << "\n Enter the details of book : \n \n";
                bk.readdata ( );
                int choice;
                do
                {
                    clsscr ( );
                    cout << "\n MAIN MENU";
                    cout << "\n 1. Issue.";
                    cout << "\n 2. Return";
                    cout << "\n 3. Display";
                    cout << "\n Exit.";
                    cout << "\n Enter the choice…";
                    cin >>choice;
                    switch(choice)
                    {
                        case 1 : Bk.issue( );
                            break;
                        case 2 : Bk.return ( );
```

```
                        break;
                case 3 : Bk. Display ( );
                        break;
                case 4 : cout << "\n Terminating program !!"
                        getch ( );
                        return;
                        default : cout <<"\n wrong choice!!!";
                }
                getch ( );
                }
                while(choice !=4);
                }
```

Exercise 2. Write a program to add two different distance - measuring units i.e., Mts, Cms with Ft, Inches.

```
# include <iostream.h>
# include <conio.h>
    class F1;
    class MC
    {
        int m;
        int cm;
        public :
            void readMeter ( )
            {
                cout << "\n Enter meter and centimeter:";
                cin >>m>>cm;
            }
            void printMeter ( )
            {
                cout <<"\n Meter and centimeter:" << m <<","<<cm;
            }
            Friend F1 sum (MC & F1 &);
            }
        meter;
        class F1
        {
            int f;
            int in;
```

```
public:
void readFeets ( )
{
cout <<"\n Enter feets and inches:";
cin >>f>>in;
}
void printFeets ( )
    {
    cout << "\n feets and inches :" <<f<<"fts"<<in<<"in";
    }
        friend F1 sum (MC & FI &);
    }
    feet, rfeet;
    void main ( )
        {
            clrscr ( );
            meter.readMeter ( );
            feet.readFeets ( );
            rfeet = Sum(meter, feet);
            rfeet.printFeets ( );
            getch ( );
        }
        F1 sum (MC & mt1, FI & ft1)
        {
            F1 ft2,ft3;
            ft2.f = (mt1.m * 100 + mt1.cm)/(2.5 * 12);
            ft2.in= (int) ((mt1.m * 100 + mt1.cm)/2.5)%12;
            ft3.f = ft2f+ft1f+(ft2.in+ft1.in)/12;
            ft3.in = (ft2.in+ft1,in)%12;
            return ft3;
        }
```

Descriptive Questions

1. **How does a class accomplish data encapsulation?**
2. **Define a class to represent an account in a bank.**
   Following are data members:
   Depositor's name

Account number

Balance

The members' functions should the following:

Initialize the data members

Display the detail of particular

Deposit amount

Withdraw amount

3. Create class to represent a floating point number. Write a program to add Subtract and multiply two such object.
4. How is a class different from an object?
5. What is scope resolution operator used for?
6. Write a C++ program using structures to create a database for hospital giving details about patients admitted:

   Patient name, age, gender, ward no, bed no, nature of illness, date of admission
7. What is difference between structure and class?
8. What is class. How object of class are created?
9. Explain following:

   (*a*) private (*b*) public.
10. What is scope resolution operator?
11. How body of member function of class is written?
12. How we create the array of class object?
13. How we pass a complete object to member function of class?
14. Can member function of class return object explain?
15. What is difference between class and object?
16. Can we write array within class explain?

Exercises

1. Write a program to implement complex number class.
2. Write a program to hold salesmen's data.
3. Write a program to hold data class.
4. Write a program to implement random class for generating psedo-random numbers.
5. Write a program to implement person class.
6. Write a program to implement matrix class.
7. Write program to implement vector class.
8. Write program to implement a polling booth.
9. Write program to implement bank account class that allows a friend function to modify balance.
10. Write program to implement bank account class that allows a friend function to modify balance.
11. Write program to implement a student structure through pointer.
12. Write a program to implement employee structure using pointer.

13. Write a program with the help of OOP concept which read the name of a person and five different account number of that and then find out account number 2323 is belong to that or not. Note that for storing account number use an array.
14. Write a program which reads the biodata of 10 employee of a factory and then print the biodata of those employee whose salary is more then 15000. The employee biodata consist following field:

    (*a*) Name (*b*) Sex (*c*) Age
    (*d*) Designation (*e*) Salary (*f*) Experience

    Write the program by object oriented approach.
15. Write a program which read two complex number and then perform following operation (Write program by OOP approach)

    (*a*) addition of complex number.
    (*b*) subtraction of complex number.
    (*c*) Multiplication of complex number.
    (*d*) Division of complex number.

    Note: If a+ib and c+id are two complex number then,

    (*a*) Addition is (a + c) +i(b + d).
    (*b*) Subtraction of complex number.
    (*c*) Multiplication is (ac–bd)+i(ad+bc).
    (*d*) Division $\dfrac{(a*c+b*d)}{c^2+d^2}+i\dfrac{(b*c-a*d)}{c^2+d^2}$.
16. Write a program to maintain account of 10 account holders.
17. Write a program to hold and process batsman's data using appropriate class.
18. Write a program to implement/simulate a ticket selling booth.
19. Write a program to hold detail of 50 items and then print largest price and sum of price.
20. Write a program to implement student-result preparation system.
21. Write a program to implement a 3-D point.
22. Write a program to implement time class.
23. Write a program to implement circle class.

11

CONSTRUCTOR AND DESTRUCTOR

In this chapter we will learn constructor and its classification. The diagrammatic presentation of the type of constructors is given below.

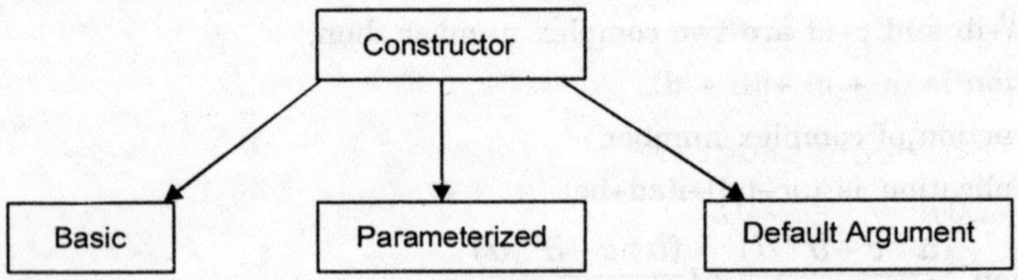

11.1 CONSTRUCTOR

A constructor is a special member function whose task is to initialize the object of its class. The name of the member function is the same as the class name. The name given to this initializing function is **constructor** because it constructs the value of the data member of a class. Constructor is creation and initialization of the object.

It is special type of member function for automatic initialization of object. Where ever an object is created the constructor will executed automatically.

The name of constructor must be same as that of its class. The constructor is declared with no return type, not even void. Constructor may not be static and virtual. Constructor should be declaring in the public section, it can be declared within the protected and in some rare case within the private. The object with a constructor (or destructor) cannot be used as a member of union.

```
class abc
 {
   int x,y;
   public :
   abc ( )
   {
```

```
x=10;  y=20;
}
void  output  ( )
{
cout  <<  a  <<  b  <<  endl;
}
```

In the above example abc is class; the constructor is

```
abc  ( )
    {  x  =  10;  y  =  20;  }
```

When we create object of above class this is automatically called and therefore 10 is assign to x and 20 is assigned to y. In the body of constructor we can write any statement and comment also

```
abc  ( )
 {cout  <<  "constructor  :"  <<endl;
  x  =  10;  y  =  20;  }
```

Characteristics of a constructor:

(*i*) It is declared in the **public** section of the class

(*ii*) It automatically initializes the data members of the object

(*iii*) It does **not return** any value

(*iv*) Constructor cannot be inherited, through a derived class can call the base class constructor.

Example 11.1: Write a program which initialized 100 and 200 to member data and calculate addition of these.

```
# include  <iostream.h>
# include  <conio.h>
class  example1
{
  int  a,b;
  public:
  example1  ( )
   {
    cout  <<  "This  is  constructor"  <<endl;
    a=100;  b=200;
   }
    int  add  ( )
    {
```

```
return (a+b);
     };
void main( )
     {
      clrscr ( );
       example1 e; //constructor called
        cout << "Output is: "<<e.add ( ) << endl;
         getch ( );
              }
```

The above output is :

This is constructor
Output is 300

The body of constructor can also be written outside the class like the other member function.

```
class abc
      {
         int x,y;
      public : abc ( );
           void output ( );
                    };
     abc :  : abc ( )
         {
            a = 10; b = 20;
          }
          void abc : : output ( )
            {
             cout << a <<b<<endl;
                }
```

11.2 CONSTRUCTOR WITH PARAMETER

The constructor abc defined in the example initializes the various data element of the object to zero. In real project we require to initialize various data elements of different objects with different value when they are created. For this we have to pass argument to the constructor function when the objects are created. Argument taking constructors are called parameterized constructors.

We can use argument in constructor as follows:

```
class abc
    {
        int x,y;
            public : abc (int x1, int y1 );
                {
                x = x1; y = y1;
                }
                void output ( )
                    {
                        cout << "x =" <<x <<endl;
                        cout << "y =" <<y <<endl;
                        };
```

When argument is used in constructor they are known as parameterized constructor. The object of such type is created as follows:

(1) abc C1 (20,30);

(2) abc C1 = abc (20,30);

The (1) declaration is called **implicit call** and (2) declaration is called **explicit call.** Generally the (1) declaration is used because this is shorthand method.

When the constructor is parameterized the actual and formal argument must match like in other function.

The two ways of passing initial values as arguments to the constructor are:

Explicit: Data-type object name = function name (arguments);

Implicit: Data-type object name (arguments)

Example 11.2: Write a program which read two numbers initialized object with these two numbers and then find out multiplication of these two.

```
# include <iostream.h>
# include <conio.h>
class xyz
    {
        int a, b;
        public : xyz (int a1, int b1)
                {
                a = a1; b = b1;
                }
                int mul ( )
                {
                    return (a * b);
```

```
            }
          };
      void main ( )
          {
            int i, j;
            clrscr ( );
            cout << "Enter first no. :";
            cin >> i;
            cout << "ZEnter second no. :";
  cin >> j;
        xyz C1 (i,j);
         cout << "Multiplication is:"
           cout << C1.mul ( ) << endl;
            getch ( );
          }
```

The simple output of above program is:

Enter first no. : 6
Enter second no. : 4
Multiplication is : 24

In the above program we cannot create object as follows:

```
xyz C1;
```

Because in the above program there is constructor, and that is parameterized. We can create object by above method if class xyz has no constructor or a constructor with no argument. A constructor with no argument is called default constructor.

Example 11.3: Write a program, which prints the object number whenever we create an object.

```
# include <iostream.h>
# include <conio.h>
   class counter
         {
        static int count;
                      public : counter ( )
                                   { count ++;
      cout << "Object number is :" <<count << endl;
            };
```

```
int counter : : count;
void main ( )
    {
clrscr ( );
cout << "We are creating C1:"<<endl;
counter C1;
 cout << "We are creating c2:" <<endl;
 counter c2;
 getch ( );
    }
```

The output of above program is:

```
We are creating C1;
Object number is :1
We are creating C2:
Object number is :2
```

11.3 MULTIPLE CONSTRUCTOR (CONSTRUCTOR OVERLOADING)

More than one constructor can be declared but they differ in arguments. So far we have considered three kinds of constructors.

construct ( ); // no argument

construct (int, int); \\ Two arguments

construct (construct &); // argument

In first case, the constructor itself supplies the data values and no values are passed by the calling program. In second case, the function call passes the approximate values for main ( ). C++ permits us to use all the above three constructs in same class definition.

```
class xyz
    {
      int m,n,p;
             public :xyz ( )
               {
      m = 0; n =0; p = 0;
      xyz (int m1, int n1)
           {
      m=m1; n =n1; p = 0;
         }
            xyz (int m1, int n1, int p1)
```

```
        {
        m  =m1;  n  =  n1;  p  =p1;
        }
            };
```

In the above example we have declared three constructors in class .xyz. The first constructor receives no arguments; the second receives two arguments and third receives three arguments. Now the question is how we create object. We can create three different type of object for above class xyz as follows:

(1) xyz C1;

(2) xyz C2 (10,20);

(3) xyz C3 (5,6,7)

When we create object like (1) then this automatically invokes the constructor which has no arguments; therefore the m,n and p of object C1 are initialized by zero (0).

When we create object like (2) then this automatically invokes the constructor which has three arguments (i.e the second one); therefore the m,n, and p of object C2 are initialized by values 10,20, and 0.

When we create object like (3) then this automatically invoke the constructor which has three arguments (i.e the third one); therefore the m,n and p of object C3 are initialized by value 5,6 and 7.

We have seen in above example that more than one constructor is possible in a class. Note that sharing the same name by two or more functions is called function overloading. When more then one constructor is defined in a class that is known as constructor overloading.

Example 11.4: Write a program which calculate the subtraction of two complex no.: a and b when a = 3+i5 and b = 4+i5.

```
# include  <iostream.h>
# include  <conio.h>
class complex
     {
    int  x,y;
    public  :  complex  (int  a)
     {
     x  =  a;  y  =  b;
     }
     void  add  (complex  C1,  complex  C2)
       {
         x  =  C1.x  -  C2.x;
         y  =  C1.y  -  C2.y;
         }
         void  show  (  )
```

```
        {
        cout <<x<< "+i" <<y<<endl;
         }
          };
void main ( )
 {
 clrscr ( );
 complex a (3,5);
 complex b (4);
 complex c (0);
  c.add (a,b);
   a.show ( );
    b.show ( )
     cout << "a - b is :"<<endl;
       c.show ( );
         getch ( );
          }
```

11.4 COPY CONSTRUCTORS

```
Classname (classname & object variable)
```

A constructor is used to declare and initialize object. The initialization of an object when done by another object is called **copy constructor**.

To declare an object and initialize with another object, we write the statement construct c2(c1);

Object c2 is defined and at the same time initialized it with the values of c1. One more way of initialization is

Construct c2 =c1;

c2 = c1; // statement

This above statement does invoke the constructor. It is assign the value of object c1 to object c2. The operator (**equal to**) = is overloaded here. This is called as **operator overloading**. An argument for **copy constructor** is a reference to an object of the same class.

Copy constructor are used to copy one object to other one

```
class xyz
 {
    int a,b;
    public: xyz (xyz & c1)
```

```
    {
     x =c1.x;  y  =  c1.y;
     }
     xyz  (  )
     {
     x  =  10;  y  =  20;
     }
         };
```

We can create for above as follows:

(1) xyz c2;

(2) xyz c3 (c2) or c3 =c2

The statement xyz c2; calls the no arguments constructor. While the statement xyz c3(c2); called first constructor that is copy constructor. This statement xyz c3 =c2 also called copy constructor. Note the header of copy constructor is written as follows-

Class-name (class-name & object-ref)

In above example we have written copy constructor as

xyz (xyz & c1)

(x =c1.x; y =c1.y)

Where xyz is name of class c1 is reference of object.

Example 11.5: Write a program which reads a complex number, copy that ino another. Use copy constructor for writing program.

```
# include <iostram.h>
# include <conio.h>
class complex
      { int r,  i;
public :  complex  (int a,  int b)
          {
               r  =  a;  i  =  b;
          }
          complex  (complex &c)
               {
                 r  =  c.r;  i=  c.i;
                 }
                    void show  (  )
                         {
                           cout  <<  r<<  "  +i<<i<<endl;
                              };
```

```
void main ( )
    {
        int x,y;
        clrscr ( );
         cout << "Enter real part:"; cin >>x;
          cout << "Enter imag part :" cin >>y;
           complex c1 (x,y); // first constructor called
           complex c2 (c1); //copy constructor called
            cout << "First no is";
             c1.show ( );
              cout << "second no. is :"
               c2.show ( );
                getch ( );
                }
```

The output of above program is:

```
Enter real part : 7
Enter imag part : 8
First no is : 7 + i8
Second no is : 7+i8
```

11.5 CONSTRUCTORS WITH DEFAULT ARGUMENTS

This method is used to initialize object with user defined parameter at the time of creation. It is possible to define a constructor with default argument like in normal function.

```
class complex
        {
         int x,y;
         public : complex (int a, int b =0)
              {
                  x = a; y = b;
                 }
                };
```

In above example the default value of b is zero i.e (0 is assigned to y). We can create the following type of object for above class:

(1) complex c1 (5);

(2) complex c2 (5,6);

If we create object like (2) then 5 is assigned to x and 6 is assigned to y.

Example 11.6: Write a program which calculate simple interest.

```
# include <iostream.h>
# include <conio.h>
# include <math.h>
class interest
    {
    int principal, rate, year;
    float amount;
    public :
    interest (int p, int n, int r=10)
    void cal (void);
      };
      interest : : interest (int p, int n, int r =10)
       {
       principal = p; year = n; rate = r;
         };
          void interest : : cal(void)
             {
                   cout << "principal" << principal;
                   cout << "\rate" <<rate;
                   cout << "year" <year;
                  amount = (float) (p*n*r)/100;
                   cout << "\amount" <<amount;
                 };
                void main ( )
                {
                 interest i1(1000,2);
                 interest i2 (1000,2,15);
                 clrscr ( );
                 i1.cal ( );
                 i2.cal ( );
                 }
```

Note two object created and initialize in main () function.

interest i1(1000,2)

interest i2(1000,2,15)

The data member principal and year of the object i1 are initialized to 1000 and 2 respectively at the time when object i1 is created. The data member rate take the default value 10 whereas when the object 12 is created, principal, year and rate are initialized to 1000, 2 and 15 respectively.

It is necessary to distinguish between **the default constructor construct: : construct ();** and default argument constructor

Construct: : construct (int=0);

The **default argument constructor** can be called with one or no arguments. When both these forms are used in a class, it cause ambiguity for a declaration like construct c1; the ambiguity is where to invoke construct: : construct() or construct : : construct(int=0)

11.6 DYNAMIC CONSTRUCTORS

Allocation of memory during the creation of objects can be done by the **constructors** too.

The memory is saved as it allocates the right amount of memory for each object (object are not of same size). Allocation of memory to object at the time of their construction is known as **dynamic construction** of object; **new** operator is used to allocate memory.

Example 11.7: Write a program to concatenate two strings. The constructor function initializes the string using constructor function which allocates memory during its creation.

```
# include <iostream.h>
# include <string.h>
class string
{
    char *name;
    int length;
    public:
    string ( )
{
        length=0;
        name = new char[length=1];
  };
    string(char*s)
    {
      length=strlen(s);
      name=new char[length+1];
      strcpy(name,s);
      };
      void display(void)
      {
        cout << "\ Name:-"<<name;
        };
        void join(string &a, string &b)
```

```
        {
        length=a.length+b.length;
        delete name;
        name = new char[length+1];
        strcpy (name, a.name);
        strcat(name,b.name);
          };
          };
          void main ( )
          {
              char*firstname= "Ram";
              string Fname(FirstName);
              string Mname("Prasad");
              string Sname("Singh");
              string Halfname, Fullname;
              Halfname.join(Fname, Sname);
              Fullname.join(Halfname, Mname);
              Fname.display ( );
              Mname.display ( );
              Sname.display ( );
              Halfname.display ( );
              Fullname.display ( );
              }
```

Output of program is:

```
Name : Ram
Name : Prasad
Name : Singh
Name : Ram.Singh
Name : Ram.Singh.Prasad
```

The above program uses **new** operator to allocate memory. The first constructor is **empty** constructor that allows us to declare an array of string. The second constructor initialize length of the string, allocates necessary space for the string to be stored and created the string itself. The member function join ( ) concatenates 2 strings. It actually adds the length of 2 strings and then allocates the memory for the combined string. After that the join function uses inbuilt string functions strcpy & strcat fulfill the action.

The output of the program will be Full Name and Half name that is Ram Singh Prasad and Ram Singh respectively.

11.7 DESTRUCTORS

A destructor as the name implies is used to destroy the object that has been created by a constructor. It is a member function like constructor whose name is the same as the class name but is preceded by **tilde.**

~construct ( ) { }

Character of destructor

- It never takes any arguments
- It does not return any value
- It is invoked implicitly by the compiler upon exit from the program

To allocate memory **new** operator is used. Similarly to free the memory we use **delete** operator.

Example

```
class  complex
      {
          int  x,y;
         public  :  complex  (  )
                {
                    x  =10,  y  =  20;
            ~complex  (  )
                    {    }
                         };
```

Output of the program is:

```
~ complex ( )
{ }
```

Solved Exercises

Exercise 1. Write program for where a constructor function takes no parameter. The copy constructor takes any object as parameter.

```
# include <iostream.h>
# include <conio.h>
class construct
      {
          int m,n;
          public  :
          construct  (  )
          {
```

```
m=0; n=0;
};
construct (intx, int y)
{
 m=x; n=y;
};
 construct (construct &c)
 {
  m=c.m; n=c.n;
  };
   void display (void);
   };
   void construct ::display(void)
    {
      cout << "value" <<rn "\t"<<n;
     };
      void main ( )
        {
              construct c1;
              construct c2;(2,4);
              construct c3(c2);
              cout << "First constructor\n";
             c1.display( );
              cout << "\nSecond constructor\n";
             c2.display ( );
              cout << "\nThird constructor\n";
             c3.display ( );
              getch ( );
               }
```

Output of the program is:

First constructor
Value 0 0
Second constructor
Value 2 4
Third constructor
Value 2 4

Exercise 2. Write a program to declare class matrix to represent the number of rows and column of matrix as well as two dimensional arrays to store the contents of matrix.

```
#include <iostream.h>
#include <stdio.h>
#include <conio.h>
 class matrix
  {
   int **p;
   int d1,d2;
   public :
   matrix(int x,int y);
   void get_value(void);
   void dis_value(void);
   void square(void);
   void cube(void);
   };
   matrx :: matrix (int x, int y)
   {
     d1=x;
     d2=y;
     p=new int *[d1];
     for (int i =0; i<d1;i++)
     p[i]=new int[d2];
     };
     void matrix :: get_value(void)
        {
          for (int i=0; i<d1; i++)
          for (int j=0; j<d2; j++)
         {
              cout << "Please Enter A No At "<<i<<j<<"position:";
              cin >>p[i][j];
               }
               };
              void matrix ::dis_value(void)
      {
          cout << "The matrix Entered";
          for (int i=0;i<d1; i++)
```

```
{
  cout << "\n";
   for (int j=0; j<d2; j++)
  cout << "\t"<<p[i][j];
  }
 };
 void matrix ::square(void)
  {
    cout<< "\n the square of matrix";
    for (int i=0; i<d1;i++)
   {
    cout<<"\n";
    for (int j=0; j<d2; j++)
    cout <<"\t"<<p[i][j]*p[i][j]*p[i][j];
    }
    };
    void main ( )
        {
         int m,n;
         clrscr ( );
         cout << "Enter Size of matrix:";
         cin>>m>>n;
         matrix mat(m,n);
         mat.get_value ( );
         mat.dis_value ( );
         getch ( );
         mat.square();
         mat.cube ();
         getch ();
         }
```

Sample output of the program is:

```
//Input
Enter size of matrix:22
Please enter A no at position 00 : 1
Please  enter A no at position 01 : 1
Please enter A no at position 10 : 2
Please enter A no at position 11 : 2
//Output
```

```
The matrix entered
11
22
The square of matrix
11
34
The cube of matrix
11
88
```

Exercise 3. Write a program to give conclusion that destructor is invoked automatically t the end of its scope.

```
#include<iostream.h>
#include<conio.h>
class add
 {
  int num1,num2,num3;
 public:
 add (int,int);
 void sum(void);
 void display(void);
 ~add(void);
   };
      add::add(int x, int y)
         {
             num1=x;
             num2=y;
             num3=0;
             cout<< "\n Constructor called object created";
          };
        void add ::sum(void)
          {
            num3=num1+num2;
           };
            void add ::display(void)
            {
              cout<< "\n num1:" num1;
              cout << "\n num2:" num2;
```

```
        cout << "\n sum :" <<num3;
      };
     add::~add(void)
      {
        num1=0;
        num 2=0;
        num 3=0;
         cout << "\n Destructor called object destroyed"
        };
        void main ( )
         {
         add a1(10,5)
         a1.sum();
         a1.display();
        }
```

Output of the program is:

Constructor called object created
num 1:10
num 2:5
sum : 15
Destructor called object destroyed

Exercise 4. Write a program declares class item to represent the price and code of th item. The constructor function initializes the object with the code and price of the item. Th copy constructor function allows you to copy the contents of one object with the contents another object.

```
 # include <iostream.h>
 # include <conio.h>
  class item
        {
          int itemcode;
          int itemprice;
          public:
          item ( ) { }
          item (int c, int p)
      {
          itemcode=c;
            itemprice=p;
```

```
        } item(item &i)
{
 itemcode=i.itemcode;
 itemprice =i.itemprice;
void display (void)
   {
      cout<< "\n itemCode:"<<itemcode;
      cout<< "\t itemprice:"<<itemprice;
   }
      };
void main ()
      itemi1(100,100);
      itemi2(i1);
      itemi3(101,200);
      itemi4=i3;
      clsscr();
      i1.display ();
    i2.display ();
    i3.display();
    i4.display ();
   }
```

Output of the program is:

Itemcode: 100	Itemprice: 100
Itemcode: 100	Itemprice: 100
Itemcode: 101	Itemprice: 200
Itemcode: 101	Itemprice: 200

Exercise 5. Write program using default constructor to calculate area and perimeter of the rectangle depending upon the argument passed.

```
#include <iostream.h>
#include <conio.h>
class rectangle
  {
      int length;
      int breadth;
      int value;
      char type;
      public :
      rectangle( )
      {
      length = 0;
```

```
 breadth  =  0;
 }
rectangle  (int  l,  int  b,  char  t  =  'P');
void  display  (void);
};
rectangle  ::rectangle  (int  l,  intb,  char  t)
{
 length  =l;
 breadth  =  b;
 if  (t=  =  'P')
 type  =  'P'
  else
  type  =  "A";
  };
  void  rectangle:  :display  (void)
  {
   cout  <<  "\  the  length  =\t"  <<length;
   cout  <<     "the  breadth  =\t"  <<breadth;
   if  (type  =  =  'P')
      {
      value   =  2  *  (length*breadth);
      cout  <<  "\n  The  perimeter  =  \t"  <<value;
       }
       else
        {
          value  =  length  *  breadth;
          cout  <<\n  The  area  =\t"<<value;
           }
          };
       void main  (  )
            {
          rectangle  R1  (10,5);
          rectangle  R2  (10,5,  'A')
          clrscr  ( );
    R1.display  (  );
    R2.display  (  );
       getch  (  );
     }
```

Descriptive Questions

1. Explain what is constructor? Give a diagrammatic description of the types of constructor and explain them.
2. Explain constructor is a function. Can we overload constructor?
3. Define dynamic constructor. Explain new and delete operator.
4. Justify destructor does not return any value. Does constructor return any value?
5. Explain multiple constructors. How do you overload constructor explain in brief?
6. How do you copy one constructor to other?
7. How can we pass parameter to constructor explain?
8. Explain constructor overloading.
9. Explain how we create constructor with default argument.
10. How and when constructor invoked?
11. Explain can we have more than one constructor in a class. If yes explain the need for such situation.

Exercises

1. Write a program to print the area of the rectangle, where the length, breadth, and char 'A' is passed to the constructor to calculate area of rectangle. By default if only the breadth and length is passed then calculate the perimeter of the rectangle if we are declaring the object R(10,5) then the perimeter of the rectangle is calculated. If the object is initialized as R2(10,5, 'A') then the area of the rectangle is calculated.
2. Create a class called time that has separate int member data for hours, minutes, and second. One constructor should initialize this data to 0, and another to fixed values. A member function should display it, in 11:59:59 format. The final member function should add two object of type passed as arguments. Main program should create two initialized time object, and one that isn't initialized. Then its should add the two initialized values together, leaving the result in the third time variable. Finally it should display the value of this third variable.
3. Write a constructor to initialize the cube with its dimensions. Find its volume. If the dimensions are not mentioned then take the default ones.
4. Write a program to initialize the data with object birth date with numeric values and display the following output

   Date of birth (14,10,75)

   October 14,1975
5. Write a program by oops which calculate the factorial of a number use constructor and destructor function.
6. Write a program which generates series of prime number using constructor member function.
7. Write an object oriented program in C++ to read an integer number and find sum of the entire digit until it reduces to a single digit using constructor, destructor and default constructor. For example if number is 4567 then

   Sum = 4 + 5 + 6 + 7 = 22

   Sum = 2 + 2 = 4

8. Write a program in C++ by oop concept which read a integer number and then Print is digit by digit words. Use constructor member function for writing program. For example if number is 4567 then output is "Four five six seven".
9. Write a program which reads an array and then short that array, after sorting Print the array use constructor member function.
10. Write a program which reads bio-data of student and then initialize an object by bio-data. The field of bio-data is:

    (*a*) name (*b*) RN (*c*) phno (*d*) Address
11. Write a program to read a string then initialize an object by string.
12. Write a program which calculates the subtraction of two complex number. The complex numbers are 4+i6 and 7+i8 use constructor.
13. Write a program which calculate the function of F where $F = ax^2 + bx + c$ and $a = 2$, $b = 3$, $c = 4$, $x = 5$. Use constructor to solve.

12

INHERITANCE

Inheritance is the most powerful feature of object-oriented programming after classes and objects. Inheritance is the process of creating a new class, called derived class from existing class, called base class. The derived class inherits some or all the traits from base class. The base class is unchanged by this process. Most important advantage of inheritance is reusability. Once a base class is written and debugged, it need not be touched again and we can use this class for deriving another class if we need.

Reusing existing code saving time and money. By reusability a programmer can use a class created by another person or company and without modifying it derive other classes from it.

Inheritance

A class is category of object, all of which share the attribute, and function of the class. An object is a particular instance of a class and every object of a class inherits the attributes and methods of that class. This is what **inheritance** means inheritance can also be extended to sub-class that a class can be derived from another class, in which case it inherits the data and methods of the **parent class.** This is a very important concept in oop and C++ which allows code reuse. Let us consider a class defined for a car. A sports car could be a subclass of the class car. A sports car shares all the general attributes of a car. Therefore it inherits properties from the car class. It may also have specific attributes in addition to what a ordinary car object has. The sports car class for example may inherits the attributes: brand name, model name, year it was made and colour of the class car

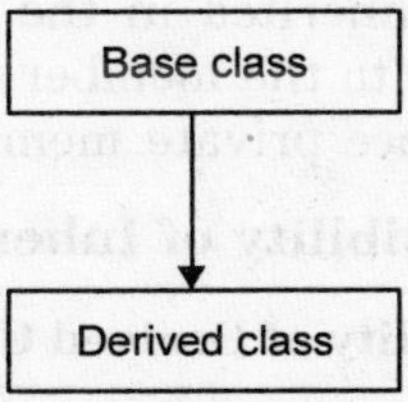

Inheritance is a mechanism, which allows a derived class to inherit properties of a base class. We say "B inherits from A". Object of class B thus have access to attributes and methods of class A without the need of redefining them, object of sub class can be used where objects of the corresponding super class are expected. This is due to the fact that objects of the subclass share the same behavior as object of the Base class.

Base class is also called **parent classes.** Subclasses may also called child **class** or just **derived classes**.

12.1 PROTECTED ACCESS SPECIFIER

If the data within a base class ware totally accessible to all classes inheriting that base class, it would be a simple matter for a programmer to inherit the base class into a derived class and have free access to all data in the parent class. This would completely override the protection affordably by the use of information hiding. For this reason, the data in class are not automatically available to the method of an inheriting class. But we may wish automatically inherit all variables directly into the subclasses and have them act just as though they were declared as part of those classes. C++ provide another visibility label protected for this reason when private data of a class needs to be accessed by derived class, it is forced to become protected.

A member declared as protected is accessible by the member function within its class and any class immediately derived from it. It cannot be accessed by function outside these two classes. A class can have all the three visibility labels as once in it as follows:

```
Class example
{
    Private
      Data members
      Member function
      Protected
      Derived class
      Data members
      Member functions
      };
```

The keyword private, protected, and public may appears in any order and in any number of times in the declaration of class.

When protected member is declared in public mode, it become protected in the derived class, and is accessible by the member function of the derived class. It is also ready for further **inheritance.** A protected member, inherited in the private mode, because private in the derived class. Although it is available to the member functions of the derived class, it is not available for further **inheritance** since private member cannot be inherited.

Table 12.1 Visibility of Inherited Members

Visibility of Base Class	Visibility of Derived Class	Visibility of Derived Class
Public	Public derivation	Private Derivation
Private	Not inherited	Not inherited
Protected	Protected	Private
Public	Public	Private

The effect of inheritance on the visibility of members in protected inheritance each public member in the base class is protected in the derived class. But the private member of each base class remains private in the base class. Hence it is visible only in base class.

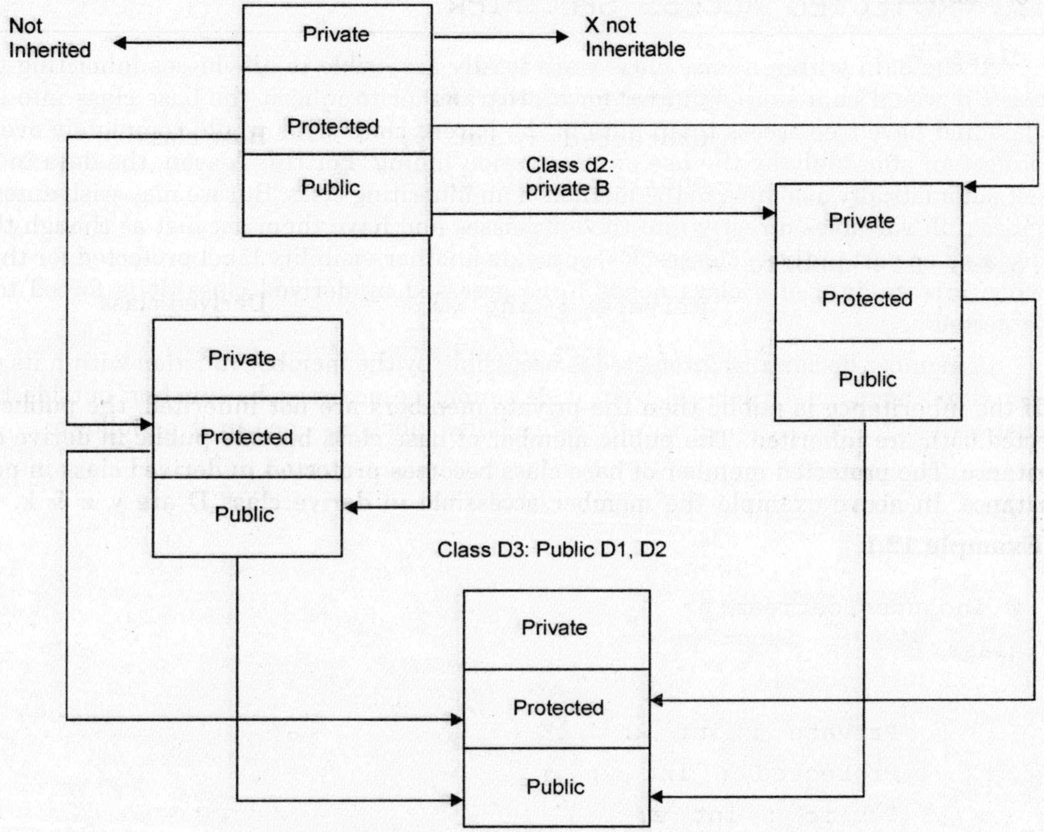

Effect of inheritance on the visibility of members

12.2 DEFINING DERIVED CLASS

A derived class is defined as follows

```
class name-of-derived-class: derivation name-base-class
      {
         member of derived class
                         };
```

The derivations are three types:

(1) public

(2) protected

(3) private

12.2.1 Public Inheritance

If the derivation type is public then inheritance is known as public inheritance.

For example:

```
class B {
                    private   : int  x;
                    protected  :  int  y;          Base class
                    public  :  int  z;
                          };
class D  :  public A  {
                    private   :  int  k;           Derived class
                        };
```

If the inheritance is public then the private members are not inherited, the public and protected both are inherited. The public member of base class become public in derive class inheritance. The protected member of base class becomes protected in derived class in public inheritance. In above example the member accessible in derive class D are y, z & k.

Example 12.1

```
#  include<iostream.h>
class  B
     {
        Private  :  int  x;
        Protected  :  int  y;
        Public  :  int  z;
         void  getdata  (  );
         void  showdata  (  );
               };
  class  D  :  public  B
           {
              private  :  k;
              public  :  void  getk  (  );
                                      void  output  (  );
                                           };

     void  B  :  getdata  (  )
                {
                     cout  <<  "Enter  first  no.  :"  cin  >>x;
                     cout  <<  "Enter  second  no.  :"  cin  >>y;
                     cout  <<  "Enter  third  no.  :"  cin  >>z;
     void  B  :   :  showdata  (  )
```

```
                    cout << "x =" << x<<endl;
                    cout << "y =" <<y<<endl;
                    cout << "z =" << z << endl;
                }
        void D : : getk ( )
                {
                    cout << "Enter K :"; cin >>k;
    void D : : output ( )
        { int s = y +z +k;
            cout << "y + z + k ="<<s<<endl;
        }
                void main ( )
                    {
                        D d1;
                        clrscr ( );
                        d1.getdata ( );
                        d1.getk ( );
                        d1.showdata ( );
                        d1.output ( );
                        getch ( );
                    }
```

The output of the program is:

```
Enter first no. : 5
Enter second no. : 6
Enter third no. : 7
Enter K : 8
    x = 5
    y = 6
    z = 7
y+z+k = 21
```

In the above example the member of class D are:

Private member K
protected member y

Public member z
getdata ( )
show data ( )
getk ( )
output ( )

In the above example x is private member of class B and cannot be inherited but object of D are able to access it through an inherited member function of B (i.e., through getdata ( ) and showdata ( ) of class B)

12.2.2 Protected Inheritance

If the derivation type is protected then inheritance is known as protected inheritance.

Example:

```
class D : protected B
      {
           private : int k
                   };
```

In the above example we have written only derive class. If the inheritance is protected then the public member of base class become protected in derived class; the protected member of base class become protected in the derive class; the private member through the inherited member function of base class.

Example 12.2

```
# include<iostream.h>
#include <conio.h>
class B
  {
  private : int x;
    protected : int y;
         public : void getdata ( );
                      void  showdata ( );
            };
class D : protected B
      {
         private : int z;
         public : void getz ( );
               void showz ( );
                   };
            void B : : getdata ( )
```

```
            {
                cout  <<  "Enter  x  :";  cin  >>x;
                cout  <<  "Enter  y  :";   cin  >>y;
       void B  :  :  showdata  ( )
                {
                       cout  <<  "x  ="  <<  x  <<endl;
                     cout  <<  "y="  <<  y  <<  endl;
       void D  :  :  getz  ( )
                {
                     cout  <<  "Enter  z=";  cin  >>   z";  cin  >>z;
                     }
            void D  :  :  showz  (  )
                {
                     cout  <<  "z  ="  <<  z  <<  endl;
                     }
                 void main  (  )
                        {
                                   d1;
      clrscr  (  );
      d1.getz  (  );
      d1.  showz  (  );
      getch  (  );
              }
```

The output of the program is:

Enter z : 4
Z = 4

In the above example the member of class d are:

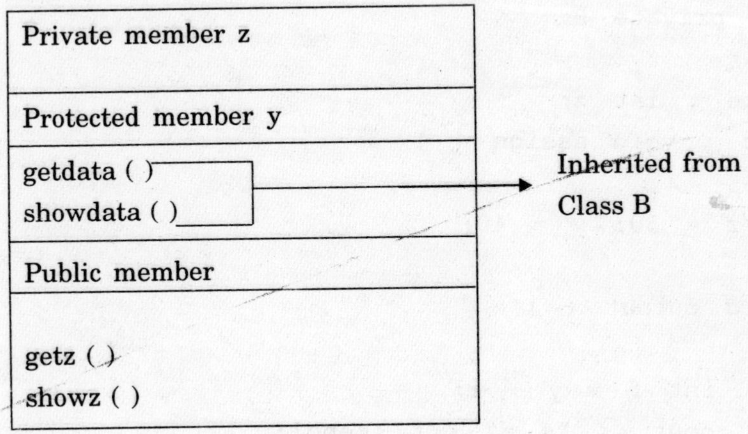

12.2.3 Private Inheritance

If the derivation type is private then inheritance is known as private inheritance.

For example:

```
Class D : private B
    {
        private : int k;
    };
```

Where B is a base class, we have written only derived class in the above example. If the inheritance is private then the public and protected both type of member of base class becomes private in derived class. The private member of base is not inherited.

Example 12.3

```
# include <iostream.h>
# include < conio.h>
class B
    {
      private : int y;
      protected : int y;
      public : void getdata ( )
            {
            cin >> x >> y;
            }
        void showdata ( )
            {
            cout <<x << y << endl;
            }
        };
      class D : private B
        {
          private : int z;
          public : void assign ( )
            {
                z = 30; y = 40;
              }
              void output ( )
                {
                    int f = y + z;
                    cout << "s =" <<f <<endl;
```

```
                }
            };
    void main ( );
            {
                D d1;
                  clrscr ( );
                d1.assign ( );
                d1.output ( );
                  getch ( );
            }
```

The output of above program is:

```
S = 70
```

In the above program, in main ( ) we cannot write

```
d1.getdata ( );
```

Because getdata ( ) function is in private mode in the class D. Similarly we cannot write

```
d1. showdata ( );
```

The member of class D in the above are:

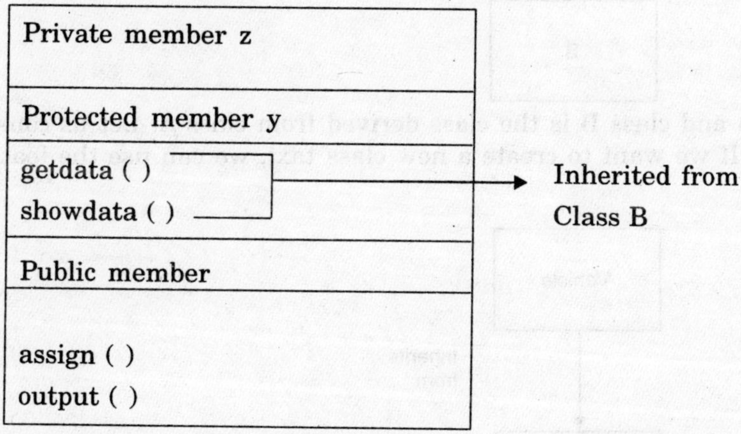

We can draw the accessibility in inheritance by following diagram.

Derivation Type	**Public**	**Protected**	**Private**
Public	Public	Public	Not accessible
Protected	Protected	Protected	Not accessible
Private	Private	Private	Not accessible

12.3 TYPE OF INHERITANCE

A class can also inherit properties from more than one class or from more than one level. According to this we can classify inheritance into following type.

(1) Single Inheritance

(2) Multiple Inheritances

(3) Multilevel Inheritance

(4) Hierarchical Inheritance

(5) Hybrid Inheritance

12.3.1 Single Inheritance

Inheritance was defined as deriving a new class from the existing base class. When only one class is derived from a single base class, the type of inheritance is called as single inheritance. This is as shown in the following figure.

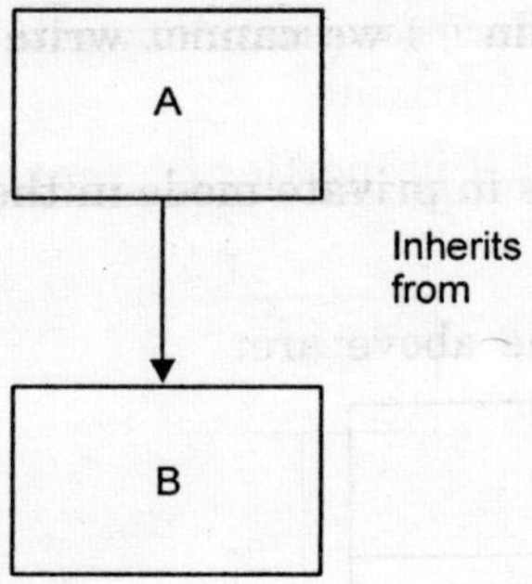

Class A is the base class and class B is the class derived from class A. Let us consider the vehicle already existing. If we want to create a new class taxi, we can use the features of the already existing class.

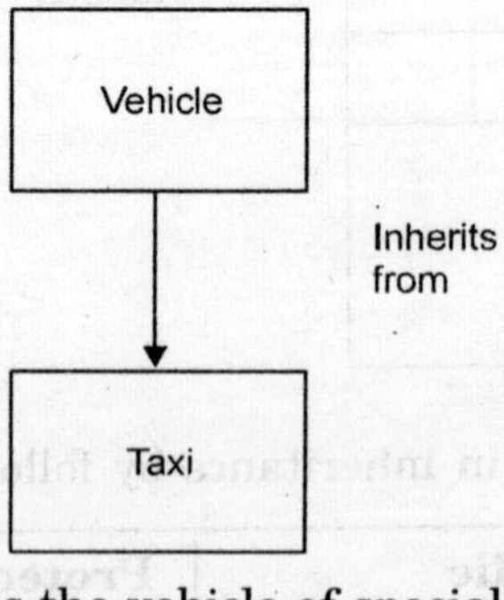

The derived class taxi describes the vehicle of special type. It already inebriated feature of the base class vehicle. It distinguishes itself from having feature of being air-conditioned or not.

```
Class taxi : private vechile
  {
      char *coolcab;
```

```
public:
   setcharges (char * coolcab);
  };
```

12.3.2 Multiple Inheritances

If a class is derived from one base class then inheritance is known as multiple inheritances. Multiple inheritances allow us to combine the features of several existing classes as a starting point for defining new class.

```
Class D: derivations B1, derivations B2, …
    {
      member of class D
    }
```

The derivation is private, public or protected. Note this is also possible that one derivation is public another one is protected or private.

This allows the subclass to inherit properties of more than one base class and to "merge" their properties as shown in figure

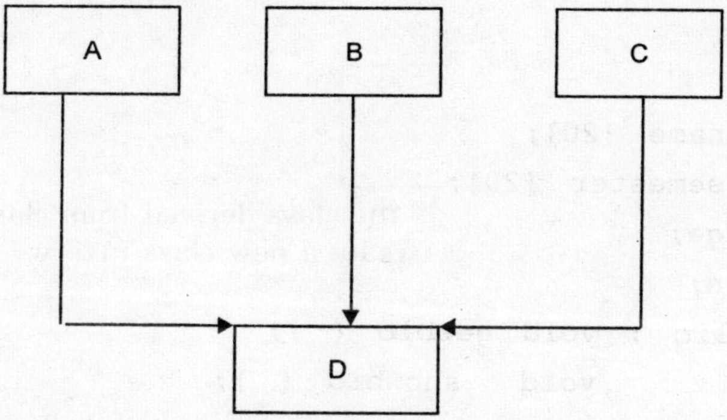

Example 1

```
class D : public B1, public B2
      {
         private : int a;
      };
```

Example 2

```
class D : public B1, protected B2
      {
        private : int a;
      };
```

Example 3

```
Class D : private B1, protected B2, public B3
       {
```

```
private : int a;
};
```

Multiple inheritances has many advantage over the single inheritance such as rich semantics and the ability to directly express complex structure. In C++, derived classes must be declared during the compilation of all possible combination of derivations and the program can choose the appropriate class at run time and create object for the application.

In the single inheritance, a derived class has a single base class. In multiple inheritances, a derived class has multiple base classes. In a single inheritance hierarchy, a derived class typically represents a specialization of its base class. In a multiple inheritance hierarchy, a derived class typically represents a combination of its base classes. But the rules of inheritance and access do not change from a single to a Multiple inheritance hierarchy. A derived class inherits data member and method from all its base classes, regardless of whether the inheritance links are private, protected or public. It can inherit publicly from one class or protected from another class or privately from still another class. Multiple inheritances can be with all public or all private or any mixed derivation.

Example 12.4

```
# include < iostream.h>
# include <conio.h>
class bio
  {
      char name [20];
      char semester [20];
      int age;
      int rn;
        public : void getbio ( );
                 void  showbio ( );
class marks
      {
      char sub [10];
        float total;
public : void getm ( );
               void showm ( );
             };
class final : public bio, public marks
        {
          long int phno;
          public : void getph ( );
void showph ( );
    };
void bio : : getbio ( )
```

```
{
    cout << "Enter name :"; cin >> name;
    cout << "Enter semester :"; cin >> semester
    cout << "Enter age:" cin >>age;
    cout << "Enter rn :"; cin >>rn;
}
void bio : : showbio ( )
{
    cout << "Name :" << name <<endl;
    cout << "Semester :" <<semester <<endl;
    cout << "Age :" <<age <<endl;
    cout << "Rn:" <<rn <<endl;
}
void marks : : getm ( )
{
    cout << "Enter subject name :" cin >>sub;
    cout << "Enter marks:" cin >>total;
}
void marks : : showm ( )
{
    cout << "subject name:" <<sub <<endl;
    cout << "marks are :" <<total << endl;
}
void final : : getph ( )
{
    cout << "Enter phone no. :"; cin >> phno;
}
void final : : showph ( )
{
    cout << "phone no:" <<phno<<endl;
}
void main ( )
{
    final f;
    clrscr ( );
    f.getbio ( );
    f.getm ( );
```

```
f.getph ( );
f.showbio ( );
f.showm ( );
f.showph ( );
getch ( );
}
```

Sample output of the program is:

```
Enter name : namrata
Enter semester : six
Enter age : 20
Enter rn : 10
Enter subject name : C++
Enter marks : 85
Enter ph no : 9451157880
```

In the above example class final is derived from class marks and class bio. Class final is derived public all by class marks therefore all the protected and public members of class marks have as are in final.

Class final derived public ally from class bio also. Therefore all the protected and public members of class bio have become as are in final. The member of final class is:

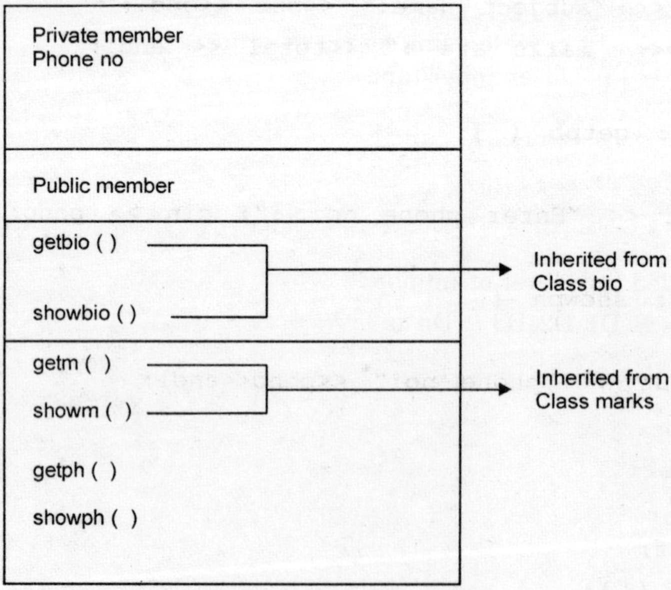

12.3.3 Multilevel Inheritance

If a class D1 is derived from class B and class D2 is derived from class D1 and so on, this type of inheritance is known as multilevel inheritance. Because there are more than one level. The diagram of multilevel inheritance is:

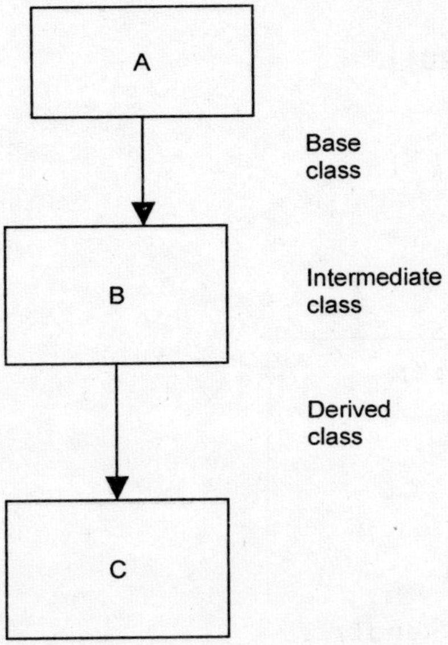

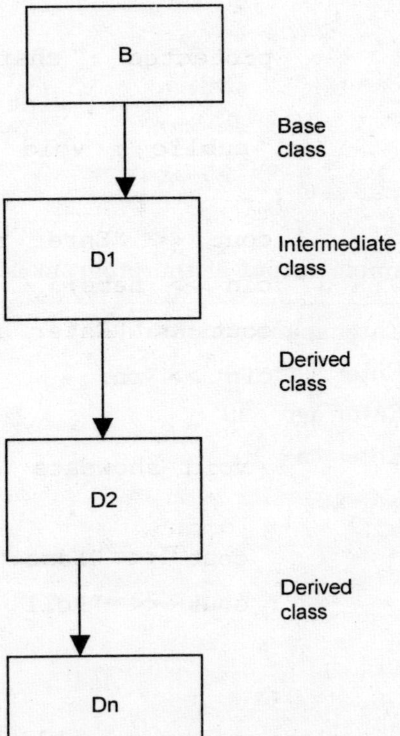

It is common that one class is derived from another derived class. The class A is base class for the derived class B. Class B is a base class for derived class C. The class B is known as intermediate base class as it provide a link for the inheritance between A and C. This chain from class A to class B is known as inheritance path.

```
class A {......}   // base class
class B public A {.....} // class B derived from class A
class C: public B {.....} // class C derived from class B
```

This can be extended any level of number

The chain B D1 or B D1 D2 D3 ...Dn is known as inheritance path

```
class B {......}   // base class
class D1 public B {.....} // class D1 derived from class B
class D2: public D1 {.....} // class D2 derived from class D1
class Dn public D2 {....} // class Dn derived from class D2
```

Example 12.5

```
# include <iostream.h>
# include <conio.h>
Class student
```

```
{
   protected : char name [20];
                    int rn;
    public : void getdata ( )
  {
   cout << "Enter name :";
   cin >> name;
   cout << "Enter roll no :";
   cin >> rn;
  }
    void showdata ( )
   {
    cout << "Name:" <<name<<endl;
    cout << "Roll no" <<rn<<endl;
   }
  };
class marks : public student
  {
    protected : float sessonal1;
                    float sessonal2;
  public : void getm ( )
  {
   cout << "Enter marks in sessonal 1:";
   cin >> sessonal1;
   cout << "Enter marks in sessonal 2:";
   cin >> sessonal 2;
  }
   void showm ( )
  {
   cout << "sessonal 1 ="<<  sessonal1 <<endl;
   cout << "sessonal 2 =" << sessonal2 <<endl;
   }
   } ;
   class result : public marks
    {
```

```
            float  total;
            public  :  void  output  ( )
                    {
                          total  =  sessonal1  +  sessonal2;
            cout  <<  "Total  marks  are  :"  <<total  <<endl;
                          }
                        };
            void  main  (  )
                    {
              result  s1;
              clrscr  ( );
              s1.getdata  (  );
              s1.  getm  (  );
              cout  <<  "the  record  of  student  is:"  <<endl;
              s1.showdata  (  );
              s1.getm  (  );
              cout  <<  "the  record  of  student  is:"  <<endl;
              s1.showdata  (  );
              s1.showm  (  );
              s1.output  (  );
              getch  (  );
```

The sample output of the above program is:

```
Enter name : Mahender
Enter Roll no : 41
Enter marks in sessonal1 : 22
Enter marks in sessonal 2: 23
The record of the student is:
Name: Mahender
Roll no : 41
Sessonal 1 = 22
Sessonal 2 = 23
Total marks are : 45
```

In the above class marks derived class student, and class result derived from class marks. The member in class marks and class result are:

Member of Class Marks:

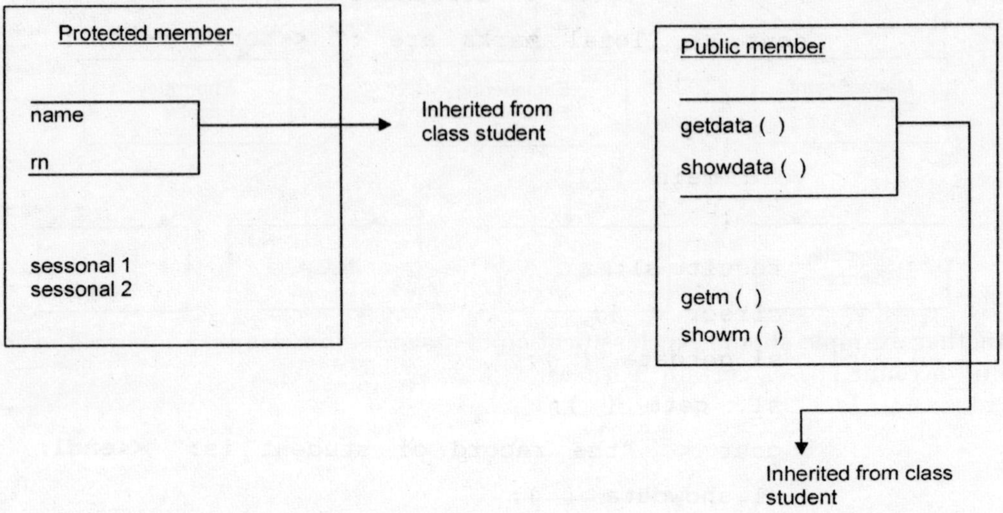

Member of Class Result:

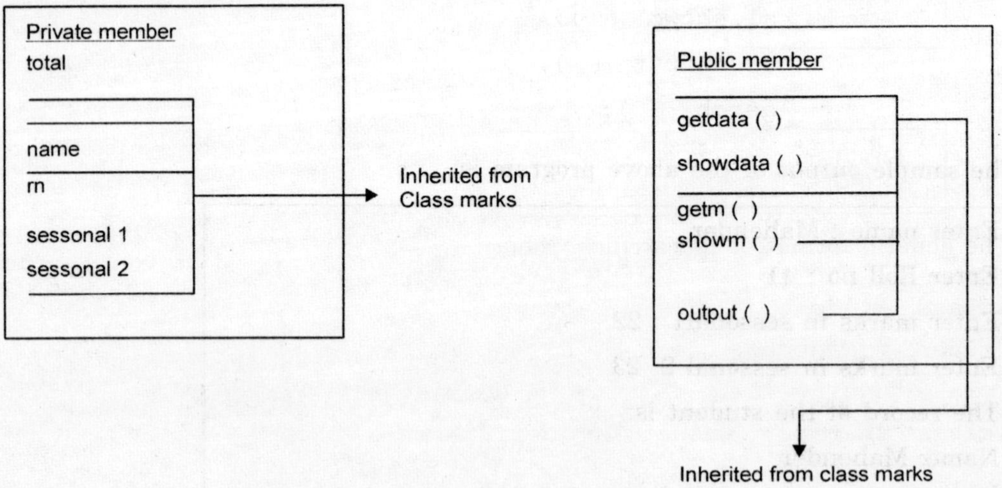

12.3.4 Hierarchical Inheritance

Many programming problems can be cast into hierarchy where certain features of one level are shared by many others below that level. Example hierarchical classification of students in university.

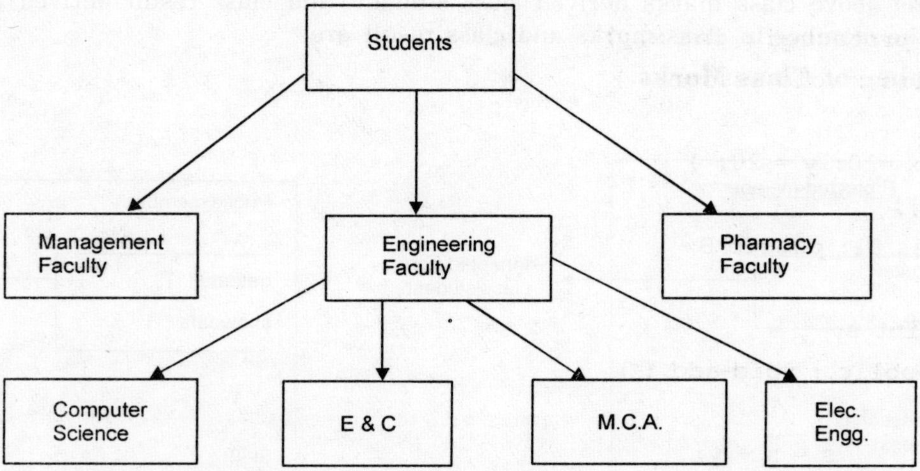

Another example should be classification of accounts in a commercial bank as shown in figure all account posses certain features

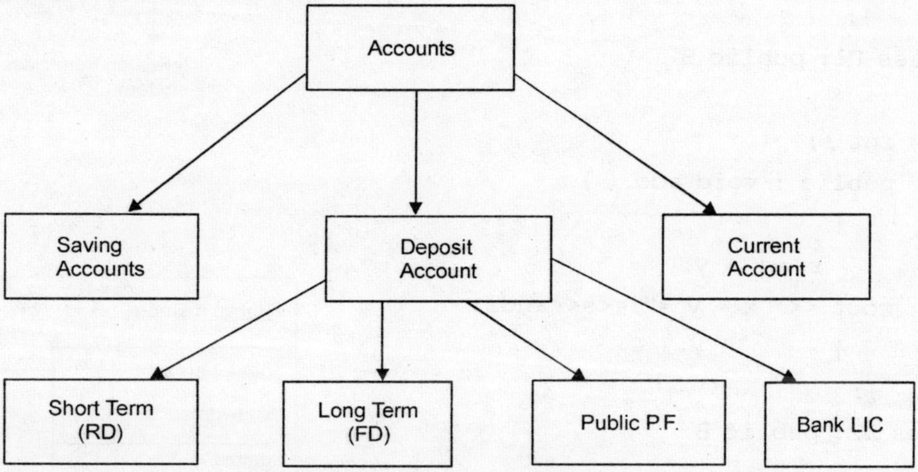

The general format of hierarchical inheritance is

```
class student {.......};
class management faculty : derivation student{.....};
class engineering faculty : derivation  student {....};
class pharmacy faculty : derivation student {...};
```

Derivation can be public protected and private type. With the help of hierarchical inheritance we can distribute the property of one class into many classes.

Example 12.6

```
# include<iostream.h>
# include <conio.h>
class B
```

```
{
  protected : int x,y;
public : void assign ( )
  {
  x =10; y = 20; }
  };
class D1: public B
  {
  int s;
  public : void add ( )
    {
     s = x + y;
   cout << " x + y =" <<s<<endl;
    }
    };
class D1: public B
  {
   int s;
   public : void add ( )
     {
      s = x + y;
   cout << "x + y =" <<s<<endl;
     }
   };
class D2: public B
  {
   int t;
   public : void sub ( )
     {
      t = x - y;
   cout << "x-y =" <<t<<endl;
     }
    };
     class D3 : public B
   {
    int m;
     public : void mul ( )
        {
```

```
                m  =  x*y;
                    cout  <<  "x*y  ="  <<m<<endl;
                }
            };
void main  ( )
    {
        D1  d1;
        D2  d2;
        D3  d3;
            clrscr  ( );
            d1.assign  ( );
             d1.  add  ( );
             d2.  assign  (  );
             d2.sub   ( );
              d3.  assign  (  );
             d3.mul  ( );
                 getch  ( );
            }
```

Output of the above program is:

```
x+y = 30
x-y = -10
x*y =200
```

The data member of D1, D2 and D3 are as follows

X	10		X	10		X	10
Y	20		Y	20		Y	20
Z	30		Z	–10		Z	200

Member of Class D1

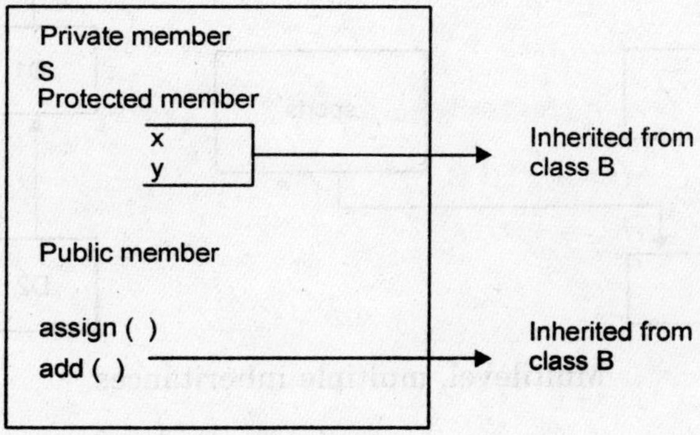

Member of Class D2

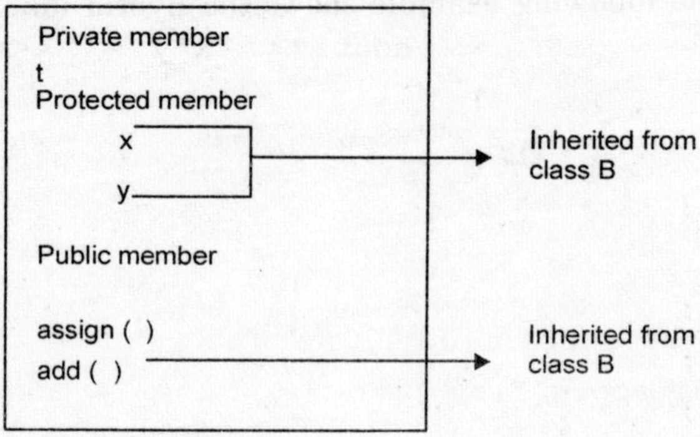

Member of Class D3

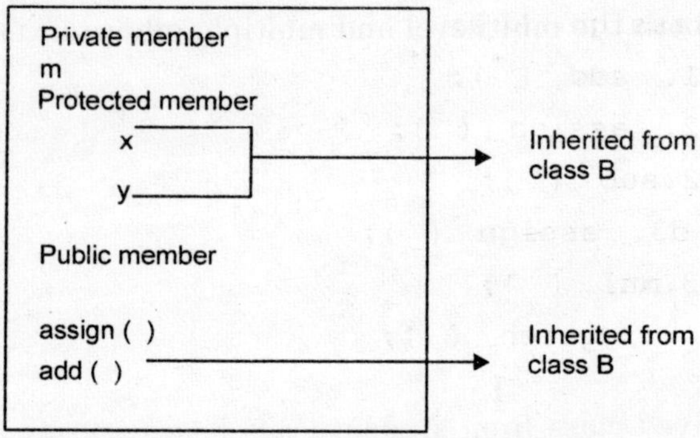

12.3.5 Hybrid Inheritance

There could be situation where we need to apply two or more types of inheritance to design a program. Consider our example of finding students results in earlier subunits. Suppose weight age for sports is stored in separate class called sports. The new inheritance relationship between the various classes would be as shown in fig. In hybrid inheritance there is multilevel inheritance existing among the classes student test and result whereas multiple inheritance exists among classes test, sports and result.

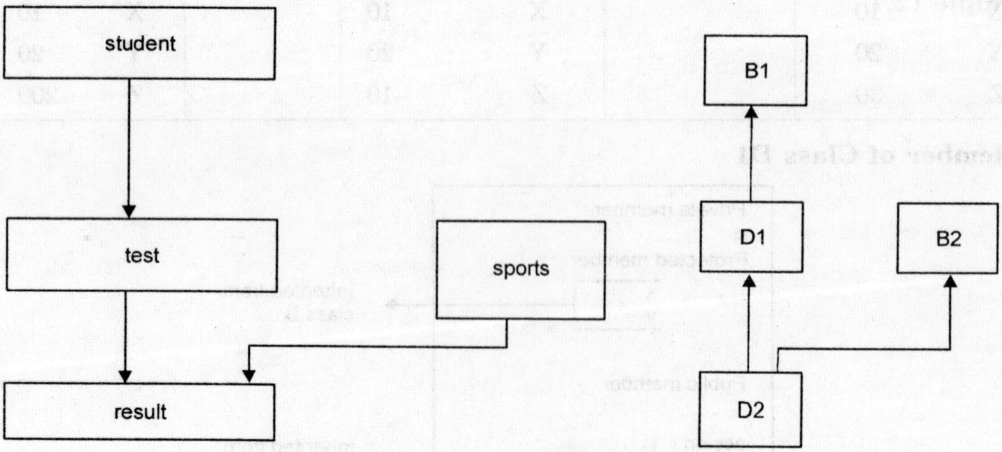

Multilevel, multiple inheritances

If we apply more than one type of inheritance to design a problem then that is known as hybrid inheritance. The following example shows the hybrid inheritance.

```
class  sports
  {
  protected:
        float  score;
  public:
            void  get_score(float);
          void  put_score(float);
  }
```

The result will have both the multilevel and multiple inheritances and its declaration is as follows:

```
class  result:  public  test,  public  sports
  {
    ......
    ......
  };
```

Where test itself derived class from student that is

```
class  test:  public  student
   {
     ......
     ......
   };
```

Example 12.7

```
#  include  <iostream.h>
#  include  <conio.h>
class  B1
    {
    protected  :  int  x;
    public  :  void assign  x  (  )
              {   x  =  20;  }  };
    class  D1  :  public  B1
         {
          protected  :  int  y;
          public  :  void  assign  y  (  )
```

```
        { y = 40; } };
      class D2 : public D1
        {
          protected : int z;
          public : void assign z ( )
                 { z = 60; } };
      class B2
        {
          protected : int k;
          public : void assign k ( )
               { k = 80; } };
      class D3 : public B2, public D2
           {
             private : int total;
             public : void output ( )
                    { total = x + y + z + k;
      cout << "x + y + z + k =" <<total<<endl;
                    };
      void main ( )
           {
             clrscr ( );
             d3 s;
              s.assign x ( );
              s. assign y ( );
              s. assign z ( );
              s. assign k ( );
              s.output ( );
              getch ( );
             }
```

The output of above program is

```
x + y + z + k = 200
```

In the above example the class D1 is derived from B1, class D2 is derived from D1 and class D3 is derived from D2 and B2. The member of class D1, D2, D3 is as follows:

Member of Class D1

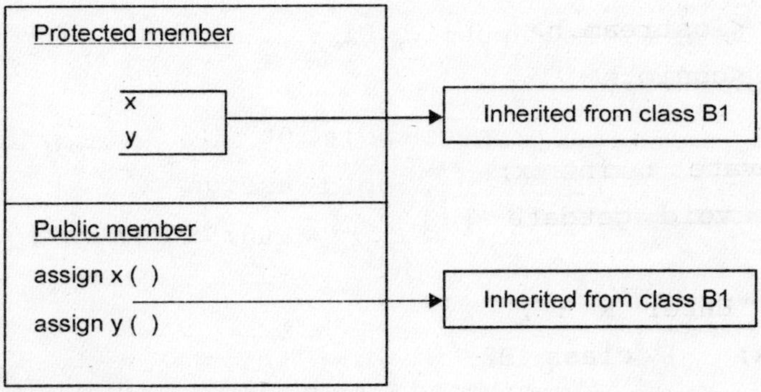

Member of Class D2

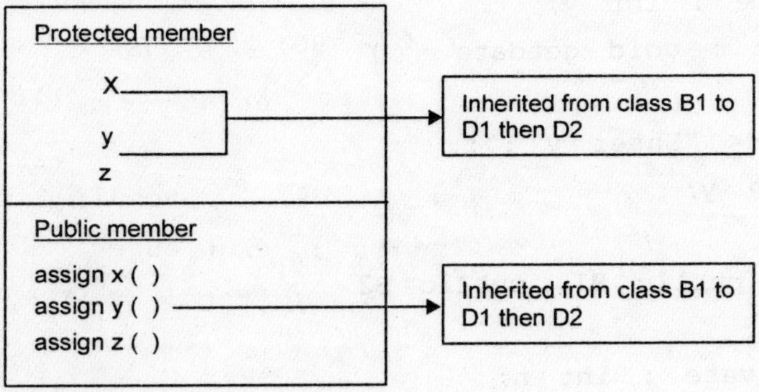

Member of Class D3

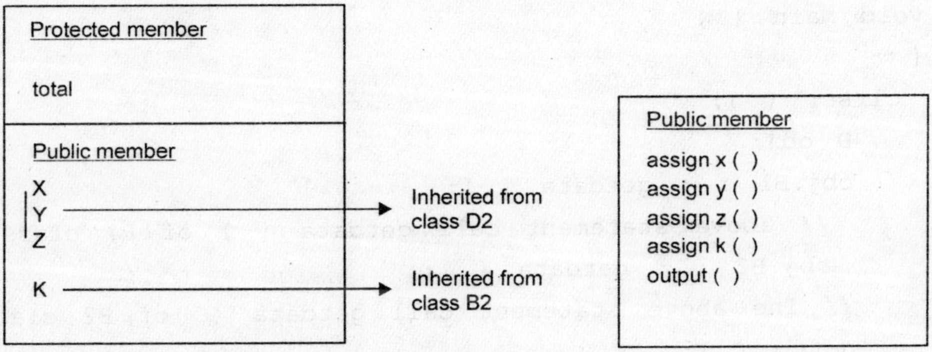

12.4 AMBIGUITY OF INHERITANCE

If a class D is derived from two classes B1 and B2; and in B1 there is member whose name is same as the member of class B2 then in class D there are two members both have same name (one member is inherited from class B1 and second from class B2). The scope resolution operator ::) differentiates these two members as follows: (if member name is x then)

B1 : : x and B2 : : x

B1 : : x means member of class B1

B2 : : x means member of class B2

Example 12.8

```
# include <iostream.h>
# include <conio.h>
class B1
  {   private : int x;
 public : void getdata ( )
{
 cout << "Enter x :";
 cin >> x;   } class B2
 {
   private : int y;
   public : void getdata ( )
   {
   cout << "Enter y :";
   cin >> y;
   }
class D : public B1, public B2
   {
     private : int n;
   };
  void main ( )
  {
   clrscr ( );
     D obj;
     obj.B1 : : getdata ( );
      // above statement call getdata ( ) of B1 class
      obj.B2 : : getdata ( );
     // The above statement call getdata ( )of B2 class
     getch ( );
   }
```

The sample output of above program is:

Enter x : 5
Enter y: 6

We can call the member function of base class in a derive class member function if both have same name then also. See the following example.

Example

```
# include <iostream.h>
class base1
    {
              private : int x;
              public : void getdata ( )
                 { x = 10; } };
              class drive1 : public base1
               {
                 private : int y;
                 public : void getdata ( )
              {
                 cout << "Enter a value:";
              cin >>y;
              if (y > 10) base1 : : getdata ( );
                     else
                         cout << "Bye" <<endl;
                                  } };
              void main ( )
                           {
                                  derive1 d1;
                                  d1.getdata ( );
                               }
```

In above program we are calling getdata ( ) function of base 1 into drive 1 within its getdata ( ) function.

In main ( ) we are calling getdata ( ) function through the object d1. In d1 there are two getdata ( ) function, one is inherited from base1 and second one is its own. But the question is how compiler knows which of the two getdata ( ) function to use.

The rule for this is:

When the same function exists in both the base class and derived class, the function in derived class will be executed. If we call the function by drive class object.

If we want to execute the base class function by the object of derive class then we call as follows:

```
d1.base1 : : getdata ( );
```

But if we create the object of base class in main ( ) as like follow:

```
base1 b1;
```

Then there is no problem in calling getdata because object b1 don't know about the derive class member, therefore the statement:

```
b1. getdata ( );
```

Call the function of base1 class. All the above concept are same for data member also. See the following example.

Example 12.9

```
# include <iostream.h>
# include <conio.h>
class base1
    {
        public : int a;
    };
class base2
    {
    public : int a;
        };
class base3
    {
        public: int a;
        }
        class drive1 : public base1, public base2, public base3
            { public : int a; };
            void main ( )
                {
                    clrscr ( );
                    base1 b1;
                    b1.a = 10;
                // above statement assigns 10 to a of b1
                // b1 has only one a
                        drive d1;
                        d1.a = 20;
                // above statement assigns 20 to a of derive class
                        d1.base1 : : a = 30;
                         d1.base2 : : a = 40;
                          d1.base3 : : a = 50;
                    }
```

On the output device (i.e., screen) no output is printed. The above program clears our concept of ambiguity

The member of object b1 in memory

a : 10

The member of object d1 in memory:

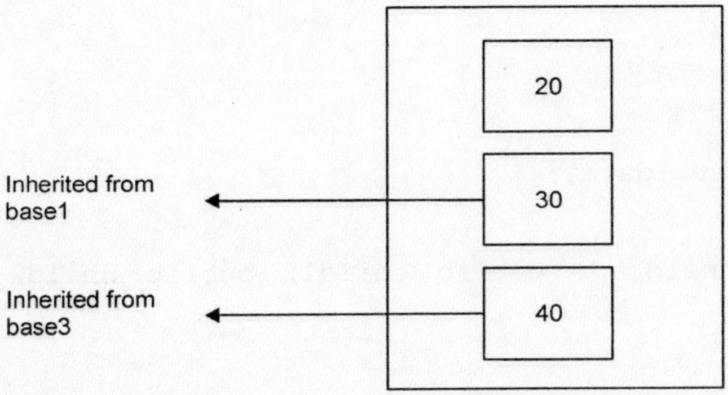

12.5 VIRTUAL BASE CLASS

In multiple inheritances class can inherit the attribute of two or more classes whereas in multilevel inheritance one derived class can serve as a base class for another derived class. Hierarchical inheritance involves the derivation of new classes from base class. All three kinds of inheritance can be merged to derive new classes from a base class and derive another class inheriting the properties from these derived classes.

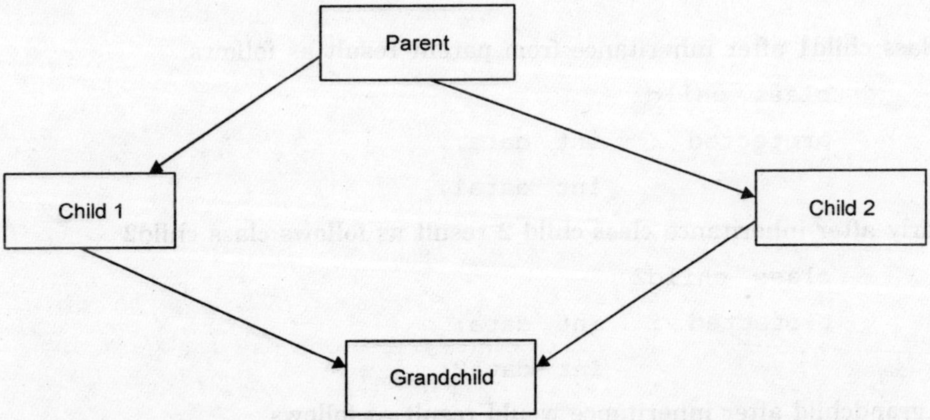

The grandchild has two direct base classes 'child1' and 'child2' which themselves have a common base class 'parent'. In this type of inheritance problem arises if a member function in the grandchild class wants to access data or function in the parent class.

```
class parent
{
protected :
    int data;
```

```
};
class child2 : public parent
{
protected :
    int data2;
};
class child1
{
protected: int data1;
};
class grandchild   : public child1, public child2
{
protected :
    int data3;
public:
int getdata ( )
{
return data;
}
};
```

The class child1 after inheritance from parent result as follows.

```
class child1
protected :  int data;
             int data1;
```

Similarly after inheritance class child 2 result as follows class child2

```
class child2
protected :  int data;
             int data2;
```

Class grandchild after inheritance would result as follows.

```
class grandchild
  protected int data      //from class child1
            int data1       //from class child1
            int data         // from class child2
            int data 2       //from class child2
  public :
```

```
getdata ( )
{
    return data;
}
```

When the getdata function of class grandchild attempts to access data of class parent there occurs a compiler error. Note that child1 and child2 each inherit a copy of data of the class parent. This copy is called as subject. The situation become ambiguous when the member function **getdata ( )** of class grandchild tries to access data. The situation is ambiguous as it is not known to class grandchild to which copy of data to refer to. The duplication of inherited member that is data in our case due to multiple paths can be avoided by making the common base that is class parent as virtual base class while declaring the direct or intermediate base classes as shown below.

```
class parent
  {
     protected : int data;
  };
class child1 : virtual public parent
      {
          protected : int data 1;
      };
class child2 : public virtual parent
            {
                  protected : int data;
            }
class grandchild : public child1,public child2
            {
                  protected : int data 3;
                  public : int getdata ( );
                        {
                              return data;
                        }
```

When a class is made virtual base class, C++ takes necessary care to see that only one copy to that base class is inherited, regardless of how many inheritance paths exist between the virtual base class and derived class. The keywords virtual and public may be used either order.

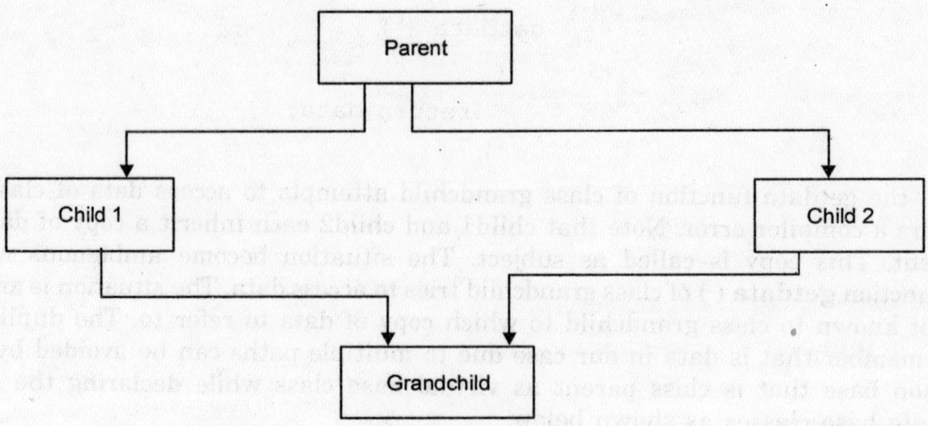

Virtual Base Class

12.6 ABSTRACT CLASS

With inheritance, we force a derived class to offer same properties like their base classes. Consequently the objects of a derived class behave like objects of their base class. An **abstract class** is designed only to act as a base class. It is the one that is used to create objects. A class is called **abstract class** if it is only used as base class for other classes.

An abstract class is one that is not used to create objects. An abstract class is used only base class (By using this other classes are derived).

Example 12.10

```
# include <iostream.h>
# include <conio.h>
  class bio-data
     {
        protected : char name [20];
        char semester [20];
        char branch [10];
         int rn;
         public : void getbio ( )
        {
          cout << "Enter name :";
          cin >> name;
          cout << "Enter branch:"
            cin >> branch;
          cout << "Enter roll no:"
          cin >> rn;
                void showbio ( )
              {
                   cout << "Name:" << name <<endl;
```

```
cout << "Semester :" <<semester <<endl;
cout << "Branch:" <<branch <<endl;
cout << "Roll no. :" <<rn<<endl;
}
}; //end class bio-data
class sessional1 : public virtual bio-data
{
protected : float total1;
public : void gettotal1 ( )
{
cout << "Enter marks in sessonal 1:";
cin >> total1;
}
void showtotal1 ( )
{
cout << "Marks in sessonal 1 =";
cout << total1 <<endl;
}
}; //end class seasonal 1
class sessional2 : public virtual bio-data
{
protected : float total2;
public : void gettotal2 ( )
{
cout << "marks in sessonal 2:";
cin << total2;
}
void showtotal2 ( )
{
cout << "Marks in sessonal 2 =";
cout << total2 <<endl:
}
};   //end of class sessonal2
class result : public sessonal1, public sessonal2
{
float total;
public : output ( )
{
```

```
                    total = total + total2;
                    showbio ( );
                    showtotal1 ( );
                    showtotal2 ( );
cout << "Total marks =" <<total <<endl;
                }
                    }
     //end of class result void main ( )
        {
            result r;
            clrcr ( );
             r.getbio ( );
             r.gettotal1 ( );
             r.gettotal2 ( );
             cout << "The students detail is:" <<endl;
             r.output ( );
             getch ( );
                }
```

The sample output of program is:

Enter name : mahender
Enter semester : 4th
Enter branch: I.T.
Enter roll no. : 1001
Enter sessonal1 : 50
Enter sessonal 2 : 50
The students detail is
Name : Mahender
Semester : 4th
Branch: I.T.
Roll no. 1001
Sessonal1 : 50
Sessonal 2 : 50
Total : 100

In the above program the class bio-data is abstract class. We have used the virtual concept also.

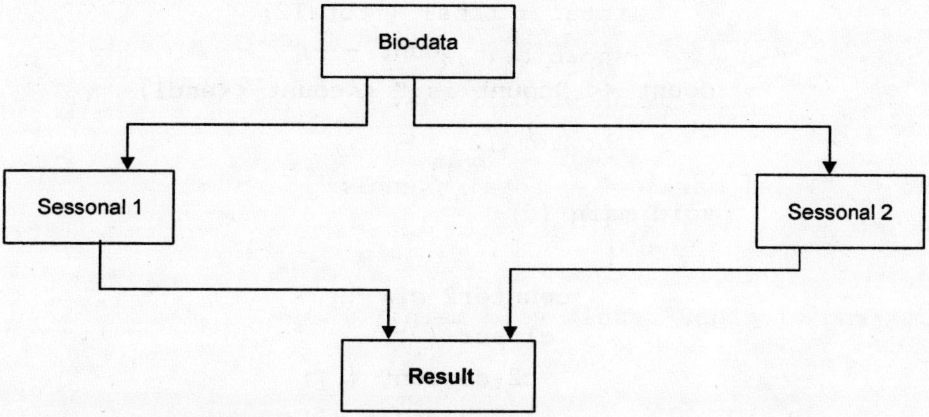

12.7 THE CONSTRUCTOR IN INHERITANCE

The constructors are used to initialize object. Upto this level in inheritance we have not used constructor in base class and also not in derived class for the sake of simplicity.

Note: **If there is no constructor specify in derived class then derived class will use the appropriate constructor (i.e., no argument constructor) of base class.**

Example 12.11

```
# include <iostream.h>
# include <conio.h>
class counter1
    {
        protected : int count;
        public : counter1 ( )
            { count = 4;
        }
        counter (int c)
        {
            count = c;
        void incount ( )
            {
            count ++;
            count << "count is:" <<count <<endl;
                }
                    };
            class counter2 :public counter1
                    {
            public : void decount ( )
```

```
                    {
                      count - -;
          count << "count is:" <<count <<endl;
                }
                    };
          void main ( )
                {
                  counter2 c2;
                  clrscr ( );
                   c2.decount ( );
                    c2.decount ( );
                     c2.incount ( );
                     getch ( );
                     }
```

The output of above program is:

Count is : 4
Count is : 3
Count is : 4

When we create object by

```
Counter2 C2;
```

This causes C2 to be created as an object of class counter 2 and initialized to four (4). Because at the time of C2 object creation the no argument counter of base class (counter1) is automatically called.

Note: **The derived class does not call the more complex constructor (i.e., one argument, two argument of base) if in derived class no constructor is specify. Like in above example the derived class can call only no argument constructor of base not the one argument constructor.**

But if we want to call complex constructor we can do this writing constructor in derived class; through the derived class constructor we can call base class constructor.

Example 12.12

```
# include <iostream.h>
# include <conio.h>
class counter1
         {
                  protected : int count;
               public : counter1 ( )
                     {
```

```
            count = 4;
        }
    counter (int c)
        {
            count = c;
        }
        void incount ( )
            {
                count ++;
            count << "count is:" <<count<<endl;
            }
        };
class counter2: public counter1
    {
        public : counter2 ( ) :counter1 ( )
            { }
    counter (int c): counter1 ( c)
            { }
        void decount ( )
            {
                count - -;
count << "count is :" <<count <<endl;
}
    };
void main ( )
    {
        counter2 c2;
        counter2 c3 (50);
        clrscr ( );
        c2.decount ( );
    c2.decount ( );
        c2.incount ( );
        c3.decount ( );
        c3.decount ( );
        c3.incount ( );
        c2.decount ( );
        getch ( );
    }
```

Explanation: In the above program two new constructors in the counter 2 class are written. The first one is

```
Counter  (  )  :  counter1  (  )
    {  }
```

In main ( ) when we have written

```
Counter2  C2;
```

The compiler will create an object C2 of type counter2 and call the no argument constructor of counter2 now the no argument constructor call the no argument constructor of counter1. In the counter2 ( ) constructor we can add additional statement if we need. In above example there is no additional statement written within counter 2( ) constructor, so the body of counter 2 ( ) between the braces { } is empty.

The second constructor in above example is:

```
counter 2  (int  c)  :  counter1  (c)
         {  }
```

The above declaration means the one arguments constructor of counter2 class call the one argument constructor counter1.

When we write the statement

```
Counter2  c3  (50);
```

The object C3 is created and the value 50 is passed to one argument constructor of counter2 class; now this constructor called the one argument constructor.

```
Counter2  (int  c)  :  counter1  (c  )
                       {  }
```

we can give the different name to these parameter i.e we can also write:

```
Counter  2  (int  D)  :  counter    (c  )
                      {     }
```

In above d is passed to counter1 c.

Note: if the inheritance is multiple and we want to call all the base constructor then we can call as follows.

```
drive-constructor  (arg)  :  base1-constructor  (arg)
base2-constructor  (arg),  -  -  -
```

12.8 CONTAINER CLASS OR (NESTING OF CLASSES)

We create object of one class within another class. This concept is called nesting of class within class as follows:

When object of a class is declared as a member of another class, it is called as **container class.**

```
class B1 { - - -    -}
class B2 {- - - - -}
class D { .........
        .........
    B1   C1;
    B2  C2;
    .........
    .........
     };
```

In above all object of D contain the objects C1 and C2, this type of relationship is called containership.

Example 12.13

```
#include <iostream.h>
#include<conio.h>
class B1
    {
      private  :  int a;
      public:  void output ( )
                 {
                    a  =  20;  cout<<a<<endl;
                 }
            };
   class  B2
           {
               private  :  int  b;
               public:  void  outputb  ( )
                          {
                             b=30;  cout<<b<<endl;
                          }
                        };
   class  D
            {
                private  :  int  c;
```

```
                    B1.obj1;
                    B2.obj2;
          public  :  void  outputc  (  )
                    {  obj1.outputa  (  );
                       Obj2.outputb  (  );
                       c  =  40;
                    cout  <<c<<endl;
                       }
                    };
void main  (  )
  {
     clrscr  ();
     D.obj3;
obj3.outputc  (  );
getch  (  );
  }
```

The output of above program is:

```
20
30
40
```

Descriptive Questions

1. **Explain inheritance how reusability is possible by inheritance.**
2. **Explain public inheritance.**
3. **What is protected access specifier?**
4. **What are the rules to be followed to declare a multiple inheritance data type?**
5. **What are the advantage and disadvantage of single inheritance over multiple inheritances?**
6. **Explain private inheritance.**
7. **What is virtual base class?**
8. **When do we make class virtual?**
9. **What is firing order of the constructors under multiple inheritances?**
10. **What is firing order of the destructor under multi level inheritance?**
11. **Define container class.**
12. **What is abstract class?**
13. **Explain Hybrid inheritance.**
14. **What is multilevel inheritance?**
15. **Explain Hierarchical inheritance.**
16. **Explain multiple inheritances.**

Exercises

1. Write a program to implement following class hierarchy person→student.
2. Design a base class which has following data (a) Name (b) Roll_no (c) Phno (d) Address. Then design a derive class from above base class in derive class the data are:

   (*a*) Marks in first sessional

   (*b*) Marks in second sessional

   (*c*) Total marks.
3. Program to implement following class hierarchy. (Hierarchical inheritance) Publication, Books, E-books.
4. Design oop program to create the payroll of an organization by the following information.

   (*a*) Employee name

   (*b*) Employee Designation

   (*c*) Account number

   (*d*) Date of joining

   (*e*) Basic Salary

   (*f*) DA, HRA, CCA

   (*g*) Deduction like PPF, GPF, CPF.
5. Develop object oriented programming in C++ to create a library information system containing the following information for books in library. Design the program using inheritance.

   (*a*) Accession number

   (*b*) Name of Author

   (*c*) Title of book

   (*d*) Publisher name

   (*e*) Year of publication

   (*f*) Cost of book.
6. The class details give the information about the students name, roll_no. Whereas the class academic_rec gives the information about his course, semester and rank. The object of this class is declared in class finance help. These can access the public function of class detail as well as class acadmic_rec.
7. Write a program in C++ which reads the two number a and b then perform following operation

   (1) a+b

   (2) a-b

   (3) a*b

   (4) a/b.

   Design the function a+b and a-b in a base class and design function a*b and a/b in a derive class.

13

OPERATOR OVERLOADING

13.1 OPERATOR OVERLOADING

Operator overloading is one of the feature of C++ language. We have already studied various types of operators provided by C++. Many of this operator s can be loaded with additional tasks to perform. We shall understand the various rules to overload any operator. Operator can be overloaded using member functions. The programs in this topic mainly focus on over-loading unary and binary operator. The concept by which we can give special meaning to an operator of language is known as operator overloading. For example +operator in C++ works only with basic type like int and float means. c = a + b is calculated by compiler if a, b and c are basic type, suppose a, b and c are objects of user defined class compiler give error. However using operator overloading we can make this statement even if a, b and c are objects of class.

13.1.1 Definition of Operator Overloading

Operator can be redefined to perform additional tasks we have seen different function with different argument list can have same name. This is known as functional overloading. Otherwise it is also known as functional polymorphism meaning function having many forms. Similarly an operator can be redefined to perform additional tasks. Consider for example the +operator so far we have used +operator to add built-in data types that is to add any integers or float etc. We can use +operator to add two strings namely to concatenate 2 strings. Overloading an operator does not change the basic template of an operator nor does it alter its order of precedence. The main advantage of using overloading operators in a program is that it is much easier to read and debug the program.

Operator overloading is done with the help of a special function. This function can be a member function or friend function. The general syntax of operator overloading is as follows. Return-type operator-to-be overloaded (argument list); operator is the keyword and it is preceded by return type of the function. Suppose we want to concatenate 2 character strings using the +operator, we would use the following declaration statement.

As said this Char operator +(char *s2); function can be member function or a fraind function. We shall have to take care while passing argument to the function.

13.1.2 Declaration of Operator Overloading

The declaration of operator overloading is done with the help of special function, called operator function. The operator is keyword in C++. The general format of operator function is:

```
return_type operator oper (arg list)
        {
                Body of function
                Which define task
                                  }
```

In above declaration operator is keyword. Oper is the operator (+, -, * , etc) of C++ which we want to overload. And arg list is argument passed to function. See the following example:

```
void operator ++ ( )
      {
            body of function
                  }
```

In above example there is no argument. The function is called operator function. When we write object with above written operator (++) the operator function is called. i.e., when we write the following statement.

```
obj ++
```

The above written function is called and executed (where obj is a object of class in which above function is written).

Note that operator function must be either member function (non static) or friend function.

13.2. OVERLOADING UNARY OPERATORS

The unary operator is overloaded using member function or friend function. When we write a member function to overload unary operators we must pass no arguments to the function. But if we write a friend function to overload the unary operator we must pass a single argument to function.

The unary operator is overloaded as follows. Let us take increment operator ++. The unary operator ++ increment the value of simple data type but if we overload this, this can increment each data member of a object.

Example 13.1: Write a program which reads a complex no. increment real and imag part of that than print.

We write above program with the operator overloading concept.

```
# include <iostream.h>
# include <conio.h>
    class complex
          {
                int r;
                int i;
```

```
public : void getdata ( )
  {
    cout << "Enter real part:";
    cin >> r;
    cout << "Enter imag part :";
    cin >> i;
void operator + + ( ) //overloaded ++
        { + +r; ++i; } // operator
            void showdata ( )
        {
    cout <<r << " +i" << i <<endl;}
        };
        void main ( )
            {
            complex C1;
            clrscr ( );
            C1. getdata ( );
        cout << "Number before increment" <<endl;
            C1.showdata ( );
            C1 ++;
        cout << "Number after increment" <<endl;
            C1.showdata ( );
            getch ( );
            }
```

The sample output of above program is:

Enter real part : 7
Enter imag part : 6
Number before increment
7 + i 6
Number after increment
8 + i7

In the above example we can write

```
+ + C1;
```

Statement in place of C1++; also both have same effect.

Within main ( ) when we write C1++ or ++C1 the member function operator ++ ( ) is called and execute.

Actually compiler check the C1 if this is basic type like int etc the compiler increment that. But if C1 is object of a class compiler execute a member function operator ++ ( ).

Note that within the body of operator function, we can write anything. But generally the statements are written which match with the meaning of operator which we want to overload, in above case the operator is ++ and operator functions operator ++ ( ).

In above example we can not write the following statement:

```
C2 = C1 ++;
```

Where C2 and C1 both are object of class complex because the return type of operator ++ ( ) function is void.

This type of problem will not come if C1 and C2 are basic type. But if C1 and C2 is object then C1++ must return a value which is assigned to object C2. We can solve this problem by changing the return type of operator ++ ( ) function.

Example 13.2

```
#include <iostream.h>
#include <conio.h>
class complex
          {
           int r;
           int i;
          public : void getdata ( )
           {
           cout << "Enter real part:" <<r <<endl;
           cout << "Enter imag part :" <<r<<endl;
               }
          complex operator ++ ( )
               {
                    complex temp;
                     temp.r = ++r;
                     temp.i = ++i;
                     return (temp);
                     }
                void showdata ( )
                         {
                     Cout <<r<< " +i" << i <<endl;
                         }
                    };
```

```
void main ( )
{
    complex C1, C2;
    C1. getdata ( );
    cout << "C1 before increment" <<endl;
    C1.showdata ( );
    cout << "C1 after increment" <<endl;
    C1. showdata ( );
    cout << "C1 after increment" <<endl;
    C1 ++;
    C1.showdata ( );
    C2 = C1 ++;
    cout << "C2 is C1+1" <<endl;
    C2.showdata ( );
    getch ( );
}
```

Output of the program is:

```
Enter real part : 5
Enter img part : 4
C1 before increment
5 + i4
C1 after increment
6+i5
C2 is C1+1
7+i6
```

In above program operator functions return a complex type data but we can write in main ( ) following statement also:

```
c1 + +;
```

This statement increment the data member C1 and we can use the following statement also

```
c2 = c1 ++;
```

These statements increment the data member of C1 and then assign those to data member of C2. We can also write following statement

```
c2 + + .showdata ( );
```

Limitation of above increment overloaded operator

In above example there is no difference between following two statements:

(1) C2 = C1 ++;

(2) C2 = ++C1;

If we write these in main ( ). Both first increment the data member of C1 and then assign to data member of C2 i.e., the prefix and postfix cannot be differentiated by the above example 13.2.

But in the current version of turbo C++ and Borland C++ there is a facility by which we can differentiate prefix and postfix by changing the header of operator function like follows-

(1) Operator ++ ( ) //does prefix

(2) Operator ++ (int); //does postfix

The (2) declaration uses a dummy int argument which is set to zero by the postfix++ operator. This extra argument allows the compiler to distinguish the tweo forms. Similarly this concept is applied for decrement operator (- -)

Operator - - ( ) //does prefix

Operator - (int) //does postfix

Note: Like the ++, unary operator - and unary - can be overloaded. In following example all these are overloaded.

Example 13.3

```
# include <iostream.h>
# include <conio.h>
        class counter
                {
                    int count;
                  public : counter ( )
                        {
                            count = 4;
                        }
        void operator + + ( ) //overloaded
                {
                    count ++;
                    }           //+ + operator
          void operator - - ( )         //overloaded
            {
            count --; } // - - operator
            void operator - ( ) //overloaded
                    {
```

```
count = - count;
} // unary - operator
void showdata ( )
{
cout << count <<endl;
}
};
void main ( )
{
counter C1, C2, C3;
clrscr ( );
C1 + +;
C2 - -;
-C3;
C1.showdata ( );
C2. showdata ( );
C3.showdata ( );
getch ( );
}
```

The output of above program is:

```
5
3
-4
```

13.3 OVERLOADING BINARY OPERATOR

Binary operator is operator which requires two operands to perform the operation. When they are overloaded by means of member function. The function takes one argument, whereas it takes two arguments in case of friend function. This will be better understood by means of the following program.

Binary operator can be overloaded very easily like unary operator. We will study the following:

(1) Overloading of arithmetic operator

(2) Overloading of comparison operator

(3) Overloading of assignment operator

13.3.1 Overloading of Arithmetic Operator

The binary arithmetic are overloaded as follows:

```
# include <iostream.h>
# include <conio.h>
      class complex
          {
                int real;
        int imag;
      public : complex ( int a, int b)
                  { real = a; imag = b;}
         void output ( )
   {
         cout <<real << "+i" <<imag <<endl;
        }
        complex operator + (complex C)
                {
                   complex temp;
                   temp.real = real + c.real;
                     temp.imag = imag + c.imag;
                                 return (temp);
                   //the above function overloaded
                 //binary + operator
      void main ( )
                   {
                          complex C1 (5,4);
                          complex C2 (3,2);
                          complex C3 (4,4);
                          clrscr ( );
                          cout << "C1 is:" <<endl;
                          C1.output ( );
                          cout << "C2 is : "<<endl;
                          C2.output ( );
                          cout << "C3 is: "<<endl;
                            C3.output ( );
                             C3 = C1+C2;
                              cout << "Now C3 = C1 +C2 is:" <<endl;
                             C3.output ( );
                                         getch ( );
                                          }
```

The output of above program is:

```
C1 is:
5+i4
C2 is:
3+i2
C3 is:
4+i4
Now C3 = C1+C2 is:
8+i6
```

In the above program declaration of operator function is:

```
complex operator + (complex C)
        {body of function }
```

When the statement C3=C1+C2 is execute the operator function is called. The operator function is called by object C1 and object C2 is passed as argument to operator function i.e the C2 object is copied into object C which is written in the header of operator function.

Inside the operator function temp.real=real+C.real;

Calculate the sum of real member of object C2 and real member of object C1 and assign this to real of temp object. In above statement real is member of C1 and C.Real is member of C2 object because C2 is copied into C at the time of call.

Similarly the statement temp.imag = imag is calculated.

The temp is returned to C3 by

```
(return (temp);
```

In above program within main ( ). We can write following type of statement also

```
C3 = C1 + C2 + C3
```

For performing this same operator function which is written in above program is called.

Note: The *, / and other binary operators are overloaded like +binary operator for example the operators function for * is as follows:

```
complex operator * (complex C)
        {
            complex temp;
              temp.real = real * c.real - imag * c,imag;
            temp.imag = real * c.imag + imag * c..real;
            return (temp);
```

This perform multiplication of two complex numbers. Within main ( ) we call this like

```
c1 = c2 *c2;
```

Where C1,C2,C3 are object of class complex.

13.3.2 *Overloading of Comparison Operator*

The comparison operator can also be overloaded like arithmetic operator return true or false, therefore we have to use enumerated data type also.

Example 13.4: Overloading of (< less than) operator

```
# include <iostream.h>
# include <conio.h>
enum boolean { false, true};
class sample
     {
          int d;
          public : sample ( ) {d = 0;}
            sample (int a1);
                  {d=a1;}
                  void show ( )
                  { cout <<d<<endl;}
            boolean operator < (sample s)
                      { if (d <s.d)
                                { return(true); }
                        else
                                { return (false); }
                                              };
     void main ( )
          {
          sample s1;
            sample s2 (4);
            sample s3 (6);
            clrscr ( );
            if (s1<s2)
                  cout << "s1 is less than s2" <<endl;
                    else
               cout << "s1 is not less than s2" <<endl;
          if (s3<s2)
                cout << "s3 is less than s2" <<endl;
            else
```

```
                        cout << "s3 is not less than s2 " <<endl;
        cout << "Member of s1 is ="; s1.show ( );
        cout << "Member of s2 is ="; s2.show ( );
        cout << "Member of s3 is ="; s3.show ( );
                                          getch ( );
                                         }
```

The output of above program

S1 is less than s2
S3 is not less than s2
Member of s1 is = 0
Member of s2 is 4
Member of s3 is = 6

In main ( ) when the following statement execute:

```
If (s1 <s2)
        cout << "S1 is less than S2" <<endl;
         else
         cout << "S1 is not less than S2" <<endl;
```

The operator function Boolean operator < (sample s) is executed.

S1<S2 means we are calling operator function, i.e object s1 calls the function and objects2 is passed as an argument.

13.3.3 Overloading of Assignment Operator

We can overload assignment operator =, +=, ,-=,*=,\=etc. See the following example.

Example 13.5: Overloading of = and + = operator

```
# include <iostream.h>
# include <conio.h>
class sample
      {
          int d;
   public : sample ( )
    { d = 0; }
      sample (int a) { d = a;}
   void show ( )
      {
          cout << d << endl;
      }
void operator = (sample s1)  //overload =
```

```
        { d=s1.d;}
void operator += (sample s2) //overload +=
        { d=d+s1.d;}
                    };
    void main ( )
        {
          sample s3;
          sample s4 (6);
          sample s5 (7);
          clrscr ( );
        s3=s4; //call the overloaded =
        s5 += s4; //call the overloaded +=
cout << "Data member of s3 is:" <<endl;
            s3.show ( );
cout << "Data member of s4 is:" <<endl;
          s4.show ( );
cout << "Data member of s5 is:" <<endl;
                s5.show ( );
                getch ( );
                    }
```

The output of above program is:

Data member of s3 is: 6
Data member of s4 is : 6
Data member of s5 is : 13

Note: similarly we load other assignment operator.

13.4 DATA TYPE CONVERSION

In mixed expression constant and variable are of different data type. The assignment operations cause automatic type conversion between the operand as per certain rules.

Consider example

```
int x;
float y = 22.123;
x=y;
```

This converts float variable y to an integer before its value assigned to x. The type conversion is automatic as far as data type involved is built in types. We can also use the assignment operator in case of objects to copy values of all data member of right hand object to object on left hand. The objects in this case are of same type. But objects are of different type we must apply conversion rule for assignment.

There are three type of situations that arise where data conversion are between incompatible type.

1. Conversion from basic type to class type
2. Conversion from class type to basic type
3. Conversion from one class type to another class type.

13.4.1 Conversion of Basic to Class Type

The conversion of basic to class type is very simple. This can be done by using constructor. We use constructor to built string type object from char*type variable. Consider the following constructor

```
string : : string (char* a)
     {
       length = strlen (a);
       name = new char[len+1];
       strcpy (name,a);
       }
```

This constructor built type object from char*type variable a. The variable length and name are data members of the class string. We define the constructor in the class string, it can be used for conversion from char*type to string type.

Example 13.6: The following example is using a class which has two data member feet and inches. These represent the distance in main ( ). We are assigning a distance which is in meter (float type) to that class.

```
#include <iostream.h>
#include <conio.h>
class distance
     {
        int feet;
        float inches;
public : distance (float mtr)
     {
        float inches;
public : distance (float mtr)
   {
        float f = 3.28*mtr;
        feet = int (f);
     inches = 12 * (f - feet);
       }
void show ( )
     {
         cout << "distance is:"<<endl;
```

```
        cout << feet << "\" "-" <<inches << '\" '<<endl;
            }
        };
void main ( )
            {
                clrscr ( );
                float meter;
                cout << "Enter a distance:";
                cin >> meter;
            distance d1 = meter; //This call the constructor which
                                    convert floating point
                                // data to class type
                d1.show ( );
                  getch ( );
                        }
```

The output of program

Enter a distance :2.3 **75′ - 5.28″**

In the above program the constructor converts basic type to class type.

In the above example mtr is multiplied by 3.28 because one meter = 3.28 feet (approx)

13.4.2 Conversion From Class to Basic Type

The constructor function does not support conversion from class to basic type. C++ allows us to define a overloaded casting operator that converts a class type data to a basic type. The general form of an overloaded casting operator function also referred to as a conversion function is:

```
operator type name ( )
            {
                function body
                        }
```

This function converts class type data to type name.

The casting operator should satisfy the following condition

1. **It must be class member**
2. **It must not specify a return type**
3. **It must have not any arguments. Since it is a member function, it is invoked by the object and therefore, the value used for. Conversion inside the function belongs to the object that invoked the function. As a result function does not need an argument.**

Example 13.7: The example is using a class that represents the distance. Same class as in example 12.7, this converts a class distance to floating type data member.

```
# include <iostream.h>
# include < conio.h>
class distance
    {
      int feet;
      float inches;
public : distance (int f, float i)
           { feet = f; inches = i; }
             void show ( )
                 {
                   cout <<feet << "\' " <<inches << '\" ' ; }
                   operator float ( )
                       {
                         float ft = inches/12;
                             ft = ft + feet;
                   return (ft/3.28);
                             }
                   };
      void main ( )
    {
      distance dl (3, 3.36);
        float m = dl;
             clrscr ( );
        cout << "distance in meter:"<<m<<endl;
        cout << "distance in feet and inches:" <<endl;
                  d.show ( );
                  getch ( );
                        }
```

The output of above program is:

distance in meter : 1.0
distance in feet and inches : 3′ - 3.36

In the above program the following function converts class type to basic type

```
operator float ( )
          {
              float ft = inches/12;
          ft    = ft + feet;
      return (ft/3.28);
          }
```

When we write

```
float m = d1;
```

In main ( ); above function is called, which take feet and inches of distance d1 and return a float type data.

13.4.3 Conversion of One Class Type to Another Class Type

We can convert one class type to another type **obj1=obj2; obj1 and obj2** are objects of different classes. Obj1 is an object of class one and obj2 is an object of class two. The class two type data is converted to class one type data and converted value is assigned to the obj1. Since the conversion takes place from two to class one, two is known as the source and one is known as the destination class.

Such conversion can be carried out by either

1. Constructor
2. Conversion function, i.e., overload casting operation function. Which from to use, depends upon where we want the type-conversion function to be located, whether in the source class or in the destination class.

We studied that the casting operation function **operation type name ( )** Converts the class object of which is a member to type name. The type name may be built-in-type or user defined (another class-type). In case of conversion between objects type name refers to the destination class. Therefore, when a class needs to be converted, a casting operator function can be used. The conversion takes place in source class and the result is given in destination class.

Let us consider a single-argument constructor function which serves as an instruction for converting the argument's type to the class type of which it is a member. The argument belongs to the source class and is placed to the destination class for conversion. Therefore the conversion constructor must be placed in destination class.

In figure summaries all the three conversion. It shows that the conversion from class to any other type (or any other type) makes use of a casting operator in the source class. To perform the conversion from any other type or class to a class type, a constructor is used in the destination class.

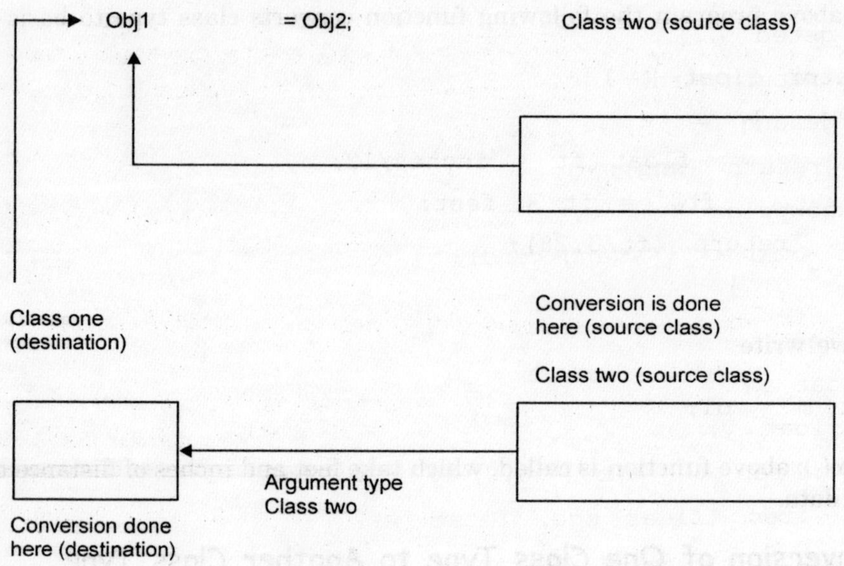

Conversion	**Conversion Between Objects**	
	Source	**Destination class**
Basic→class	**Not applicable**	**Constructor**
Class→Basic	**Casting operator**	**Not applicable**
Class→class	**Casting operator**	**Constructor**

When conversion using a constructor is performed in the destination class, we must be able to access the data member of the object sent (by source class) as an argument. Since data member of the source class are private, we must use special access function in the source class to facilitate its data flow to the destination class.

Example 13.8

```
#include  <iostream.h>
#include  <math.h>
#include<conio.h>
class  polar
    {
        float  rd;
        float  ang;
public  :  polar  (  )
    {  rd  =  0.0;  ang  =  0.0;}
polar  (float  r,  float  a)
        {  rd  =  r;  ang  =  a;}
```

```
float geted ( )
    { return (rd); }
float getang ( )
    { return (ang); }
void showpolar ( )
{ cout <<rd <<","<<ang<<endl; }
                        };
class rec
  { float x;
      float y;
public : rec ( ) {x = 0.0; y = 0.0; }
        rec (float xco, float yco)
              { x = xco; y = yco; }
        rec (polar p)
              {
                   float r = p.getrd ( );
                   float a = p.getang ( );
                   x = r * cos (a);
                   y = r* sin (a);
              }
   void showrec ( )
        {
           cout<< x << "," <<y <<endl;
           };
   void main ( )
         { rec r1;
         polar p1 (2.0 , 90.0);
           clrscr ( );
             r1 = p1; //convert polar to rec by calling one
argument constructor
           count << "polar co. :"<<endl;
               p1.showpolar ( );
           cout << "rec co. :" <<endl;
               r1.showrec ( );
         getch ( );
              }
```

The output of program

```
Polar co. :
        2.0 .90
Rec co.
0.0, 2.0
```

In above program the following constructor converts polar class type to rec class type

```
rec (polar p)
    {
        float r = p.getrd ( );
        float a = p.getang ( );
          x = r* cos (a);
          y = r* sin (a);
```

This is written in destination i.e., in rec class.

In this constructor object of polar class p is passed as an argument. Within polar class rd and ang are private data we can not access these outside the class therefore getrd ( ) and getang ( ) function are written within polar class by using these function. We can get rd and ang; by following function.

p.getrd ( );

p. getang ( );

The statement

r1=p1;

Called one argument constructor of class rec i.e., the above written constructor.

Conversion function: When the conversion routine is in source class, it is implemented as a conversion function.

Example 13.9

```
# include <iostream.h>
# include <math.h>
# include <conio.h>
class rec
      {
            float x;
            float y;
   public : rec ( )
   {
      x =0.0; y = 0.0;
   }
rec (float xco, float yco)
```

```
{ x=xco;  y=yco;}
  void  showrec  ( )
   {
     cout  <<x  <<","  <<y  <<endl;  }
 class  polar
   {
     float  x;
     float  y;
public  :  rec  (  )
     {  rd=0.0;  ang  =0.0;  }
     polar  (float  r,  float  a)
          {  rd  =  r;  ang  =a;}
   operator  rec  (  )
         {
          float  x1  =  red*  cos(ang);
         float  y1=rd  *sin  (ang);
         return  rec  (x1,y1);  }
     void  showpolar  (  )
         {
          cout  <<rd<<  ","  <<ang<<endl;  }
                  };

     void  main  (  )
                 {
         rec  r1;
         polar  p1  (2.0,  90.0);
        r1  =p1;  //converts  polar  to  rec  by  calling  conversion
function
         cout  <<  "  polar  co.  :"  <<endl;
         p1.showpolar  (  );
         cout  <<'"rec  co.  :"  <<endl
         r1.showrec  (  );
         getch  (   );
              }
```

The output of above program

Polar co. :
2.0, 90.0
Rec co. :
0.0, 2.0

In the above program conversion function is written in class polar, which is source class. When we write the following statement.

```
r1 = p1;
```

This is called the conversion function

```
operator rec ( )
    {
        float x1 = rd* cos (ang);
        float y1 = rd* sin (ang);
        return rec (x1, y1);
    }
```

This function uses the rd and ang of p1 and returns an object of rec type class to r1. In above function return rec (x1,y1); create a temporary object and assign the data member of that by value x1 and y1.

Solved Exercises

Exercise 1. Write a program to overload unary operator to negate an object.

```
#include<iostream.h>
#include <conio.h>
class integer
{
    z;
public:
void getdata(int a, int b, int c);
void disp(void);
void operator-( ); //overloading unary operator minus
};
void integer::getdata(int a, int b, intc)
{
     x=a;
     y=b;
     z=c;
}
void integer::disp(void)
{
    cout<<x<< " ";
   cout<<y<< " ";
```

```
cout<<z<< " ";
}
void integer::operator-( ) //defining operator-( )
{
   x=-x;
   y=-y;
   z=-z;
}
main ( )
{
      integer s;
      s.getdata(11,-21,-31)
      cout << "s:";
      s.disp ( );
      -s;
      cout << "s:";
      s.disp ( );
      getch ( );
   }
```

Output of the above program is:

```
S: 11-21-31
S: -11 21 31
```

Exercise 2. Write a program to find Fibonacci series illustrate overloading prefix.++ increment operator.

```
# include <iostream.h>
#include <conio.h>
class fibo {
 private:
int f0,f1,fib;
public:
fib0 ( ); //constructor
void operator ++( );
void display ( );
};
fibo::fibo ( )
{
  f0=0;
  f1=1;
```

```
    fib=f0+f1;
  }
  void  fibo::display  ( )
  {
     cout  <<fib<<  '\t';
  }
   void  fib0::operator++( )
   {
     f0=f1;
     f1=fib;
     fib=f0+f1;
  }
   void  main  ( )
  {
    fibo  obj;
    int  n;
    cout  <<  "Enter  a  value  to  display  the  Fibonacci  series";
    cin>>n;
    for  (int  i=0;  i<=n-1;  ++i)
    {
     obj.display  ( )
     ++obj;
     }
     getch  ( );
      }
```

Output of the above program is:

Enter a value to display the Fibonacci series 7
1 2 3 5 8 13 21

Exercise 3. Write a program create objects of class integer and overload the + operator to add two object value.

```
# include<iostream.h>
#include<conio.h>
class  integer
  {
    private:
    int  val;
```

```
public:
  integer ( );
  integer  (int  one);
  integer  operator+(integer  objb);
  void  disp  (  );
   };
   integer::integer  (  )
   {
     val=0;
    }
    integer::integer(int  one)
   {
    val=one;
   }
   integer  integer::operator+(integer  objb)
   {
     integer  objsum;
    objsum.val=val+obj.val;
     return(objsum);
    }
    void  integer::disp  (  )
    {
     cout<<  "value="  <<val<<endl;
     }
    void  main  (  )
    {
     integer  obj1(11);
     integer  obj2(22);
     integer  objsum;
     objsum=obj1+obj2;
     obj1.disp  (  );
     obj2.disp  (  );
     objsum.disp  (  );
 getch  ( );
 }
```

Output of the above program is:

```
value=11
value=22
value=33
```

Exercise 4. Create a class to represent a character string. Write constructor function to initialize the object using operator overloading, concatenate the two strings compare the two objects representing string display the longest both.

```
#include<string.h>
#include<iostream.h>
#include<conio.h>
class string
 {
   char*p;
   int len;
   public:
   string ( )
   {len=0;p=NULL;}
    string (const char*s);
    string (const string &s);
    ~string ( ) {delete p;}
    friend string operator+(const string s, const string t);
    friend int operator <=(const string &s, const string &t);
    friend void show(const string s);
    };
    string::string(const char *s)
      {
        len=strlen(s);
        p=new char[len+1];
        ctrcpy(p,s);
        }
        string::string(const chat*s)
          {
            len=strlen(s);
            p=new char[len+1];
            strcpy(p,s)
            }
            string::string(const string &s)
              {
                len=s.len;
                p=new char[len+1];
                strcpy(p,s,p);
                }
```

```
string operator+(const string s, const string t)
{
    string temp;
    temp.len=s.len+t.len;
    temp.p=NULL;
    temp.p=new char[temp.len+1];
    strcpy(temp.p,s.p);
    strcat(temp.p,t.p);
    return (temp);
}
int operator <=(const string &s, const string &t)
{
  int m=strlen(s,p);
  int n=strlen(t,p);
  if (m<=n)return (1); else return(0);
  }
 void show(const string s)
  {
   cout<<s.p;
   }
  main ( )
   {
    string s1= "kamlesh"
    string s1= "kumar"
    string s3= "yadav"
      t1=s1;
      t2=s2;
      string t3=s1+s2;
      t4=s1+s3;
      cout<<endl;
      cout << "t1:";
      show(t1);
      cout <<endl;
      cout << " t2:":
      show (t2);
      cout <<endl;
      cout << "t3:";
```

```
        show (t3);
            cout <<endl;
            cout << "t4:";
            show(t4);
            cout<<end<<endl;
            cout<< "string comparison result:"<<endl<<endl;
            if(t3<=t4)
              {
                        cout<< "    ";
show(t4);
cout<< "larger than";
show(t3);
cout <<endl;
}
else
{
    cout << "    ";
    show(t3);
    cout<< "larger than";
    show (t4);
    cout<<endl;
    }
    getche( );
    }
```

Descriptive Type Questions

1. How are the preferment and post decrement taken care of while declaring operator overloading?
2. What is meant by operator overloading?
3. How will you overload input and output operator?
4. Explain how memory management operator are used for overloading in C++.
5. A class abc has constructor (int a, double b, float c); can this constructor be used to convert type.
6. Explain the use of fraind function in operator overloading.
7. Explain overloading of comparison operator..
8. Explain overloading of assignment operator.
9. Explain conversion from basic type to class type.
10. Explain conversion from class type to basic type.
11. Explain conversion from one class type to another class type.

12. What is the difference between operator overloading and constructor overloading.
13. When used in postfix form, what does the overload ++operator do differently for what it does in the prefix form.

Exercises

1. Write a program to overload operators +,-,>>,<<,= for point class.
2. Write a program to overload operator +, =, = =, >>, << [ ] for string class.
3. Write a program to overload operator +, =, = =, >>, << for measure class.
4. Write a program to overload operators >>, <<,=, = =, >, < + (days) for date class.
5. Write a program to overload operators >>, <<,=, = =, [] for vector class.
6. Write a program to overload operators +,-<,= for ratio class.
7. Write a program to overload operators of complex number class.
8. Write a program to overload operators of matrix class.
9. Write a program to overload operators of time class.
10. Write a program to overload operators - - operator.
11. Write a program to overload operators % operator.
12. Write a program to overload operators * operator.
13. Write a program to overload operators = = and != operator.
14. Write a program to overload operators >= operator.
15. Write a program to overload operators *=, -=, /=, %= operators.
16. Write a program to convert one basic type to class type.
17. Write a program to convert class type to basic type.
18. Write a program to convert class type to another class type.
19. Write a program in C++ which compare two string objects and return the smallest.
20. Write a C++ program using operator overloading to find the factorial of a given number 5.
21. Write a C++ program to overload +=operator for strings. The operator should also permit the result of the operation to be used in other calculations as in s3 = s1 + s2;
22. Write a C++ program using operator overloading to find the simple interest (I) of a given principal (P), rate of interest (R) and number of year (N).

14

POINTER IN C++

Pointer is a variable which stores the address of another data type. It provides an essential tool for increasing the power of C++, a powerful technique by which we can access data by indirect reference. Pointer is stored in memory but holds the address of another variable. Every byte in the memory has an address. When program is loaded into memory it occupies a certain range of address, the address of a variable can be got by using the & operator.

For example

```
cout<<& var;
```

Displays the address where the variable var is stored. Each variable starts at a unique address. A variable can hold address value is called as a **pointer**. We know that pointer variable to int data type is declared as

```
int *ptr;
```

The asterisk means pointer to.

Consider the following program segment.

```
int var1, var2;
int *ptr;   //ptr declared as pointer to integer
datatype
ptr=&var1;     //ptr points to var1
*ptr=50;   //contents at ptr=50//i.e., pointer ptr
points to var1   //var2 is initialized with content at ptr
stores 50 at location var2 //
cout <<var2;
```

Ptr points to var1

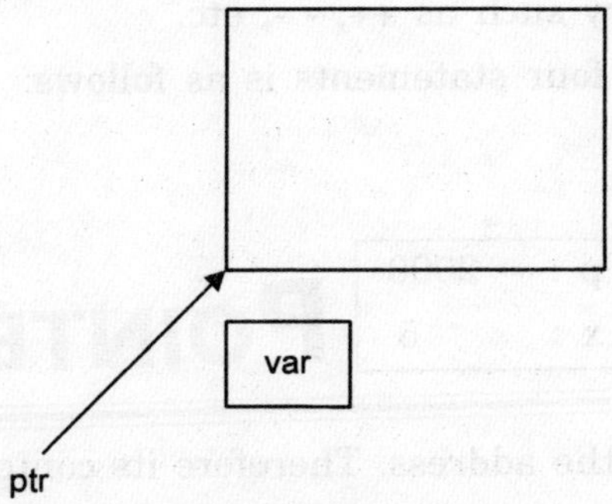

***ptr means contents at ptr. But ptr holds the address of var1. Therefore the *ptr means contents at the address of var1. Therefore *ptr=50; store 50 at the location of var1.**

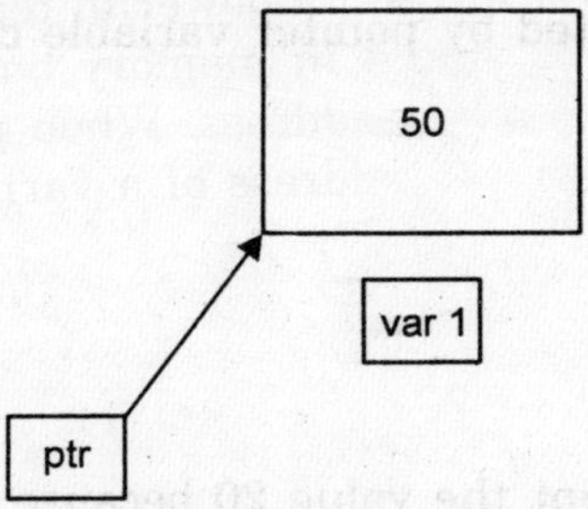

var2=*ptr initializes var2 to 50. Therefore the output statement would display 50.

14.1 DECLARATION OF POINTER

The general format of the pointer declaration is.

```
data - type * pointer - variable;
```

for example → int *p

means the p is pointer variable which can store the address of int type data i.e p points to integer type data.

Pointer-variable is any identifier and data-type is any data-type of C++, like int, float etc.

When a name is preceded by asterisk (*) then that is pointer -variable.

When we declare pointer variable that can store the address of data-type which is written in front of that. Now next point is to assign the address of a variable to pointer variable as follows:

```
int * ; //declaration of pointer
int x; //declaration of variable
p = &x;
x = 5;
```

The statement p=&x; assigns the address of x to p. The & is a unary operator that returns the memory address of its operands.

The * is known as **pointer operator** and & is **address operator** both has same precedence as the other unary such as ++, - -, etc.

The memory for above four statements is as follows:

Address of memory

```
1000 :
1001 :        | p :   2000 |
=====         | x :      5 |
2000 :
```

Note that pointer stores the address. Therefore its contents are unsigned integer type.

14.2 ACCESSING THE VARIABLE POINTED TO

The variable which is pointed by pointer variable can be accessed as follows:

```
int * p;
int x;
x = 20;
p = &x;
cout << *p;
```

The statement cout <<*p; print the value 20 because *p means value at the address p. Similarly,

```
*p = *p+10;
```

Is same as -

```
x = x +10;
```

Note that if we write the following statement-

```
cout << p;
```

this prints the address of x. Similarly the statement-

```
cout << &x;
```

also prints the address of x.

Example 14.1

```
#include<iostream.h>
#include<conio.h>
void main ( )
 {
   int *p;
   int x;
   clrscr ( );
   cout << "Enter a value:"
   cin >>x;
```

```
    p = &x; //assigns of x to p
      *p = * p +10; //same as x = x+10
      cout << "now x is :" <<x<<endl;
      cout << "value of x through p:"<<*p<<endl;
      cout << "The address of x is" <<&x<<endl;
      cout << "The address of x is" <<p<<endl;
      getch ( );
          }
```

Output of the above program is:

Enter a value : 25
Now x is : 35
Value of x through p: 35
The address of x is 0 x 8f51fff4
The address of x is 0 x 8f51fff4

14.3 POINTED TO VOID

Note that we can assign the address of a float type variable to a pointer to int for example:

```
float y;
int *p;
p = &y; //illegal statements;
```

```
float *p;
int x;
p = &x; //illegal statement
```

That means if variable type and pointer type is same then we can assign the address of variable to pointer variable. And if both are different type then we can not assign the address of variable to pointer variable but this is also possible in c++ by declaring pointer variable as a void as follows:

```
void *p;
```

The above pointer is called pointer to void type. That means pointer p point any type of data int, float etc. For example:

```
void *p;
int x;
float y;
p = & x;
p = & y;
```

14.4 POINTER ARITHMETIC

Pointer is permitted to perform following arithmetic operations

Pointer Arithmetic	Description
ptr++	ptr= ptr+size of (data_type) use original value of ptr and then ptr is incremented after statement execution.
++ptr	ptr=ptr+size of (data_type) use original value of ptr and then ptr is decremented after statement execution.
ptr - -	ptr=ptr-size of (data_type) use original value of ptr and then ptr is decremented after statement execution.
- -ptr	ptr=ptr+size of (data_type) original ptr is decremented before execution of statement.
*ptr++	*(ptr++) retrieve the contents of the location pointed to be pointer and then increment ptr.
*(ptr)++	Increment contents of the location pointed to by ptr. For pointer type contents, use pointer arithmetic else use standard arithmetic.
++*ptr	++*(ptr) Increment the contents of the location pointed to by ptr depending on the type of the contents.
- - *ptr	- -*(ptr) Decrement contents of the location pointed to by ptr depending on the type of the content.
*ptr - -	*(ptr- -) retrieve the content of the location pointed to by ptr and then decrement ptr
*- -ptr	*(- -ptr) decrement ptr, then retrieve the content of the new location pointed to by ptr
(*ptr)- -	Retrieve contents *ptr of the location printed to by ptr, then decrement the content of the location; ptr is not changed

1. Increment

If p is a pointer type then ++p; is possible with pointer. Note that ++p or p++ not add 1 to p but add size of that data type with p which is pointed by pointer. Example:

```
int  x,  *p;
p=&x;
p++;
```

If p is 1000 after the statement p=&x then after p++ the p will be 1002 because the size of (x) is 2 byte.

The difference between p++, ++p is same as postfix and prefix increment with basic type. For example:

```
int  x,  *p1,  *p2,  *p3;
p1=  &x;
p2  =  p1++;
p3  =  ++p1;
```

If location of x is 1000 then after execution of p=&x; the value 1000 is assigned to p1; After statement p2=p1++; the value p1 is assigned to p2 first then p1 is incremented i.e P2=1000, and p1=1002 after above statement because size of x is 2 byte.

After statement p3=++p1; the value of p1 is incremented first then assigned to p3 i.e P1=1004, and p3=1004.

P1 is 1004 because p1 is 1002 after statement p2 = p1++;

Note: we can assign a pointer to another pointer if both points to same type of variable, as in above example.

2. Decrement

If p is pointer type then p - - of - -p is possible. p- - or - - p not decrement 1 but the size of data type which is pointed by p.

p - - is postfix decrement and - -p is prefix decrement. The difference is same like p++ and ++p.

For example

```
int  x  *p1,  *p2,  *p3;
p1  =  &x;
p2  =  p1  -  -;
p3  =  -  -p1;
```

If address of x is 1000 then after statement p1 = &x; p1 contain 1000.

Address statement p2 = p1 - -; p2 is 1000 and p1 is 998(p1-size of x)

After statement p3 = - -p1; p1 is 996 and p3 is also 996.

3. We can add integer value with pointer

We can add any integer value to pointer like follows:

P2=p1+6; where p2 and p1 both are pointer type, point to same type of data.

After p2=p1+6; p2 to points to the sixth element of the pointer type beyond the element pointed to by 1.

See the following statement

```
int x. *pl, *p2, *p3;
pl=&x;
p2 = pl - -;
p3 = - -pl;
```

If address of x is 1000 then p is 1000 after statement p = &x.

After p2=p+7; now p is → 1000+14=1014 integer type element take 2 byte. The memory for above is:

X: → 1000	10
1001	
1002	
1003	
1004	
1005	
1006	
P:	1000

After statement p=&x;

X: →1000	10 }2 byte
1001	
1002	}2 byte
1003	
1004	
1005	
1006	
1014	
P:	1014

After statement p=p+7;

4. We can subtract integer value from pointer

We can subtract an integer number from pointer type like addition, for example p=p-9; (where p is a pointer type) after above statement now p points to an element which is ninth element back from an element which currently points to.

For example:

```
float x, *p;
p = &x;
p = p -3;
```

After statement p= &x; the address of x is assigned to p if address of x is 2000 then p is assigned to value 2000.

After p = p-3; the value of p is 1088 (i.e 2000-3*4) because float type takes 4 byte.

Note: Only above arithmetic operators are allowed with pointer type other than above are not allowed. i.e., following are not allowed with pointer type:

1. To multiply or divide
2. To add or subtract type float or double to pointer
3. To operate the bitwise shift etc.

14.5 POINTER AND ARRAY

There is closed association between pointer and array. Array name is pointer to itself. For example:

int a[5], *p;

p = & a[0];

after statement p = &a[0]; p points the array i.e the p contains the address of a[0], first element of array)

p++;

after this statement p points to a[1] element.

Example 14.2

```
# include <iostream.h>
# include <conio.h>
void main ( )
  {
     int a[5] = {5,6,7,8,9}
     int *p;
      p = &a [0];
      clrscr ( );
      for (int i = 0; i <=4; i++)
           cout << * (p+i) <<endl;
          getch ( );
              }
```

The output of above program is:

5
6
7
8
9

Because the statement cout<<*(p+i)<<endl; execute 5 times from i= 0 to 4.

When i = 0 then * (p+i) is *(p+0) means *p therefore this print the value which store at location p.

Similarly *(p+1) means the value of second element, because p+1 is pointer to the second element of array. Similarly other elements are printed.

We know that array name is also pointer to that so the above program can be written as follows also:

Example 14.3

```
#include<iostream.h>
#include<conio.h>
void main ( )
{
    int a[2] [3] = { {5,6,7}, {8,9,10}};
    clrscr ( );
    for (int i =0; i <=1; i++)
    for (int j=0; j <=2; j++)
cout <<*(*(a+i)+j << '\t';
        cout <<endl;
        }
        getch ( );
        }
```

The output of above program is

5	6	7
8	9	10

14.6 POINTER AND STRING

We know string is array of char. Therefore pointer notation can be applied to the characters in string, just as it can to the elements of an array. But in case of string if we initialized the string at the time of declaration then the string name is constant. Therefore we cannot perform pointer arithmetic operation with that.

Example

```
# include <iostream.h>
# include <conio.h>
void main ( )
    {
        char str [ ] = "Saurabh Pal";
        clrscr ( );
        cout << str; //display the string
            str++ //illegal
            getch ( );
                }
```

Above program give an error because str is constant we can not write statement like str++. But if we declare the string by pointer then we can perform arithmetic operation.

Example 14.4

```
# include <iostream.h>
# include <conio.h>
void main ( )
    {
        char * str1 = "Anju Lata"
        clrscr ( );
        cout << str1 << endl;
        str1++; //ok
cout << str1 <<endl;
getch ( );
    }
```

The above program is ok the output of above program is:

Anju lata **nju lata**

str1 is a pointer type variable therefore we can perform arithmetic operation str1++, pointer string from second character.

But in example1 the str is an array name, that is a pointer to string. Which contains a address which is constant, i.e., we can say that is a pointer constant.

14.6.1 String with Pointer Notation as a Function Arguments

We represent a string using pointer that is known as string with pointer notation as in the above example2 i.e.,

```
char *s;
```

s is a pointer which point to character type data but this also uses for string.

```
# include <iostream.h>
#include <conio.h>
void main ( )
  {
      void display (char * str)
        char s [ ] = "kamlesh";
        clrscr ( );
        display (s);
        getch ( );
              }
void display (char * str)
      {
          while (*str)
              cout <<* str++<<endl;
                  }
```

The output of above program is:

```
K
m
l
e
s
h
```

In the above program s is pointer constant but this is passed to function where str is pointer variable within the body of function the loop.

```
while (*str)
      cout << *str++<<endl;
```

Terminate when *str is 0 i.e., upto the end of string.

str++ first print constants pointed by str then incremented.

Example 14.5

Copy of one string by using pointer.

```
# include <iostream.h>
# include <conio.h>
void main ( )
  {
     void copy (char *, char *);
     clrscr ( );
     char *s1 = "Yadav";
     char s2 [80];
      copy (s2, s1);
      cout << s2 <<endl;
      getch ( );
         }
void copy (char *d, char *s)
      { while (*s)
             *d++ = * s ++;
             *d = '\0';
                }
```

Output of above program is:

```
Yadav
```

In the above program the statement

```
*d ++ = * s ++;
```

means first the value pointed by s is assigned to *d then both d and s increment, because the increment is postfix increment.

14.7 ARRAY OF POINTER

We know that array is homogeneous collection of data. This is also possible that an array element can be pointer type that array is known as array of pointer. The array of pointer is declared as follows:

```
data - type * array - name [size]
```

for example

```
int * a[10]
```

makes an array of 10 elements. Each element is a pointer type which points to int type data.

```
char *a [10];
```

makes on array of pointer to string, because char *s; makes an pointer to string, therefore an array which each element points to string is a string type.

Example 14.6

```
# include < iostream.h>
# include <conio.h>
void main ( )
      {
        char *a [3] = { "NITIN YADAV"};
      clrscr ( );
         for (int i = 0, i < = 2,      i++)
      cout << a << a[i] <<endl;
      getch ( );
           }
```

The output of above program is:

NITIN
YADAV

14.8 POINTER TO POINTER

An array of pointer is same as pointer to pointer type. The pointer to pointer type declared as follows:

```
data-type ** pointer - variable - name;
```

For example:

```
int **p;
```

Where p is pointer which holds the address of the pointer.

Example 14.7

```
# include <iostream.h>
# include <conio.h>
  void main ( )
     {
        int data;
        int *p1;
        int **p2;
        data = 16;
        cout << "Data =" <<data <<endl;
        p1 =& data;
        p2 = & p1;
        cout << "data through p1=" <<*p1<<endl;
        cout << "data through p2=" <<**p2<<endl;
             getch ( );
                  }
```

The output of above program is:

```
data = 16
data through p1 = 16
data through p2 = 16
```

14.9 POINTER TO FUNCTION

C++ allows function to be referenced by a pointer. A pointer to a function must be declared to be a pointer to the data type returned by the functions. The argument type of the function must also be specified when the pointer is declared.

The general syntax of a pointer to a function is:

```
return-type (*pointer-name) (list of parameter);
```

For example:

```
void (*p) (float, int);
```

In the above declaration a pointer to a function returns void and takes the two formal arguments float and int types.

After declaring of pointer to a function the address of the function must be assigned to a pointer like follow:

```
p = & function - name;
```

where p is pointer variable.

Through pointer to function the function is called as follows:

```
A = (*p) (x,y);
```

Where x and y are actual parameters and A is variable in which the function return value. P is a pointer name which points to function.

Example 14.8

```
# include <iostream.h>
# include <conio.h>
void main ( )
  { float add (float, float);
  float a, b, s;
     float (*p) (float, float);
        p = & add;
        a = 20.5;
        b = 10.3;
```

```
        s  =  (**p)  (a,b);
        cout  <<  "s  =  <<  s  <<  endl;
            getch  (  );
    float  add  float  a1,  float  b1)
                {
                        int  sum;
                        sum  =  a1  +  b1;
                        return  (sum);
                                }
```

The above program is:

s = 30.8

In the above program the statement:

```
Float  (*p)  (float,  float);
```

Declare a pointer p which is point to function.
The statement →

```
s  =  (*p)  (a,b);
```

calls the function which is pointed to p (i.e., add) and then returned the value of function is assigned to s.

Note: **If in the pointer to function declaration we skip the brackets in which pointer name is written then C++ compiler interprets it as a function which returns a pointer type value.**

```
float *p (float,  float);
```

This statement means p is a function which returns pointer and the pointer points to float type data i.e., function return a pointer to float.

14.10 POINTER AS AN ARGUMENT TO FUNCTION

If pointer is passed as an argument to a function that is known as pass by address or pass by pointer. The concept is also called call by reference. Actually call by reference concept is interpreted in C++ by two way-

1. **pass by reference**
2. **pass by address**

The following example interpreted the pass by address concept

Example 14.9

```
# include <iostream.h>
# include <conio.h>
void main ( )
     {
          int a, b;
          void swap (int *, int *)
          a = 10; b= 20;
            clrscr ( );
            swap ( &a, &b)
            cout << "a="<<a<<"b"<<b<<endl;
                getch ( );
                      }
              swap (int *a1, int *b1)
                      {int t;
       t = *a1;
       *a1 = *b1;
     *b1 = t;
              }
```

The output of above program is

a = 20, b = 10

If we change the header of the function is as follows:

```
swap(int & a1, int & b1)
```

then this is called pass by reference.

Example 14.10

```
# include <iostream.h>
#include <conio.h>
void main ( )
    {
      int a, b;
      void swap (int &, int &);
        a = 10; b = 20;
          clrscr ( );
          swap (a,b);
   cout << "a=" <<a<<"b =" <<b <<endl;
          getch ( );
              }
```

```
void swap (int &a1, int &b1)
        {
          int t;
                t = a1;
                a1=b1;
                b1= t;
              }
```

The output of above program is:

```
a = 10, b = 20
```

By the above example we can say that we pass argument as a call by value then any change in formal parameter does not effect on the actual parameter but if we pass argument as a pass by address or pass by reference then any change in formal parameter effect on actual parameter also.

14.11 POINTER AND STRUCTURE

A pointer to structure is defined as follows

```
structure - name * pointer - variable;
```

After this the address of any structure variable is assigned to pointer variable as follows:

```
pointer - variable = & structure - variable;
```

for example:

1.
```
struct A { int a; float b;}
           A a1;
           A *p;
           p = & a1
```

But note that a1 must be A type structure because p is point to A type structure

1.
```
struct A {int a; float b;};
struct B {char a, float b; };
    A *p;
    B a1;
P = & a1;   //wrong
```

The statement p = &a1; is wrong because a1 is B type structure while p points to A type structure. The next point is through pointer how we can access the structure variable.

p → member of structure

1.
```
structure A {int x; float y;};
A a1;
```

```
A   *p;
p = & a1              //now p point to a1 structure
p→x = 10;            //equal to a1.x =10
p→y = 20;            //equal to a1.y = 20
```

If we pass structure variable to function that is call by value but if we pass address of structure that is pass by address

Example 14.11

```
#include <iostream.h>
#include <conio.h>
#include <string.h>
   struct employee
      {
         char name [20];
         int age;
         long int salary;
      };
 void main ( )
{
  void modify (employee *);
   void output (employee);
   clrscr ( );
 employee a = {"Rajesh", 26,8000};
   modify (& a);
   output (a);
   getch ( )
         }
 void modify (employee *a1)
   { strcpy (a1 → name, "Noopur");
       a1 → age = 35;
          a1 → salary = 18000;
 void output (employee a2)
   {
     cout << "Name =" <<a2.name <<endl;
    cout << "Age =" <<a2.age <<endl;
    cout << "Salary =" <<a2.salary <<endl;
   }
```

The output of above program is

```
Name : Noopur
Age : 35
Salary : 18000
```

14.12 POINTER AND CLASS

Pointer can also with class like structure. That means pointer can also points to object of class like in structure pointer can point to structure variable.

Object pointer are very useful in creating objects are run time. We also use object pointer to access the public member of an object.

```
#include  <iostream.h>
#include<conio.h>
  class  student
          {
              int  rn;
             char  name  [20]
   public  :  void  getdata  (  )
                   {
                      cin  >>  rn;
                      cin  >>name;
          void  showdata  (  )
                 {
                      cout  <<  name  <<  endl;
                      cout  <<  rn<<endl;
                              };
             student  s1;
             student  *p;
                   p  =  &  s1;  //now  p  points  to  s1
             p->  getdata  (  );
             p  ->  showdata    (  )
```

In above p→ getdata ( ) is equal to s1.getdata ( ) and p→ showdata ( ) is same as s1 showdata ( ). Through pointer we can access only public member like through object but we can not access private or protected through pointer..

14.12.1 This Pointer

In C++ this is a keyword; this represents an object that invokes a member function. The address of that object called its member function this pointer is automatically set and contains the address of that object. The pointer acts as an implicit argument to all the member function.

```
class xyz
{
        float a;
        int b;
        - -
        - - -
        - -};
```

The private member a and b can be used directly inside any member function as follows:

```
a = 10.5;
b = 20;
```

We can also use the following statement inside any member function of xyz

this → a = 10.5;

this → b = 20;

Because the statement form is

```
a = 10.5;
b = 20;
```

therefore no need to use this. An important application of this is to return the object, it points to as follow.

```
Return *this;
```

Example 14.12

```
# include <string.h>
# include <iostream.h>
class student
    {
        int rn;
        int total;
          char name [20];
public : student (int r1, int t1, char *s)
      {
       rn = r1;
        total =t1;
        strcpy (name, s ); }
        student ( ) { }
void output ( ) {cout << "Roll No" <<rn<<endl;
```

```
                    cout <<"Total Marks"<,total<,endl;
                    cout << "Name"<,Name<,endl;
        students & students : : topper (student & st)
                  { if (st.total > total)
                              return st;
                        else
                    return *this;
                  }
                 };
void main ( )
  {
    student s1 (5, 450, "Nitin");
    student s2 (6, 425. "Dheeraj");
    student s3;
   student s4 (7, 500, "Sneha");
   s3 = s1.topper (s2);
    clrscr ( );
   cout << "Topper in s1 and s2 is :" <<endl;
   s3.output ( );
   s3 = s1.topper (s4);
   cout << "Topper in s1 and s4 is :" <<endl;
   s3.output ( );
   getch ( );
       }
```

The output of above s1 and s2 is:

Topper in s1 and s2 is: Roll no. 5 Total Marks 450
Name Nitin
Topper in s1 and s4 is: Roll no. 7
Total marks 500
Name Sneha

14.12.2 Pointer to Derived Classes

Pointer to object class is type compatible with pointer to object of a derived class.

```
class base1
 {- - - -}
class drive1 : public base1
 {- - - -};
   base *p;
   base1 b1;
   derive1 d1;
   p = &b1;
   p = &d1;
```

In the above statement the statement p = &d1 is also valid because the pointer of base is type compatible to derive class.

14.12.3 Dynamic Constructor

The constructor can also used to allocate memory while creating objects. Allocating of to objects at the time of their construction is possible by dynamic constructor.

For example we are creating a matrix dynamically.

Note that pointer means pointer to array i.e pointer to matrix (two dimensional array)

```
int   **p;
```

now p is pointer to matrix and we can create the space as follows.

```
p  =  new  int  *  [r];
```

Where r is any integer value. This statement creates an array of pointer and assigns that to p. New is a keyword in C++ used for creating space. Now with the following statement we can create space for each row as follows.

```
for  (int  i  =  0;  I  <  =  (r-1);  i++)
          p[i]  =  new  int   [ c];
```

The statement → p[i] = new int (c); is execute r times therefore this create space for r row and each space length is equal to space for c int type elements.

Note that the new is a keyword in C++ by using which we can create space for a variable.

The format of new is:

```
new  x;
```

Example 14.13

```
#  include  <iostream  .h>
#  include  <conio.h>
class  matrix
      {
          int  **p;
          int  row;
          int  col;
   public  :  matrix  (int  r,  int  c);
   void  input  (int  i,  int  j,  int  v);
   int  &  output  (int  i,  int  j);
 matrix  :  :  matrix  (int  r,  int  c)
      {
```

```
        row = r;
        col = c;
        p = new int * [row];
    for (int k =0; k <=(row-1); k++)
      p[k] = new int [col]; }
  void matrix : : input (int i, int j, int v)
         {
            p [i] [j] = v;
         }
  int & matrix : : output (int i, int j)
        {
          return p [i] [j];
        }
  void main ( )
         {
        matrix m1 [2] [3];
          matrix m2 [2] [2];
          int i, j, value;
          clrscr ( );
  cout << "Enter element for matrix m1"<<endl;
        for (i = 0; i < = 1; i++)
          for (j = 0; j < = 2; j++)
          {
             cin >> value;
             m1.input (i,j, value);
             cout <<endl;
                 }
  cout << "Enter element for matrix m2"<<endl;
        for (i = 0; i < = 1; i++)
        for (j = 0; j < = 2; j++)
          {
             cin >> value;
             m2.input (i,j, value);
             cout <<endl;
             }
  cout << "matrix m1 is" <<endl;
     for (i = 0; i < = 1; i++)
```

```
{ for (j = 0; j < = 2; j++)
            cout <<m1.output (i,j) << '\t';
            cout <<endl;
        cout << "Matrix m2 is" <<endl;
    for (i =0; i < = 1; i++)
        { for (j = 0; j < = 1; j++)
                cout << m2.output (i,j) <<'\t';
  cout <<endl;
        }
  getch ( );
        }
```

The sample output of above program is:

```
Enter element for matrix m1
4
5
6
7
8
9
Enter element for matrix m2
1
2
3
4
Matrix m1 is
4   5   6
7   8   9
Matrix m2 is
    1 2
    3 4
```

14.13 MEMORY MANAGEMENT THROUGH POINTER

If we create an array as follows:

```
int a [100]
```

Then compiler reserve 100 space for array a, but suppose we want to create space for array at the run time. Then without using pointer we can not do this.

In C++ we know that array is finite collection of same type of element that means the size of array must be defined at the time of declaration i.e we can not do following.

```
int a [size]
cin >> size;
```

The size of array must be constant which value is defined before declaration of array size is integer value.

But suppose we want to create a list but we don't know how many element in then with the help of pointer we can do.

In C++ **new** operator can create space dynamically i.e at the run time, and similarly **delete** operator is also available which release the memory taken by variable and return memory to operating system. With the help of new and delete we can manage the memory.

There are other function by which we can create space in memory **malloc ( ) and calloc ( ).**

If space is created variable at compile time that approach is known as **Static.** If space is created at run time for a variable that is called dynamic.

Solved Exercises

Exercise 1. Write a program to copy one string to other string using pointer

```
#include <iostream.h>
#include <conio.h>
void main (void)
     {
          static int a [2] [3] = { {11,12,13}
                                             {14,15,16}};
  int *ptr;
  int i, j,n,m,temp;
 n =  2;
 m = 3;
 cout << "Contents of the array" <<endl;
 for (i = 0; i <=n-1; ++i) {
 for (j =0; j <=m-1; ++j) {
 temp = *(*(a+i)+j);
 cout <<temp<<'\t';
   }
  cout <<endl;
   }
 getche ( );
}
```

Output of the above program is"

Contents of array
11 12 13
14 15 16

Exercise 2. **Write a program to declare a class person with two variable name and age. Function greater takes single argument and return object with greater age else the this pointer returns reference of the object which is used to invoke the greater function**

```
# include < iostream.h>
# include <string.h>
#include <conio.h>
class person
    {
    char name [20];
    float age;
  public :
    person (char *s, float a)
   {
    strcpy (name,s)
    age = a;
    }
    person & person : : greater (person & x)
    {
         if (x.age >=age)
         return x;
         else
         return *this;
     }
     void display (void)
      {
      cout << "Name :"<<name<<"\n"<< "age:"<<age<< "\n";
      }
     };
     void main (void)
      {
         person P1 ("ANIL", 40.50),
                               P2 (" MAHENDER", 29.0),
                               P3 (" ROHIT",48.25);
         Person P ( '\0', 0);
```

```
        P=P1.greater  (P3);
        cout  <<  "Elder  Person  is:"     //P3.greater  (P1)
    P.display  (  );
    P=P1.greater  (P2);  //P2.greater  (P1)
    cout  <<  "Elder  person  is:\n";
    P.display (  );
    getche  (  );
    }
```

Output of above program is:

Elder person is :
Name : ROHIT
Age : 48.25
Elder Person is :
Name : ANIL
Age: 48.5

Descriptive Questions

1. What pointer to void? Explain pointer in brief?
2. Explain pointer arithmetic?
3. Explain relation between array and pointer.
4. How array of pointer created?
5. What is difference between pointer to pointer and array to pointer explain?
6. Explain pointer to function. What do you mean by call by value and call by reference?
7. Explain the following (*i*) new (*ii*) Delete.
8. What is pointer? Explain use of pointer.
9. How can you concatenate two strings?
10. What does this pointer point to?

Exercises

1. Program to find larger of two given numbers.
2. Program to swap values of to given integer variables.
3. Program to encrypt a given string using an encryption technique.
4. Program to store roll-numbers and marks of some student in dynamically created two parallel arrays.
5. Program to create a copy of an array using pointer.
6. Program to search for memory address integer in an array. If the number exists in the array, its memory address is returned otherwise NULL is returned.
7. Program to obtain address of minimum value of a given array.

8. Program to create a copy of a given string.
9. Program to search for a given chapter inside a given string. If the character is found in the string, the character onwards.
10. Program to exchange position of string stored in an array.
11. Program to check presence of a substring in main string using printers.
12. Program to reserve the contents of an array of pointer.
13. Program to obtain sum of number pointed by first given *n* pointer in a pointer array.
14. Program to change each negative element of an array with its absolute value.
15. Program to replace a substring with another substring in a given string.
16. Program to create an array containing some values whose pointer are passed in it the form of a pointer-array.
17. Program to concatenate two string using pointers.
18. Program to sort an array using pointer, applying BUBBLE SORT.
19. Program to sort an array using pointer, applying SELECTION SORT.
20. Program to sort an array using pointer, applying INSERTION SORT.
21. Program to use pointer to function to calculate Σ square (*n*) or Σ cube (*n*) where square ( ) and cube ( ) are pointer to by pointers-to-functions.
22. Program to use array of pointers-to-function to invoke specific function depending upon user's choice.

    User can calculate square, cube or factorial of a number. The function square ( ), cube ( ) and factorial ( ) are pointed to by pointers-to-function.
23. Program to read student detail (roll no, name, stream, marks) using Structure pointers.
24. Program to increase salaries of employees having experience of 10 or more years by passing structure pointer to function.
25. Program to illustrate functioning of this pointer using some object of salesman class.
26. To count the number of 1 bits in a number's equivalent binary number.

15

POLYMORPHISM, VIRTUAL FUNCTION AND FRIEND FUNCTION

Polymorphism means one name many forms. The concept of function overloading has already introduced polymorphism, we say how to carry out the different processing steps by function having same message. The operator overloading allowed overloading a operator with additional task i.e., + operator is used to add any two number and concatenate two strings. Having different functions with same function name as in function overloading and choosing the overload member function by matching argument (both type of data) during compilation time is called **early binding or static binding**. During compilation determines which function is used based on the parameters passed to the function or functions return type. With early binding one can achieve greater efficiency as function calls are faster as information necessary to call the function are hard coded.

15.1 POLYMORPHISM

Polymorphism is very important feature of object oriented programming. **Polymorphism means one name, multiple forms.** We have already studied the concept of operator overloading. It is also a part of polymorphism. Similarly we have studied the constructor overloading that is also part of polymorphism.

Because constructor is a function that means function overloading is possible. The following example also implements concept of polymorphism through function overloading.

Example 15.1

```
# include <iostream.h>
# include <conio.h>
void area (float r);
void area (float l; float b);
void main ( )
    { float r1, l1,b1;
        clrscr ( );
cout << "Enter value of r1:";
cout <<r1;
cout <<"Enter value of l1:";
```

```
cout <<b1;
cout << "Area of circle is "<<endl;
area (r1);
cout << "Area of rectangle is "<<endl;
area (l1, b1);
getch ( );
  }
void area  (float r)
  { float a = 3.14 * r* r;
    cout << "Area =" <<a<<endl;
       }
     void area (float l, float b)
         {
              float a1 = l * b;
              cout << "Area =" <<a1<<endl;
                      }
```

The sample output of the above program

Enter value of r1 :2
Enter value of r2 : 4
Enter value of r3 : 6
Area of circle is
Area = 12.56
Area of of rectangle is
Area = 24

In the above program two functions have same name but question is how compiler differentiate these two. In C++ compiler differentiate these two by argument. In one area function there is only one argument which is float type but in second area function there are two arguments both are float type.

In any program has two functions both have same name and number of argument is also same then compiler differentiate these by type of argument.

Example 15.2

```
 # include <iostream.h>
 # include <conio.h>
void line (char f );
void line  (int c);
void main ( )
```

```
{ int c1;
        char   f1;
        clrscr  ( );
        cout  <<  "Enter  an  integer  number:";
        cin  >>  c1;
        cout  <<  "Enter  a  character";
        cin  >>  f1;
  cout  <<  "Line  by  integer  number"<<endl;
     line  (c1);
  cout  <<  "Line  by  character"  <<endl;
     line  (c1);
     getch  ( );
          }
void  line  (char  f)
  {  for  (int  i  =  1;  i  <=1;  i<  =  4;  i++)
     cout  <<  f;
        }
void  line  (int  c)
   {  for  (int  j  =  1;  j  =  1;  j  <  =  4;  j++)
   cout  <<  c;
        }
```

Output of the above program is:

```
Enter an integer number : 2
Enter a character : a
Line by integer number :
2 2 2 2
Line by character :
a  a  a  a
```

We have seen overloaded member function of a class also with constructor. We know that constructor is also member function, therefore constructor overloading means member function overloading. The overloaded member function is selected for invoking by matching arguments, both type and number. This information is known to the compiler at the compile time, therefore compiler, can select appropriate function. This is called **Early binding or static binding.** Early binding means that object is bound to its function call at compile time. Therefore this is known as **compile time polymorphism.**

If member function is selected while program is running then is called **runtime polymorphism**. In C++ runtime polymorphism is also possible with the help of virtual function concept. In run time polymorphism the function link with a class very late after compilation therefore this is also called **Late binding or dynamic binding.** This is called dynamic binding because function selected dynamically at runtime.

- **Compile time Polymorphism:** The compile time polymorphism can be done by
  (*a*) Operator overloading
  (*b*) Function overloading
- **Runtime Polymorphism:** The runtime polymorphism is done by
  (*a*) Virtual Function

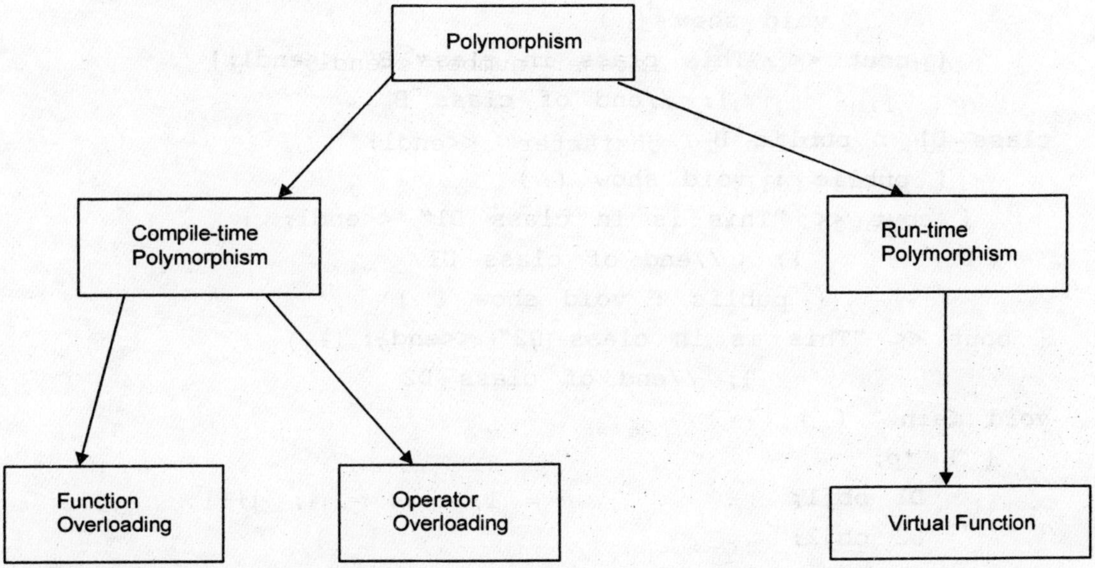

15.2 VIRTUAL FUNCTIONS

Virtual Function, one of the advance features of OOP is one that does not really exists but appears real in some of a program. This section deals with the polymorphic feature which is incorporated using the virtual functions.

The general syntax of virtual function declaration is:

```
virtual return type function_name1 (arguments);
virtual return type function_name2 (arguments);
virtual return type function_name3 (arguments);
......
......
};
```

To make a member function virtual, the keyword virtual is used in the methods which it is declared in the class definition but not in the member function definition. The keyword virtual precedes the return type of the function name. The compiler gets information from the keyword virtual function and not a conventional function declaration.

Virtual means existing in effect but not in reality. A Function is declared virtual by writing keyword virtual in front of the function header.

Example 15.3

```
# include <iostream.h>
# include <conio.h>
class B
      { public:
                  void show ( )
      { cout << "This class in class B" <<endl;}
                      }; //end of class B
class D1  : public B
      { public  : void show ( )
     { cout << "This is in class D1" <<endl; }
              };   //end of class D1
             { public : void show  ( )
{ cout << "This is in class D2" <<endl; }
                    }; //end of class D2
void main   ( )
    { B *p;
        D1 obj1;
        D2 obj2;
        B objbase;
        p = & objbase;
        p → show ( );
        p = & obj1;
        p → show ( );
        p = & obj2;
        p → show ( );
        getch ( );
          }
```

In above program p is pointer of base type. We know that the base pointer is compatible to its drive class.

Therefore the statement

```
p = & obj1;
p = & obj2;
```

The output of above program is :

This is in class B
This is in class B
This is in class B

That means p→ show ( ); statement execute every time the show function which is in class B.

When we assign address of objbase to p by statement p = & objbase to p by statement p = &objbase, then function of class B is called by the statement p → show ( ) because objbase is object of class B.

But when we assign address of obj1 to p → show ( ); statement again called the function show ( ) of class B while obj1 is object of class D1 because in class D1 there are two function both have name show ( ), one is inherited from class B and second is its own. The pointer p is actually pointer of B type by the declaration statement B*p.

Similarly after statement p = & obj2; and p→ show ( ) compiler again executes the function which is inherited from class B.

Whenever this type of situation occurs i.e derived class there are two function both have same name, one is inherited from base, second is its own, and pointer is base type. Then if we want to execute the function through pointer compiler chose the function of base (i.e., which is inherited from base). But when this situation does not occurs compiler executes the function of derived class because base type pointer is compatible with the derived class also.

If we want to execute the function of derived class in above example that is possible in C++ by virtual function concept. If we make the function show ( ) of base B as virtual function then the output of the program is different.

When a function is made virtual, C++ compiler determine which function to use at run time based on the contents of base pointer rather than the type of pointer (i.e., if base pointer has address of derived class objects then that execute the function of derived).

Note that if base pointer contains the address of a derived class objects then that is called objects points to by base pointer.

Example 15.4

```
# include <iostream.h>
# include <conio.h>
class B
      {
        public :
           virtual void show ( )
{ cout << "This is in class B" <<endl; }
                            }; //end of class B
class D1 : public B
         { public : void show ( )
  { cout << "This is in class D1" <<endl;}
              }; //end of class D1
  class D2 : public B
           { public : void show ( )
                { cout << "This is in class D2" <<endl;}
                  }; //end of class D2
                        void main ( )
```

```
{ B*p;
    D1. obj1;
    D2.obj2;
    B objbase;
    p = & objbase;
    p-> show ( );
      p = & obj1;
      p -> show ( );
      p = & obj2;
      p-> show ( );
      getch ( );
          }
```

The output of the program is :

This is in class B
This is in class D1
This is in class D2

In the above program the member function of class B i.e., show ( ) is virtual function, therefore the output of the above program is different.

Example 15.5

```
class point {
int x;
int y;
public:
virtual int length ( );
virtual void display ( );
};
```

To make a member function virtual, the keyword virtual is used in methods while it is declared in the class definition but not in member function definition. The keyword virtual precedes the return type of the function name. The compiler gets information from keyword virtual that is a virtual function and not conventional function declaration.

Example 15.6

```
class point {
int x;
int y;
public:
```

```
virtual void display ( );
  };
virtual void point ::display ( ) //error
{
Function body
}
```

Remember that the keyword virtual should not be repeated in the definition if the definition occurs outside the class declaration. The use of a function specifier virtual in the function definition is invalid.

Example 15.7

```
class point {
int x;
int y;
public:
virtual static int length ( ); //error
 };
 int point : : length ( )
 {
 function body
  }
```

A virtual function cannot be a static member since a virtual member is always a member of a particular object in a class rather than a member of the class as a whole.

15.2.1 Late Binding

Late binding means selecting function during the execution. Though late binding requires some overhead it provides increased power and flexibility. The late binding is implemented through virtual function as a result we have to declare an object of a class either as a pointer to a class or reference to a class

Example 15.8

```
    class base {
        private:
        int x;
        float y;
        public:
        virtual void display ( );
          int sum ( );
            };
          class derived: public base A
```

```
{
    private:
    int x;
    float y;
    public:
    void display ( ); //virtual
    int sum ( );
    };
  void main ( )
  {
    base A*ptr;
  derived objd;
   ptr = &objd;
   ptr->display ( ); //run time binding
   ptr-> sum ( ); //compile time binding
   }
```

Note that the keyword virtual is be followed by the return type of a member function if a run time is to be bound. Otherwise, the compile time binding will be effected as usual. In the above program segment, only display ( ) function has been declared as virtual in the base class, whereas the sum ( ) is non virtual. Even though the message is given from the pointer of the base class to the objects of the derived class, it will not access the sum ( ) function of the derived class as it has been declared as non virtual. The sum ( ) function compiles only the static binding.

15.2.2 Virtual Function with Inline Code Substitution

Through virtual function can be declared as an inline code, being the run time binding of the compiler, the inline code does not affect much of the programming efficiency. For inline code substitution, the compiler must get information about the function, like from where they have to be invoked etc. these must be defined during compilation time.

The general syntax of virtual function with inline code substitution.

```
class base {
private:
data members
member functions
public:
virtual inline void getdata ( );
virtual inline void display ( );
   };
void main ( )
```

```
{
        base obja;
        obja->getdata ( );
        obja->display ( );
   }
```

15.3 PURE VIRTUAL FUNCTION

A pure virtual function declared in a base class that has no definition relative to the base class. In such cases, the compiler requires each derived class to either defines the function or redeclare it as a pure virtual function. A class which contains the pure virtual function is called abstract base class i.e., that class is used for deriving other classes from it.

If we delete the body of virtual function then it is called pure virtual function.

```
# include <iostream.h>
# include <conio.h>
class B
      {
        public :
          virtual void show ( ) = 0;  //pure virtual function
{ cout << "This is in class B" <<endl; }
                        }; //end of class B
   class D1 : public B
            { public : void show ( )
  { cout << "This is in class D1" <<endl;}
            }; //end of class D1
  class D2 : public B
            {public: void show ( )
            { cout << "This is in class D2" <<endl;}
                       }; //end of class D2
void main ( )
   { B*p;
        D1. obj1;
        D2.obj2;
        B objbase;
        p = & objbase;
        p-> show ( );
          p = & obj1;
          p -> show ( );
```

```
        p  =  &  obj2;
         p->  show  (  );
         getch  (  );
              }
```

When a virtual function is declared within the class declaration itself. The virtual function may be equated to zero if it does have a function definition. Such function are also called as do-nothing function.

```
// pure virtual functions
# include <iostream.h>
class base {
private :
int  x,y;
public:
virtual  void  getdata  ( )  =  0;
virtual  void  display  ( )  =  0;
    };
class  derived  B::public  base{
data  members
member  functions
      };
```

15.4 FRIEND FUNCTION

We know that private member of a class cannot be accessed from outside the class i.e a non member function cannot access to the private data of a class. But may be in some situation one class wants to access private data of second class and second wants to access private data of first class, or may be an outside function wants to access the private data of a class. Then for solving these situations in C++ there is a concept that is called **friend function**.

If an outside function can access the private data of a class. Then that is called friendly to class.

To make outside function friendly to a class, we have to declare this function as a friend function. The friend function declares as follows.

```
class  B
          {
                member  function1;
                member  function2;
                member  function3;
```

```
        public :
            member function1;
            member function2;
            member function3;
friend return-type function-name (arg);
                        };
```

The body of function is written outside the class (i.e definition of function is written outside the class)

When the body is written the keyword friend is not used and scope resolution operator is also not used. The body of function is written as follows:

```
return-type function-name (arg)
    {
        body of function
                    }
```

Note that the friend function can be declared either in the public or private part of a class without affecting its meaning.

Example 15.9

```
# include <iostream.h>
# include <conio.h>
class sample
    { int x,
        int y;
      public :
          sample (int a, int b)
              {x = a; y = b;}
          friend int add (sample s1);
                };

 int add (sample s1)
        {return (s1.x+s1.y);}
 void main ( )
    { sample s2 ( 30,40);
        int sum;
        clrscr ( );
        sum = add (s2);
        cout << "sum of private data of object s2=";
        cout << sum<<endl;
            getch ( );
                }
```

The output of above program is

```
sum of private data object s2=70
```

Note that the friend function accessed the private data of class through dot operator, like in above example the private data of class are accessed like follow in function add ( ).

```
s1.x and s1.y;
```

The friend function is call by its name, like

```
sum = add (s2);
```

The function add ( ) is out of scope of class sample therefore it is not call like object-name. Function-name add ( ) is a friend function are not in the scope of the class in which they are defined. So the **friend function is call like normal function, not like member function of a class.**

We can make a friend function which is friend of two different classes by declaring that into both classes, any body of function is written outside the both classes as follows:

```
class A; //forward declaration
class B
    { -
          -
public :
          friend void add (B b1, A a1);
          -
          -
          };
class A
  { -
      -
public :
friend void add (B b1, A a1);
      -
      -
      };
void add (B b1, A a1)
  {
body of function }
```

In above format class A is declared before class B but the body of class A is written after class B this is necessary because within function we are using argument which is object of class A. So compiler must know that class A exists. This type of declaration is called **forward declaration**.

Example 15.10

```
# include <iostream.h>
# include <conio.h>
class sample2;
class sample1;
      { int x;
    public : sample1(int x1)
          { x = x1;}
     friend void small ( sample1 s1, sample2 s2);
                   };
      class sample2
                  { int y;
        public : sample2 (int y1)
                     { y = y1; }
        friend void small (sample1 s1, sample2 s2);
                             };
          void small (sample1 s1, sample2 s2)
                     {
                        if (s1.x < s2.y)
          cout << " The data of object s1 is small" <<endl;
            else
           cout << " The data of object s2 is small" <<endl;
                 }
            void main ( )
      {
           sample s1 (40);
           sample s2 (50);
           clrscr ( );
            small (s1,s2);
            getch ( );
```

The output will show the data object s1 is small. In above program the function small is friend to both the classes' sample1 and sample2. Therefore this can access the private data of sample 1 class and also private data of sample2 class.

Solved Exercises

Exercise 1. Write a program to demonstrate the run-time binding of the member function of a class. The same message is given to access the derived class member functions from the array of pointers. As functions are declared as virtual, the C++ compiler invokes the dynamic binding.

```
#include <iostream.h>
#include <conio.h>
class base A
public:
virtual void display ( )
   {
     cout << "one\n";
      }
      };
      class deriveB: public baseA
        {
                public:
                virtual void display ( )
                {
                  cout <<"Two\n";
                 };
                 class deriveC:public deriveB
                 {
                   public:
                   virtual void display ( ){
                   cout <<"Three\n"; }
                   };
                   void main ( )
                   {
                     //define there objects
                     baseA obja;
                     deriveB objb;
                      deriveC objc;
             baseA* ptr[3]; //define an array of pointers to base A
                      ptr [0] = &obja;
                 ptr [1] = &objb;
                 ptr [2] = &objc;
                 for (int i = 0;i<=2; i++)
          ptr[i]->display ( ); //same message for all objects
                 getche ( );
                 }
```

Output of the program is:

```
One
Two
Three
```

Exercise 2. Write a program to demonstrate how to define virtual functions with inline code substitution for run time binding of the member functions of a class. The programs have two such as student and physique. The functions getdata ( ) and display ( ) are declared virtual inline in the class student the sanctions the getdata ( ) and display ( ) functions of class physique are invoked with help of pointer in main function.

```
#include<iostream.h>
#include <conio.h>
class student {
private:
int rollno;
char name[20];
public:
virtual inline void getdata ( );
virtual inline void display ( );
   };
class physique : public student {
private:
float height, weight;
public :
void getdata ( );
void display ( );
};
inline void student :: getdata ( )
  {
    cout << "\n enter roll";
    cout >>rollno;
    cout << "\n enter name";
    cin >>name;
  }
  inline void student :: display ( )
  {
  cout << "entered details for student" rollno<< "and name="<<name
    cout <<endl;
     }
    void physique ::getdata ( )
     {
        cout << "enter height of a student : \n";
```

```
cin >>height;
   cout << "enter weight of the student:\n";
   cin >> weight;
   }
   void physique: display ( )
     {
     cout << "Height weight\n";
     cout<<height<< '\t'<<weight <<endl;
     }
     void main ( )
     {
       student*ptr;
       physique obj;
       ptr = &obj;
       ptr->getdata ( );
       ptr ->display ( );
       getche ( );
     }
```

Output of the program is :

```
Enter height of student:
156
Enter weight of student:
54
Height weight
156 54
```

Exercise 3. Write a program using two classes employee and grade. The class employee is base class and the grade is derived class. The functions getdata ( ) and display ( ) are declared for both the classes. For the class employee the functions are defined with empty body or no code inside the function. The code is written for the grade class. The methods of the derived class are invoked by the pointer to the base class. Demonstrate how pure virtual function defined, declared and invoked from the object of derived class through pointer of base class.

```
#include<iostream.h>
#include<conio.h>
class employee
{
int code;
```

```
char name [20];
public:
virtual void getdata ( );
virtual void display ( );
};
class grade: public employee
{
   char grade[90];
   float salary;
public:
   void getdata ( );
   void display ( );
   };
   void employee::getdata ( )
   {
   }
   void employee ::display ( )
   {
   }
    void grade::getdata ( )
        {
         cout << "enter employee's grade:;
         cin >>grade;
         cout << "\n enter the salary";
         cin >>salary;
        }
        void grade::display ( )
        {
         cout << "Grade salary\n";
         cout <<grade<< " "<<salary<<endl;
        }
          void main ( )
          {
            employee *ptr;
            grade obj;
            ptr = &obj;
            ptr->getdata ( );
```

```
        ptr->display  ( );
            getche  ( );
        }
```

Output of the program is :

```
Enter employee's grade A
enter the salary 250000
Grade salary
  A    250000
```

Descriptive Questions

1. Explain the following (a) Run time polymorphism (b) Compile Time Polymorphism.
2. What is virtual function and what are the advantage of declaring a virtual function in a program?
3. Why do we make a virtual function pure?
4. Explain the concept of static binding and late binding with the help of example.
5. How will achieve polymorphism using keyword virtual?
6. Write a declaration for virtual function getdata ( ) that returns type void and takes one argument of type int.
7. Discuss the constructor member function cannot be virtual.
8. What is friend function?
9. How functions create friendly for two classes?
10. Explain the advantage of friend function.

Exercises

1. Write a program to calculate area of various shapes.
2. Write a program to check divisibility of two numbers. If second number is not provided, then the number should be tested for prime-ness.
3. Write program to add operation on two integers, two floats, two doubles, a double an int, float an int.
4. Write a program to obtain largest of three integers, three floats, and three double
5. Write a program to perform integer division and floating point division
6. Write a program to find sum of all elements of an integer array and a double array
7. Write a program to calculate a^b where a can be double or integer and b in integer only.
8. Write a program to implement replicate function, which in case of no parameter prints a string of 12' + 's. If a character argument is passed then it prints string of 12 such character and if an integer argument is passed then it points a string of n"*s. If both a character and integer argument are passed, it prints a string of a given character replicate given number of time.
9. Write a program to implement class hierarchy shape, circle, rectangle, square. The functions and shape is an abstract class
10. Write a program to implement following class hierarchy point, 3d shape, sphere, and cube, cuboids. The shape should be an abstract class. The function getvolume ( ) and draw ( ) are implemented virtually

11. Write a program to implement following class hierarchy, implement function virtually wherever possible Animal, Mammal, cat, lion, tiger, birds, duck.
12. Write a program which calculate the multiplication of two integer number and also calculate multiplication of two complex number use the function overloading concept.
13. Write a program which calculate the sum of following series

    (*a*) $1 + 2 + 3 + 4 + 5 + \text{------------} + n$

    (*b*) $\frac{1^2}{x^2} + \frac{2^2}{x^2} + \frac{3^2}{x^2} + ------ + \frac{n^2}{x^2} +$
14. Write a program which calculate arc of circle, area of rectangle, area of triangle using virtual function
15. Write a program which calculates the addition of private fdata of a class use friend function.
16. Write a program which calculates the following function:

    (*a*) $f(x) = 2x^2 + 3x + 5$

    (*b*) $f(x) = 3x^4 + b$

    (*c*) $f(x) = 4x^4 + 7x^3 + 9$

    (*d*) $f(x) = 8x^5 + 7x^4 + 3x^3 + 5$
17. There are two class 'student and academic'. The class academic is derived from class student. The two member function getdata and display are defined for both the classes. *obj is defined for class student, the address of which is stored in the object of class academic. The functions getdata ( ) and display ( ) of student class are invoked by the pointer to the class. Illustrate the static binding of the member function of a class.
18. Write a program using two classes 'student and academic'. The class academic is derived from student. Student function has two virtual functions getdata ( ) and display ( ). The pointer for the student class is defined and objects for academic class are created. The pointer is assigned the address of the object and function of derived class is invoked by pointer to student.
19. Write a program to access member function with array of pointer, take three classes' student, academic and array of physique. The classes' academic and physique are derived from the class student. In main program an array of pointer *ptr[3] is declared. The 0th element of pointer array is assigned the address of object of the class academic and first element is assigned the address of the object of the class physique. The functions of the academic and physique classes are called with the respective pointers.
20. A publication company market both books and audio-cassette. Create a class publication that shows the title and price of the publication. Derive two classes' book which adds a page count and type which adds playing time in minutes. These three classes should have a getdata () function to get its data from the user and display function to display its data. Write main () program that creates an array of pointers to publication. In a loop, ask the user for data about a particular book or tape and use new to create an object of type book or tape to hold the data. Put the pointer to the data for all books and tapes, display the entire details of books and tapes entered using the following program statement.

    ```
    pubarr[i]->putdata ( );
    ```

    to display the data from each object on the array.

16

FILES AND STREAMS

As we know, every program takes some data as input and generates the required data as output. Therefore it is essential to know how to provide input data and how to produce the result of desired form. In the previous chapter we have used cin and cout with the insertion and extraction operator. C++ provides I/O functions, these are advanced feature of C++. The C++ programmer note that approach to disk I/O used in C++ is quite different from that in C. The old C functions, such as **fread ( ) and fwrite ( )**, will still work in C++, but they are not so well suited to the object-oriented environment.

16.1 STREAM

Stream is a general name given to flow of data. In C++ there are different types of stream. Each stream is associated with a particular class, which contains member function and definition for dealing with file. The stream class hierarchy means how the different streams are linked with each other i.e., how they are derived from other.

By the above hierarchy the class iostram is derived from both classes istream and ostream are derived from ios. Similarly the class fstream is derived from iostream and fstreambase. Generally two main header files are used iostream.h and fstream.h, the classes used for input to the video display and keyboard are declared in the header file iostream.h and the classes used for disk file input output in fstream.h.

In the iostream.h following classes are declared:

1. ios
2. istream
3. ostream
4. streambuf
5. iostream
6. istream withassign
7. ostrem withassign

In the fstream.h following classes are declared:

1. fstreambase
2. filebuf
3. ifstream

4. ofstream
5. fstream
6. iostream withassign
7. ostream withassign

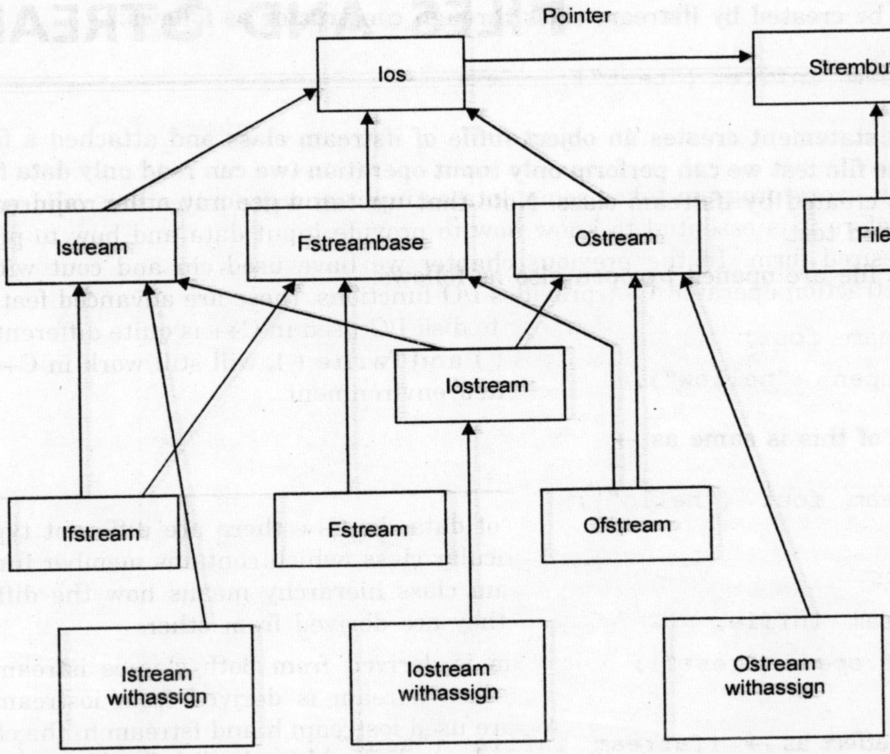

When we include the header file fstream.h header file in our program then there is no need to include iostream.h header file. Because all the classes which are in fstream.h they are derived from classes which are in iostream.h therefore we can use all the functions of these classes also.

16.2 OPERATION WITH CLASS

First we will see how files are opened and closed. A file can be defined by following class ifstream, ofstream, fstream, all these are defined in fstream.h header file.

If a file declared by ifstream class then that can be used for reading from file purpose.

If a file is declared by ofstream class then that can be used for only writing onto file purpose.

If a file is declared by fstream class then that can be used for both reading and writing purpose.

16.2.1 Opening a File

A file can be created by constructor as follows:

```
ofstream fout ("hellow");
```

The above statement creates an object fout we can give other name also of stream class and this object with a file hello we can give any other valid name. The operating system takes the name of file hello. But in file hello we can only write the data because this is created by ofstream class.

A file can be created by ifstream class through constructor as follows:

```
ifstream infile ("test");
```

The above statement creates an object infile of ifstream class and attached a file test with this. In the file test we can perform only input operation (we can read only data from it) because this is created by ifstream class. Note that we can write any other valid name in place of infile and test.

The above file are opened by open also as follows:

```
 ofsream fout;
fout.open ("hellow");
```

The effect of this is same as →

```
ofstream fout ("hello");
```

and

```
ifstream infile;
infile.open ("test");
```

has same effect as → `ifstream infile ("test");`

Note: open is keyword in C++.

16.2.2 Closing a File

A file is closed as follows:

Example

1. `fout.close ( );`
2. `infile.close ( );`

i.e., the general syntax is

```
file_object _name.close ( );
```

In the above two example fout and infile both are file_object_name.

16.2.3 Reading and Writing String

By using the insertion and extraction operator string data can be write and read. See the following example.

Example 16.1 (*a*)

```
# include <fstream.h>
void main  ( )
  { ofstream outfile ("result");
     outfile << "Sneha"  <<\n";
     outfile << "marks"  <<\n";
     outfile << "450" << "\n";
     outfile.close  ( );
     }
```

The above program stores Sneha, marks and 450 onto file result on the separate line. For reading above file result the following code is written.

(*b*)

```
# include <fstream.h>
void main  ( )
    { ifstream infile ("result");
     char name [80], name [80], name2 [80];
    infile >> name; infile >> name1;
    infile >>name 2;
   cout << name << name1 << name2 <<endl;
    infile.close  ( );
         }
```

The program (*b*) is read the first line of file store into name, read second line store into name1, read third line store into name2.

The program (*b*) can be written as follows also:

```
# include <fstream.h>
void main  ( )
    {
     char name [80];
      ifstream infile ("result");
      while (infile)
       {
         infile.getline (name, 80);
         cout << name << endl;
                }
          }
```

The above program reads a line by getline ( ) function. The while loop execute upto end of file.

16.2.4 Reading and Writing Character

The character can be written on the file or read from file by using put ( ) and get ( ) function.

Example 16.2 (*a*)

```
# include < fstream.h>
void main  ( )
      {
            char  c;
          ofstream  outfile  ("test");
for  (int  i  =1;  i  < =  16;  i++)
      {  cout  <<  "Enter  a  character:";
          cin  >>  c;
          outfile.put  (c);
                }
          outfile.close  (  );
                }
```

The above program reads 16 characters and stores in file test.

For reading the file test character by character following program is written:

(*b*)

```
# include <fstream.h>
void main  (  )
    {   char  c;
         ifstream  infile  ("test");
         while  (infile)
              {  infile.get  (c)  ;
                   cout  <<  c  <<  endl;
                        }
              }
```

16.2.5 Multiple File with Same Stream

In the following files open by open ( ) function and same stream object is used for all the files.

Example 16.3

In the program the file open ( ) function and same stream object is used for all the files.

```
# include <fstram.h>
void main ( )
  {
    ofstream outfile;
      outfile.open ("file1");
      outfile.open ("file1");
      outfile << "Kamlesh yadav" << "\n";
      outfile << "Dheeraj yadav" << "\n";
      outfile.close ( );
      outfile.open ("File2");
      outfile << "Rajesh Panday" <<"\n";
              outfile.close ( );
// reading file
char line [80];
ifstream infile;
infile.open ("file1");
cout << "The contents of file 1" <<endl;
      while (infile)
            { infile.getline (line, 80);
                  cout << line << endl;
                  }
        infile.open ("file2");
        cout << "The contents of file2" << endl;
              while (infile)
                  { infile.getline (line, 80);
                  cout << line << endl; }
                      }
```

16.2.6 File Modes

We know that constructors and open ( ) both can be used to open a existing file as well as to create a new file.

The open ( ) function is in general form is:

```
file stream object. Open ("filename", mode);
```

The second argument mode specifies the purpose for which the file is opened. The mode is following type:

Mode	Meaning
1. ios ::app	Append to end of file
2. ios : : atc	Go to end of file on opening
3. ios : : in	Open file for reading
4. ios : : out	Open file for writing only
5. ios : : binary	Binary file
6. ios : : trunk	Delete contents of file if it exists
7. ios : : no create	Open file if exist otherwise open fails
8. ios : : no replace	Open file if does not exist otherwise open files

Note: When file create by stream ifstream and ofstream then the mode is default. In the ofstream the default mode is ios::out and in case of ifstream the default mode is ios : : in

The two modes can be combined also by bitwise or operator as follows:

```
fstream  fout;
fout.open  ("test",  ios  :  :  app  |  ios  :  :nocreate);
```

This opens the file in the append mode but open fails if file does not exist.

16.2.7 File Pointer and their Manipulator

Each file has two pointers one is called input pointer and second is output pointer. The input pointer is called get pointer and output pointer is called put pointer.

When input and output operation takes place, the appropriate pointer is automatically set according to mode.

For example when we open a file in reading mode file pointer is automatically set to start of file. And when we open a file in appended mode the file pointer is automatically set at the end of file.

In C++ there are some manipulators by which we can control the movement of pointer. The available manipulator in C++ is:

1. seekg ( )
2. seekp ( )
3. tellg ( )
4. tellp ( )

1. Seekg ( )

This move gets pointer *i.e.*, input pointer to specific location.

For example

```
infile.seekg  (5);
```

Move the file pointer to the byte number 5 from starting point.

2. **Seekp ( ): This move puts pointer (output pointer) to specific location for example:**

```
outfile.seekp (5);
```

3. **tellg ( ): This gives the current position of get pointer (input pointer)**

4. **tellp ( ): This gives the current position of put pointer (output pointer)**

For example

```
ofstream fileout;
fileout.open ("test", ios : : app);
int length = fileout.tellp ( );
```

By the above statement in length, the total number byte of files is assigned. Because file opened in append mode that are file pointer is at last of file.

16.2.8 Reading and Writing Object

The object of a class can be read and written in a file as follows:

Example 16.4

```
# include <fstream.h>
class student
        { protected :
                        char name [20];
                        int rn;
                public :
                      void getdata ( )
                    { cout << "Enter name :" cin >>name
         cout <<"Enter roll no" ; cin >>rn;
                                    }
         void showdata ( )
                 { cout << "Name =" << name << "\n";
              cout << "Roll no. =" <<rn<< "\n";
                             };
              void main ( )
                   { student std;
                          fstream file;
              file.open ("test.dat", ios : : out);
         file (int i =1; i < = 4; i++)
```

```
            {cout << "student data" << "\n";
               std.getdata  (  );
               file.write (  (char*)  & std,  sizeof  (std))
                         }
                  file.close  (  );
                  file.open  ("test.dat",  ios  :  :in);
                  file.read  ((char*)  & std,  sizeof  (std));
                        while  (!file.eof  (  ))
                              {
                                 cout  <<  "student  is"  <<  "\n";
                                 std.showdata  (  );
                          file.read  ((char*)  &  std,  sizeof  (std));
                              }
                                         }
```

The above program stores four objects to into and then print all. In above program read ( ) and write ( ) function are used and eof ( ) function is also used. The format of read is-

```
read  ((char*)  & name of object,  sizeof  (name of object));
```

The format of write is

```
write  ((char  *)  & name of object,  sizeof  (name of object));
```

The eof ( ) is a function, the while loop quit on endof file in above example.

Example 16.5

```
# include <fstream.h>
class  student
      { protected  :
                        char  name  [20];
                          int  rn;
          public  :
                    void  getdata  (  )
                       {cout  <<  "Enter  name";
                          cin  >>  name;
                          cout  <<  "Enter  roll  no";
                          cin  >>rn;
                void  showdata  (  )
        {  cout  <<  "Name  ="  <<name  <<  "\n"
           cout  <<  "Roll  no="  <<rn  <<"\n";
```

```
            }
        };
void main ( ).
    {
        student std;
        fstream file;
        file.open ("result.dat", ios : : out);
        for (int i =1; i <=4; i++)
        {
    cout << "Enter data" << "\n";
    std.getdata ( );
    file.read ((char *) &std, sizeof (std));
            }
        file.close ( );
    file.open ("result.dat", ios : : in);
        file.seekg (0, ios : :end);
        int length = file.tellg ( );
        int n = length/sizeof (std);
        int m;
        cout << "The total student in file =" <<n<<"\n";
        cout << "Enter which no student you want to read";
        cin>>m;
        int position = (m-1) * sizeof (std);
        file.seekg (position)
          file.read ((char *) & std, sizeof (std));
                std.showdata ( );
                    }
```

The above program reads four objects and stores into file, then print the total student number in file. After that read an integer number then that student which stores in this number in file. After this print that student onto screen.

In the seekp ( ) and seekg ( ) we can give argument also like in above program. The statement

```
file.seekg (o, ios : : end);
```

Means the file pointer (input pointer go to zero byte from end of file *i.e.*, go to at last). The first argument in seekg is called offset and second argument is tell about the position from where pointer move. This can be three types.

1. ios : : end
2. ios : : beg
3. ios : : cur

ios : : beg means from start of file

ios : : cur means from current position of file.

ios : : end means from end of file.

The offset is negative also as follows-

file.seekg(-5, ios : :cur);

This statement means file pointer move five byte back from current position.

Similarly, l above concepts are same for seekp();

16.2.9 Error Handling in File

In c++ for handling error in file operation following functions is available:

1. eof ( )
2. fail ( )
3. bad ( )
4. good ( )

1. **eof ( ):** This function return true if end of file encountered while reading otherwise return false.
2. **fail ( ):** This function return true when an input and output operation has failed otherwise return false.
3. **bad ( ):** Return true if no error occurred otherwise false.
4. **good ( ):** Return true if no error occurred otherwise false.

These functions are used as follows:

```
f stream file;
file.open ("Add", ios : :in);
if (file.eof ( )){-----}
if (file.fail ( )) {-----}
if (file.bad ( ) {-----}
                                    etc
```

16.2.10 Binary File

When we open a file in binary mode that is called binary file. When a file is in binary mode the data stored is different from the character format. For example suppose we have a int value. In binary format int takes two byte to store a value but in character format int takes space according to character in value.

Example

Suppose we have integer value 240 then the character format and binary format are:

2	4	0
1st byte	2nd byte	3rd byte

Binary format:

binary of 240
2 byte

Solved Exercises

Exercise 1. Write a program for reading and writing multiple objects in files

```
# include <fstream.h>
class employees
  {
   protected:
   int empno;
   char name [25];
   char dept [25];
   char desig [25];
   double basic;
   double deds;
   public:
   void getdata(void)
     {
    cout <<endl << "enter empno :";cin>>empno;
    cout <<endl << "enter empname :"cin >>name;
    cout <<endl << "enter department :"cin>>dept;
    cout <<endl << "enter designation":cin >>design;
    cout <<endl << "enter basic pay";cin >>basic;
    cout <<endl << "enter deductions";cin>>deds;
     }
     void showdata(void)
     {
    cout<<endl<< "employee number:"<<empno;
     cout<<endl<< "empname:"<<name;
     cout<<endl<< "department:"<<dept;
     cout<<endl<< "designation:"<<design;
     cout<<endl<< "basic pay"<<basic;
```

```
cout<<endl<< "deductions:<<deds;
}
};
void main(void)
{
char ch;
employees emp;
fstream file;
file.open("pay.fil", ios::applios::outlios::in);
do
{
cout << "enter employee data"<<endl;
emp.getdata ( );
file.write(char*)&emp,sizeof(emp));
cout<<endl<<"any more employees? (y/n)"<<endl;
cin>>ch;
}
while(ch= ='y');
file.seekg(0);
file.red((char*)&emp,sizeof(emp));
while(!file.eof())
{ cout<<endl<<"employee file:"<<endl;
played only
after loop
emp.showdata();
file.read((char*)&emp,sizeof(emp));
}
}
employee file:
employee number: 1
empname: Anjulata
department: finance control
designation: lecturer
basic pay:10000.00
deductions:1000.0C
```

16.3 TEMPLATES AND EXCEPTION HANDLING

Templates are very important feature. By using templates we can define generic classes both classes and function.

16.3.1 Class Template

For example, suppose we want to create a class which has three private data all are int type. And the classes has two member function one get the data from keyboard and second perform the addition of two private data, store the result into third private data, then print the result. The class looks as follows:

```
class  sample
   {
      private  :  int  a,  b,  c;
      public  :  void  getdata  (  );
                           void  sum  (  );
                                 };
      void  sample  :  :  getdata  (  )
            {
            cout  <<  "Enter  first  number:";
            cin  >>a;
            cout  <<  "Enter  second  number:";
            cin  >>b;
                 }
            void  sample  :  :  sum  (  )
                {
                 c=a+b;
                 cout  <<  "sum="  <<C<<endl;
                 }
```

But suppose we want to perform same operation with float type data then what we do? The solution is we have to change the type of private data a,b and c from int to float, or design a new class which private data are float type. But with the help of templates we can solve problem. Because template facility allows the data type to be specified as a parameter i.e., We can design generic classes.

The template class for above problem looks as:

```
templates  <class  T>
class  sample
        {  private  :  T  a,  b,  c;
```

```
                public : void getdata ( );
                                    void sum ( );
                                          };
                    templates <class T>
                    void sample <T> : :getdata ( )
                    {
                        cout << "Enter first number:";
                        cin >>a;
            cout << "Enter second number:";
            cin >>b;
            void sample <T> : : sum ( )
                {
                  c = a + b;
                    cout << "sum =" <<c<<endl;
```

Now the objects of template class is declared as follows:

```
sample <int>s1;
```

The object s1 works like same as the object of class in which a,b and c are int type. The call procedure for member function is also same as normal class.

If we declare the object of template class as follows:

```
sample <float> s2;
```

The object s2 works like the object of class in which a, b and c are float type. That means only one template class is used for creating such different type of object. Now we can write the general format template class that looks as:

```
template <class T>
class classname
   {
     ---
     ---
     ---
     ---
       };
```

If we write the member function body outside the class then declaration is:

```
template <class T>
class classname
    {
        ---
        ---
        ---
        };
```

Body of member function is written as follows:

```
template <class T>
return type class name <T> : : function name1 (arg)
            {
                body of function1
                    }
return type classname <T> : : function name2 (arg)
                {
                    body of function 2
                    }

return type classname <T> : : function name n (arg)
                    {
                        body of function n
                        }
```

Note that class member type can be written T whenever appropriate.

The object of template class are created as follows:

```
class name <data type> object name (arg);
```

The arg are used when constructor are in template class otherwise skipped. Note that template is keyword in C++.

Example 16.6

```
#includes <iostream.h>
#include <conio.h>
template <class T>
class add
    {
      private : T a, b;
```

```
        public :
    void getdata ( )
            {
                cout << "Enter first data =";
              cin >>a;
              cout << "Enter second data =";
              cin >>b;
          }
          t sum ( )
            { T C;
                  c = a + b;
                  return ( c);
              }
            };
    void main ( )
        {
          add <int> obj1;
          add <float> obj2;
          cout << "Enter integer number "<<endı;
          obj1.getdata ( );
          cout << "sum of integer data="<<obj1.sum ( );
          cout <<endl;
    cout << "Enter float type data" <<endl;
        obj.getdata ( );
    cout << "sum of float type data=" <<obj2.sum ( );
        cout << endl;
          getch ( );
            }
```

Output of the program is :

```
Enter integer number
Enter first data = 6
Enter second data = 7
Sum of integer data = 11
Enter float type data
Enter first data = 7.5
Enter second data = 8.3
Sum of float type data = 15.8
```

Example 16.7

```
# include <iostream.h>
# include <conio.h>
template <class T>
class sample
      {
            private : T a, b;
            public : sample (T a1, Tb1)
      { a= a1; b=b1; }
t small ( )
    {
      if (a<b) return (a);
     else return (b);
      }
  };
void main ( )
  {
     sample <int> obj1 (10,5);
cout << "smaller is in integer=" <<obj1.small ( );
cout <<endl;
cout << "smaller in float =" <<obj2.small ( );
cout <<endl;
     getch ( );
       }
```

The output of above program is:

Smaller is in integer = 5
Smaller in float = 10.5

16.4 FUNCTION TEMPLATE

Similar to class template, the function template will be used to create a family of function with different type. The function template creates as follows:

```
template <class t>
return_type function_name (arg)
      {
            body of  function the type t
               is used whenever appropriate
                     }
```

Example 16.8

Write a function which swap two numbers by function template call this into main program.

```
# include <iostream.h>
# include <conio.h>
template <class t>
void swap (t &a, t &b);
void swap (float &a1, float &b1);
void swap (char &a1, char &b1);
void main ( )
         { int i1, i2;
         float f1, f2;
         char c1,c2;
cout << "Enter first integer"; cin>>i1;
cout << "Enter second integer"; cin>>i2;
cout << "Enter first float no"; cin>>f1;
cout << "Enter second float no"; cin>>f2;
cout << "Enter first character no"; cin>>c1;
cout << "Enter first integer"; cin>>c2;
swap (i1, i2);
cout << "After swapping the integer no"<<endl;
cout << "first no="<<i1<<endl;
cout << "second no="<<i2<<endl;
swap (f1, f2);
cout << "After swapping the float no"<<endl;
cout << "first no ="<<f1<<endl;
cout << "second no="<<f2<<endl;
swap(c1,c2);
cout << "After swapping the char"<<endl;
cout << "first no="<<c1<<endl;
cout << "second no="<<c2<<endl;
  getch ( );
      }
```

Output of the above program is:

Enter first integer : 4
Enter Second integer : 5
Enter first float no : 5.7
Enter second float no : 8.7
Enter first character no a
Enter second character no b
After swapping the integer no
first no = 5
second no = 4

16.5 EXCEPTION HANDLING

In C++ there is some keyword by using which the exception (*i.e.*, unusual condition) can be handled.

These keywords are:

(*a*) try

(*b*) throw

(*c*) catch

These keyword try, throws and catch are implemented as follows:

(1) When an error condition occurs, the function throws an expression. The syntax of a throw expression is :

```
throw expression;
```

Example 16.9

```
float divide (float dividend, float divisor)
     {
          if (divisor = = 0)
          throw "division by zero";
       else
     return dividend/divisor;
          }
```

The try and catch block are used as follows:

```
try
  {
    call the function
  }
  catch (one formal argument)
  {
    take an action depending upon the exception
  }
```

Example 16.10

```
          try
               {
                 cout << "dividend/divisor="
                 cout <<divide (dividend, divisor);
                 cout << endl;
               }
```

```
catch (const char * message)
        {
            cerr << message <<endl;
        }
```

Descriptive Type Questions

1. State different input stream.
2. State different output stream.
3. Which are the different pre-defined streams?
4. What is task of width ( ) function?
5. Explain put ( ) and get ( ) function.
6. In which header file are all disk file I/O operation included?
7. Explain extraction operation with example.
8. Explain different formatted and unformatted I/O functions.
9. Which are streams in C++?
10. Write a program to display the contents of file on the screen.
11. What is file explain? Explain different file mode?
12. How we can open a file and close a file in C++?
13. Explain the following:
    (*a*) seekg
    (*b*) seekp
    (*c*) tellg
    (*d*) tellp
14. How can we read and write objects into class by read ( ) and write ( ) function in C++ ? Explain.
15. What are the three modes in which a file can be opened?
16. Explain what is template.
17. Explain how class templates are defined.
18. Explain how function templates are defined.
19. Explain what is advantage of templates.
20. Explain difference between function templates and class templates.
21. What type of function available for handling exception?
22. Explain try, catch and throws.

Exercises

1. Write program to count number of characters in a given file **abc.txt.**
2. Write a program to count the number of lines in a given file **abc.txt.**
3. Write a program to count number of vowels in a given file **abc.txt.**
4. Write a program to count uppercase, lowercase letter, digits and special symbols in a given file.

5. Write a program to append file to another.
6. Write a invert case of each character of file.
7. Write a program to merge contents of two files to third file.
8. Write a program to determine size of file in byte.
9. Write a program to maintain students data file namely **students.dat.**
10. Write a program which design a template that perform multiplication of:
    (*a*) int type data
    (*b*) float type data
11. Write a program which calculate area of rectangle for:
    (*a*) int type data
    (*b*) float type data

    For solving above problem use function template.

17

OBJECT-ORIENTED PROGRAMMING AND SOFTWARE DEVELOPMENT SYSTEMS

Object-oriented programming (OOP) has been developed with the purpose to produce clear, reliable and easily maintainable products. In order to understand OOP it is necessary to have a clear perspective of some basic concepts like the software process, life cycle of waterfall model, conventional concepts and introduces OOP along with its characteristics.

17.1 SOFTWARE PROCESS

Software concept is related to tools, methods and procedure to develop the software. The software systems developed are so large, abstract and complex that there arises a need to make them visible in various documents like users manuals, systems designs etc. This documentation package henceforth becomes a part of software engineering process.

The software engineers have been targeting for high quality software with increase in productivity using various tools, methods and procedures to minimize the cost of development methods. Now let us understand the terms method, tools and procedure.

Method. The software are related to procedures for developing the software.

Tools. Tools provide automated or semi-automated support for methods.

Procedures. Procedures are nothing but methods and tools integrated together for the timely development of the software.

Therefore "Software process is a set of activities and associated results to develop software".

The set of activities are as follows:

1. *Software specification:* During this activity the functionality of the software and constraints on its operation must be defined.
2. *Software development:* After the software specification is ready, the software required to meet this specification must be produced.
3. *Software validation:* The software must be validated to ensure that it is satisfies the customer's requirement.
4. *Software evolution:* The software must be evolved to meet the changing needs of the customer.

17.2 PROCEDURE-ORIENTED PARADIGM

These above activities are decomposed in numerous ways. Industries choose different processes to produce the same product. The product still differs in the type of make, considering the quality standards. One of the classic software process model known as **"The waterfall model"** offers the way of making the development process more visible.

Let us look at figure 1.1 where the typical waterfall model displays six different stage of software development process.

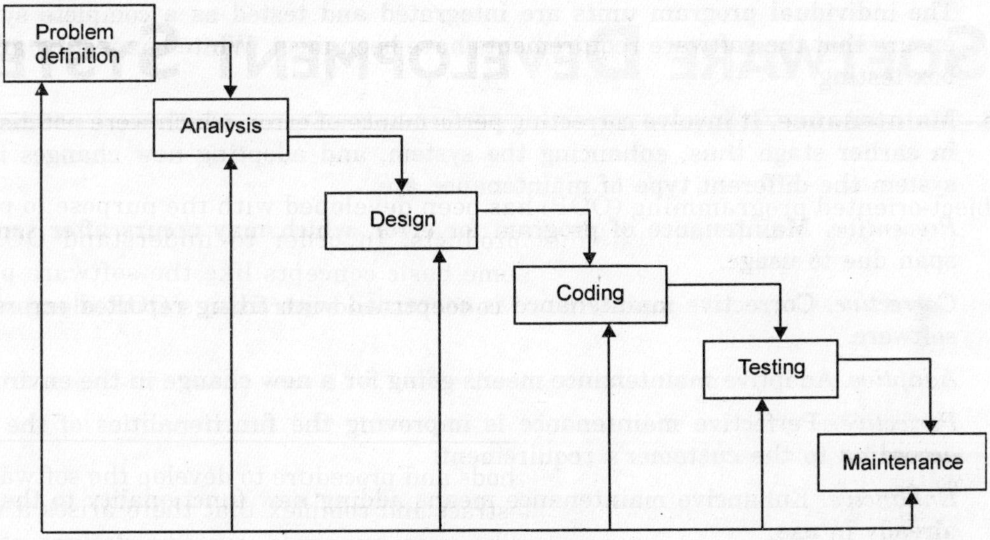

Waterfall Model

The waterfall model is the base of software engineering process. The life cycle of software development comprises problem definition to maintenance and the cycle repeat again. It follows top down design approach. Let us consider each phase of process.

1. **Problem definition.** In this problem (i.e., for which we want to write software) is defined properly. It helps not only the development but also the user to understand the problem better.
2. **Analysis.** In this we study the requirement of both the user and software. In this we find out mainly following:
   (*a*) What are the input?
   (*b*) What are the output expected?
   (*c*) What are the process required?
3. **Design.** The design phase deals with various concepts of system design, such as data structure and algorithms. The goal of the design phase is to transform the requirement specification into structure that is suitable for implementation in some programming language. It describes the related procedures for developing the software, designing can be categorized into two stages: architecture design and detail design.

   Architecture design. Data Flow Diagram (DFD) entity means the flow of data in the system.
   Relationship Diagram (ERD)

Detail design. Algorithm, flow charts, step-by-step procedure written in simple english to solve a given problem.

4. **Code.** To implement the project we should choose the appropriate tools for programming. Coding is the instruction written in some programming language to execute the program. We choose applications and then the platform to develop the application.
5. **Testing (Validation).** Testing is a process, which uncovers the errors. Testing is various types. Unit testing involves verifying that each unit meets its specification. The individual program units are integrated and tested as a complete system to ensure that the software requirements have been meet. White box testing and black box testing.
6. **Maintenance.** It involve correcting performance of error, which were not discovered in earlier stage thus, enhancing the system, and adopting new changes into the system the different type of maintenance are:

   Preventive. Maintenance of program for error, which may occurs after some time span due to usage.

   Corrective. Corrective maintenance is concerned with fixing reported errors in the software.

   Adaptive. Adaptive maintenance means going for a new change in the environment.

   Perfective. Perfective maintenance is improving the functionalities of the system according to the customer's requirement.

   Enhancive. Enhancive maintenance means adding new functionality to the project already in use.

17.3 OBJECT-ORIENTED PARADIGM

Software development system based on the object-oriented paradigm is system which is a collection of entities that together to accomplish certain objectives. In object-oriented paradigm the entities are objects. As the name indicates, the object-oriented paradigm places greater emphasis on the objects that encapsulate data and functions.

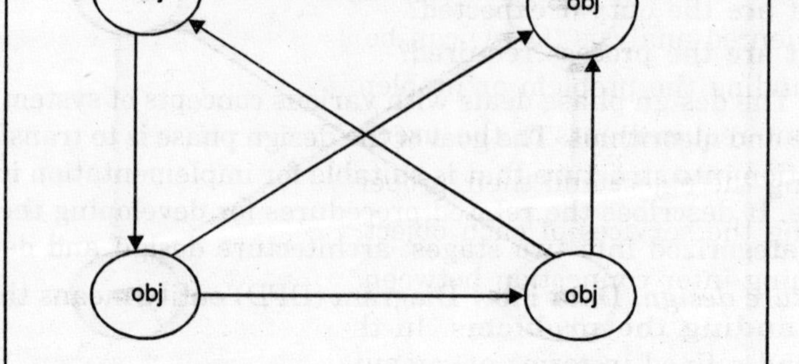

If we want to design a problem by object-oriented concept then the software development system consist mainly following steps:

1. Object-oriented analysis (OOA)
2. Object-oriented design (OOD)
3. Object-oriented programming(OOP)

We will study in detail about OOA, OOD, and OOP in separate section.

By combining above steps of object-oriented software development system we can draw software development life cycle.

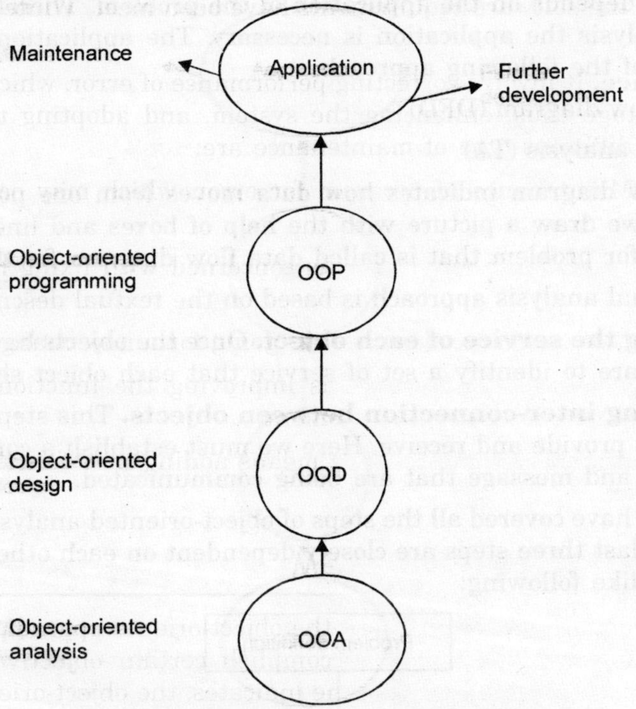

Object-oriented software development life cycle

17.3.1 Object-Oriented Analysis (OOA)

OOA is basically concerned with the decomposition of problem into its components parts. OOA provide us with a sample, but powerful mechanism for identifying objects.

The object-oriented analysis (OOA) can be divided into following steps:

1. Understanding the problem or problem definition.
2. To find out requirements of the user and software.
3. Identifying the object and their properties.
4. Identifying the services of each object.
5. Establishing inter connection between objects.

1. **Understanding the problems.** In these steps the problem statement should be refined and refined in terms of computer system engineering. By using statements computer based solution is easy. This statement is also called problem definition.

2. **To find out requirement.** Once the problem is defined, next step is to find out requirements. For finding the requirement the developer should state following points:
   (*i*) What output are required
   (*ii*) What input are necessary
   (*iii*) What resource are required
   (*iv*) What process are involved to produce required output.
3. **Identify the objects and their property.** In this step the objects are identify in terms of real world objects and abstract objects. The identification of objects for a problem is depends on the application of the problem. Therefore before identifying objects analysis the application is necessary. The application may be analyzed by using one of the following approaches.
   (*i*) Data flow diagram (DFD)
   (*ii*) Textual analysis (TA)

   Data flow diagram indicates how data moves from one point to another in the system. If we draw a picture with the help of boxes and line which describe data movement for problem that is called data flow diagram for that problem.

   The textual analysis approach is based on the textual description of the problem.
4. **Identifying the service of each object.** Once the objects have been identified, the next steps are to identify a set of service that each object should offers.
5. **Establishing inter-connection between objects.** This step identifies the service that objects provide and receive. Here we must establish a correspondence between the service and message that are being communicated.

Now we have covered all the steps of object-oriented analysis (OOA) approach. In OOA steps last three steps are closely dependent on each other. The OOA steps can be written like following:

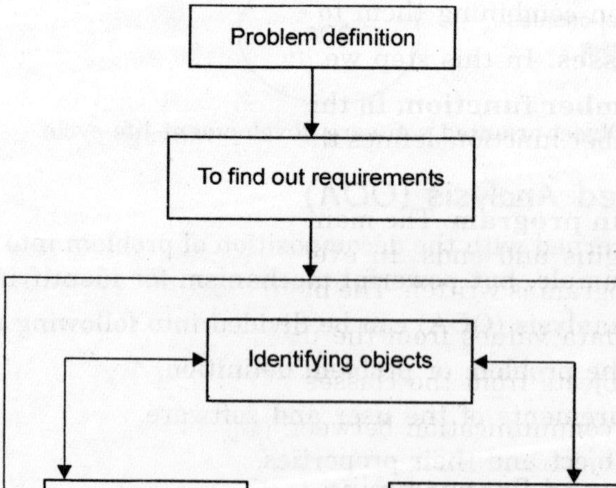

Object-oriented analysis steps

17.3.2 Object-Oriented Design (OOD)

The object-oriented design approach involves the following steps:

1. Review of objects created in the analysis phase
2. Specification of class dependencies
3. Derive class hierarchies
4. Design of classes
5. Design of member function's
6. Design of main program

1. **Review of object created in analysis phase.** The main objective of this is to refine the objects in terms of their attributes and operations and to identify other objects.
2. **Specification of class dependencies.** The main objective of this is to analysis of relationships between the classes. The major relationship that are important in the context of design are:

   (*a*) Inheritance relationship

   (*b*) Containment relationship

   (*c*) Use relationship

   The knowledge of such relationship is important to design of a program. Inheritance relationship is most powerful in c++. We know about this containment relationship means the use of an object of a class as a member of another class. Use relationship gives information such as the various classes a class uses and the way it uses them.
3. **Derive class hierarchies.** In previous steps, we examined the class dependencies. We must re-examine them and create a class hierarchy. Derive class hierarchy involves identification of common attributes and functions among a group of related classes and then combining them to form a new class.
4. **Design of classes.** In this step we design the complete details of each class.
5. **Design of member function.** In this step we design the member functions of each class. The member function defines the operations that are performed on the member data.
6. **Design of main program.** The main program is a part of software where execution of software begins and ends. In every program there is a main ( ) function code where main program is written. The main program is mainly responsible for following:

   (*a*) Receiving data values from the user

   (*b*) Creating objects from the classes

   (*c*) Arranging communication between objects.

17.3.3 Object-Oriented Programming (OOP)

In this we design all classes and their relationship in C++ or any other OOP language.

Descriptive Type Questions

1. Describe why the testing of software is important.
2. Distinguish between water-fall model and the functional model.

3. Explain procedure oriented paradigm.
4. Explain object-oriented paradigm..
5. What is OOA?
6. What is OOD?
7. Why DFD is used? Explain data flow diagram.
8. What do you mean by maintenance of software? How and when it is done?
9. What is OOP ?

Objective Type Questions

Give the answer is true or false for the following questions:

1. An important consideration when designing a new system is the end user.
2. The user has no role in analysis and design of system.
3. The only one step OOD is sufficient is object-oriented paradigm.
4. Water-fall model is used in object-oriented paradigm.

18

SOLVED PAPERS OF UP TECHNICAL UNIVERSITY

THIRD SEMESTER EXAMINATION, 2001-2002

OBJECT-ORIENTED PROGRAMMING AND C^{++}

Time—3 hours Total Marks—100

Note: *1. Attempt **ALL** questions.*

2. All questions carry equal marks.

Q.1. Answer any FOUR of the following parts:

Q.1 (*a*) *Define a class for an object that can be used to perform operations on paragraph written in English language. Operations that can be performed are-left justify, right justify, word count and search for a word in paragraph.*

Ans. A class describes the group of objects with similar properties (attributes), common behaviour (operations), common relationships to other objects and common semantics e.g., person and process are class. Each person has an age, IQ and may work at a job. Similarly, each process has an owner, priority and list of required resources. Objects in a class have the same attributes and behaviour pattern.

```
class english
    {
  int word count (char * p)
    {
      int x;
    while (*p! = NULL)
    {
      x++;
      p++;
    }  cont<<x  ;
       return x;
    }
```

```
int word charsearch (char*p, char*p)
{
while (*p! = NULL)
  {
    p++;
  }
```

Q.1 (b) *Differentiate between generalization and aggregation.*

Ans.

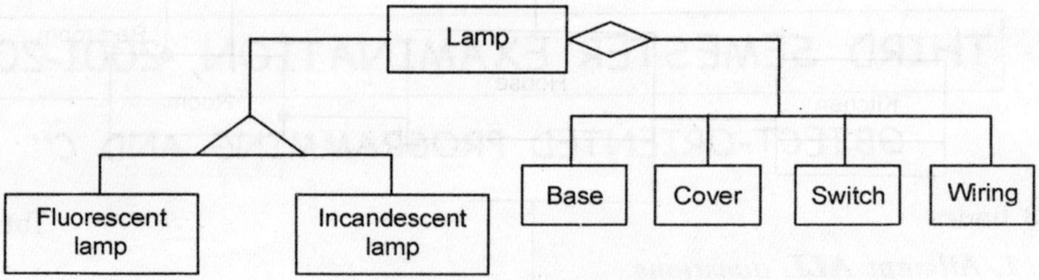

Generalization and Aggregation

This figure illustrates difference of aggregation and generalization for the case of a lamp. Base, cover-switch are all parts of a lamp i.e., aggregation while lamp class can be subdivided into several different sub class i.e., of generalization.

Aggregation	Generalization
1. Aggregation is "part-whole" a part of relationship in which objects representing the components of something are associated with an object representing the entire assembly.	1. Generalization is the relationship between a class and one or more refined version of it. The class being refined is called the super class and each refined version is called a sub class.
2. Aggregation relates instances. Two distinct objects are involved, one of them is a part of the other.	2. Generalization relates classes and is a way of structuring the description of a single object.
3. An aggregation tree is composed of object instances that are all part of a composite object.	3. A generalization tree is composed of classes that describe an object.
4. Aggregation is often called "a-part of" relationship.	4. Generalization is often called "a-kind-of" or "is a" relationship.
5. Aggregation is sometimes called an "and-relationship".	5. Generalization is sometimes called an "or relationship.

Q.1 (c) *What is an abstract class? Take suitable example from real life.*

Ans. An abstract class is a class that has direct instances but whose descendant classes have direct instances. An abstract class is designed only to act as a base class (to be inherited by other classes). It is a design concept in program development and provides a base upon which other classes may be built. A concrete class is a class that is instantiable i.e., it can have direct instances. A concrete class may have sub-classes.

Q.1 (*d*) *Design and draw class diagram for a house structure. Make realistic assumptions about room, kitchen etc.*

Ans.

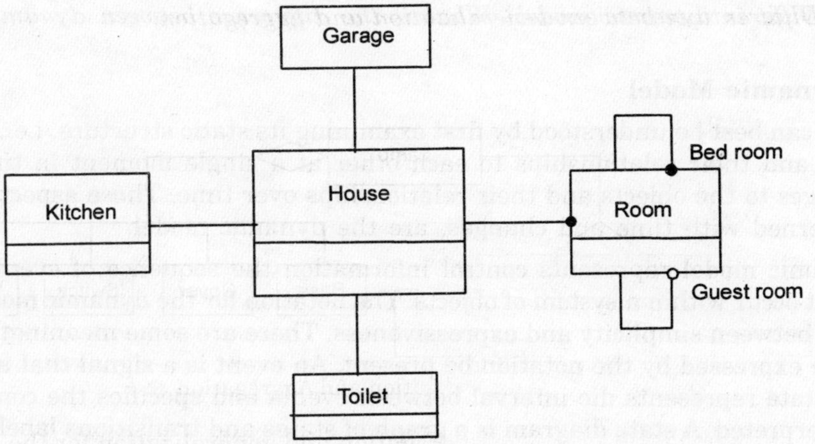

Q.1 (*e*) *Represent association using diagram between following classes:*

(*i*) *Employee* — *Company*

(*ii*) *Capital* — *Country*

(*iii*) *Computer* — *User*

(*iv*) *Car* — *Wheel*

Ans. Association using diagram

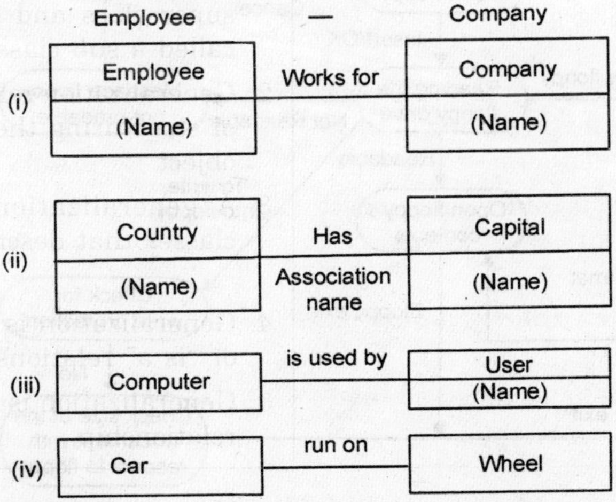

Q.1 (*f*) *What is metadata?*

Ans. Metadata. Metadata is the data that describes other data. For example, the definition of a class is metadata. Models are **inheretently** metadata since they describe the things being modelled (rather than being the things).

Many real-world applications have metadata such as parts catalogues, blueprints and dictionaries. Computer language implementation also use metadata heavily.

Relational database management system also use meta data. A person can define database tables for storing information. Similarly, a relation DBMS has several meta tables that store table definitions. For example, if a data table may store the fact that the capital of Japan is Tokyo, then a meta-table would store the fact that a country has a capital city.

Q.2. Answer any TWO of the following parts:

Q. 2(*a*) *What is dynamic model? What is the difference between dynamic model and object model?*

Ans. Dynamic Model

A system can best be understood by first examining its static structure, i.e., the structure of the objects and their relationships to each other at a single moment in time. Then, we examine changes to the objects and their relationships over time. Those aspects of a system, that are concerned with time and changes, are the dynamic model.

The dynamic model represents control information the sequence of events, states and operations that occur within a system of objects. The notation for the dynamic model represents a compromise between simplicity and expressiveness. There are some meaningful constraints that cannot be expressed by the notation be present. An event is a signal that something has happened. A state represents die interval between events and specifies the context in which events are interpreted. A state diagram is a graph of states and transitions labelled by events.

Q.2 (*b*) *Identify various states in which a floppy drive in a computer system can exist. Draw state transition diagram.*

Ans.

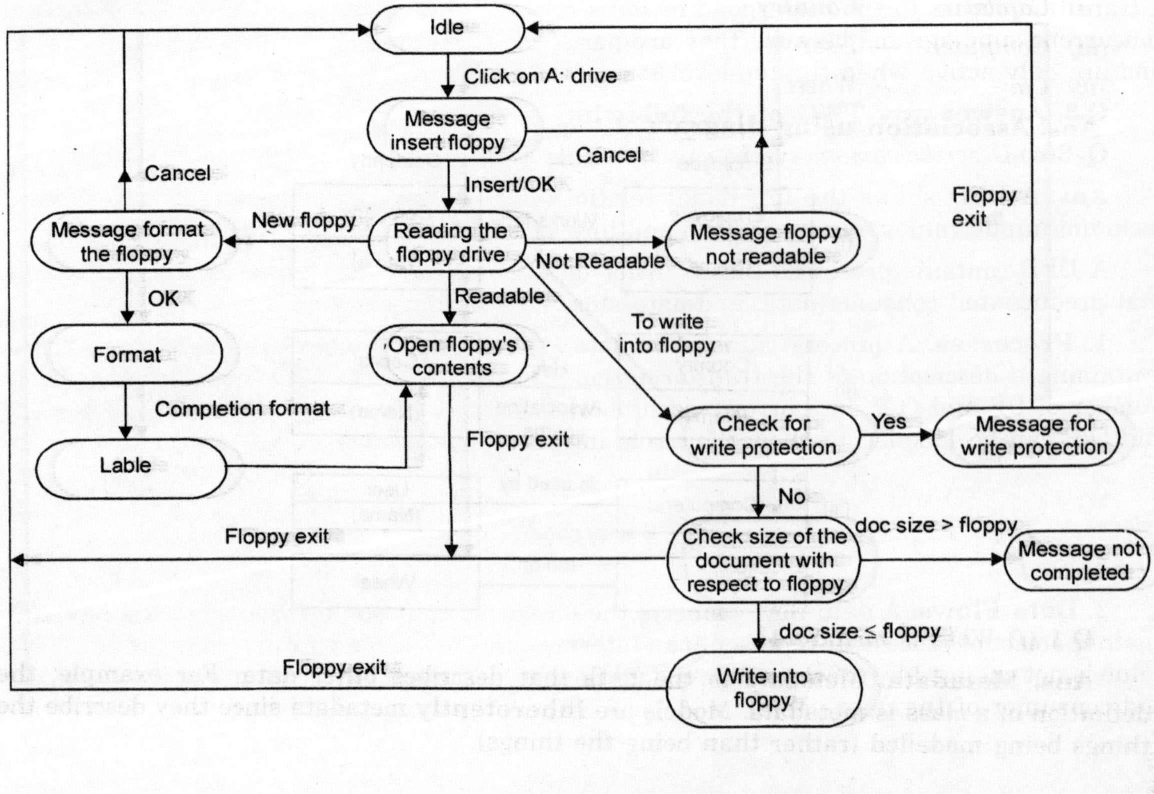

Q.2 (c) *How is concurrency within states of a single object represented?*

Ans. Concurrency within the state of a single object arises when the object can be partitioned into subsets of attributes or links; each of which has its own subdiagram. The subdiagrams need not be independent; the same event can cause transitions in more than one subdiagram. Concurrency within a single composite state of an object is shown by partitioning the composite state into subdiagrams with dotted lines. The name of the overall composite state can be written in a separate region of the box, separated by a sided line from the concurrent subdiagrams. For example, the state diagram for the play of a bridge rubber.

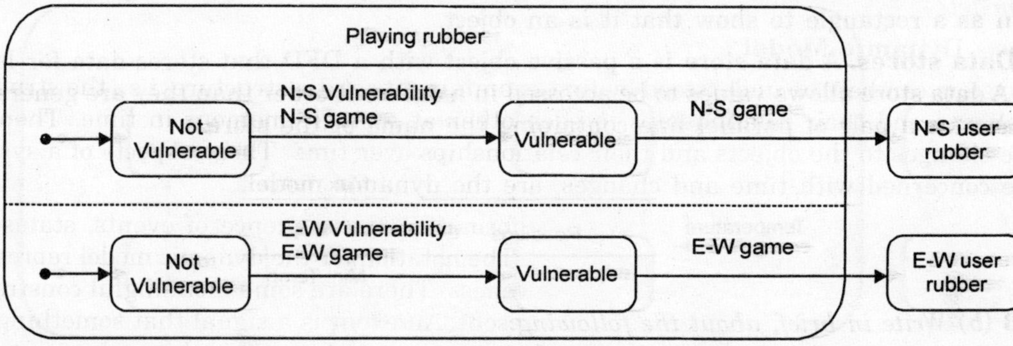

When a side wins a game, it becomes "vulnerable"; the first side to win, two games wins the rubber. During the play of the rubber, the state of the rubber consists of one state from each subdiagram. When the playing rubber composite state is extended, both subdiagrams are initially in their respective default states "Not vulnerable". Each subdiagram can independently advance to state 'vulnerable' when its side wins a game. When one side wins a second game, a transition occurs to the corresponding wins rubber state. This transition terminates both concurrent subdiagrams because they are part of the same composite state playing rubber and are only active when the top-level state diagram is in that state.

Q.3. Answer any TWO of the following parts:

Q. 3(*a*) *Describe various symbols used in data-flow diagram along with their significance.*

Ans. A DFD shows the functional relationships of the values computed by a system, including input values, output values, and internal data stores.

A DFD contains processes that transfer data, data flows that move data, actor objects that produce and consume data, and data store objects that store data passively.

1. **Processes.** A process transforms data values. A processes is drawn as an ellipse containing a description of the transformation, usually its name. Each process has a fixed number of I/P and O/P data arrows each of which carries a value of a given type. The I/P and O/P can be labelled to show their role in the computation.

2. **Data Flows.** A data flow connects the output of an object or process to the input of another object of process. It represents an intermediate data value within a computation. The value is not changed by the data flow. A data flow is drawn as an arrow between the producer and consumer of the data value.

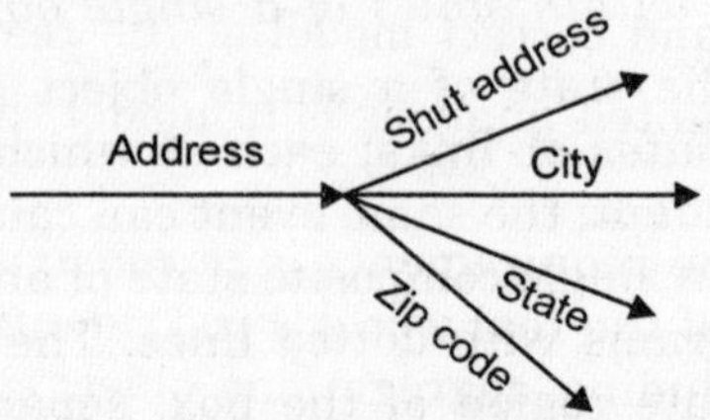

3. **Actors.** An actor is an active object that drives the data flow graph by producing or consuming values. Actors are attached to the inputs and outputs of a dataflow graph. An actor is drawn as a rectangle to show that it is an object.

4. **Data stores.** A data store is a passive object with a DFD that stores data for latter access. A data store allows values to be accessed in a different order than they are generated. It is drawn as a pair of parallel line containing the name of the store.

Q.3 (*b*) *Write in brief, about the following:*

(i) Nested Data-Flow Diagram.

(ii) Functional Constraint

Ans. 3(*b*) (*i*) Nested DFD. A DFD is particularly useful by showing the high-level functionality of a system and its breakdown into smaller functional unit. A process can be expanded into another DFD. Each input and output of the process is an input or output of the new diagram. The new diagram may have data stores that are not shown in the higher-level diagram. Diagrams can be nested to be an arbitrary depth, and entire set of nested diagrams forms a tree. Nesting of data flow diagram permits each level to be coherent and understandable yet overall functionality can be arbitrary complex. A diagram that references itself, represents a recursive computation. The nesting of diagrams has also been called levelling. Since the diagrams are organized into different levels, eventually the nesting of diagrams terminates with simple functions.

Ans. 3(*b*). (*ii*) Functional Constraint. A constraint shows the relationship between two objects at the same time (such as frequency and wavelength) or between different values of the same object at different times (such as the number of outstanding shares of the mutual fund). A constraint may be expressed as a total function (one value is completely specified by another) or a partial function (one value is restricted, but not completely specified, by another), e.g., a coordinate transformation might specify that the scale factor for the x-coordinate and the y-coordinate will be equal; this constraints totally defines one value in term of the other. The second law of thermodynamics express a partial, constraint. It states that the entrophy (disorder) of the universe can never decrease.

Constraints can appear in each kinds of the model. Object constraints specify that some objects depend entirely relationships among the states or events of different objects. Functional constraints specify restrictions on operations. A constraint between values of an object over time is often called an invariant.

Q. 3(c) *During analysis phase of OMT, object model, functional model and dynamic model are prepared.' Describe contents of these models.*

Ans. Analysis, the first step of the OMT methodology is concerned with diversing a precise, concise, understandable and correct model of the rest-world.

The purpose of the object-oriented analysis is to model the real-world system so that it can be understood.

The first step in analyzing the requirements is to construct an object model. The object model shows the static structure of the real world. First, identify object classes, then identify associations between objects, including aggregations object attributes and links should be identified, although minor ones can be deferred. Inheritance should be used to organize and simplify the class structure. Organize tightly-coupled classes and associates into models. Information in object models should be supplemented with brief textual descriptions, including the purpose and scope of each entity.

The dynamic model shows the time-dependent behaviour of the system and the objects in it. The dynamic model is insignificant for a purely static data repository such as a database. The dynamic model is important for interactive systems.

First prepare scenarios of typical and exceptional sessions. Then identify external events between the system and the outside world. Build a state diagram for each active object showing the patterns of events it receives and sends, together with actions that it performs. Match events between state diagrams to verify consistency, the resulting set of diagrams constitute the dynamic model.

The functional model shows the functional derivations of values, without regard for when they are computed. First identify input and output values of the system as parameters of external events. Then construct data flow diagrams to show the computation of each output value from other values and ultimately input values. Data flow diagrams interact with internal objects that serve as data stores between interactions. Finally, specify constraints and optimization criteria.

Q.4. Answer any FOUR of the following parts:

Q. 4(*a*) *Give complete definition of a class in C++ to implement a stack of integer.*

Ans. Simplate <Class itype>

```
class stack
{
 protected :
    int * S ;
    int top_ptr, size ;
    public :
    stack (unsigned int n)
    {
     S = new inf [n];
     top_ptr = - 1;
     size = n;
    }
     void push ( )
```

Q.4 (*b*) ***Overload '+' operator in C++ to perform addition of complex numbers.***

Ans. Program to overload '+' operator in C++ to perform addition of complex numbers.

```
# include<iostream>
 class complex
 {
   float x;
   float y;
   public:
    complex ()      { }
   complex (float real, float imag)
   {x = real; y = imag;}
   complex operator + (complex);
   void display (void):
   } ;
 complex complex:: operator + (complex C)
   {
   complex temp;
   temp. x = x + c . x;
   temp. y = y + c . y;
   return (temp);
   }
 void complex : : display (void)
   {
    cout<<x <<''+j'' << y << ''\n'';
   }
 int main ()
   {
    complex C1, C2, C3;
    C1 = complex (2.5, 3.5);
    C2 = complex (1.6, 2.7);
    C3 = C1 + C2;
    cout <<''C1 ='' ; C1 . display ();
    cout <<''C2 ='' ; C2 . display ();
    cout <<''C3 ='' ; C3 . display ();
     return 0;
     }
```

Q.4 (*c*) ***Is definition of multiple constructors within a C++ class permitted? Why are multiple constructors needed?***

Ans. Yes, multiple constructors within a C++ is permitted in such a condition if we are defining constructors with no argument, with one argument, with two, three or multiple arguments and default arguments.

Multiple constructed can initialize the values of an object when it creates.

The values can be given by default argument, by default constructors with arguments.

Example:

```
class ABC
  { int a,b,c;
    public:
    ABC ( )
    {a = 10; b=20; C=3b;}
    ABC (int x int y, int z = 3)
    {a=x; b=y; c = z;}
    ABC (int x)
    {a = x; b = 2, c = 3;}
  void putdata (void)
    { cout <<a<< b<<c; }
    } ;
  int main ()
  { ABC P;
    ABC Q (10);
    ABC R (1, 2) ;
    ABC S (5, 4, 9);
    P. putdata ();
    Q. putdata ();
    R. putdata ();
    S. putdata ();
    return 0;
  }
```

Output will be :

10	20	30	//	for P object
10	2	3	//	for Q object
1	2	3	//	for R object
5	4	9	//	for S object

Q.4. (*d*) *Write, in brief, about the following keywords of C++:*

Public, Private, Protected.

Ans. Public. The keyword public is known as visibility label and is used in terms of members, (functions and variables are collectively called). A class member that is accessible to all users of the class. The access is not restricted to the member and friend functions of the class alone. A public member of a base class is inherited by a derived class.

Private. The class members that have been declared as private, can be accessed only from within the class. By default, the members of a class are private. Such a class is completely hidden from the outside world and does not serve any purpose. A private member of a base class is not inherited by a derived class.

Protected. A protected member is the same as a private member except that a protected member of a base class is inherited by a derived class, whereas a private member is not. A member declared as protected, is accessible the member functions within its class and any class immediately derived from it.

Q.4 (*e*) *Write a suitable example, demonstrating need for a user defined destructor.*

Ans. A destructor, as the name implies is used to destroy the objects that have been created by a constructor. Like a constructor, the destructor is a member function whose name is the same as the class name but is preceded by a tilde. For example, the destructor for the class integer can be defined as shown below:

~integer ( ) { }

A destructor never takes any argument, nor does it return any value. It will be involved implicitly by the compiler upon exit from the program to clean up storage that is no longer accessible. It is a good practice to declare destructors in a program since it releases memory space for future use.

Q.4 (*f*) *How does a static member differ from non-static member of a C++ class?*

Ans. A member function that is declared static has the following properties:

1. A static function can have access to only other static members (functions or variables) declared in the same class.
2. A static member function can be called using the class name (instead of its objects) as follows:

```
class name:: function-name;
```

Whereas non-static member functions have some special characteristics different from static member functions:

1. Several different classes can use the same function name. The membership label will resolve their scope.
2. Member functions can access the private data of the class. A non-member function cannot do so.
3. A member function can call another member function directly, without using the dot-operator.

Q.5. Answer any TWO of the following parts:

Q.5(*a*) *What is virtual function? Explain with a suitable example.*

Ans. Virtual function. When we use the same function name in both the base and derived classes, the function in base class is declared as virtual using the keyboard virtual preceding its normal declaration. When a function is made virtual, C++ determines which function to use at run time based on the type of object pointed to by the base pointer, rather than the type of the pointer. Thus, by making the base pointer to point to different objects, we can execute different versions of the virtual function.

Run time polymorphism is achieved only when a virtual function is accessed through a pointer to the base class. It cannot be achieved using object name along with the dot operator to access virtual function. We can have virtual distributors but not virtual constructors. A virtual function equated to use is called a pure virtual function. It is a function declared in a base class that has no definition relative to the base class. A class containing such pure function is called an abstract class.

Equation of virtual functions:

```
# include <iostream>
  class base
  {
    public
    void display ( ) {cout <<''\n display base'';}
    virtual void show () {cout <<''\n show base'';}
    } ;
    class derived : public base
    {
     public :
     void display ( ) {cout <<''\n display derived'';}
     void show ( ) {cout <<''\n show derived'';}
    } ;
        int main ( )
        base B;
        derived D;
        base * bptr;
    cout << ''\n bptr points to base\n'';
    bptr = & B;
    bptr → display ( ); || calls base version
    bptr → show ( ); || class base version
    cout << ''\n bptr points to derived \n'';
    bptr = & D;
    bptr → display ( ); || calls base version
    bptr → show ( ); || calls derived version
    return 0;
    }
```

Output:

bptr points to base Display base show base bptr points to derived display base show derived

Q.5 (*b*) *Differentiate between JSD and OMT approaches of software engineering.*

Ans. OMT. One of the most popular object-oriented development techniques today is the object modelling technique (OMT). It is primarily used by system and software developers supporting full life-cycle development, targeting object-oriented implementations. It continues to be successful in many application domains–telecommunication, transportation, compliers etc.

OMT graphically defines a system through 3 kinds of model:

1. **Object model.** It defines the object classes in the system and their relationships, as well as their attributes and operations. The object model is represented graphically by a class diagram.

2. **Dynamic model.** Indicates the dynamics of the objects and their changes in state. By exploring the behaviour of the objects over time, and the flow of control and events among the objects, the dynamic model capture the essential behaviour of the system.

3. **Functional model.** Functional model is a DFD of the system and describes what the system does, but not how it is done.

JSD i.e., Jackson structured development is another mature methodology. JSD does not distinguish between analysis and design and instead lumps both phases together as specification:

1. JSD first determines the 'what' and then 'how'.
2. JSD is intended especially for applications in which timing is important.
3. JSD model describes the real world in terms of entities, actions and ordering of actions. Entities usually appear as nouns in requirement statements and action appears as verbs.
4. JSD software development consists of sequential steps: entity action step, entity structure step, initial model step, function step, system timing step, implementa-tion step.
5. JSD approach is complex and difficult to comprehend. It is more obscure than data flow and object-oriented approaches because of its heavy reliance on pseudecode.
6. JSD places more emphasis on actions and less on attributes then we do.
7. JSD is ineffective at abstraction and simplification.
8. JSD is useful for concurrent software where processes must synchronize with each other and real time software etc.

Q.5 (*c*) *Can a base class pointer be type casted to derived class pointer? Give reason.*

Ans. Pointers to objects of a base class are type compatible with pointers to objects of a derived class. Therefore, a single pointer variable can be made to point to objects belonging to different classes.

However, there is a problem in using a pointer of base class to access public members of the derived class because we can access only those members which were inherited from base class and not the members that originally belong to derived class.

MCA

THIRD SEMESTER EXAMINATION, 2002-2003

OBJECT-ORIENTED PROGRAMMING AND C^{++}

Time—3 hours Total Marks—100

Note: *1. Attempt* ***ALL*** *questions.*

2. All questions carry equal marks.

Q.1. Attempt any FOUR of the following:

Q.1(*a*) *Prepare a class diagram from the instance diagram of Figure. Explain your multiplicity decisions. Each point has a x-coordinate and a y-coordinate. What is the smallest number of points required to construct a polygon? Does it make a difference whether or not a given point may be shared between several polygons? How can you express the fact that points are in a sequence?*

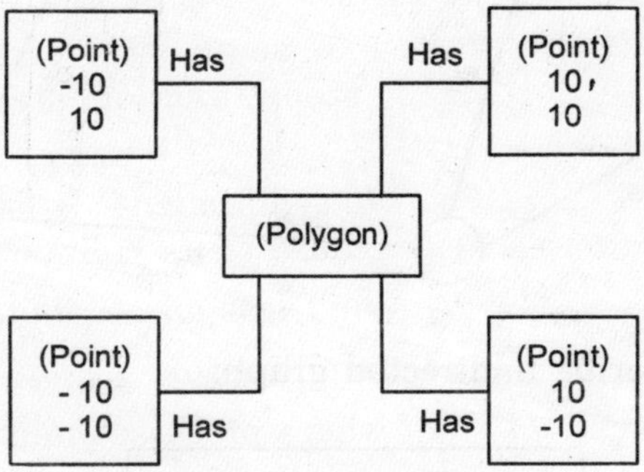

Ans. Instance diagram of figure given in question.

Class diagram:

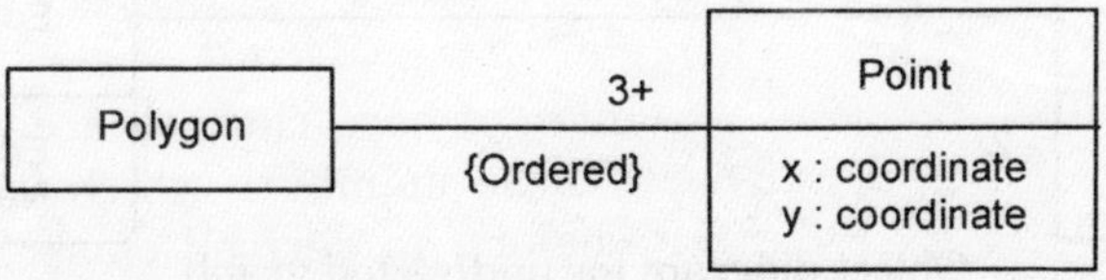

The smallest number of points required to construct a polygon is three. One way to express the fact that points are in a sequence is to indicate that the association is ordered. The multiplicity of the association depends on how points are identified. If a point is identified by its location, then points are shared and the association is many-to-many. On the other hand if each point belongs to exactly one polygon, then several points may have the same coordinates.

Q.1 (*b*) *Differentiate between aggregation and association with suitable examples.*

Ans. Aggregation is a special form of association not an independent concept. If two objects are tightly bound by a part-whole relationship, it is an aggregation. If two objects are usually considered as independent, even though they may often be linked, it is an association. For example,

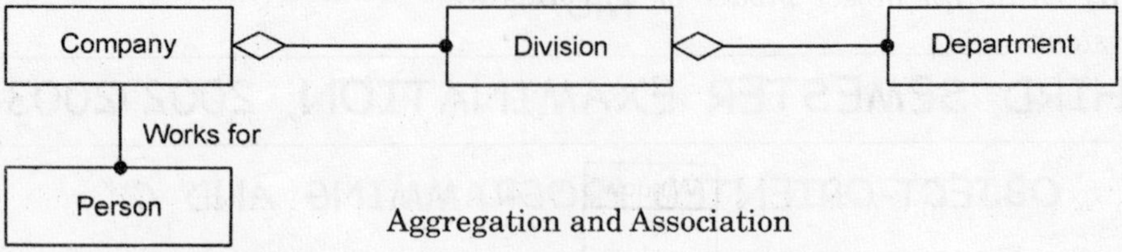

Aggregation and Association

A company is an aggregation of its divisions, which are in turn aggregation of their departments. A company is indirectly an aggregation of departments. A company is not an aggregation of its employees, since company and person are independent objects of equal stature.

Q. 1 (c) *Prepare an object model to describe undirected graph. Your model should capture only the structure of graphs (i.e., connectivity) and need not be concerned with geometrical details such as location of vertices or length of edges.*

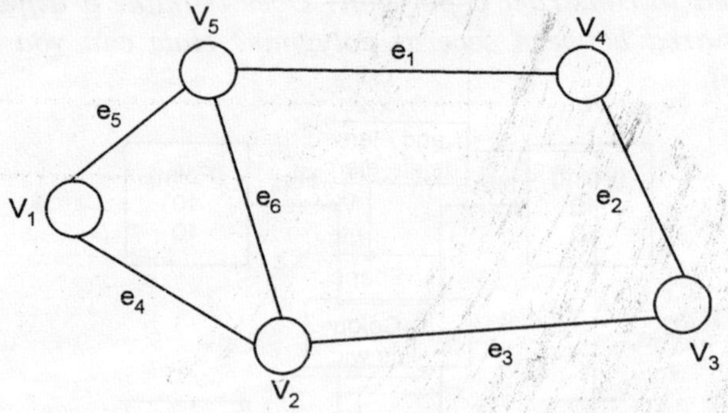

Ans. Object model to describe undirected graph:

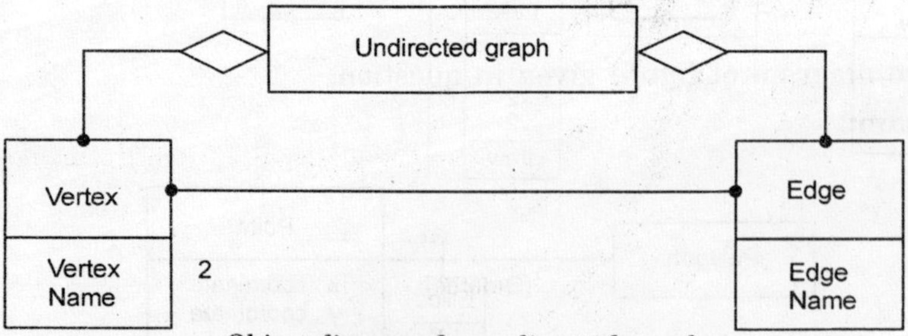

Object diagram for undirected graph

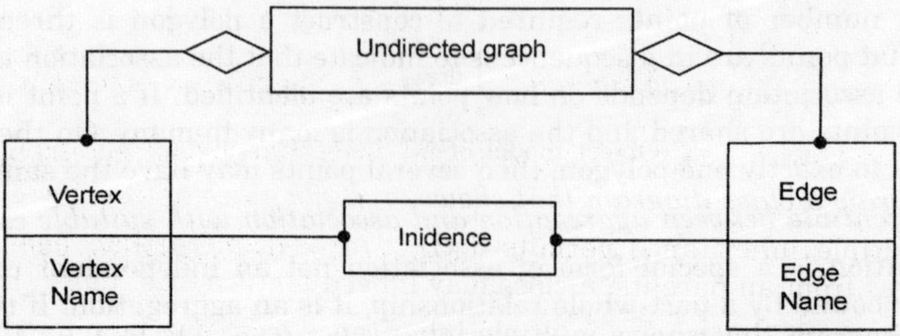

Object diagram for undirected graphs in which the incidence between vertices and edges is treated as an object class

Q. 1(*d*) *Draw an object model of a workstation window management system (e.g., X Window system).*

Ans.

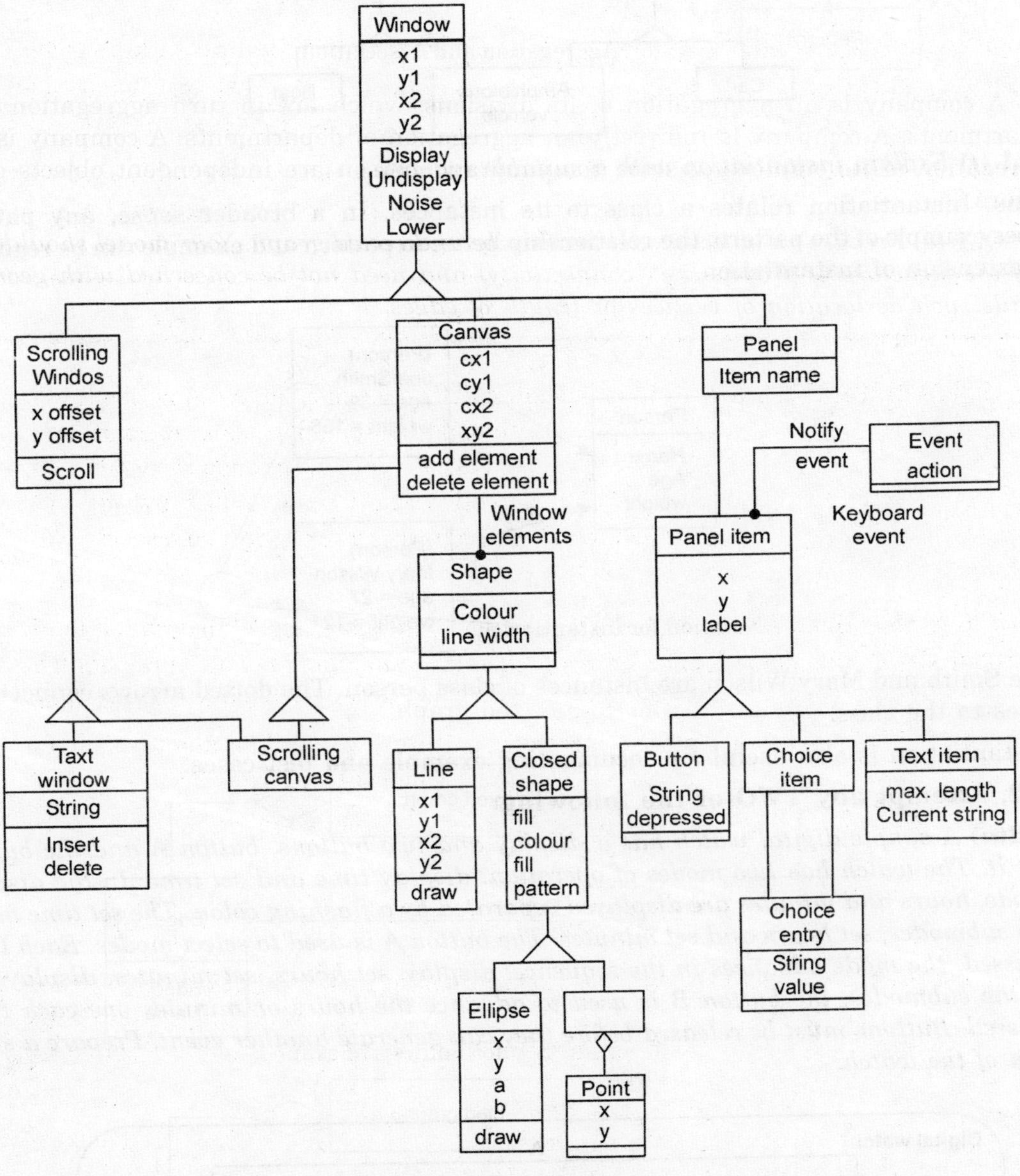

(Object model of window ring system)

Q.1 (*e*) *Draw a class diagram that shows multiple inheritance from overlapping classes.*

Ans. Multiple inheritance permits a class to have more than one superclass and to inherit features from all parents. A class may inherit feature from more than one superclass.

A class diagram that shows multiple inheritance from overlapping classes.

Amphibious vehicle is both land vehicle and water vehicle shows overlapping classes.

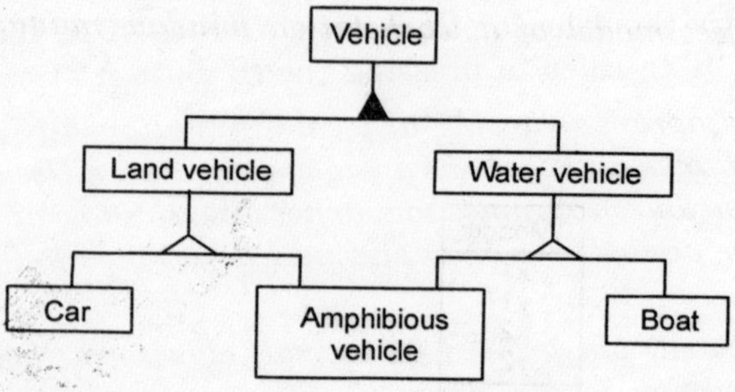

Q.1 (*f*) *Explain instantiation with a suitable example.*

Ans. Instantiation relates a class to its instances. In a broader sense, any pattern describes example of the pattern, the relationship between pattern and example can be regarded as an extension of instantiation.

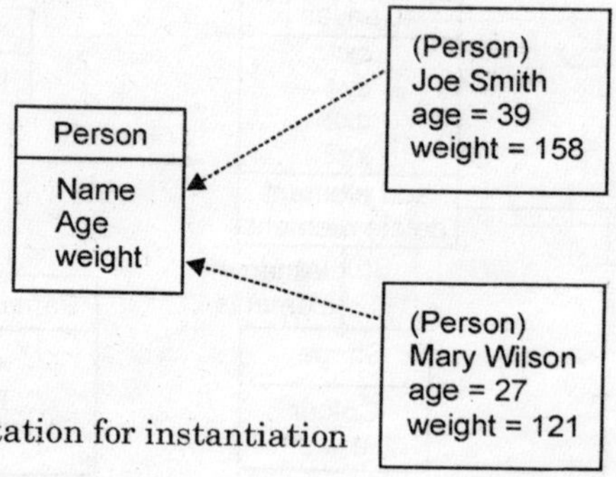

Notation for instantiation

Joe Smith and Mary Wilson are instances of class person. The dotted arrows connect the instances to the class.

Instantiation is also useful for documenting example and test cases.

Q.2. Attempt any TWO of the following:

Q.2(*a*) *A simple digital watch has a display and two buttons, button A and the button B to set it. The watch has two modes of operation: display time and set time. In the display time mode, hours and minutes are displayed separated by a flashing colon. The set time mode has two submodes, set hours and set minutes. The button A is used to select modes. Each time it is pressed, the mode advances in the sequence: display, set hours, set minutes, display etc. Within the submodes, the button B is used to advance the hours or minutes one each time it is pressed. Buttons must be released before they can generate another event. Prepare a state diagram of the watch.*

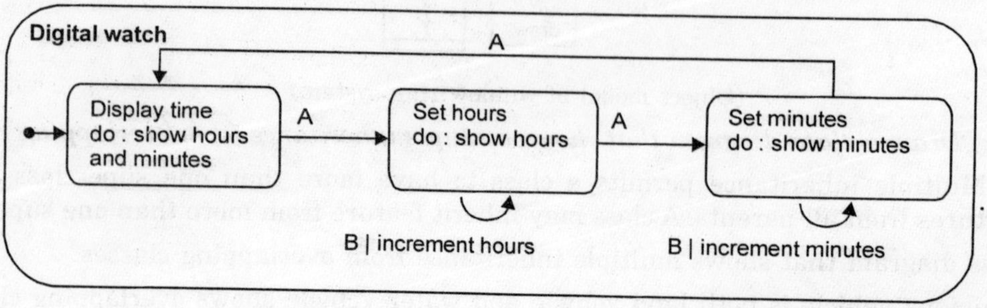

Ans. A state diagram for a simple digital watch we assume that persuing a button is an event and that we may ignore the release of a button. We use 'A' in the diagram to refer to pressing the 'A' button and 'B' to refer to pressing the 'B' button.

Q.2 (*b*) *Prepare object diagrams showing at least 10 relationships among the following object classes. Include associations, aggregations and generalizations. Use qualified associations and show multiplicity balls in your diagrams. You do not need to show attributes of operations. Use association names where needed. You may add additional object classes, as you prepare the diagrams.*

OBJECT CLASSES: school, playground, principal, classroom, book, student, teacher, cafeteria, restroom, desk computer, chair, door.

Ans.

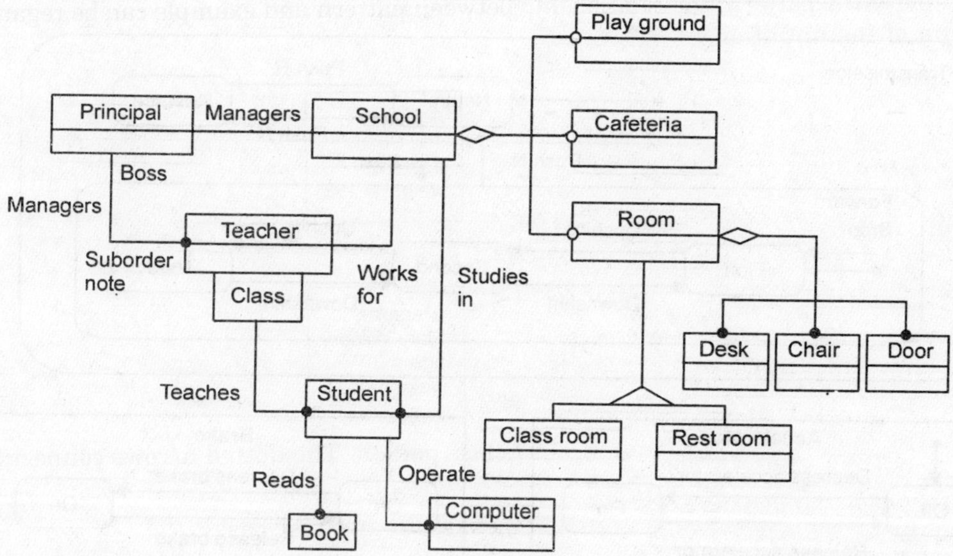

Q.2 (*c*) *Discuss aggregation concurrency and concurrency within object with the help of suitable state diagrams.*

Ans. A dynamic model describes a set of concurrent objects, each with its own state diagram. The objects in a system are inherently concurrent and can change state independently. The state of the entire system cannot be represented by a single state in a single object, it is the product of the states of all the objects in it. For example, the state of a car has an aggregation of component states the ignition, transmission, accelerator and brake. Each component state also has substates.

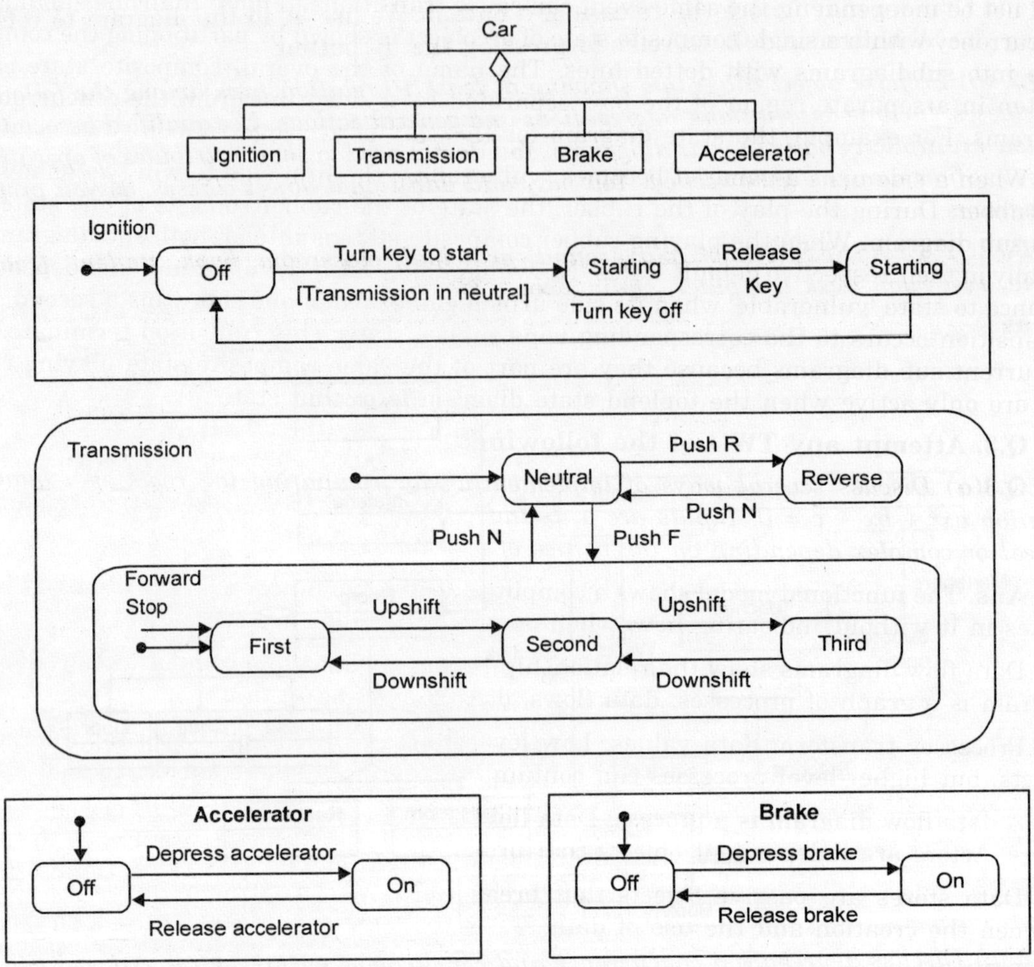

Aggregation and its concurrent state diagram

Concurrency within the object:

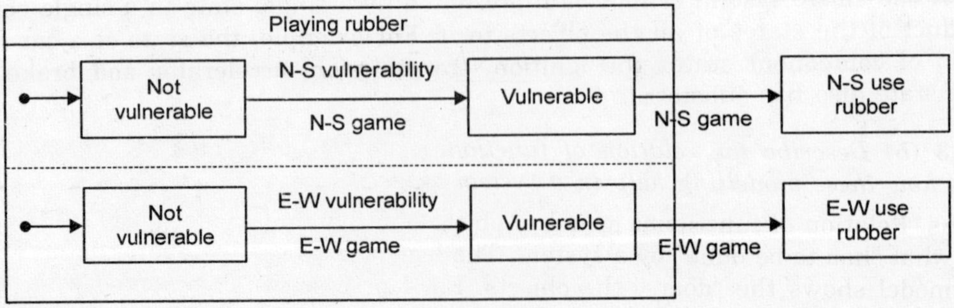

Bridge game with concurrent states

Concurrency within the state of a single object arises when the object can be partitioned into subsets of attributes or links; each of which has its own subdiagram. The subdiagrams need not be independent; the same event can cause transitions in more than one subdiagram. Concurrency within a single composite state of an object is shown by partitioning the composite state into subdiagrams with dotted lines. The name of the overall composite state can be written in a separate region of the box, separated by a sided line from the concurrent sub diagrams. For example, the state diagram for the play of a bridge rubber.

When a side urns a game, it becomes "vulnerable"; the first side to win two games urns the rubber. During the play of the rubber, the state of the rubber consists of one state from each sub diagram. When the playing rubber composite state is intend, both sub diagrams are initially in their respective default states "Not vulnerable". Each sub diagram can independently advance to state 'vulnerable' when its side urns a game. When one side wins a second game, a transition occurs to the corresponding wins rubber state. This transition terminates both concurrent sub diagrams because they are part of the same composite state playing rubber and are only active when the toplend state diagram is in that state.

Q.3. Attempt any TWO of the following:

Q.3(*a*) *Discuss several ways of implementing for computing the roots of a quadratic equation $ax^2 + bx + c = 0$. Inputs are a, b and c. Outputs are roots R_1 and R_2 which may be real or complex depending on the values of a, b and c.*

Ans. The functional model shows a computation and the functional derivation of the data values in it without indicating how, when or why the values are computed.

Data flow diagrams show the relationship between values in a computation. A data flow diagram is a graph of processes, data flows, data stores and actors.

Processes transform data values. Low level processes are simple operation on single objects, but higher-level processes can contain internal data stores subject to side effects.

A data flow diagram is a process. Data flows relate values on processes, data stores and actors. Actors are independent objects that produce and consume values.

Data stores are passive objects that break the flow of control by introducing delays between the creation and the use of data.

DFD for computing the roots of a quadratic equation $ax + bx + c = 0$. Inputs are a, b and c.

Input root: a, b and c **Output roots:** $R_1 + R_2$

Quadratic formula for R_1 and R_2 is:

$$\frac{-b \pm \sqrt{b^2 - 4ac}}{2a}$$

Q.3 (*b*) *Describe the relation of function model to object and dynamic models. Also discuss how these modelling help in a system model?*

Ans. Relation of functional model to object and dynamic models. The functional model shows what "has to be done" by a system. The leaf process are the operation on objects. The object model shows the "doers" the objects. Each process is implemented by a method on some object. The dynamic model shows the sequences in which the operations are performed. Each sequence is implemented as a sequence, loop or alteration of statements within some method.

The processes in the functional model correspond to operations in the object model.

Actors are explicit objects in the object models. Data flows to or from actors represent operations on or by the objects. Because actors are self-motivated objects, the functional model is not sufficient to indicate when they act. The dynamic model for an actor object specifies when it acts.

Data stores are also objects in the object model or atleast fragments of objects such as attributes. Data stores are passive objects that respond to queries and updates so the dynamic model of the data store is irrelevant of to its behaviour. Data flows are values in the object model. Many data flows are simply pure values, such as numbers, strings or lists of pure values. A pure value is not a container whose value can change but just the value itself-A pure value, therefore, has no state and no dynamic model.

Relative to the functional model. The object model shows the structure of the actors, data stores and flows in the functional model. The dynamic model shows the sequence in which processes and performed.

Relative to the object model. The functional model shows the operations on the classes and the arguments of each operation. It, therefore, shows the supplier client relationship among classes. The dynamic model shows the states of each object and the operations that are performed as it receives events and change state.

Relative to the dynamic model. The functional model shows the definitions of the leaf actions and activities that are undefined with the dynamic model. The object model shows that changes state and undergoes operations.

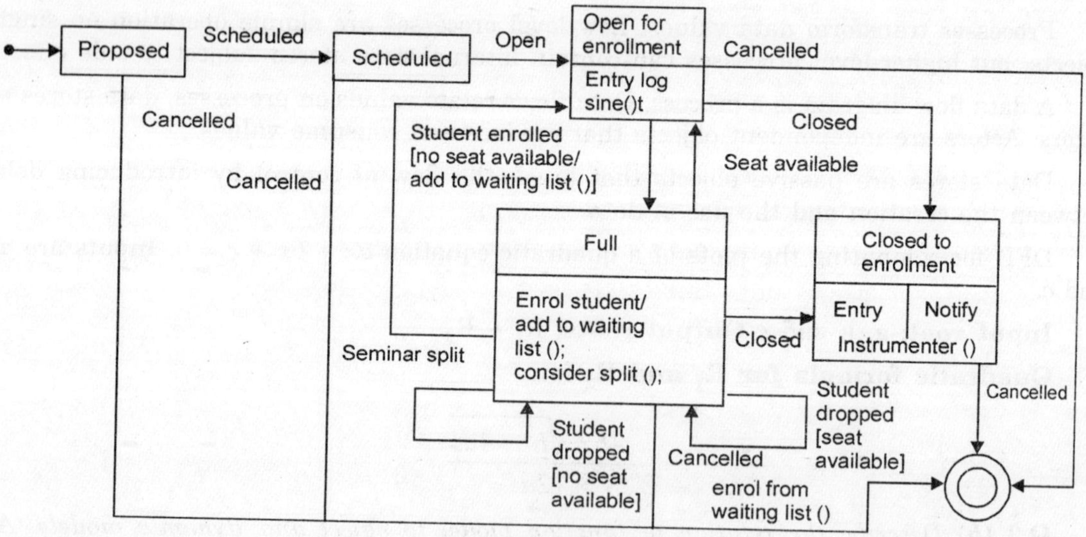

Q. 3. (*c*) *What is OMT object model. Draw OMT object model for participant's registration system for seminar.*

Ans. The OMT object model describes the static structure of the objects in a system and their relationship. The object model contains object diagrams. An object diagram is a graph nodes are object classes and whose arcs are relationships among classes.

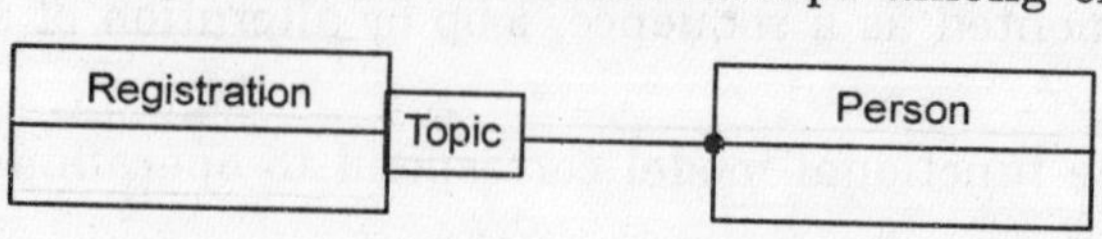

Q.4. Attempt any FOUR of the following:

Q.4(*a*) *Define and implement a class Date and Overload + operator to add two Date objects.*

Ans.
```
class Date
  { int yr, mon, day;
    public:
    void getdata (int d, int m, int y)
    { day = d; mon = m ; yr = y;}
    void putdata (void)
      { cout<< day << mon << yr;}
    Date operator + (Date tm);
      }
    Date Date:: Operator + (Date t1)
      { Date t;
        t. day = t1. day + day
        t. mon = t. day % 30;
        t. day = t. mon + t1. day + day
        t. yr = t.mon / 12
        t. mon = t.mon % 12;
        t. yr = t. yr + t1. yr + yr;
      return t;
}
    int main ();
        { Data d1, d2, d3;
        d1 . get data (08, 05, 76)
        d2 . get data (06, 02, 81)
        d3 = d1. + d2
        d1 . put data ();
        d2 . put data ();
        d3 . putdata ();
    return 0;
```

Q.4 (*b*) *What is copy constructor? Explain with an example.*

Ans. Copy constructor. The constructor that creates a new class object from an existing object of the same class. A copy constructor is used to declare and initialize an object from another object.

A copy construction takes a reference to an object of the same class as itself as an argument.

Example:
```
# include <iostream>
      class code
```

```
{
int id;
public:
  Code () {}                // Constructor
Code (int a) {id=a:]        // Constructor
Code (Code & x)             // Copy constructor
{
  id = x. id                // Copy in the value
}
void display (void)
{
  cout << id;
} ;
int main ()
{
  code A (100); // Object 'A' is created and inhibitor
  code B (A);   // Copy constructor called
  code C = A;   // Copy constructor called again
  code D;       // D is created and not initialised
  D = A
  cout <<''\n id of A:''; A. display ( );
  cout <<''\n id of B:''; B. display ( );
  cout <<''\n id of C:''; C. display ( );
  cout <<''\n id of D:''; D. display ( );
  return D;
  }
```

Output of the program is:

id of A : 100
id of B : 100
id of B : 100
id of D : 100

Q.4 (c) ***Find the errors in the following macro definitions and correct them:***

(i) *# define PI = 3.141593*

(ii) *# defineMAX(a,b)a>b?a:b*

(iii) *# define fac (a) (a) * fac (a) – 1)*

Ans. (*i*) There should not '='

define PI 3.141593

(*ii*) a > b has error. The correct syntax is :

define MAX (a . b) (a > b) ? a : b.

(*iii*) In the given macro fac (a – 1) is wrong have parentheses mistake.

define fac (a) (a) * fac (a – l).

Q.4 (*d*) *Justify, why a friend function cannot be used to overload the assignment operator =*

Ans. A friend function can not be used to overhead =, [ ], (), →. In particular, operator =, operator [ ], operator ( ), and operator → must be non-static member functions; this ensures that their first operands will be I values. If a friend function be used to overload operator =, then we need to pass two arguments and the first argument can be inadvertently value, which is not possible because 2 = *i* is not possible. Hence, a friend function cannot be used to overload an assignment operator.

Q.4 (*e*) *What is a virtual base class. When do we use such class? Explain with an example.*

Ans. Virtual base class. A base class that has been qualified as virtual in the inheritance definition. In multiple inheritance, a derived class can inherit the number of a base class via two or more inheritance paths. If the box class is not virtual, the derived class will inherit more than one copy of the member of the base class. For a virtual base class, however, only one copy of its members will be inherited regardless of the number of inheritance paths between the base class and the derived class.

We use virtual base class when we require both the multiple and multilevel inheritance. For example,

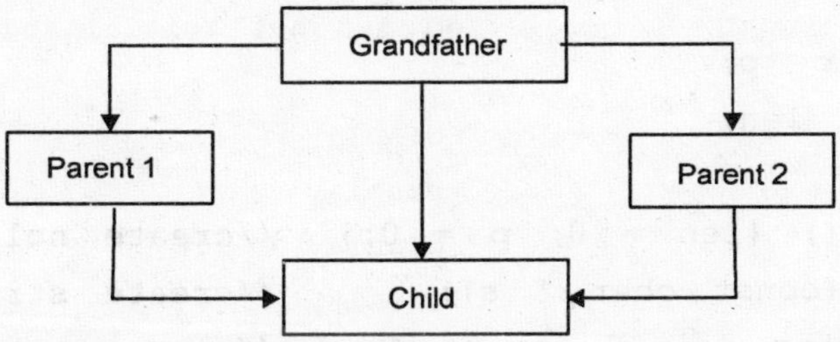

The child has 2 direct base classes "parent 1" and "parent 2" which themselves have a common base class "grandparent". The "child" inherits the traits of "grandparent" via 2 separate paths. It can also inherit directly as shown by the broken line. All the public and protected members of "grandparent" are inherited into child twice. This duplication of inherited members due to these multiple paths can be avoided by making the common base class (ancestor class) as virtual base class.

Q.4 (*f*) *What is explicit constructors? How does it differ from other constructors? Explain.*

Ans. The *explicit* keyboard is used to declare class construction to be "explicit" constructors. While the simple constructor performs *implicit conversion* in which the type received by the constructor is converted to an object of the class in which the constructor is defined. Since, the conversion is automatic, we need not apply any costing. In case, we do not want such automatic conversion to take place, we may do so by declaring the one argument constructor as explicit as:

```
class ABC
  {
   int n;
```

```
public:
  explicit ABC (inti)  || Constructor
  {
    m= i;
     }
  };
```

ABC abc 1 (100) || Objects of A B C class is created

Q. 5. Attempt any TWO of following:

Q.5(*a*) *Create and implement a string class having the following functional requirements:*

(i) The class should have copy constructor in addition to overloading constructors.

(ii) Maximum length of string is not limited.

(iii) There should be a destructor in the class. Also define the need of this destructor.

(iv) There should be friend functions for input, output and comparison.

(v) Assignment operator should be allowed on string.

Ans.

```
# include <string.h>
# include <iostream.h>
class string
{
    char *p;
    int len;
public:
    string () {len = 0; p = 0;}  //create null string
    string (const char * s);     //create string from arrays
      string (const string & s); //copy constructor
      string () {delete p;}      //destructor
      // + operator
    friend string operatorl- (const string &s, const string & t);
      //< = operator
     print int operator <=(const string & s, const string & t);
        friend void show (const string s);
}
string :: string (const char * s)
{
        len = strelen (s);
        p = new char [len+1];
        strcpy (p, s);
}
string :: string {const string & s)
```

```
{
            len = s. len;
            p = new char [len+ 1];
            strcpy (p, s, p);
}
//overloading + operator
string operator + (const string & s. const string & t)
{
            string temp;
            temp, len = s. len + 1 . len;
            temp, p =new char [temp. len+1];
            strcpy (temp. p.s.p):
            strcat (temp, p.t.p);
            return(temp);
}
//overloading <= operator
int operator <= (const string &s, const string &t)
{
            intm = strlen(s.p);
            int n = strlen (t.p);
            if (m <=n)
            return(1);
            else return (0);
}
void show (const string s)
{
            cout<< s.p;
}
int main()
{
            string s1 = ''New'';
            string s2 = ''York";
            string s3 = "Delhi";
            string t1, t2, t3;
t1 = s1;
t2 = s2;
t3 = s1 + s3
cout << ''\nt1 = '' ; show (t1);
```

```
cout << "\nt2" ; show (t2);
cout << "\n" ;
cout << "\nt3 = " ; show (t3);
cout << "\n\n" ;
if (t1, <= t3)
{
        show (t1);
        cout << "smaller than";
        show(t3);
        cout << "\n";
}
else
        show (t3);
        cout << "smaller than";
        show (t1);
        cout << "\n";
}
return 0;
}
```

Q.5 (*b*) *Discuss the syntax for creating, user-defined manipulators. Design a single manipulator to provide the following output specifications for printing float values:*

(*i*) *10 columns width*

(*ii*) *Right justified*

(*iii*) *Two digits precision*

(*iv*) *Filling the unused places with*

(*v*) *Trailing zeros shown*

Ans. Manipulators are formatting instructions inserted directly into a stream.

(*i*) cout . setw (10)

(*ii*) cout self (ios :: right);

(*iii*) cout. set precision (2);

(*iv*) cout setfm ('*');

(*v*) cout trail zero ();

Q.5 (*c*) *Differentiate between JSD and SA/SD methodology for item development.*

Ans. SA/SD includes a variety of notations for formally specifying software. During the analysis phase, data flow diagrams, process specifications, a data dictionary, state transition diagrams, and entity-relationship diagrams are used to logically describe a system. In the design phase, details are added to the analysis models and the data flow diagrams are converted into structure chart descriptions of programming language code.

Data flow diagrams model the transformations of data as it flows through a system and are the focus of SA/SD. A data flow diagram consists of processes, data flows, actors, and data stores. Starting from the top level data flow diagram. SA/SD recursively divides complex processes into sub-diagrams, until many small processes are left that are easy to implement. When the resulting processes are simple enough, the decomposition stops, and a process specification is written for each lowest-level process. Process specifications may be expressed with decision tables, pseudocode, or other techniques.

The data dictionary contains details missing from data flow diagrams. The data dictionary defines data flows and data stores and the meaning of various names.

State transition diagrams model time dependent behaviour and are similar to the dynamic model. Most state transition diagrams describe control processes or timing of function execution and data access triggered by events.

Entity-relationship (ER) diagrams highlight relationships between data stores that otherwise would only be seen in the process specifications. Each ER data element corresponds to one data flow diagram data store. The object modelling notation described in this book (primarily Chapter 3) is an enhanced form of ER diagram.

The above tools are used during the process of structured analysis. Structured design follows structured analysis and addresses low-level details. For example, during structured design, data flow diagram processes are grouped into tasks and allocated to operating system processes and CPUs. Data flow diagram processes are converted into programming language functions, and a structure chart is created showing the procedure call tree.

Jackson Structural Development (JSD) is a methodology different from SA/SD or OMT. JSD uses graphical models.

Simpler problems. Jackson places more emphasis on actions and less on attributes than we do. Some JSD actions look similar to OMT associations. For example, a clerk allocates product to an order. We call allocates an association; Jackson calls it an action. Jackson finds attributes confusing and prefers to avoid them. Actions have such a prominent role in JSD modelling that they permet attributes, in much the same way that attributes diminish the importance of operations in OMT object models.

JSD is a useful methodology for the following types of applications: Concurrent software where processes must synchronize with each other.

Real time software. JSD modelling is extremely detailed and focuses to time.

Microcode. JSD is thorough, makes no assumptions about the availability of an operating system, and considers concurrent processing and timing.

Programming parallel computers. The JSD paradigm of many processes may be helpful here. JSD is ill-suited for some other applications.

High level analysis. JSD does not foster broad understanding of a problem. JSD is ineffective at abstraction and simplification. JSD meticulously handles details but does not help a developer grasp the essence of a problem.

Databases. Database design is a more complex topic than Jackson implies. JSD modelling is biased towards actions and away from entities and attributes. As a natural consequence, it is a poor technique for database design.

Conventional software running under an operating system. JSD's abstraction of hundreds or thousands of processes is confusing and unnecessary.

MCA

THIRD SEMESTER EXAMINATION, 2003-2004

OBJECT-ORIENTED PROGRAMMING AND C++

Time—3 hours **Total Marks—100**

Note: *Attempt ALL questions.*

Q.1 (*a*) Choose the correct alternative out of the following (i) to (xi):

(*i*) *A derived class inherits all members of its base class, but can only use the*

(*a*) *public and protected members of its base class.*

(*b*) *private and public members of its base class.*

(*c*) *protected and private members of its base class.*

(*d*) *none of above*

Ans. (*a*)

(*ii*) *Which of the following keywords cannot be used to define classes in C++?*

(*a*) *struct*

(*b*) *union*

(*c*) *classes*

(*d*) *none of above*

Ans. (*d*)

(*iii*) *Identify the incorrect statement about the keyword, "this"*

(*a*) *The this keyword is a pointer.*

(*b*) *The this keyword is available only in the public member functions.*

(*c*) *The this keyword is available only in the public member function.*

(*d*) *The this keyword holds the address of the object that invokes the member function.*

Ans. (*b*)

(*iv*) *Consider the following:*

int x=65;

cout Set f (ios:: oct, ios:: basefield);

cout << "Value:" << x ++ << endl;

The output is

(*a*) *Value: 65*

(*b*) *Value: 66*

(*c*) *Value: 101*

(*d*) *Value: 41*

Ans. (*c*)

(v) Operator in C++ can be overload using the function named:

(a) Overload

(b) Op + ovr

(c) Ovr – op

(d) None of these

Ans. *(d)*

(vi) The key word friend appears in (identify the incorrect statement).

(a) the class that grants access to another class.

(b) the class that desired access to another class.

(c) the private or protected section of a class.

(d) the public section of a class.

Ans. *(b)*

(vii) Which of the following operators have the same precedence and group left to right?

(a) + =and – =

(b) ::and–>

(c) ++ and – –

(d) None of these

Ans. *(b)*

(viii) What is the return type of a constructor?

(a) void

(b) int

(c) float

(d) None of these

Ans. *(d)*

(ix) The delete operator is used to:

(a) delete a variable name.

(b) delete a member function.

(c) deallocate storage.

(d) None of the above

Ans. *(c)*

(x) Find out the maximum number of constructors that can be defined for a given class:

(a) 0

(b) 1

(c) 2

(d) None of these

Ans. *(d)*

(xi) When no return type is specified for a function:

(a) it may be a constructor.

(b) it may be a destructor.

(c) *it may be a function with default type void.*

(d) *it may be a conversion function.*

Ans. (*a*), (*b*) and (*d*)

Q.1 (*b*) Attempt any five of the following:

(*i*) *What is the significance of scope resolution operator ::?*

(*ii*) *How is matching done in the case of overloaded functions?*

(*iii*) *Explain the role of a default constructor.*

(*iv*) *How can C++ achieve dynamic binding yet also static typing?*

(*v*) *What is a copy constructor? What is its significance?*

(*vi*) *What is a virtual function? Why do we need virtual functions?*

Ans.

(*i*) Resolution operator tells the compiler that the given function belongs to that particular class and also tells the scope of the function is restricted to the class specified in the header.

(*ii*) In case of function over loading, matching is done by the number of arguments passing through the function and data types are used (in order) in function arguments.

(*iii*) A constructor that accepts no parameter is called default constructor. It is used to invoke when an object is created with no arguments.

(*iv*) At run time, when it is known what class objects are under consideration, the approximate version of the function is invoked. And at run time function is linked with a particular class, much after the compilation. This process is called dynamic binding. But what it links at the compile time then it is called static binding.

(*v*) A copy constructor is invoked and initialize an object from another object when a new object is created.

(*vi*) A base class pointer, even when it is made to contain the address of a derived class always executes the function in the base class. To execute the function is derived class when base and derived classes have same function. The function in base class is declared as virtual using the keyword virtual preceding its normal declaration.

Q.2. Attempt any TWO:

Q. 2(*i*) *Write a C++ program to simulate an arithmetic calculate for integers. The program should be able to produce the test result calculated and the number of arithmetic operations performed so far. Any wrong operation is to be reported.*

Ans.
```
# include <iostream.h>
# include <conio.h>
int main ()
{
    int a, b;
    static intent;
    char ch; clrscr();
    cout << "\n Enter the expression";
    cin >> a >ch;
```

```
while (ch! = '=')
{
    cin>>b;
    switch (ch)
{
    case '+':                 // for int sum
    a = a + b;  Cnt ++;
    break;
    case '-':
    a = a - b;  Cnt ++;  // for int sub.
    break;
    case '*':
    a = a * b;  Cnt++;   // for int multiplication
    break;
    case '/':
    a = a/b; Cnt++;     // for int division
    break;
    default;
    cout "Wrong operation is performed";
}
    cout << a;    Cin>>ch;
    clrscr();}
    cout<< "No of operation performed ="<< Cnt;
    return 0;
}
```

Q.2 *(ii) Write a C++ program to evaluate a post-fix expression using stack.*

Ans. Evaluation of postfin enp

```
# include <stream.h>
# define maxcols 80
    class stack
{
  private:
  int position;
  static int top = -1;
  double expr [MAX OLS];
public;
  void input ()
  {
   position = 0;
```

```
    while ((expr {position++} = getchar()) ='/n)
    expr [- -position] = '/0';
  }
  void push (double item)
  {
  expr = item;
  return;
  }
  double pop ()
  {
  double item;
  return expr [top- -];
  }
  friend double eval (stack &s);
}
  double eval (stack &s)
{
  int c;
  double op1, op2, value;
  stack opstk;
  for (s.position = 0; (c.s.expr [s.position])! = '\0';s.position++)
  if(isdigic (c))
  opstk.push ((double) (c-'0'));
else
{ op1 = opstk.pop()
  op2 = opstk.pop ();
  value = oper (c, op1, op2);
  opstk push (value);
}
  return (opstk pop ());
}
  int isdigit (class y)
{
  return (sy >= 'o' && sy <= 'g');
}
  double open (int sy, double op1, double op2)
{
  switch (sy)
{
```

```
    case '+': return (op1 + op2);
    case '-': return (op1 - op2);
    case '*': return (op1 * op2);
    case '/': return (op1/op2);
    case '/': return (pop (op1, op2));
    default exit (1);
  }
  }
    void main ()
  {
    stack st;
    st.input();
    st.output ();
    cout<< ''postfin enp evaluation is"<< eval (&st);
```

Q. 2 (*iii*) ***A class ONE with data members int a and char b inherits from another class TWO with data members float f and int x. Write definitions for ONE and Two for the following situations:***

(a) ***Objects of both the classes are able to access all the data members of both the classes.***

(b) ***Only the members of the class ONE can access all the data members of both the classes.***

Ans. (*a*).

```
class TWO
{
public:
            float t;
            int x;
}
            class ONE; public TWO
            {
            public:
            {
            int a
            float b;
            }
```

(*b*).

```
class TWO
{
protected:
```

```
        int x;
        float f;
    }
    class ONE; public TWO
    {
        int a;
        char b;
    }
```

Use friend function

Q.3. Attempt any two:

Q.3(*i*) *Create a class called rational that represents a rational number p/q as two integers p and q. Besides the constructors, the following operations:*

(a) Overloaded >> and << operators so that the objects of rational can be read and displayed using cin and cout streams respectively.

(b) Three overloaded + operators such that rational + rational, rational + integer and integer + rational can be specified. While adding an integer with rational, the integer value should be treated as a rational with a denominator of 1.

(c) A function simplify () that simplifies the rational number p/q by cancelling the highest common factor of p and q. For example, 28/42 after simplification should be 2/3.

Ans.

```
class rational
{
    int p, q;
public:
    rational (int x, int y)          //constructor
{ p = x; q = y;}
rational operator + (rational, rational);
friend rational operator + (int a, rational b);
friend rational operator + (rational b, int a);
friend rational operator >> (istream &, rational &);
friend rational operator << (ostrearm &, rational &);
rational simplify (rational);
};
```

(*a*)

```
istream & operator >> (istream & din, rational & b)
{
  cin>>b.p;
  cin>>b.q;
  retun(din)
}
ostream & operator << (ostream & cout, rational & b)
```

```
{
  cout << b.p << "/'' <<  b.q;
}
```

(*b*)
```
rational operator (int a, rational b)
{
  rational c;
c.p = b.p + (a * b.q);
c.q = b.q;            // Assume denometor 1
return c;
}
rational operator+ ( rational b, int a)
{
rational c;
c.p = n.p + (a*b.q)
c.q = b.q;
return (c)
}
rational rational:: operator + (rational a)
{ rational c;
c.q = a.q * q
c.p = (a.p * q) + (p*aq);
return c;
}
```

(*c*)
```
rational rational ::simplify (rational r)
{ rational s; int t;
  t = (r.p>r.q)? r.q : r.p;
  for (int i = t; i > 1; i--)
  { if (r.p % t == 0 && r.q % i == 0)
    { s.p = r.p/i;
      s.q = r.q/i;
    }
  }
    return 0 ;
  }
```

Q.3 (*ii*) ***Write definition for two versions of an overload functions. This function's 1st version sum () takes an argument, int array, and return the sum of all the elements of the passed array. The 2nd version of sum () takes two arguments, an int array and a character ('E' or 'O'). If the passed character is 'E', it returns the sum of even elements of the passed array and if the passed character is 'O', it returns the sum of odd elements. Incase of any other character, it returns 0.***

Ans.

```
Class ABC
    { public:
    int arr[10];
void get data (void)
    { cin<< "Enter the 10 values in the array:'';
    for (int i = o; i < 10; i++)
    cin<< arr[i];
    }
    int sum (int*);
    int sum (int* char);
    }
    in ABC ::sum(int*x)
    { int sum = 0; int i;
    for (i = 0; i < 10; i++)
    {
        return (sum);
    }
     int ABC : : sum(int* x, char ch)
    { int sum = 0; int i;
    if (ch = = '/0')
    i = 0;
    else if (ch == '/0')
    i = 1;
    else i=2;
    if (i==2)
    return;
    else while (i< 10)
    { sum = sum + x [i];
    i = i + 2
    return (sum);
    }
```

Q.3 *(iii)* *Write C++ module to perform the following functions using two strings s1 and s2:*

(a) Display the characters common to s1 and s2.

(b) Display the characters appearing in s1 but not in s2.

(c) Swap s1 and s2.

Ans.

```
# include < iostream.h >
# include <string.h>
```

```
class string
{ char name [s];
string ( ) {out << "Enter the string upto schar";
for (int i = 0; i < 6; i++)
cin >> namd [i]
}
void common char (string & a)
{ int i, j;
 for (i = 0; i < 6; i++)
 for (j = 0; j < 6; j++)
{ if (name [i] ==aname[i])
 cout << name [ i]
 }
}
```

(*b*)

```
void uncommon (string & a)
{ int i, j; int flag;
for (i = 0; i < 6; i++)
{ flag = 1
  for(i=0; j < 6; i++)
{ if (name [i] = n. name [i])
     flag = 0;
{
        if (flag)
cout << name [i];
}
```

(*c*)

```
void swap (string & a)
{       string emp;
   strcpy (temp. name, a1 name);
   strcpy (a1. name, name);
   strcpy (name, temp. name);
}
```

Q.4. Attempt any TWO:

***Q.4 (i)** Prepare object diagram showing at least 10 relationships among the following object classes. Include associations, aggregations and generalizations. Use qualified associations and show multiplicity balls in your diagrams. You do not need to show attributes or operations. Use associations names where needed. As you prepare the diagrams, you may add additional object classes.*

(a) School, playground, principal, school board, classroom, book, student, teacher, cafeteria, rest room, computer, desk, chair, ruler, door, swing.

Ans.

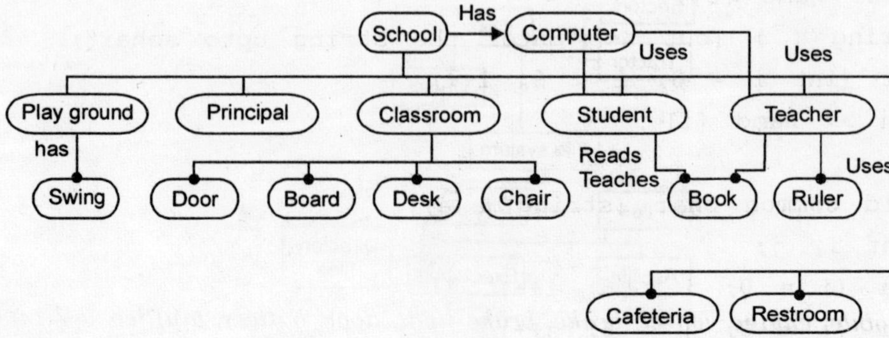

(b) Castle, moat, drawbridge, tower, ghost, stairs, dungeon, floor, corridor, room, window, stone, lord, lady, cook.

Ans.

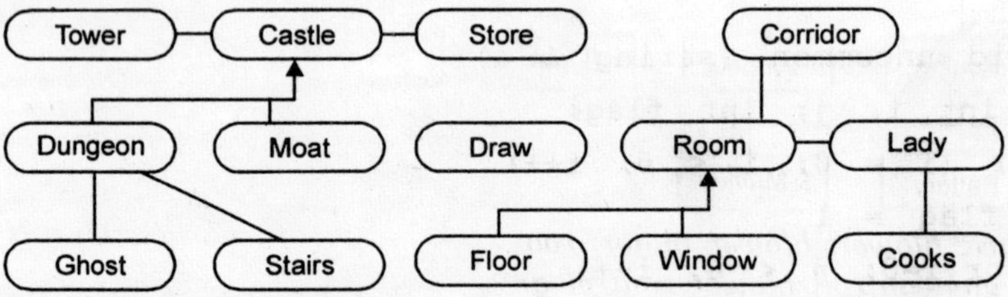

(c) Expression, constant, variable, function, argument list, relational operator, term, factor, arithmetic operator, statement, program.

Ans.

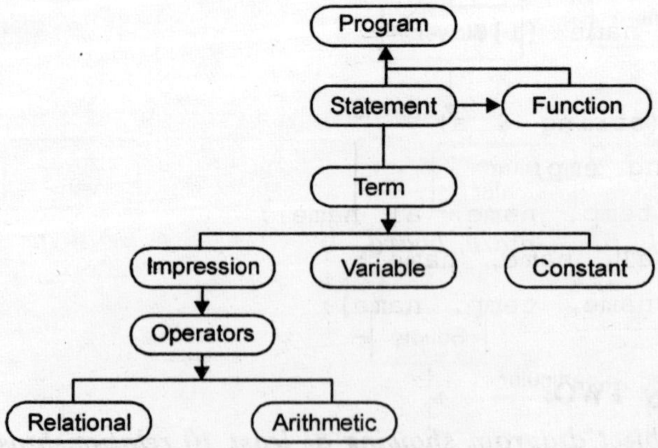

(d) File system, file, directory file name, ASCII file, executable file, directory file, disk, drive, track and sector.

Ans.

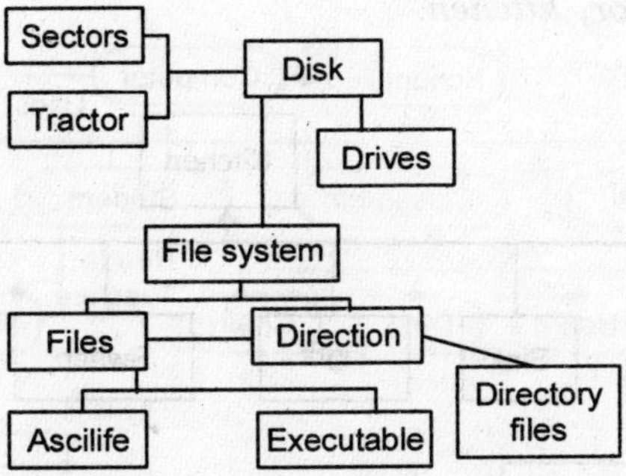

(e) Automobile, engine, wheel, brake, brake light, door, battery, muffler, tail pipe.

Ans.

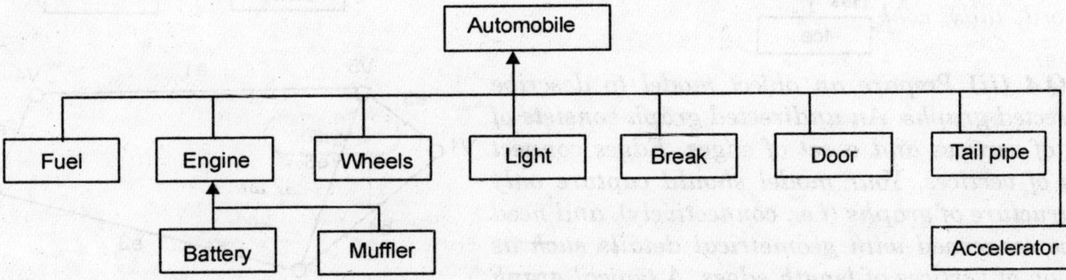

(f) Gas furnace, blower, blower motor, room thermostat, furnace termostat, humidifier, humidity sensor, gas control, blower control and hot air vents.

Ans.

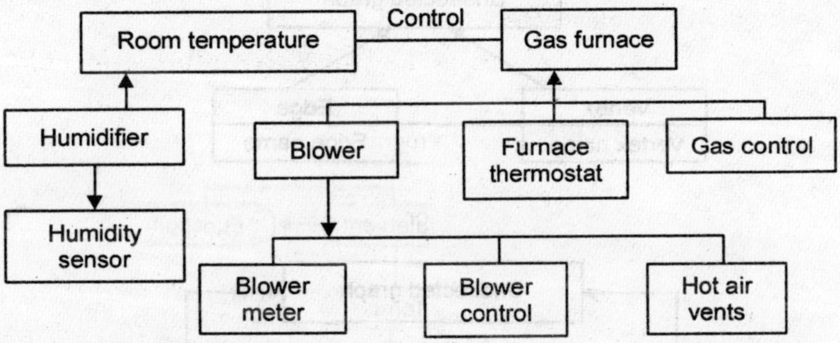

(g) Chess piece, rank, file, square, board, move, position, sequence of moves.

Ans.

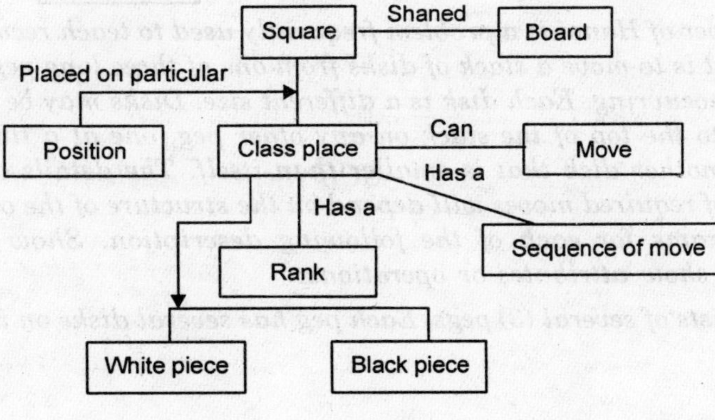

(h) Sink, freezer, refrigerator, table, light, switch, window, smoke alarm, burglar alarm, cabinet, bread, cheese, ice, door, kitchen.

Ans.

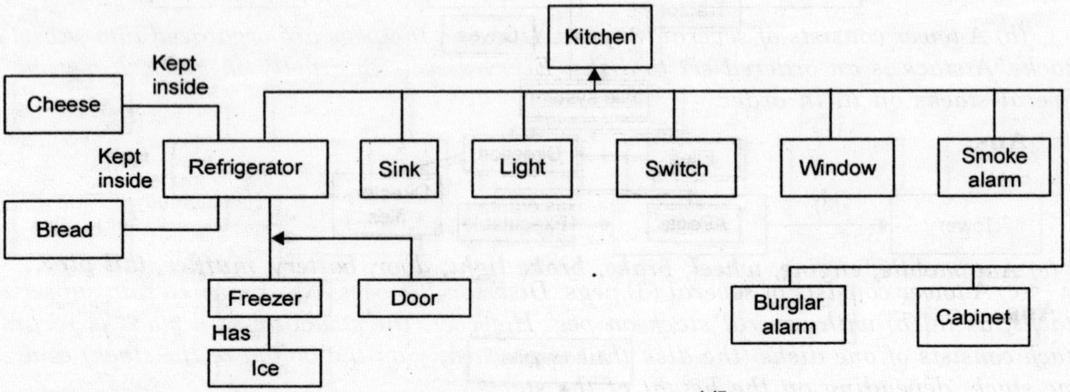

Q.4 (ii) *Prepare an object model to describe undirected graphs. An undirected graph consists of a set of vertices and a set of edges. Edges connect pairs of vertices. Your model should capture only the structure of graphs (i.e., connectively), and need not be concerned with geometrical details such as location of vertices of length edges. A typical graph is shown in figure:*

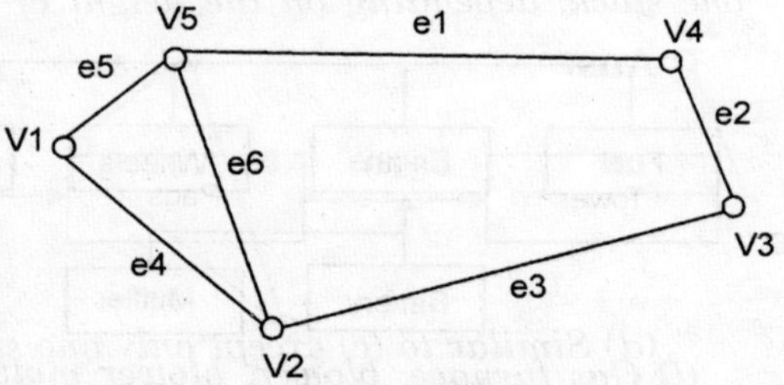

Undirected Graph

Ans.

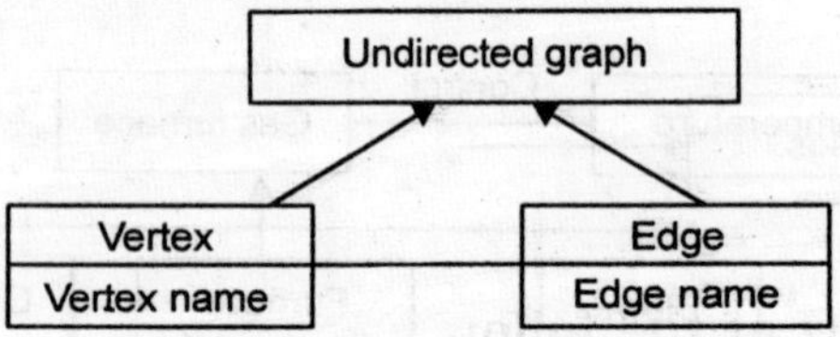

or

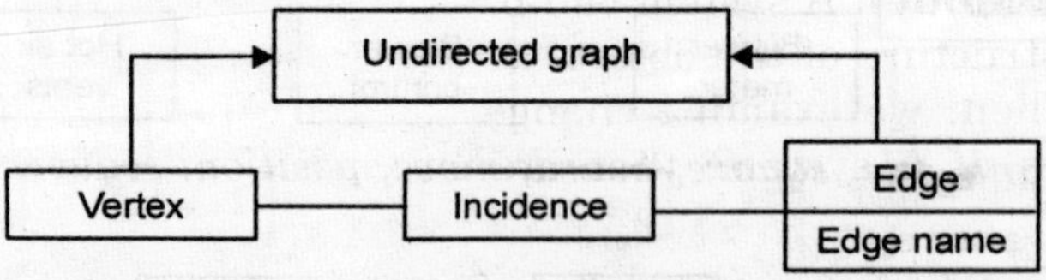

Q.4 (iii) *The tower of Hanoi is a problem frequently used to teach recursive programming techniques. The object is to move a stack of disks from one of three long pegs to another. Using the third peg for manoeuvring. Each disk is a different size. Disks may be moved from the top of a stack on a peg to the top of the stack on any other peg, one at a time, provided a disk is never placed on another disk that is smaller than itself. The details of the algorithm for listing the sequence of required moves will depend on the structure of the object diagram used. Prepare object diagrams for each of the following description. Show object classes and associations. Do not show attributes or operations:*

(a) A tower consists of several (3) pegs. Each peg has several disks on it, in a certain order.

Ans.

(b) A tower consists of several (3) pegs. Disks on the pegs are organized into subset called stacks. A stack is an ordered set to disks. Every disk is in exactly on stack. A peg may have several stacks on it, in order.

Ans.

(c) A tower consists of several (3) pegs. Disks on the pegs are organized into subsets called stacks, as in (b) with several stack on peg. However, the structure of a stack is recursive. A stack consists of one disks (the disk that is physically on the botton of the stack) and zero or one stack, depending on the height of the stack.

Ans.

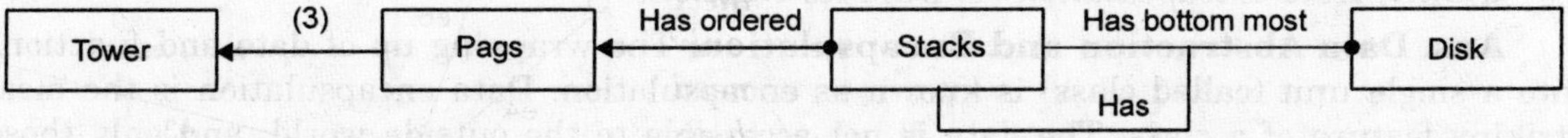

(d) Similar to (c) except only one stack is associated with a peg. Other stacks on the peg are associated in a linked list.

Ans.

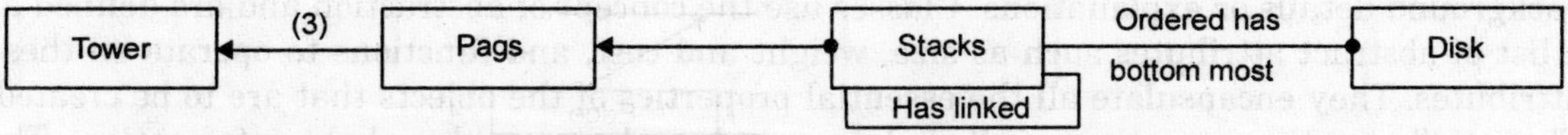

Q. 5. Explain any TWO of the following:

Q.5 (*i*) *Object Modelling vs. Dynamic Modelling*

Ans. Dynamic Model: A system can best be understood by first examining its static structure, i.e., the structure of the objects and their relationships to each other at a single moment in time. Then, we examine changes to the objects and their relationships over time. Those aspects of a system, that are concerned with time and changes, are the dynamic model.

The dynamic model represents control information the sequence of events, states and operations that occur within a system of objects. The notation for the dynamic model represents a compromise between simplicity and expressiveness. There are some meaningful constraints that cannot be expressed by the notation be present. An event is a signal that something has happened. A state represents the interval between events and specifies the context in which events are interpreted. A state diagram is a graph of states and transitions labelled by events.

Q.5 (*ii*) *Polymorphism*

Ans. Polymorphism: It means the ability to take more than one form. An option may exhibit different behaviours in different instances. The behaviour depends upon the types of data used in the operation. It is also known as overloading.

Example: Function add ()is works as polymorphism in the following manner.

```
class ABC
{ public int a, b, c, d, sum;
 void add (int x)
{ a = x; b = 10,
  sum = a + b;
}
 void add (int x, int y)
{ a = x; b = y,
  sum= a + b;}
 void add (int x, int y, int 2;)
  sum = a + b + c + d;
 }
```

there add is a function which is used many times to add many values, so it is polymorphic property.

Q.5(*iii*) *Data Encapsulation vs. Data Abstraction.*

Ans. Data Abstraction and Encapsulation: The wrapping up of date and functions into a single unit (called class) is known as encapsulation. Data encapsulation is the most striking feature of a class. The data is not accessible to the outside world, and only those functions which are wrapped in the class can access it. These functions provide the interface between the objects data and the program. This insulation of the data from direct access by the program is called data hiding or information hiding.

Abstraction refers to the set of representing essential features without including the background details or explanations. Classes use the concept of abstraction and are defined as a list of abstract attributes such as size, weight and cost, and functions to operate on these attributes. They encapsulate all the essential properties of the objects that are to be created. The attributes are sometimes called data members because they hold information. The functions that operate on these data ate sometimes called methods or member functions.

Q.5 (*iv*) *I/O in C++.*

Ans. C++ supports a rich set of functions and operations to perform I/O. It uses the concept of stream classes to implement its I/O operation with the onsole and disk files.

The stream is a sequence of bytes.

Source stream or I/P stream provides data to the program.

Destination stream or O/P stream get data from I/P stream.

C++ has several predefined stream that the automatically opened when a program beings its execution.

C++ contains of classes that are used to define various streams these classes are called stream classes.

>> operator is overloaded in istream op is overloaded in ostream get () is in istream I/P single character.

Put () is in ostream to O/P single character.

Write () is to O/P a whole line of tout.

Syntax:

cout write (line, size).

MCA

THIRD SEMESTER EXAMINATION, 2004-2005

OBJECT-ORIENTED PROGRAMMING AND C++

Time—3 hours Total Marks—100

Note: *1. Attempt **ALL** questions.*

2. All questions carry equal marks.

Q.1. Attempt any FOUR of the following:

Q.1(*a*) *What are inline functions? Explain with example.*

Ans. Inline functions. To eliminate the cost of calls to small functions, C++ proposes a new feature called inline function. An inline function is a function that is expanded in time when it is involved. That is, the compiler replaces the function call with the corresponding function code (something similar to macros expansion). The inline functions are defined as follows:

```
inline function header
{
  function body
```

Inline expansion makes a program run faster because the overhead of a function call and return is eliminated.

For Example,

```
# include <iostream>
inline float null (float x, float y)
{
return (x * y)
}
inline double div (double p, double q)
{
return (p/q)
  }
int main ()
  {
     float a = 12.345;
     float b = 9.82;
     cout<< null (a, b) << "\n";
     cout << div (a, b) << "\n";
     return 0;
     }
```

Output:

```
121.228
1.25713
```

The speed benefits of inline functions diminish as the function grows in size, usually, the functions are made inline, when they are small enough to be defined in one or two lines.

Q.1 (*b*) *What is reference? How it is similar and/or different to pointers?*

Ans. When the address of a variable is stored in some other variable name then this is called reference.

Example: b = & a

a has reference of b or

a contains address of b.

Pointer points the value of the variable whose address is stored in another variable.

Reference indicates address of variable but pointer indicate value of the variable at that address.

Example:
```
int a = 5, *b;
b = & a
printf ('`b = %d, a = %d', b, *b);
```

Here, b is reference of a and *b is the pointer of a.

Q.1 (*c*) *What are general rules for overloading functions in C++.*

Ans. Function overloading means that we can use the same function name to create functions that perform a variety of different tasks.

General rules for overloading functions in C++ are:

1. The compiler first tries to find an exact match in which the type of actual argument are the same, and use that function.
2. If an exact match is not found, the compiler uses the integral promotions to the actual arguments such as to

   Char to int

   Float to double

   To find a match
3. When either of them fails, the compiler tries to use the built in conversions (the implicit assignment conversions) to the actual arguments and then uses the function whose match is unique. If the conversion is possible to have a multiple matches, then the complier will generate an error message. Suppose, we use the following 2 functions:

   Long square (long n)

   Double square (double x)

   A function call such as square (10) will cause an error because in argument can be converted to either long or double, thereby creating an ambiguous situations as to which version of square () should be used.
4. If all of the steps fail, then the complier will try the user-defined conversions in combination with integral promotions and built-in conversions to find a unique match. User defined conversions are often used in handling class objects.

Q.1 (*d*) *What are virtual functions? Explain how run-time polymorphism can be achieved using them?*

Ans. Virtual functions. A function qualified by the virtual keyword. When we use the same function name in both the base and derived classes, the function in base class is declared as virtual using the keyword virtual preceding its normal declaration.

When a function is made virtual, C++ determines which function to use at run time based on the type of object pointed to by the base pointer, rather than the type of the pointer. Thus, by making the base pointer to point to different objects, we can execute different versions of the virtual function.

Run time polymorphism is achieved only when a virtual function is accessed through a pointer to the base class. It cannot be achieved using object name along with the dot operator to access virtual operation.

Q.1 (*e*) *What is 'this' operator? Explain its distinct use?*

Ans. This is a pointer that pointer to the object for which '*this*' function was called. C++ used a unique keyword called '*this*' to represent an object that involves a member function.

This unique pointer is automatically passed to a member function when it is called. The pointer '*this*' acts as an implicit argument to all the member function.

For example,

```
Class ABC
{
int a;
........
........
} ;
```

this → a = 123; (| | in place of a = 123)

One important application of the pointer 'this' is to return the object it points to.

Q.1 (*f*) *Explain the hierarchy for C++ STREAM classes.*

Ans. The C++ I/O system contains a hierarchy of classes that are used to define various streams to deal with both the console and disk files. These classes are called stream classes.

The hierarchical diagram of stream classes:

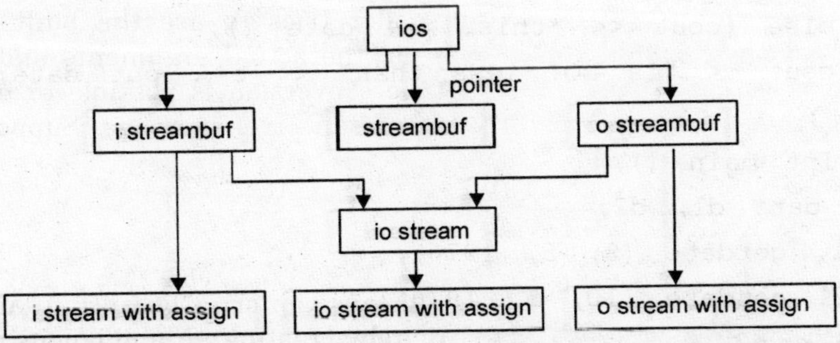

These classes that are declared in the header file iostream. This file should be included in all the programs that communicate with the console unit, ios is the base class for istream (input stream) and ostream (output stream) which are in turn base, classes for iostream (I/o stream). The class ios is declared as the virtual base class so that only one copy of its members are inherited by the iostream.

The class ios provides the basic support for formatted and unformatted I/O operations. The class istream provides the facilities for formatted and unformatted input while the class ostream (through inheritance) provides the facilities for formatted output. The class *iostream* provides the facilities for handling both input and output stream Three classes namely, istream with assign, ostream with assign and iostream with assign add assignment operators to these classes.

Q.2. Attempt any two of the following:

Q.2 (*a*) *Overload '<' operator to find out whether a given date is less than or not with respect to another given date.*

Ans.
```
class date
  { int day,  month,  year;
    public:
void get date  (int  x,  int  y,  int  z)
    { day  =  x;  month  =  y;  year  =  z;}
void put data  (void)
    {  cout  <<  day  <<  ":"  <<  month
          <<  ":"  <<  year;}
void operator  <  (date  t)
    {  if  (year  <t.  year)
          {  Cout  <<  *this.  put  data  ();
cout<<  "is  less  than"  <<  t  .  put  data  ();
    }
  else if  (year==  t.  year  &&  month  <t  .  month)
      {  cout  <<  *  this  .  put data  ();
        cout<<  "is  less  than"  <<  t.put  data  ();}
  else if  (year  =  t.year  &&  month  =  t.month  &&  day  <  t.day)
{ cout << * this  . put data  ()  "is less than"  << t.  put data;
    }
  else  {cout  <<  *this.  put  data  ();
  cout  <<  "is  NOT  less  than"  <<  t  .  put  data;
}  ;
  int  main  ()
{  data  d1,  d2;
d1.  getdate  (8,  5,  1976);
d2.  getdate  (10,  5,  1976);
d1  <  d2
return  0;
}
```

Q.2 (*b*) *Write a program 'AREA' in C++, which calculate area of the circle, square, rectangle, triangle depending upon user's choice. Use function overloading.*

Ans.
```
class area
{
void area (x, double r)
{
cout << "area of circle";
a1 = B.4 * r * r;
cout << "a1";
void area (int x, int y)
{
cout << "Area of rectangle";
a2 = x * y
cout << "a2";
}
void area (int 2)
{
cout << "Area of square";
a3 = z * z;
cout << "a3";
}
main ()
{
  int C;
cout << "Enter choice";
cout << "1- circle";
cout << "2 - rectangle";
cout << "3 - square";
cin >> C;
if (C==1)
{
cout << "Enter radius";
cin >> r;
area (r);
}
if (C == 2)
{
cout << "Enter x";
cin >>"x";
cout << "Enter y";
```

```
cin >> y;
  area (x, y);
}
if (C == 3)
{
cout << "Enter 2";
cin >> 2;
area (2);
    }
```

Q.2 (c) *Write a program in C++, which asks for 'system-in' and 'system-out' time from user and calculates 'system-use-time'. Use classes and objects.*

Ans.

```
class system
{ int hin, min, sin;
  int hout, mout, sout;
void get data (void)
      { cout << ''Enter the system in time:";
    cin >> hin >> min >> sin ;
        cout << "Enter system out time:";
        cin >> hout >> mout > sout;
void use time (void)
    { int hr, mnt, sec;
        sec = sout - sin;
        if (sec < 0)
      { sec = 60 + sec;
       mout--;
      }
       mnt = mout - min;
    if (mnt<0)
       { mnt = 60+mnt;
         hout--;
       }
        hr = hout - hin;
    cout << "System use time is" << hr<< mnt << sec;
      }
      } ;
        int main ()
      { system A;
       A . get data ();
       A . use time ();
       return 0;
      }
```

Q.3. Attempt any two of the following:

Q.3 ***(a)*** *A directory file contains information about flies in a directory, including both ordinary flies as well as directory files.*

Ans.

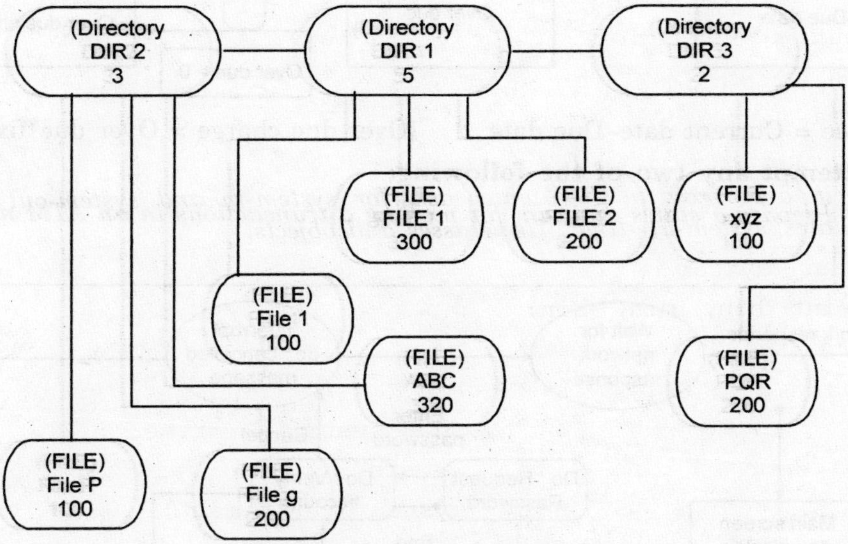

Instance diagram

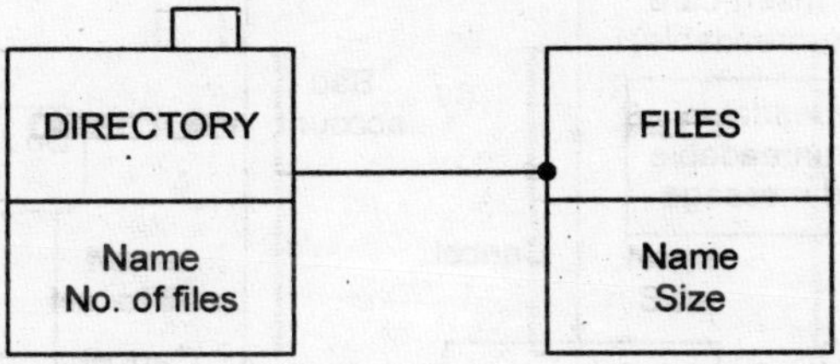

Q.3 ***(b)*** *Prepare an object diagram for the dining-philosopher's problem. There are 5 philosophers and 5 forks around a circular table. Each philosopher has access to two forks on either on the table or in use by one philosopher. A philosopher must have 2 forks to eat.*

Ans. Object diagram for the Dining-Philosophers problem.

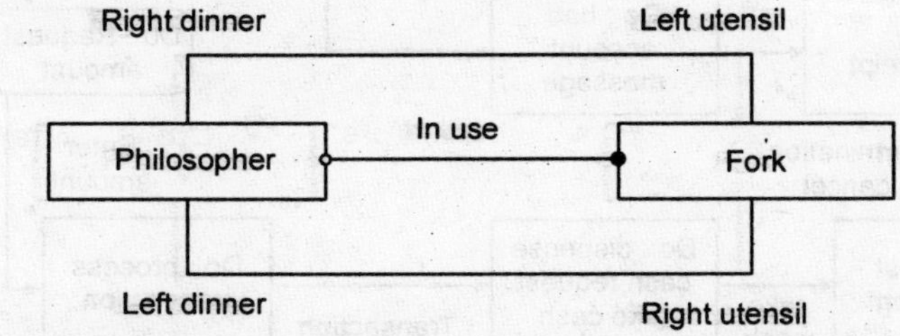

The one-to-one associations describe the relative locations of philosophers and forks. The 'In use' association describes who is using which is forks. Other representations are possible, depending on your view point.

Q.3 ***(c)*** *Prepare a portion of an object diagram for a library book check out system that shows the date of a book is due and the late charges for an overdue book as derived objects.*

Ans.

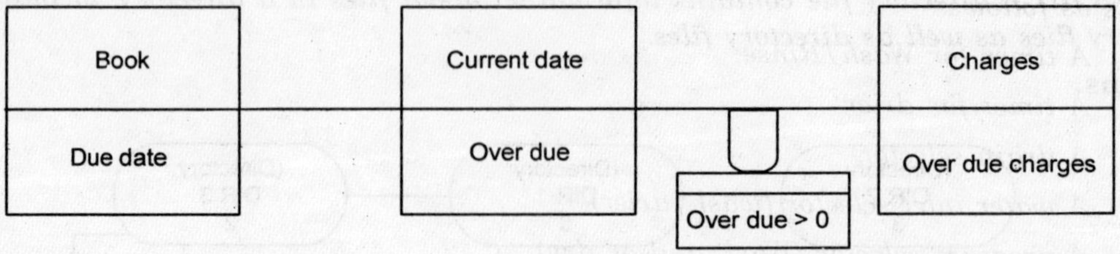

Over due = Current date–Due date {Over due charge = Over due*fixed charge}

Q.4. Attempt any two of the following:

Q.4 (a) *Prepare a states diagram for making a transactions in an ATM machine.*

Ans.

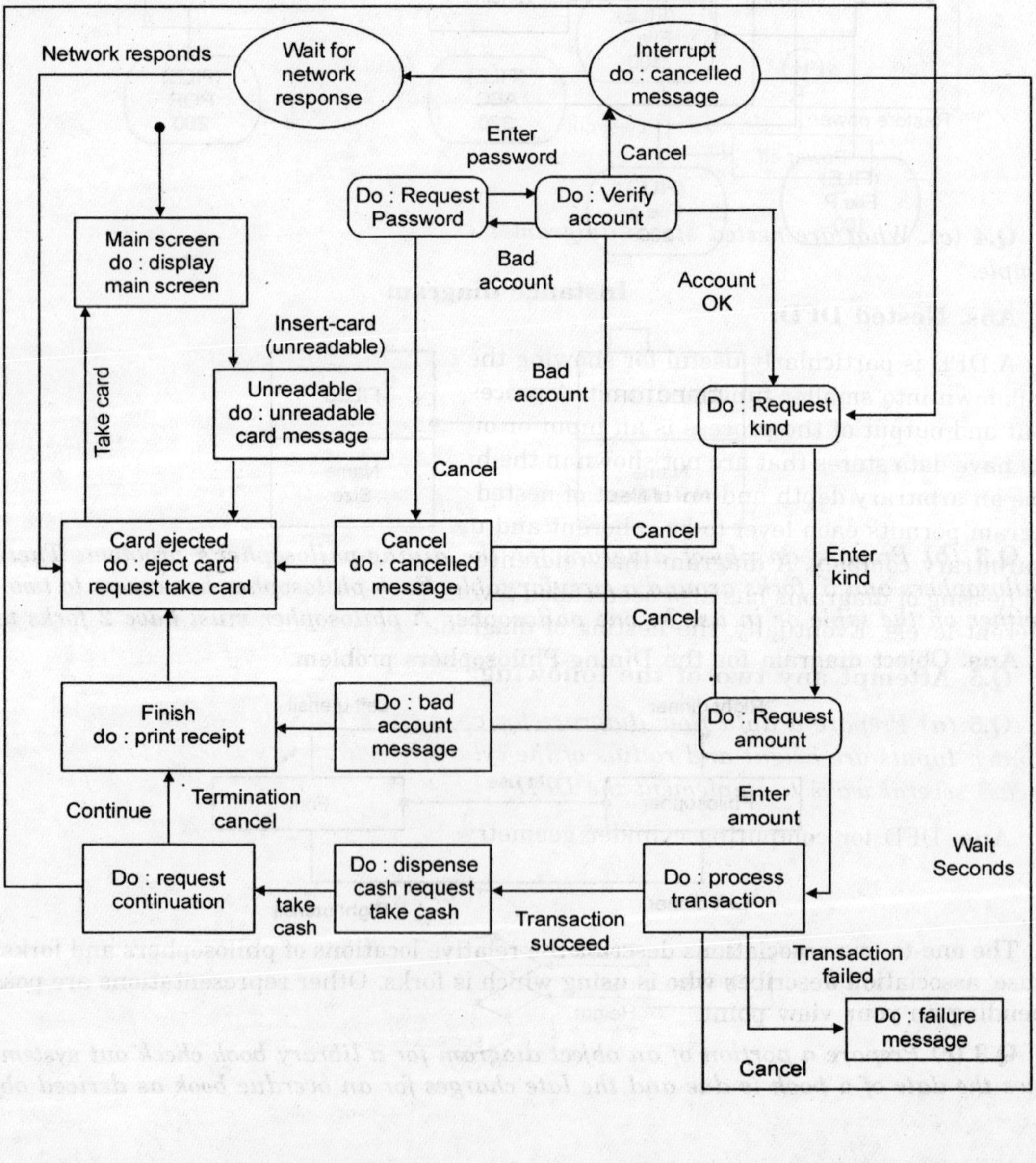

Q.4 (*b*) *Prepare states diagram for a Twin-Tub, semiautomatic machine having usual controls as follows:*

(i) A timer for Wash/Rinse.

(ii) A timer for drier.

(iii) A drain selector.

(iv) A water inlet selector (wash/drier)

(v) A program selector (Wash and or dry)

Ans. Washing machine:

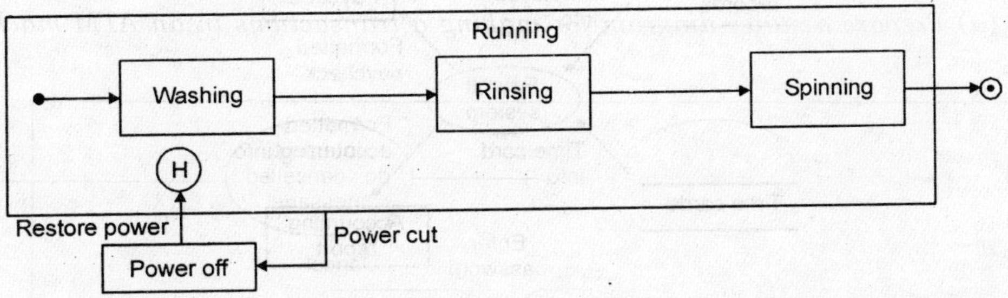

Q.4 (*c*). *What are nested states diagrams? Why they are useful? Explain with suitable example.*

Ans. Nested DFD:

A DFD is particularly useful for showing the high-level functionality of a system and its breakdown into smaller functional unit. A process can be expanded into another DFD. Each input and output of the process is an input or output of the new diagram. The new diagram may have data stores that are not shown in the higher-level diagram. Diagrams can be nested to be an arbitrary depth and entire set of nested diagrams forms a tree. Nesting of data flow diagram permits each level to be coherent and understandable; yet overall functionality can be arbitrary complex. A diagram that references itself represents a recursive computation. The nesting of diagrams has also been called levelling. Since the diagrams are organized into different levels. Eventually, the nesting of diagrams terminates with simple functions.

Q.5. Attempt any two of the following:

Q.5 *(a)* *Prepare a data flow diagram for computing the volume and surface area of a cylinder. Inputs are height and radius of the cylinder, outputs are volume and surface area. Discuss several ways to implement the DFD.*

Ans. DFD for computing cylinder geometry:

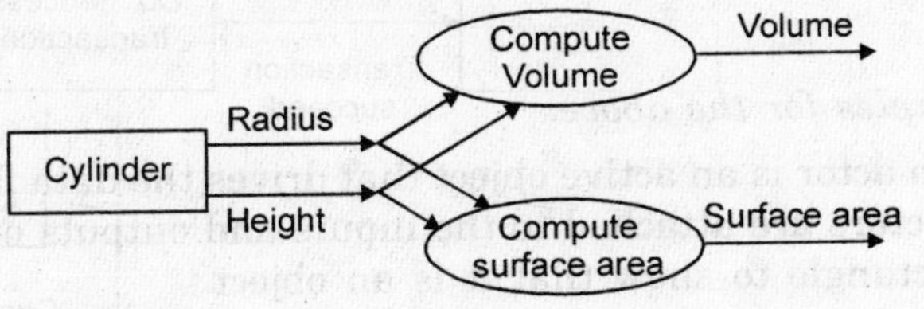

Formula:

Volume $= \pi r^2 h$

Surface area = $2 \pi r h$ (r = radius, h = height)

Q.5 ***(b) Prepare a DFD for payroll system in a company.***

Ans. Level 0: Payroll system

Level 1:

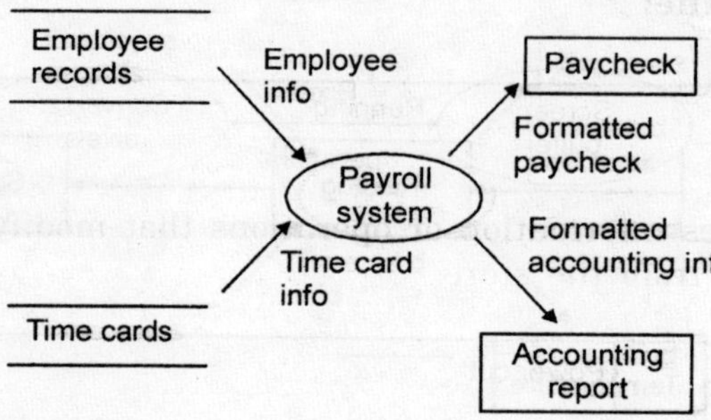

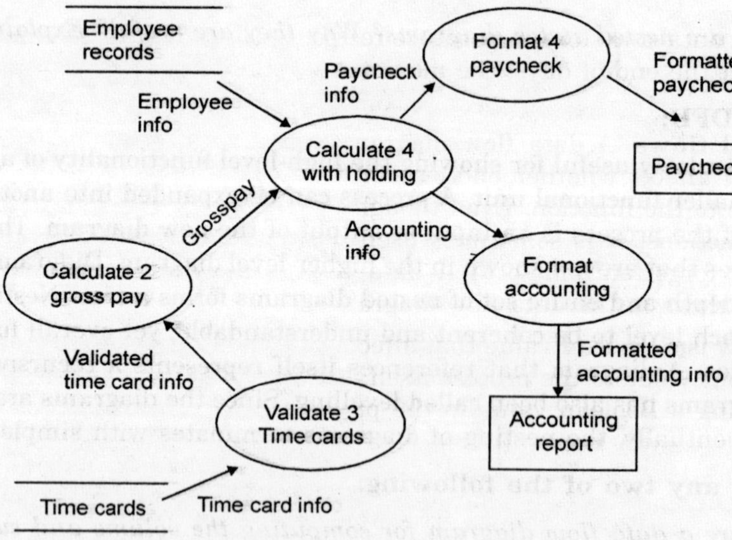

Q.5 ***(c) Explain the following with reference to data flow diagrams:***

(i) Actors

(ii) Data stores

(iii) Control flows

Give suitable examples for the above.

Ans. (*i*) Actors. An actor is an active object that drives the data flow graph by producing or consuming values. Actors are attached to the inputs and outputs of a data flow graph. An actor is drawn as a rectangle to show that it is an object.

(*ii*) Data stores. It is a passive object within a data flow diagram that stores data for later access unlike an actor, a data store does not generate any operations on its own but merely responds to request to store and access data.

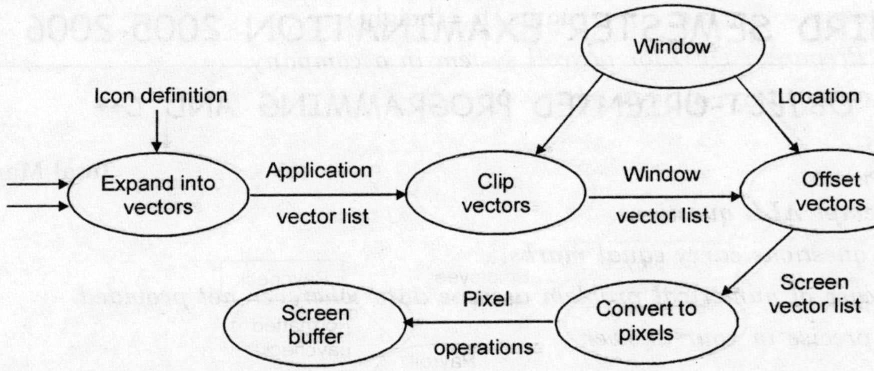

Input arrows indicates information or operations that modify the stored data. Output arrows indicate retrieved from the store.

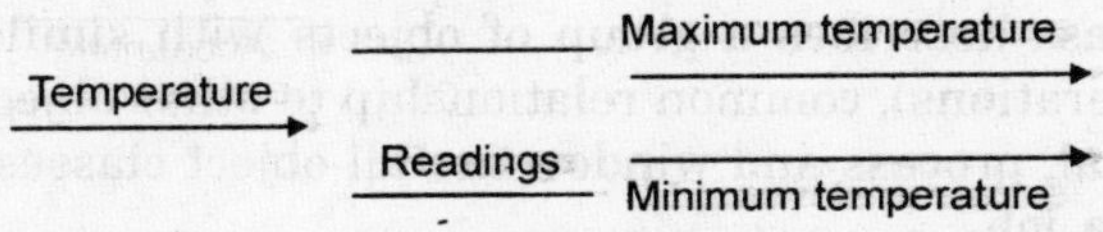

'Reading' is a data store for temperature readings. Every hour new temperature readings enter the store. At the end of days, the maximum and minimum reading are retrieved from the store.

***(iii)* Control flows.** A data flow diagram shows all possible computations paths for values. A decision affects whether one or more functions are even performed, rather than supplying a value to the function. Even though the functions do not have input values from these decision functions. It is sometimes useful to include than in the functional model so that they are not forgotten and so their data dependencies can be shown. This is done by including control flows in the data flow diagram.

A central flow is a boolean value that affects whether a process is evaluated. The control flow is not an input value to the process itself. A control flow is shown by a dotted line from a process producing a Boolean value to the process being controlled.

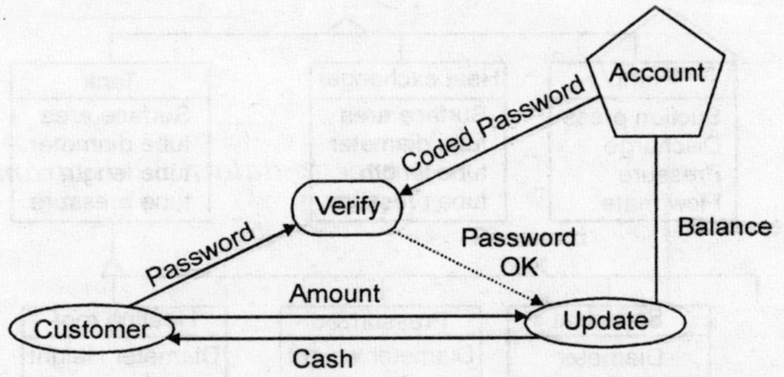

A data flow diagram for a withdrawal from a bank account. The customer supplies a password and an amount. The withdrawl occurs only if the password is successfully verified.

The update process could be branded with a similar control flow to guard against overdrafts.

MCA

THIRD SEMESTER EXAMINATION 2005-2006

OBJECT-ORIENTED PROGRAMMING AND C++

Time—3 hours | Total Marks—100

Note: *1. Attempt* ***ALL*** *questions.*

2. All questions carry equal marks.

3. In case of numerical problem assume data wherever not provided.

4. Be precise in your answer.

Q.1. Attempt *any four* parts of the following: (5×4=20)

Q.1 *(a)* *What are object class? Discuss how they are different from Normal class.*

Ans. An object class describes a group of objects with similar properties (attributes), common behaviour (operations), common relationship to other objects and common semantics person, company, animal, process and window are all object classes. Each person has an age, IQ, and may work at a job.

The abbreviation class is often used instead of object class.

Q.1 *(b)* *How does inheritance differ from generalisation? Explain with an example.*

Ans. Difference between inheritance and generalisation:

Generalization and inheritance are powerful abstractions for sharing similarities among classes while preserving their differences.

Inheritance refers to the mechanism of sharing attributes and operations using the generalization concepts.

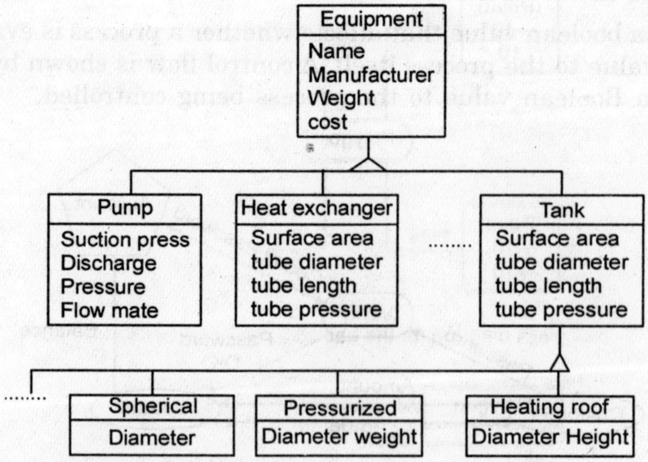

A Multilevel inheritance hierarchi with instances

Generalization is the relationship between a class and one or more refined versions of it. The class being refined is called the **superclass** and each refined version is called a **subclass**. For example, Equipment is the superclass of **Pump** and **Tank**.

Q.1 ***(c) Design a template class for implement a LINKED LIST.***

Ans.

```
template < class T>
class sample
{
private : data, T * Link ;
}
T oppend ( )
{
T C ;
C = n ;
return (c) ;
} ;
};
void main ( )
{ add <int> obj 1;
cout<< "the integer added is = "<< obj 1 append ();
getch ( );
}
```

Q.1 ***(d) Draw a class and instance diagram for loopping statement in C programming language.***

Ans. Instance diagram of a polygon that happens to be square

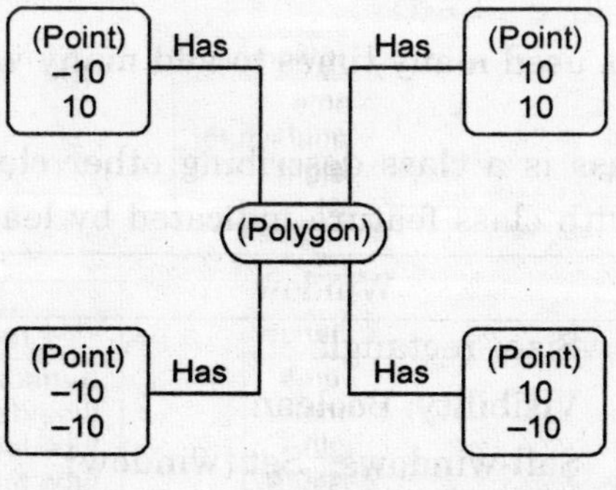

class diagram for the above instance diagram

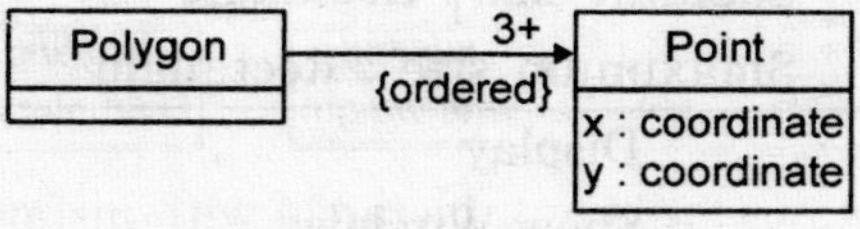

Q.1 ***(e) What is aggregation? Explain with an example and a suitable diagram.***

Ans. Aggregation is the "Parts whole or 'a-part'-of" relationship in which objects representing the components of something are associated with an object representing the entire assembly.

Example. The bill-of-materials or parts explosion tree, A name, argument-list and a compound statement are part-of a C-language function definition, which in turn is part of an entire programme.

Company office organisation officer person

Q.1 ***(f)*** *Define the following term, giving at least one example of each.*

(i) Polymorphism (ii) Meta class

Ans. (*i*) Polymorphism. It means the ability to take more than one form. An option may exhibit different behaviours in different instances. The behaviour depends upon the types of data used in the operation. It is also known as overloading.

Example. Function add () is works as polymorphism in the following manner.

```
class ABC
{ public int a, b, c, d sum;
 void add (int x)
{ a = x; b = 10,
 sum = a + b;
}
 void add (int x, int y)
{ a = x; b = y;
 sum = a + b; }
 void add (int x, int y, int 2)
     sum = a + b + c + d;
```

there add is a function which is used many times to add many values. So it is polymorphisim property.

(*ii*) Meta class. Meta class is a class describing other classes.

Example. Class window with class feature indicated by leading dollar sign.

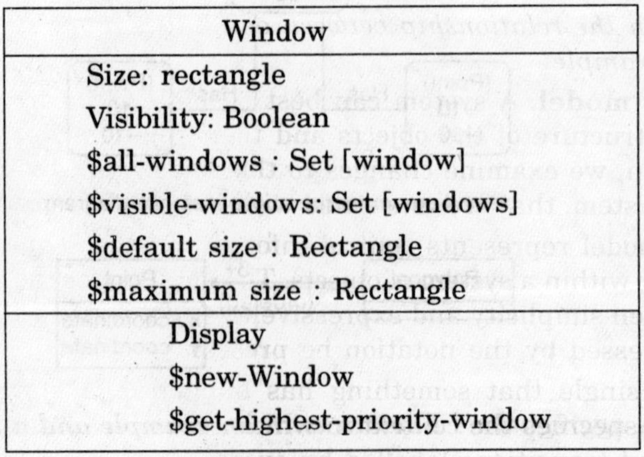

Class with class feature

Q.2. Attempt *any four* parts of the following: **(5×4=20)**

Q.2 (*a*) *What is dynamic model? Explain how events between two object are identified, with the help of an example.*

Ans. Dynamic model. A system can best be understood by first examining its static structure i.e., the structure of the objects and their relationships to each other at a single moment in time. Then, we examine changes to the objects and their relationships over time. Those aspects of a system, that are concerned with time and changes, are the dynamic model.

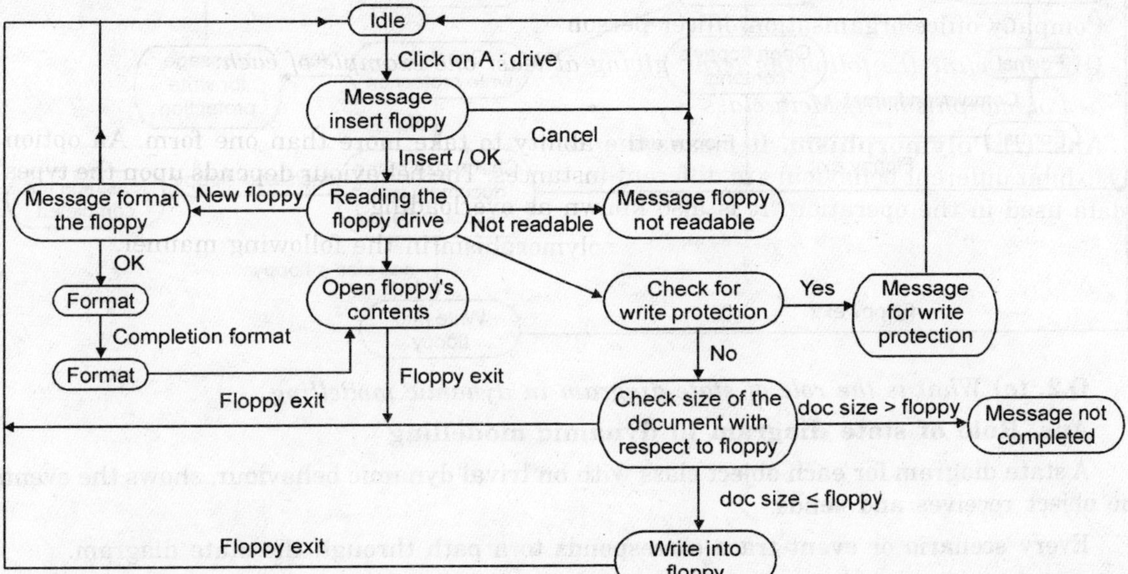

The dynamic model represents control information the sequence of events, states and operations that occur within a system of objects. The notation for the dynamic model represents a compromise between simplicity and expressiveness. There are some meaningful constraints that cannot be expressed by the notation be present.

An event is a single that something has happened. A state represents the interval between events and specifies the context in which events are interpreted. A state diagram is a graph of states and transitions labelled by events.

Example. State diagram for floppy drive of a computer system.

Q.2. (*b*) *Explain the relationship between object and dynamic model. Your explanation should include an example.*

Ans. Dynamic model. A system can best be understood by first examining its static structure, i.e., the structure of the objects and their relationships to each other at a single moment in time then, we examine changes to the objects and their relationships over time. Those aspects of a system, that are concerned with time and changes, are the dynamic model.

The dynamic model represents control information the sequence of events, states and operations that occur within a system of objects. The notation for the dynamic model represents a compromise between simplicity and expressiveness. There are some meaningful constraints that cannot be expressed by the notation be present.

An event is a single that something has happened. A state represents the interval between events and specifies the context in which events are interpreted. A state diagram is a graph of states and transitions labelled by events.

Example. State diagram for floppy drive of a computer system.

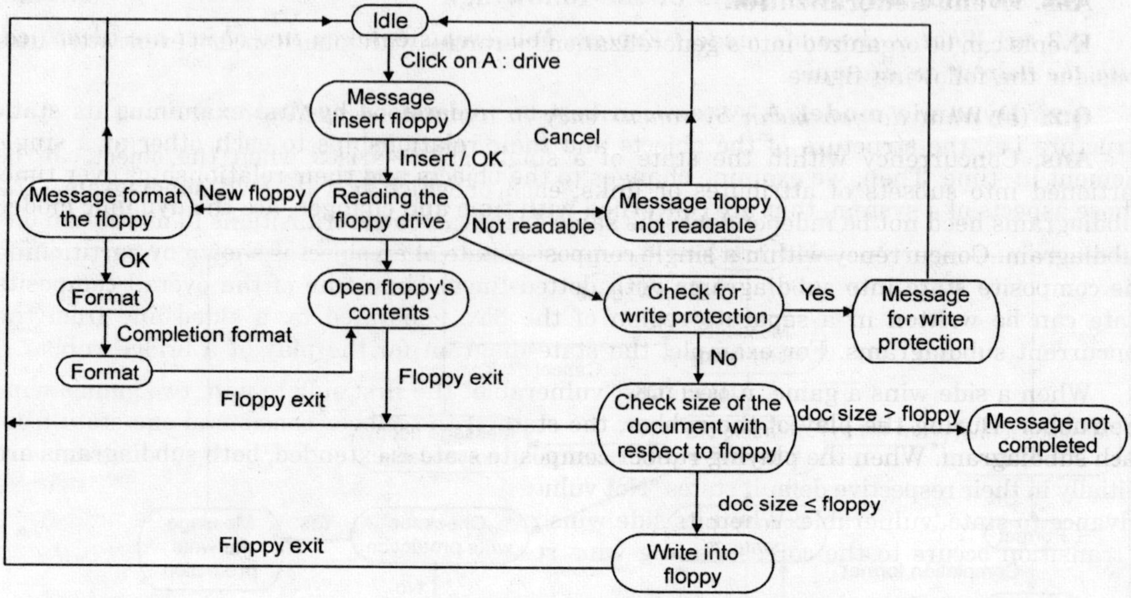

Q.2. **(c)** *What is the role of state diagram in dynamic modelling.*

Ans. Role of state diagram in dynamic modelling

A state diagram for each object class with on trival dynamic behaviour, shows the events the object receives and sends.

Every scenario or event trace corresponds to a path through the state diagram.

The interval between any two event is a state.

Q.2. **(d)** *Explain the event generalisation with the help of suitable example.*

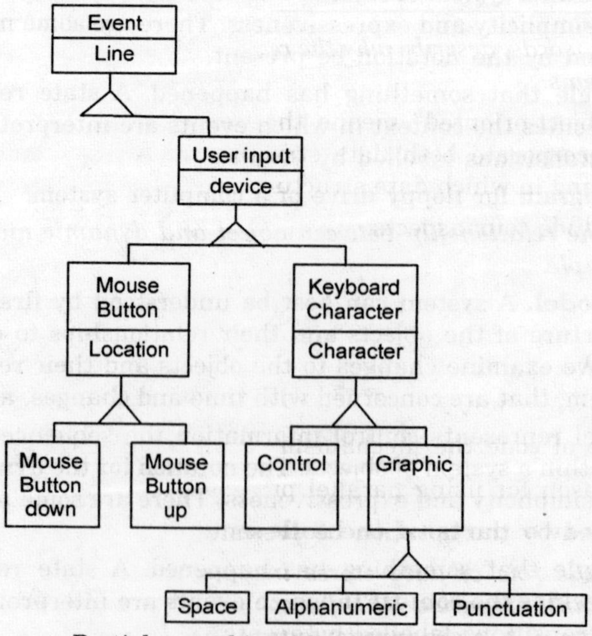

Partial event hierarchy for K.B. events

Ans. Event Generalization

Events can be organized into a generalization hierarchy with inheritance of event attributes consider the following figure.

Q.2. *(e) What do you mean by concurrency in dynamic modelling?*

Ans. Concurrency within the state of a single object arises when the object can be partioned into subsets of attributes or links; each of which has its own subdiagram. The subdiagrams need not be independent; the same event can cause transitions in more than one subdiagram. Concurrency within a single composite state of an object is shown by partitioning the composite state into subdiagrams with dotted lines. The name of the overall composite state can be written in a separate region of the box, separated by a sided line from the concurrent subdiagrams. For example, the state diagram for the play of a bridge rubber.

When a side wins a game, it becomes "vulnerable" the first side to win, two games wins the rubber. During the play of the rubber, the state of the rubber consists of one state from each subdiagram. When the playing rubber composite state is extended, both subdiagrams are initially in their respective default states "Not vulnerable". "Each subdiagrams can independently advance to state 'vulnerable' When its side wins a game. When one side wins a second game, a transition occurs to the corresponding wins rubber state.

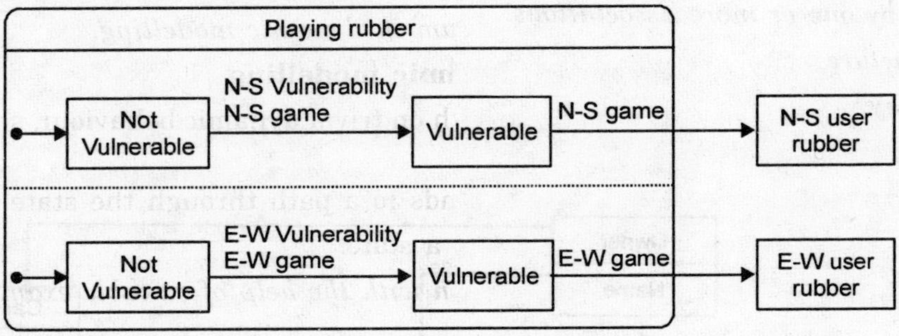

Q. 2 *(f) In your own words, describe why the recursive / parallel process model is appropriate for object oriented systems.*

Ans. The term "object-oriented" means that we organise software as a collection of discrete objects that incorporate both data structure and behaviour. This is in control to conventional programming in which data structure and behaviour are only loosely connected.

They generally include four aspects:

→ identity

→ classification

→ poly, morphism

→ Inheritance

To make the reuse of code the mechanism called inheritance is used.

And this is the reason for using parallel process model in object-oriented systems.

Q.3. Attempt any two parts of the following: (10×2=20)

Q.3. *(a) What is the role of data stores in data flow diagram? Using the quadratic formula as a starting point, prepare a DFD for computing the roots of quadratic equation* $ax^2 + bx + c = 0$ *real numbers a, b, c are inputs, outputs are values of* $x = R1$ *and* $x = R2$*, which* *satisfy the equation. Remember R1 and R2 may be real or complex depending on the values of a, b and c. The quadratic formula for R1 and R2 is* $\frac{-b \pm \sqrt{b^2 - 4ac}}{2a}$.

Ans. Data Stores. It is a passive object within a data flow diagram that stores data for later access unlike an actor, a data store does not generate operations on its own but merely responds to request to store and access data.

Input arrows indicates information or operations that modify the stored data. Output arrows indicate retrieved from the store.

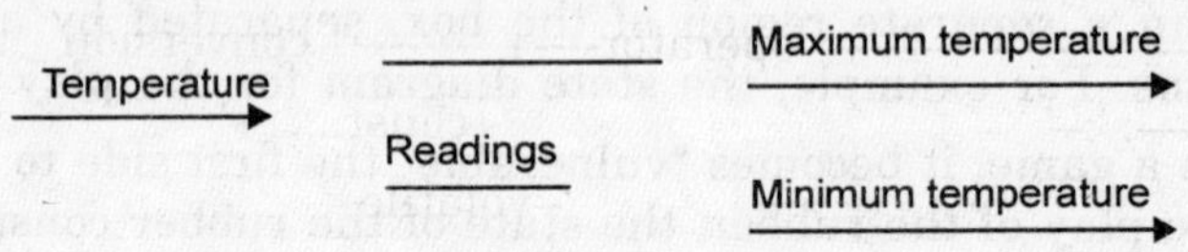

'Reading' is a data store for temperature readings. Every hour new temperature readings enter the store. At the end of days, the maximum and minimum reading are retrieved from the store.

Q.3 (*b*) *Draw object diagram in which each of the following conventional data structures is replaced by one or more associations.*

(i) *Structure*

(ii) *Array*

Ans.

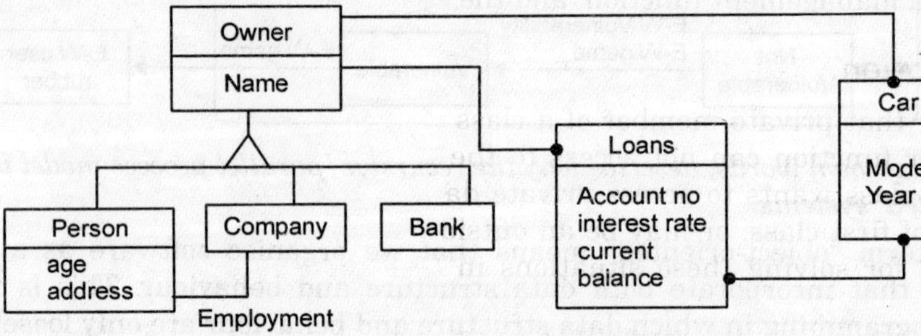

Proper object model for car loans

Q.3 (*c*) *For each of the following system*

(*i*) *Chess player*

(*ii*) *Software to mail merge*

Identify the relative importance of three aspects of modelling:

(*i*) *Object modelling*

(*ii*) *Dynamic modelling*

(*iii*) *Functional modelling. Explain your answer.*

Ans. (*i*) For chess player system dynamic modelling is most important since in dynamic modelling, the states and events are considered.

As the state changed due to any event, the chess player decides how to move so that he could win or prevent himself from losing the game.

(*ii*) In software to mail merge, functional modelling can be considered became of using same data to be sent to various destinations.

Q.4. Attempt any two parts of the following: (10×2=20)

Q.4. (*a*) *What is a conversion function? How is it created? Explain its syntax. Also describe operator function and friend function with the help of suitable examples.*

Ans. Conversion Function. We can define a member function of a class, called a conversion function, that converts from the type of its class to another specified type.

```
>---------------------------+ –operator----+ -------+- conversion _ type -------->
'—class—: :–'                          '+const......+'
                                       '–volatile–'

>------------------------------------------+ (--)------------------ + --------------------X
|----------------------------------|                    '-{---function_body--}-'
| V                              | |
'---- pointer_operator -+-'
```

Operation Function. The operation functions of the subscriber line terminal consists of control from the remote operation terminal (WS), and control from the PC that is directly connected. Remote operation terminal interface.

SNMP (Simple Network Management Protocol) is used for the interface between the remote operation terminal (WS) and the subscriber line terminal. The remote operation terminal has a management function, and the subscriber line terminal has an agent function.

Friend Function

We know that private member of a class cannot be accessed from outside the class *i.e.*, a non-member function can not access to the private data of a class. But may be in some, situation one class wants to access private data of second class and second wants to access private data of first class, or may be an outside function wants to access the private data of a class. Then for solving these situations in C++ there is a concept that is called **friend function.**

The friend function can be illustrated by following example:

```
# include <iostream.h>
class sample
{
int x;
int y;
public:
sample (int a, int b)
  { x = a, y = b; }
friend int add (sample si)
{
```

```
int add (sample sl)
{
return (sl x + sl . y) ; }
void main)
{
sample s2 (20, 30);
int sum;
clrscr cs;
sum = add (s2)
cout << "sum is="
cout << sum << end;
}
```

Q.4. (*b*) ***What is a constructor? Is it mandatory to use constructor in a class? How do we invoke the constructor function? What is Parameterized constructor?***

Ans. **A constructor is a special member function which is invoked automatically when objects are created.**

It is mandatory to use constructors to initialize instance variable in a class. One the object for the class is created.

Invoking constructor

```
# Include <ostream.h>
class sample
{
int a, b;
public ;
sample ( )
{ cout << "This is constructor "<<endl};
a = 100; b = 200;}
int add ( )
{ return (a + b);
}
};
void main ( )
{ clrscr ( );
  sample S ; || constructor invoked
cout << "Output is : " << S. add ( );
}
```

Parameterized Constructor

In parameterized constructor we can use arguments in constructor. When arguments are used in constructor they are known as parameterized constructor.

Example:

```
class  xyz
{  int  a,  b
Public  :
x  y  z  (int  a  1,  int  b  1)
{ a  =  a1
b  =  b1;}
void  show  (  )
{  cout  <<  "a  ="  <<  a  ;}
```

Q.4. (c) ***Design a doubly linked list class. The class should include all functionalities relating to a doubly linked list like creation, deletion of elements, insertion, printing of elements etc. observe the following while designing classes;***

(i) Clearly indicate public and private elements

(ii) Design constructors and explain their purpose.

(iii) Identify data structure and methods which can be inherited.

(iv) Implementation should be in C++.

Ans.

```
# include  <  iostream.h  >
# include  <alloc.h>
struct  dnode
{  struct  ,dnode  *  prev  ;
intdata  ;
struct  dnode  *  neset;
public:
void  d-append  (structdnode  **,  int);
void  d-addatbeg  (structurednode  **,  int)  ;
void  d-display  (struct  node  .*.);
void  d-delete  (struct  -node  `**,  int);
} ;
void  main  ()
{
struct  denode  *  p  ;
    p  =  NULL;
d-append  (p,  11);
d-display  (p,  11);  .
d-delete  (p,  55);
}
void  d-append  (struct  node  **  s,  int  num)
{  strutd  dnode  *  r,  *q,  =  *  s;
```

```
    if  (*s  =  NULL)
    {  *s  =  malloc  (size of  (structd  node));
       (*  s)  →  prev  =  Null  ;
       (*  s)  →  data  =  num  ;
       (*  s)  →  next  =  Null;
    }
  else
       {
       while  (q  →  next  !  =  NULL)
       q  =  q  →  next;
       r  =  malloc  (size  of  (struct  dnode));
       r  =  data  =  num;
       r  =  next  =  NULL;
       r  =  prev  =q;
       q  =  next  =  r;
    }
  }
```

Q.5. Attempt any two parts of the following: (10×2=20)

Q.5 (a) *What is object modelling technique? Draw OMT object model for participant's registration system for a seminar.*

Ans. Object modelling technique

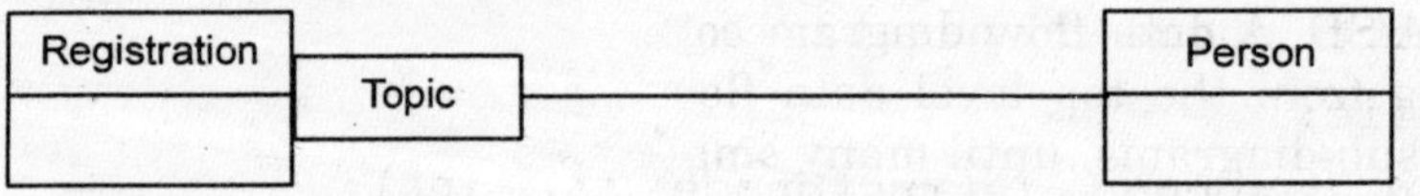

OMT. One of the most popular object-oriented development techniques today is the object modelling technique (OMT). It is primarily used by system and software developers supporting full life-cycle development, targeting object-oriented implementations. It continues to be successful in many application domains telecommunication, transportation, compilers etc.

Q.5 (b) *Apply Booch's methodology for object-oriented analysis ad design specifications of sales office automation.*

Ans. The Booch method encompasses both a micro development process add a macro development process. The micro level defines a set of analysis tasks that are re-applied for each step in the macro process.

Q.5 (c) *Write short notes on Jackson structured development (JSD).*

Ans. Jackson structural development (JSD) is a methodology different from SA/SD or OMI/JSD uses graphical models.

Simple Problems. Jackson places more emphasis on actions and less on attributes than we do. Some JSD actions look similar to OMT associations. For example, a clerk allocates product to an order. We call allocates an association; Jackson calls it an action. Jackson finds attributes confusing and prefers to avoid them. Actions have such a prominent role in JSD modelling that they prompt attributes, in much the same way that attributes diminish the importance of operations in OMT object models.

JSD is a useful methodology for the following types of applications: Concurrent software where processes must synchronize with each other.

Real time software. JSD modelling is extremely detailed and focuses to time.

Microcode. JSD is through, makes no assumptions about the availability of an operating system and considers concurrent processing ad timing.

Programming parallel computers. The JSD paradigm of many processes may be helpful here. JSD is ill-suited for some other applications.

High level analysis. JSD does not foster broad understanding of a problem. JSD is ineffective at abstraction and simplification. JSD meticulously handles details but does not help a developer grasp the essence of a problem.

Databases. Databases design is a more complex topic than Jackson implies. JSD modelling is based towards actions and away from entities and attributes. As a natural consequence, it is a poor technique for data base design.

Conventional software running under an operating system. JSD's abstraction of hundreds or thousands of processes is confusing and unnecessary.

Q.5 *(c) (ii) Structured analysis/structured design (SA/SD)*

Ans. SA/SD includes a variety of notations for formally specifying software. During the analysis, phase data flow diagrams, process specifications, a data dictionary, state transition diagrams, and entity-relationship diagrams are used to logically describe a system. In the design phase, details are added to the analysis models and the data flow diagrams are converted small to structure chart descriptions of programming language code.

Data flow diagrams model the transformations of data as it flows through a system are the focus of SA/SD. A data flow diagram consists of processes, data flows, actors and data stores. Starting from the top level data flow diagram. SA/SD recursively divides complex processes into sub-diagrams, until many small processes are left that are easy to implement. When the resulting processes are simple enough, the decomposition stops, and a process specification is written for each lowest-level process. Process specifications may be expressed with decision tables, pseudo-code, or other techniques.

The data dictionary contains details missing from data flow diagrams. The data dictionary defines data flows and data stores and the meaning of various names.

State transition diagrams model time dependent behaviour and are similar to the dynamic model. Most state transition diagrams describe control processes or timing of function execution and data access triggered by events.

Entity relationship (ER) diagrams highlight relationships between data stores that otherwise would only be seen in the process specifications. Each ER data element corresponds to one data flow diagram data store. The object modelling notation described is an enhanced form of ER diagram.

The above tools are used during the process of structured analysis. Structured design follows structured analysis and addresses low-level details. For example, during structured design, data flow diagram processes are grouped into tasks and allocated to operating system processes and CPUs. Data flow diagram processes are converted into programming language functions, and a structure chart is created showing the procedure call tree.

APPENDIX I

STANDARD LIBRARY FUNCTION

1. 'abs' function—This function provide the absolute value of an integer number.
2. 'pow' function—This function calculation power of any number.
3. 'sin' function—This function calculates sine of angle.
4. 'sqrt' function—This function calculate the positive square root of value.
5. 'tan' function—This function calculates the positive square root of value.
6. 'atoi' function—This function converts a string to an integer.
7. 'gent' function—Converts floating point number to a string.
8. 'atoa' function—Converts integer to string.
9. 'isspace' function—Specifies the value by table look-up using ASCII coded integer value use the library file to include the function.
10. 'tolower' function—This function translates all character to lowercase alphabate.
11. 'toupper' function—This function translate all character of upper alphabate.
12. 'strcapt' function—This function concatenate one string with another.
13. 'strlen' function—This function find the length of string.
14. 'strcmp' function—This function compare one string to another.
15. 'ftell' function—This function indicates the current position of file pointer.
16. 'inportb' function—This function reads words from hardware port.
17. 'getcwd' function—This function provide current working directory.
18. 'memmove' function—This function copies block of *n* bytes.
19. 'memcpy' function—This function copies a specified number of character from one buffer to another.
20. 'memget' function—This sets *n* bytes of block of memory to byte *c*.
21. 'setdisk' function—This function sets current disk drive.
22. 'calloc' function—This function allocate main memory.
23. 'relloc' function—This function reallocate main memory.

APPENDIX II

C++ LANGUAGE KEYWORDS

Keyword cannot be used as name for variables or other users defined program elements. Following are some C++ keywords:

Auto	near
Break	**new**
Case	operator
Catch	pascal
Char	private
Class	protected
Const	public
Continue	register
Default	return
Do	short
Double	signed
Else	size of
Enum	static
Extern	struct
For	switch
Float	template
Far	this
Friend	type def
Goto	union
Hung	unsigned
If	virtual
Inline	void
Int	while
Interrupt	
long	

INDEX

O

P

Q

R